AF576677

AKRON ART MUSEUM: ART SINCE 1850
AN INTRODUCTION TO THE COLLECTION

AKRON ART MUSEUM
ART SINCE 1850

AN INTRODUCTION TO the Collection

By
BARBARA TANNENBAUM
MITCHELL D. KAHAN
JEFFREY GROVE

With additional contributions by
Graham W. J. Beal
Jack Becker
Russell Bowman
Carolyn Kinder Carr
Sheryl Conkelton
Keith F. Davis
Jean E. Feinberg
Mona Hadler
Susan A. Hobbs
Judith Keller
Wendy Kendall-Hess
Nicholas Kilmer
Gerald Nordland
Naomi Rosenblum
Luc Sante
Sachi Yanari-Rizzo

Akron Art Museum
Akron, Ohio
Distributed by University of Washington Press, Seattle
Printed and bound in China

70 East Market Street
Akron, Ohio 44308-2084
330-376-9185
www.akronartmuseum.org

Distributed by
University of Washington Press
P.O. Box 50096
Seattle, Washington 98145-5096
206-543-8870

Editors: Barbara Tannenbaum and Mitchell D. Kahan
Text editor: Norma Roberts, Lexington, Ohio
Design: Lowie and Lowrey Design, Los Angeles
Printed and bound in China by Dai Nippon

Photo credits
All reproduction photographs taken by Richman Haire, except Lydia Dull, 14, 22, 59, 99, 139, 229; ©1988 Robert Glenn Ketchum, 207; John Seyfried, 47; Michael Tropea, 16, 53, 57, 61, 63, 65, 69, 71, 73, 75, 77; John Tsantes, 107, 131; Carrie Mae Weems, 241; Ellen Page Wilson, 231; Brian Ulrich, 34; Courtesy Anthony d'Offay Limited, 243; Courtesy Lennon, Weinberg, Inc., 129; Courtesy PaceWildenstein, 205; Courtesy Universal Limited Art Editions, Inc., 237.

Library of Congress Cataloging-in-Publication Data

Akron Art Museum
Akron Art Museum : art since 1850, an introduction to the collection / by Barbara Tannenbaum, Mitchell D. Kahan, Jeffrey Grove: with additional contributions by Graham W.J. Beal . . . [et al.].
p. cm.
Includes bibliographical references and index.
ISBN 0-940665-05-0
1. Akron Art Museum--Catalogs. 2. Art--Ohio--Akron--Catalogs. I. Tannenbaum, Barbara. II. Kahan, Mitchell Douglas, 1951- III. Grove, Jeffrey D. I V Title.
N512.A4A53 1997 708.171'36--dc21 97–19721
CIP

Contents

PUBLICATION OF THIS BOOK HAS BEEN GENEROUSLY UNDERWRITTEN BY THE FOLLOWING CONTRIBUTORS:

ELIZABETH FIRESTONE GRAHAM FOUNDATION
NATIONAL ENDOWMENT FOR THE ARTS

THE MIRAPAUL FOUNDATION
THE GEORGE GUND FOUNDATION
ROBERT W. KOCH
C. COLMERY GIBSON POLSKY FUND OF AKRON COMMUNITY FOUNDATION

DONNA R. BENDER
CHEMSTRESS CONSULTANT COMPANY
GEORGE AND JOANNE DAVERIO
KATHLEEN AND GORDON EWERS
MR. AND MRS. C. COLMERY GIBSON
PATRICIA L. GRAVES
BILL HENRY
CLIFFORD AND JUDITH ISROFF
THE KLEIN FAMILY
PHILIP A. LLOYD
BEATRICE KNAPP MCDOWELL
HERB AND DIANNE NEWMAN
OMNOVA SOLUTIONS FOUNDATION
RORY AND DEDEE O'NEIL
IRVING AND HARRIETT SANDS
CAROLYN AND LARRY SAULINO

1996 AKRON ART MUSEUM ANNUAL APPEAL
1997 AKRON WINE AUCTION

Dedication

This book is gratefully dedicated to Mary Schiller Myers. She has served the museum with the most exemplary commitment since she and her late husband Louis S. Myers first became members in 1947.

Entranced by the visual arts since her youth, Mary obtained an undergraduate degree in art from the University of Akron. She brought both that academic training and her intuitive eye to the accessions committee during the crucial years after the Akron Art Institute closed its school and began to explore the concept of becoming a modern art museum, a goal that she vigorously championed. Important works by Andy Warhol and Donald Judd were acquired during those years, setting a new standard for acquisitions. Her enthusiasm converted her husband into an articulate champion for the institution that she loved, so much so that he not only served as board president but also as general chairman of the capital campaign for the museum's current facility. At that time, the Myerses donated funds to create the Mary S. and Louis S. Myers Sculpture Courtyard, which also contains two of their major donations. The rare bronze by Emile-Antoine Bourdelle dates from the end of the nineteenth century and reflects the period when the museum's current facility was originally built. Most unforgettable is another gift, the sensuous and pink *Inverted Q*, which resulted from Mary's invitation to Claes Oldenburg to come to Akron to create an outdoor sculpture. Many other objects pictured on the following pages are gifts from Mary and her family.

Additionally, Mary initiated the museum's first major fund-raising campaign designated exclusively for endowment. As part of this campaign, she created in 1987 the first restricted fund exclusively for the purchase of art. It guarantees annual purchase funds for painting and sculpture, fulfilling a longtime goal of this institution. Four works on the following pages have been acquired with proceeds from this endowment.

Mary's leadership became evident during the fiftieth anniversary year, when she served as president of the Arts Council, the organization's key support group. In 1981 she chaired the black-tie gala during opening week of the museum's new facility. She served a total of thirteen years on the Board of Trustees, including two years in the demanding role of president, a task that requires energy and involvement throughout the community and in virtually every aspect of the museum's operations. It has been an honor for her fellow trustees to work with her and be inspired by her passion and her vision for the museum.

That vision springs from her deep intellectual and emotional understanding of art and her belief that works of art communicate essential ideas and heartfelt insights. As a collector, Mary has had a great impact on museum staff over the years. She has generously loaned and donated works of art and assisted in recruiting several directors. But most importantly, she has inspired staff and trustees by her pursuit of excellence, her patience in seeking just the right work of art, and her commitment to individual artists over many years.

Mary's devotion to art extends to other institutions locally, regionally, and nationally, including the Mary Schiller Myers School of Art of the University of Akron, the Cleveland Museum of Art, the Metropolitan Museum of Art, and the Whitney Museum of American Art. Her philanthropy and involvement have benefited many institutions but none more than the Akron Art Museum. For this, the Board of Trustees and the community salute her.

Philip A. Lloyd, President, Board of Trustees

Presidents of the Board of Trustees

Edwin C. Shaw, Chair, Founding Committee 1920–21
The Rev. Franklyn Cole Sherman 1922
Edwin C. Shaw 1923
Marvin M. Mell 1924–27
Dr. D. W. Stevenson 1928–32
Judge A. F. O'Neil 1932–35
A. I. Spanton 1935–37
Dr. B. Z. Stambaugh 1937–39
John F. Suppes 1939–41
Dr. Edgar B. Foltz 1941–44
Elmer Jackson 1944–45
Walter P. Keith Sr. 1945–51
Robert W. Koch 1951–53
Walter P. Keith Sr. 1953–57
Norman E. Malone 1957–60
Bernard Schulman 1960–64
Walter P. Keith Sr. 1964–65
Frank M. Whiteman 1965–66
John F. Floberg 1966–67
John N. Hart 1967–69
Sam S. McKeel 1969–71
Charles E. Pierson 1971–73
Louis S. Myers 1973–77
Mary A. Saalfield 1977–79
John V. Frank 1979–82
Lawrence H. Pomeroy 1982–84
M. Donald McClusky 1984–87
Mary S. Myers 1987–89
C. Gordon Ewers 1989–90
Judith B. Isroff 1990–92
Thomas R. Merryweather 1992–95
Donna R. Bender 1995–97
Fred Bidwell 1997–99
Philip A. Lloyd 1999 to present

Directors

Wilbur Peat 1924-29
Theodore Hanford Pond 1929-31
No Director 1931-45
Charles Val Clear 1945-49
George G. Culler 1949-55
Robert Luck 1955-56
Leroy Flint 1956-65
Forrest H. Selvig 1966-68
Orrel E. Thompson 1969-73
Robert M. Doty 1974-77
John Coplans 1978-79
I. Michael Danoff 1980-84
Kathleen M. Monaghan 1984-85
Mitchell D. Kahan 1986 to present

Preface

As the Akron Art Museum embarks on an exciting plan to expand its facilities, it is a great pleasure to publish this overview of the museum's holdings in painting, sculpture, and photography, its areas of strength. The publication began as a project for the institution's seventy-fifth anniversary in 1997 and has taken many years to complete. It is the first publication to survey the collection, which spans the years from 1850 to the present. One hundred works are reproduced and discussed here.

The purpose of this publication is three-fold. The Board of Trustees and staff trust that the works of art pictured on the following pages will inspire community pride and lead to further efforts to build a world-class collection in the twenty-first century. In addition, this publication will have an educational role. It will inform the public and colleagues in the field about Akron's holdings, which are available for scholarly research and for loan to significant exhibitions. And not least, this publication adds a necessary dimension to the history of Akron and calls attention to those who sought to raise the banner of culture in a city dedicated to industry.

Prior to this book, the only significant publication on the museum's holdings was a 1986 catalogue raisonné documenting works from the collection of Edwin C. Shaw, who chaired the committee established in 1920 to create an art museum for Akron. The committee's efforts bore fruit, and on February 1, 1922, the Akron Art Institute opened in the basement of the city's main library. Though a significant part of Mr. Shaw's collection had been dispersed during his lifetime, several dozen works came to the institute from his estate a decade after his death. That key gift and many others are outlined in the accompanying history of the collection.

It should be noted that because of space and time limitations the introductory essay is not a complete history of this institution. Instead, it focuses on the growth and evolution of the collection. Many people played key roles in other achievements, including the legendary Masked Balls; the successful fund-raisers A Day at the Races and Akron Wine Auction; several building campaigns; major educational programs; and innovative outreach activities. Although those efforts are not detailed here they deserve our respect and gratitude. It is hoped that a future publication will provide a more detailed accounting of the entire history of the museum.

What is most unusual about the institution's development is its changing focus over seventy-five years, as it responded to donors, professional staff, and the community. In sum, the organization shifted its direction several times, with the result that the majority of works described in the following pages have been acquired over the past thirty years. Earlier trustees deserve our admiration for implementing complex changes and focusing the institution's efforts, for they have bequeathed to us a vital museum prepared for the new millennium. More recently, board leadership has supported this publication project and created an ambitious plan for the future. The trustees' unstinting efforts and their belief in our abilities have led to one success after another. I am particularly grateful to Thomas R. Merryweather and Donna R. Bender, both of whom served as president of the Board of Trustees during the fund-raising for this book.

A publishing enterprise of this complexity and expense is made possible not only by the labor of staff and guest writers but most importantly by the generosity of many funders. On behalf of the Board of Trustees, I am most happy to offer enthusiastic appreciation to all the donors, many of whom have supported the institution for decades. Their past gifts have underwritten exhibitions, educational programs, acquisitions, and routine operating costs, allowing the museum to remain open free of charge to the public for its entire history. Their most recent gifts have allowed this anniversary project to be undertaken at the highest level of quality. The trustees and I particularly acknowledge Honorary Trustee Ray A. Graham III of the Elizabeth Firestone Graham Foundation, who provided the initial impetus for this project with a generous three-year grant. Completion of this undertaking was ensured by a large grant from the National Endowment for the Arts, one of many awarded to the museum over the past three decades.

Appreciation is gratefully extended to the many people who helped bring this publication to fruition. All of the museum's staff contributed to its success. I particularly want to thank the following individuals. Registrar Arnold Tunstall coordinated both the conservation and photography for the project. Preparators James Williams and Thaddeus Gregory, assisted by Jason Byers, expertly prepared works for display and assisted with photography. Conservation of several works was conducted by the staff of the Intermuseum Conservation Association in Oberlin, Ohio. Richman Haire produced most of the beautiful transparencies from which the illustrations have been made. Librarians Kay Downey, Jody Perkins, and Lyndsey Shaeffer provided assistance over several years. Now retired, former Development Director Arlene Rossen assisted in securing funding, aided by Cindy Kellett. Executive Secretary Lenore DeLong Fiedorek and Curatorial Assistant Gary Setzer helped with fact-finding and coordination of various materials for the text. Nicholas Lowie, Sheridan Lowrey, and Lida Lowrey in Los Angeles designed a graceful and impressive format for our efforts. Editor Norma Roberts edited and revised the text. Numerous colleagues reviewed and commented on the one hundred entries. Several long-time patrons and staff members kindly read the introductory essay and offered helpful comments. I thank all of the above for their hard work and others unnamed for sharing their knowledge.

With her usual expertise and dependable sleuthing, Chief Curator and Head of Public Programs Barbara Tannenbaum edited the book and wrote the concise yet fascinating history of the collection despite a dearth of material covering the first thirty years. In cases where conflicting accounts exist, she relied on available documentary evidence. She, former Curator of Exhibitions Jeffrey Grove, and I wrote most of the essays on works in the collection. We delighted in the opportunity to conduct research and explore in depth many of the museum's best works. It was a pleasure to work with such creative and energetic curators and I thank them for their inspiration. In addition, I offer special appreciation to the sixteen guest writers who contributed thirty-one short essays on artists about whom they are acknowledged experts. Their contributions add great variety and insight to this publication.

This project reminds donors, staff, and the public that the collection is the soul of every art museum. The collection is what remains in perpetuity to enlighten the community long after lectures and traveling exhibitions, parties and concerts have ended. The collection expresses pride in our past and stands as our gift to the future. It is a testament to art's universal power.

Mitchell D. Kahan
Director

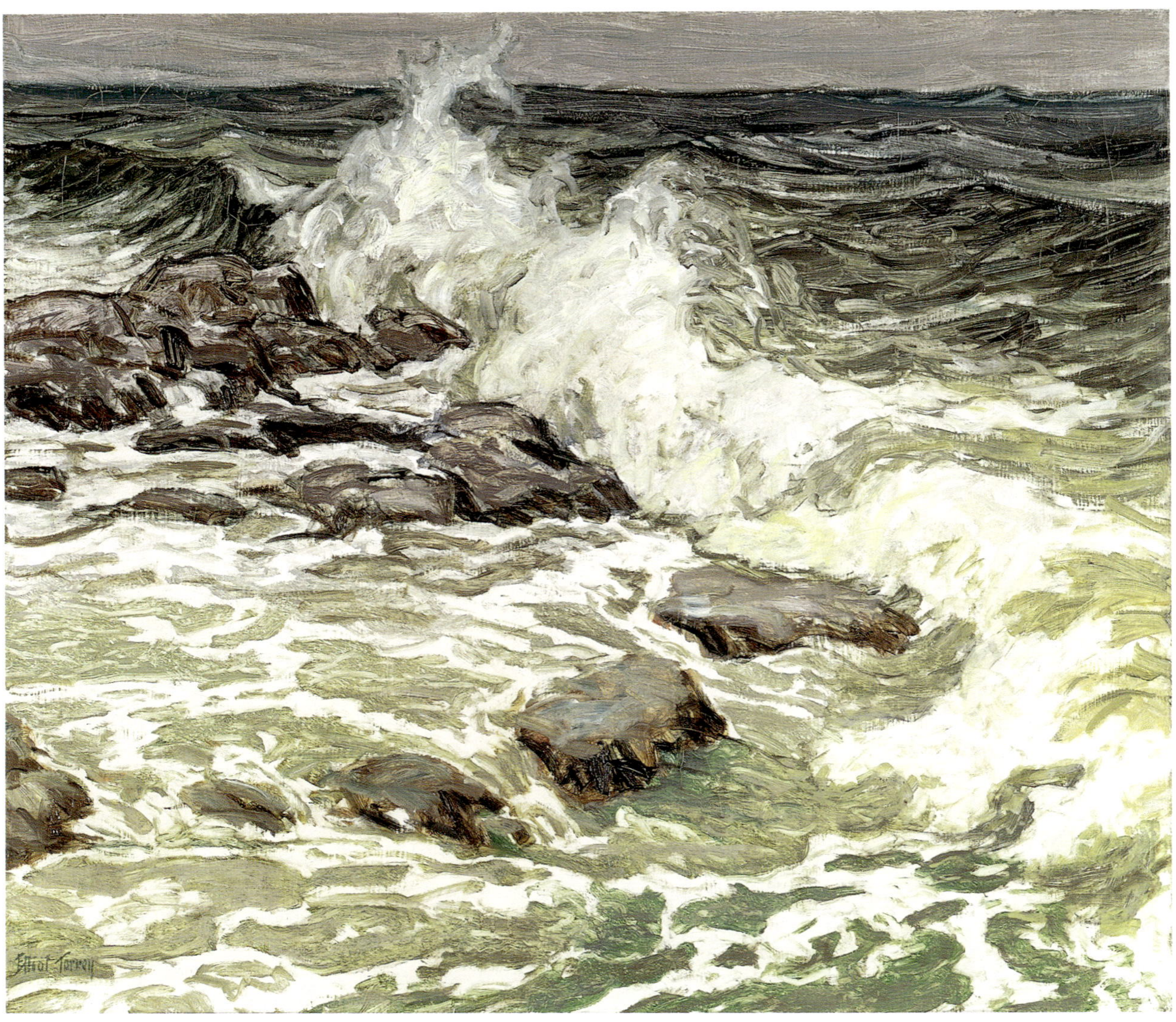

Elliot Torrey's *Surf* was painted around 1920, the year that plans were initiated for an art institute in Akron. That coincidence may have inspired A. H. Marks to donate this work from his collection to the fledgling institution in 1923.

Birth and Rebirth

A History of the Collection of the Akron Art Museum

Barbara Tannenbaum

It may seem purely fortuitous that the first piece to enter the collection of the Akron Art Institute—Elliot Torrey's *Surf*—would someday fall within the much more limited collecting focus of the institute's successor, the Akron Art Museum. In fact, viewed with the wisdom of hindsight, the Torrey painting was but one of many factors that prefigured the institute's transformation in the 1970s into a museum with a significant collection of modern and contemporary art.[1]

1. The factual information in this essay is based primarily on documentary materials in the archives and files of the Akron Art Museum. Unfortunately, these records are often incomplete, especially for the institution's early years, and sometimes provide contradictory information. Although attempts were made to confirm information from more than one source, this was rarely possible. It is hoped that any errors or omissions that remain will be corrected in the future when a detailed history of the museum is written.

For their assistance in researching obscure materials, I want to thank the staffs of the Language, Literature and History and the Fine Arts Divisions of the Akron-Summit County Public Library; and David B. Cooper and the *Akron Beacon Journal* staff. At the Akron Art Museum, special assistance for this essay came from Mitchell Kahan, Arnold Tunstall, Lenore DeLong Fiedorek, and Jody Perkins. Last but certainly not least, I owe a debt of gratitude to the many past trustees, museum supporters, and staff members who have shared their stories and answered my questions over the years.

The collection of the Akron Art Museum consists of over three thousand objects and contains only works of fine art created since 1850, with the emphasis on American achievements. This book focuses on one hundred works selected from the collection, which has particular strengths in the areas of photography, turn-of-the-twentieth-century American painting, and painting and sculpture since 1960.

When the institution opened its doors in 1922 as the Akron Art Institute, its constitution put no limits of any kind on what it might collect. The founders undoubtedly hoped that the fledgling institution would eventually be able to build a comprehensive historical collection like those of their larger, wealthier neighbors to the north and west, the Cleveland Museum of Art and the Toledo Museum of Art. The fifty-year journey from the unreachable ideal of a general museum to the realizable goal of a specialized collection followed a path that was anything but smooth. Twists and turns occurred throughout the institute's tumultuous history, which in turn was influenced by Akron's cyclical boom-and-bust economy.

Akron had just become the capital of the U.S. rubber industry in 1920 when thirty-four artists, prominent citizens, and representatives of various civic organizations met to establish an art institution. It was the fastest growing city in the nation, "a place where money, and nothing else, counts—an overgrown village without semblance of culture—an expression of only the more sordid side of modern commercial life."[2] The blue-collar nature of the city and its concentration on manufacturing attracted far more laborers, engineers, and businessmen than aesthetes. The chair of the institute's founding committee, BFGoodrich executive Edwin C. Shaw, felt "compelled to confess that our community has not yet truly awakened to a true appreciation [of art]. I believe, however, it will in time and that is one of the real purposes of the effort in conjunction with our Art Institute."[3]

The institute's other purposes, as outlined in the constitution, were "to provide a place for the exhibition of art, to secure lecturers and programs, to exhibit art in the schools, and to hold and obtain art objects."[4] Its founders hoped that the institute could be both a regional art center offering exhibits and instruction *and* a collecting institution, in

2. A. I. Spanton, "Music, Art, Books," in *A Centennial History of Akron* (Akron: The Summit County Historical Society, 1925), 352.

3. Letter from Shaw to H. Dudley Murphy, March 8, 1924; quoted in Carolyn Kinder Carr, "The Art Collection of Edwin Coupland Shaw," *The Edwin C. Shaw Collection of American Impressionist and Tonalist Painting* (Akron: Akron Art Museum, 1986), 26.

4. "E. C. Shaw Heads Art Association," *Akron Beacon Journal*, November 18, 1920, 6.

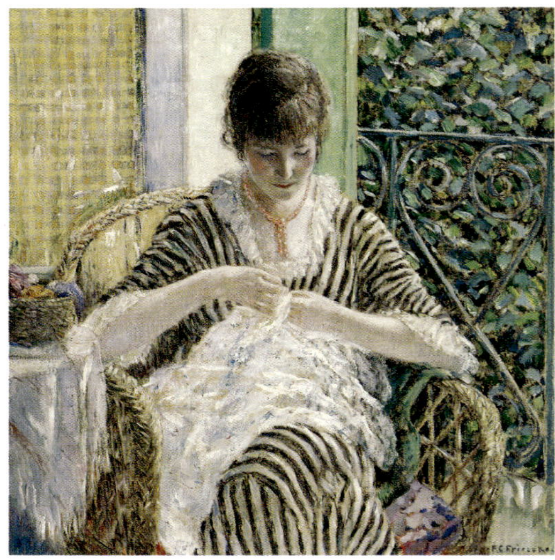

Frederick C. Frieseke's *On the Balcony,* 1912–15, is one of thirty-nine works in the collection originally owned by the chair of the institute's founding committee, Edwin C. Shaw.

time holding work of national significance. The fact that collecting was their last, not first, priority made the latter objective unlikely. This would remain the case throughout the entire first phase of the collection's history, which lasted until 1945. During that time, the institute had only a tiny collection and functioned primarily as an art center, not a museum.

The lack of emphasis on collecting may have been dictated by practicality. When it opened on February 1, 1922, the institute did not own a single work. Raising enough money just to open the doors had taken two years—and that was with a totally volunteer staff working in two rooms of donated space on the ground floor of the Akron Public Library at 69 East Market Street. Every penny that could be raised was needed for operating expenses; there was no money with which to purchase art. Nor were there immediate hopes of major gifts upon which to build a collection. There were few significant art collections in Akron, and even by 1940 only three were considered worthy of special note: those of Edwin C. Shaw, Elizabeth Parke Firestone, and F. A. Seiberling.[5] Of the three, Shaw's was not only the most highly regarded, it was also the only one that would eventually (but not until 1955) yield significant gifts for the institute.

In the meantime, Shaw may have solicited the first two works to enter the institution's collection. These were gifts from Shaw's friends and colleagues, A. H. Marks and Andrew H. Noah, which arrived shortly before the institute's second birthday. Both men possessed modest collections of post-Civil War American paintings that had been exhibited at the institute—with Shaw's far more extensive holdings in the same area—at the end of the gallery's first year. Indeed, it was probably Marks and Noah who had earlier encouraged Shaw to begin collecting and directed his taste toward recent American art—again, a prefiguration of the museum's later emphasis.

No evidence exists as to why these three men chose to "buy American." It may have been because American art was easier to purchase in the United States than European art or because of American patriotic fervor surrounding World War I. Marks, who had moved to New York in 1921, may have selected the Torrey painting as a gift from his collection because it was created around the same year (1920) that the plans for the institute

5. Cora Dodd, "Federal Writers' Project, Ohio: History of Akron and Summit County," Ohio Writers' Project No. 19417, pp. 121–22; typescript in Akron-Summit County Public Library.

were established. The month following Marks's gift, Noah gave the second work to enter the institute's collection, a large blue-and-white Chinese vase. With only two items, the collection was already eclectic.

Only three more items had entered the collection when the institute's first professional staff member, twenty-six-year-old Wilbur D. Peat, was hired as director in August 1924. Enthusiastic, energetic, and an excellent lecturer, Peat raised the community's awareness of art. His exhibition program attracted visitors to the institute, perhaps because of his far-ranging ideas about what materials were appropriate for museums. Under his aegis, the institute's displays included not only painting and sculpture but also photography (a medium just gaining acceptance as art), crafts, traditional folk art from the homelands of Akron's immigrant workers, Native American art, posters, children's book illustrations, soap sculptures from Proctor & Gamble, furniture, fabric design, and ethnographic art. Peat's imaginative and eclectic exhibition schedule may unintentionally have set the pattern for the institution's future collecting—an unfortunate pattern, because hindsight reveals there was little hope that the small, ill-funded institution could build a high-quality, comprehensive collection.

When Peat left in 1929, funds were already tightening due to the onset of the Depression. The next director, Theodore Hanford Pond, was hired on a half-time basis. After two years, even that proved unaffordable. The institute was forced to dismiss Pond and rely almost entirely on board members and volunteers, a situation that lasted until 1945. At the conclusion of its first decade, the institute had no professional staff, had yet to find funds to secure a permanent home, and had been asked to give up the free space it occupied in the library.

During the long period of crisis between 1931 and 1945, when there were insufficient funds to retain a professional staff, the institute turned to its community. A small group of dedicated volunteers kept the institute alive, performing all the duties surrounding the organization of exhibitions, lectures, and art classes. In addition to trustees, the group included Harvey A. Valentine and Jane Barnhardt, who were in charge of exhibitions and accessions for most of this period, and Effie B. Stevens, who served as secretary from 1928 to 1938. For most of the 1930s the only paid employee was a gallery attendant.

The institute began to promote itself as a local art center rather than a museum, and its exhibition program emphasized the work of local artists. The 1933 Annual Report explained that, faced with "the difficult and ungrateful task of arranging and presenting exhibitions of art, without spending much money,...it was necessary to hunt out many local works of art." Even during this period, however, the trustees did not revise the mission to exclude collecting, nor did they mandate limiting the institute's focus to regional art.

Nonetheless, the precariousness of the institute's existence made it nearly impossible to attract gifts of art. A registration book ending in 1931 lists only twenty-six entries of original artworks into the collection, all of them gifts and none of them particularly distinguished works. The majority—seventeen pieces—were examples of the decorative arts from the United States and Asia, many from the home of Mrs. J. J. Tracy Sr. of Cleveland. This miscellany included an American lap desk, oriental vases, a carved couch believed to have belonged to one of the rajahs of India, a Japanese cabinet, and a pair of lotus-shaped brass floor lamps from India.

At this time the institute had only four paintings, all by American artists who were living at the time their works were acquired. The most valuable was *Circe and Anatole* by Robert Reid. An indefinite loan through the National Academy of Design in New York, the painting was purchased with funds from the Henry Ward Ranger bequest and assigned to Akron in a national loan and gift program. Reid's work and Torrey's *Surf* were joined by the works of two women artists who were born in Ohio but worked elsewhere. Akron-born Jessie Evans's *The Arroyo* was donated by the Akron and Summit County Federation of Women's Clubs and Florence Gotthold's *Spikes and Bells* was given by a New York collector at the artist's request.

In 1924, to the institute's credit (and perhaps because of Wilbur Peat's open-mindedness), it accepted the gift of a group of portrait and landscape photographs by local artist Hervey W. Minns.[6] Minns, who made a living by operating a commercial portrait studio, won recognition in international competitions for his artistic photography in the Pictorialist style. Acquiring photography and treating it as fine art at such an early date was a bold move for an arts institution. Unfortunately, in spite of nearly annual exhibitions of photography,

6. Minns's name is sometimes cited as Harvey. The surviving records about this gift do not give a total number of photographs, nor do they list the works individually.

staff members in later years were far less certain about the medium's legitimacy as art. Minns's were the only photographs to enter the collection until 1967.

During the second decade of the institute's existence, the situation worsened. In 1936, when it was located in two rented rooms at 36 South Howard Street, attendance, which had been around 20,000 annually, dropped to 2,300. Membership, a major source of income, dropped to thirty-seven. Board president A. I. Spanton immediately initiated a search for a new, more desirable home.

Salvation came the very next year thanks to the efforts of Effie B. Stevens and her husband Vincent. In 1937 the Stevenses secured a gift of $7,500 from Mrs. Russell L. Robinson—half the purchase price of the Commins mansion on Fir Hill. Mrs. Robinson's generosity inspired other donations to help finance remodeling and operation. In November 1937 the institute finally occupied its first permanent home. Within the year, attendance rose to 21,500 and membership to 270.

Even after this rebirth, significant financial problems continued, to the point that board president B. Z. Stambaugh decided to create a citizens' committee in early 1939 "to discuss the advisability of continuing the operation of the Akron Art Institute." Happily, the committee's unanimous opinion that spring was "that we could ill afford to let the Institute close."[7] The board of trustees agreed and immediately mounted a fund-raising campaign. Led by Penfield Seiberling and Noel Michell, the campaign raised $20,000 to pay off debts and complete the remodeling. In 1941 Mrs. Robinson donated the other half of the building's purchase price, allowing the institute to pay off its mortgage. Things were once again looking up.

Disaster struck on Saturday, January 2, 1942. "A blaze which mounted to uncontrollable proportions fanned by a 20-mile-an-hour wind" destroyed the institute's new home and much of its contents.[8] Losses of art were estimated at around $160,000. Of that, $150,000 represented a group of over 300 Chinese and rare ninth-century Siamese ceramics, religious relics, and handicrafts on permanent loan from the University of Akron. Insured for

7. Board minutes for February and April 1939, cited in typescript history of the institute, Akron Art Museum archives.

8. Alan Rosenfeld, "Blaze Destroys Akron Art Treasures," *Akron Beacon Journal*, January 3, 1942. Information on the fire and its results is drawn from articles in the *Akron Beacon Journal* on January 3, 4, 5, 8, 9, 16, 20, 21, 25, 29; February 17; June 23; July 2; October 8; and November 27, 1942.

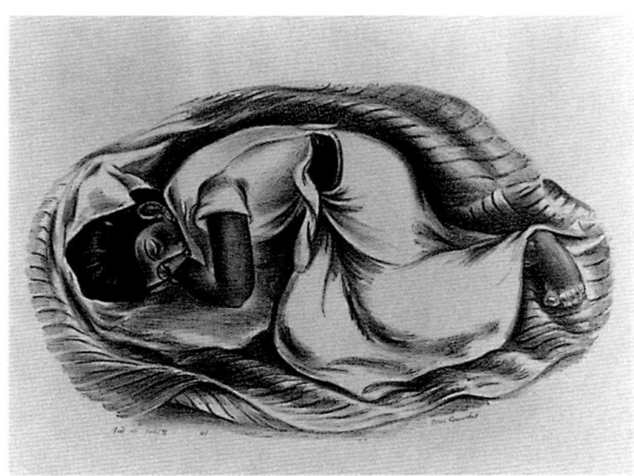

Doris Rosenthal's *Girl in White* was the first work to be purchased for the collection. This 1945 lithograph was acquired in 1946, the twenty-fourth year of the institute's existence.

less than half their value, these works were almost a total loss. Three temporary exhibitions on view at the time were also incinerated. An exhibition of new acquisitions from the collection, valued at around $4,000 by the secretary of the board of trustees, had been protected somewhat from the fire because it was housed temporarily in a storage area built into a wall.

Because there had been no professional staff for so many years and because records were destroyed in the fire, little reliable information remains about exactly what works were in the collection on that fateful night. Of the forty works listed in a 1931 collections ledger, only the four paintings mentioned earlier seem to have survived. Also making it through the fire was a group of gifts that entered the collection during the 1930s and early 1940s. Most were prints, but there were also two more paintings by Ohio-born women that had been donated by the Summit County Federation of Women's Clubs; a portrait by Akron artist Julius Faysash of poet Orlando Potter; and a suit of Japanese armor. Also surviving was the institute's first bequest: five etchings of travel scenes from the estate of Harvey Valentine, donated in 1940. Given the works that survived the fire and the insurance values of those that perished, it seems clear that the collection was still small and eclectic and contained objects of minor significance.

The fire threw the institute into a tailspin. It continued to hold a few activities in borrowed spaces, but membership dropped to an all-time low of four in April 1944. Once again the institution's very existence seemed in peril. And once again it rose, phoenixlike, from the ashes. In 1944 newly elected board president Elmer Jackson, assisted by Frances Herron and Alice Schell, began a total reorganization of the institute beginning with a consideration of its mission. A planning committee was appointed, headed by Walter P. Keith Sr. A number of museum and art professionals were brought to Akron to give advice in 1944–45. Keith would carry out some of these recommendations as the board's next president, the first of three times he served in that office.

The report given the most attention was that of Daniel S. Defenbacher, director of the Walker Art Center in Minneapolis. Board minutes for November 15, 1944, report that he urged the trustees to hire a professional director. What is most interesting is that Defenbacher stressed "an approach to industry and to labor." This idea may have originated in discussions with the trustees, for the concept had already been broached in a "Resumé and Program" written for the institute in late 1938 or early 1939.[9]

9. "The Akron Art Institute: A Resumé and A Program," 1; typescript in the Akron Art Museum archives.

It is unclear who authored the "Resumé" or whether it was ever officially adopted. Even if it remained unofficial, its content certainly shaped the institute's goals and activities into the 1960s. The program called for an art center, as opposed to a museum. Its author did not believe that a collection was important for an organization whose primary purpose would be "to develop appreciation of fine and applied arts, past and contemporary" by exploring the American aesthetic, "not only...in fine arts but in color and design of business products, advertising, architecture, photography, interior decoration and in numberless other field[s] in which it has permeated the lives of our people." A collection ranked fifth (and last) among the priorities: the institute would "provide to those interested in acquisition the facilities for inspection and comparison of art objects."

In 1945, with the consultants' recommendations and perhaps those of the "Resumé" in mind, the trustees officially voted to make the institute an art center instead of a museum. This decision implied a focus on current art, as opposed to the history of art, and a continuation of the emphasis on exhibitions, lectures, and classes rather than collections. The trustees accelerated their search for a new, permanent home for the institute and, ironically, hired a director for whom collecting was a high priority. His advent marked the beginning of the collection's second phase, which would last until 1970. This was a period of collection building, but without a plan or focus.

Charles Val Clear, the first professional staff member since 1931, served from 1945 to 1949. He was "an amazingly active young man with decided ideas about how to run a community museum."[10] He championed the acquisition of contemporary art by American artists, which helped set the stage for the museum's eventual identity. His priorities were clear from the first two shows he organized, *40 American Artists* and *40 More American Artists*. These exhibitions were wish lists of works from colonial to modern times to "show the Akron Public what the Institute might well have in a permanent collection of American painting." The new director was clearly hoping that "the first purchases for this collection will be of works of living artists."

His wish came true in January 1946, the twenty-fourth year of the institution's existence, when the first purchase of art was finally made. The modest expenditure of $10 for a lithograph by contemporary New York artist Doris Rosenthal did not, of course, represent the level of ambition demonstrated by *40 American Painters*.[11] However, prospects

10. Quotations in this paragraph are from Alonzo Lansford, "Akron Proves Value of Community Museum," *Art Digest* 22 (December 15, 1947): 12.

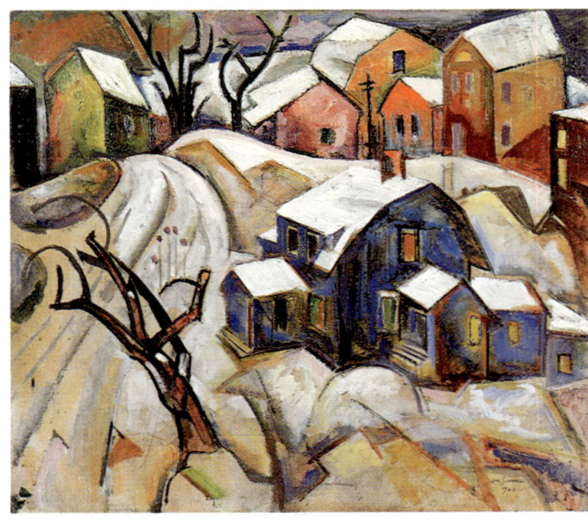

William Sommer's *Bach Chord,* 1923, was donated in 1992 by Russell Munn in memory of his wife, Helen. Other works by Sommer were among the institute's earliest purchases.

for the future had brightened considerably. In the month that Val Clear arrived, the board, under the leadership of Walter Keith, had allocated the institute's first regularly budgeted sum for the purchase of art. The 1946 operating budget of $30,000 included $2,500 to be used for acquisitions. This decision to purchase art was an unprecedented step, one that moved the supposed "art center" toward becoming a museum. Allocation of operating funds for acquisitions would remain a practice for many years, although the amount was often modest, sometimes only a few hundred dollars. Through purchases, a director could hope to focus the collection, fill in its gaps, and raise its quality.

Although the first purchases were prints by New York artists, the majority of works bought over the next decade would be by local artists, including such area notables as William Sommer and Raphael Gleitsmann. In the mid-1940s, the tradition of purchasing work from the annual spring artists' show was initiated; this practice continued through the mid-1960s. Works by area artists entered the collection in fairly large numbers by gift as well. Over the years, a number of Akronites supported local artists, often purchasing their works at the institute's sales and rental gallery. Some of these works eventually were donated to the institute, and many artists generously presented their own work and that of their peers. The largest single acquisition of regional work was the result of government patronage. In 1948 the Art Department of the Akron Board of Education transferred to the institute seventy-five prints by artists working as part of the local Works Progress Administration program.

In the late 1940s gifts greatly enlarged the collection. It more than tripled in size with the addition of 201 new pieces in 1946; during the rest of the 1940s several hundred works, most of them gifts, were added annually. These numbers contrast sharply with those from the period 1940 to 1944, when six works entered the collection (five from a bequest and one a damaged work donated by an insurance company). However, the bountiful numbers of the late 1940s are somewhat misleading, for many of the works turned out not to be of museum quality. Nonetheless, now that the institute had, for the first time, both a professional staff and plans for a permanent home, people were willing to entrust their gifts to it.

Unfortunately, few of the subsequent donations fit in with Val Clear's desire to focus acquisitions on American art. Perhaps because of the international nature of the

11. The accessions number for this item—45.1, which indicates that it was the first item acquired in 1945—must have been assigned retroactively. The purchase of the Rosenthal print was presented to and approved by the executive committee of the board of trustees at their January 11, 1946 meeting.

rubber business, a large number of well-to-do Akronites were interested in European art and also in the cultures of South America and Asia. As a result, the collection grew to be quite international in character. The first large bequest, the estate of Dr. Edgar B. Foltz, contained items bought during his many travels: among the works were European and American paintings, Egyptian and Mayan sculpture, Asian art, Guatemalan weavings, Native American baskets and pottery, period furniture, and ancient jewelry. A prominent Akron physician, Foltz had helped operate the institute when it lacked a director; he had been a trustee for many years, was board president from 1941 to 1944, and was an enthusiastic collector. Unfortunately many of his donations turned out to be tourist art or were not of museum quality. Some were deaccessioned (officially removed from the collection) as early as 1949. Over the years, a number of Pre-Columbian works were donated by Dr. and Mrs. George Oenslager, whose first gift, in 1946, was a group of Peruvian textiles. In 1948 the Baird Collection of 110 items of Asian art, including eight Siamese paintings, was transferred from the University of Akron. The same year, Mrs. Allan Johnson gave a large collection of Japanese prints.

In addition to building the institute's collection, Val Clear also vastly enlarged its educational offerings. When he arrived in Akron in 1945, servicemen and women were beginning to return home in large numbers from World War II. The demand for art programs boomed, thanks to the G.I. Bill, which provided money for people to whom study in the arts would have been an unaffordable luxury five years earlier. The institute's adult educational offerings in studio art and design proliferated after the war, leading in 1947 to the creation of a professional art school with a four-year degree program. The school, which was later accredited, continued until 1965.

The design arts received major emphasis in both the instructional and exhibition programs into the 1960s. Val Clear "brought the Institute into Akron's factories by showing that modern industrial design was art by another name."[12] According to a student who attended in the 1950s, the school was a "mini-Bauhaus…a working, teaching, and exhibiting institution that made no distinction between artist, artisan, or design."[13] This path, first suggested in the 1938–39 "Resumé," proved to be wise. Few other small museums had the courage and foresight to embrace such a direction, one in which the institute, despite its limited resources, could pioneer and finally achieve a national reputation.

12. Kenneth Nichols, "Surprise of the Half Century: 50 Years for Art Institute," *Akron Beacon Journal*, December 28, 1969, D5.

13. Nomination of Leroy Flint for the Ohio Governor's Awards in the Arts, 1990; typescript in the Akron Art Museum archives. The typescript does not reveal the identity of the nominator.

To organize the design shows, Val Clear hired the institute's first curator, Luke Lietzke, in 1946. Lietzke served as curator of design until 1964; regrettably, most of that time her position was only part-time. She organized a remarkable series of exhibitions that brought to Akron the best contemporary furniture, textiles, architecture, and industrial design and placed the institute firmly in the forefront of design programs across the country. Although Lietzke saw to it that a few items were acquired by donation, there was no correspondingly strong emphasis on contemporary design in the collection.

Modern styling was also brought to the interior design of the institute's new home at 69 East Market Street. In June 1950, the "new" building—the former public library, where the institute began in 1922—opened. Renovation of the building, which cost around $300,000, was financed through a fund-raising campaign led by Roger Firestone and B. A. Polsky. Val Clear worked with the board and its president, Walter Keith Sr., to acquire and prepare the site, but he left for another position in 1949. It was left to Keith and the next director, George D. Culler, to complete the project and actually open the new building. With the move into its largest home yet, the institute established a new mission statement that raised collecting to second priority among its aims. As opposed to the 1945 definition of the institute as an art center, this statement referred to it as "a museum where works of art may be housed for the enjoyment and education of the people."

Culler, who served from 1949 to 1955, was committed to the importance of contemporary art. Under his direction, Lietzke's design shows continued while contemporary painting and sculpture received renewed emphasis. The major acquisitions of Culler's term, however, would be gifts of turn-of-the-century American painting including, at long last, the Shaw collection.

Shaw began collecting in 1916 and stopped in 1922, at which point his holdings included sixty-eight major works and a number of prints. He sold a portion of his collection in the late 1920s, but among the high points that remained were William Merritt Chase's spectacular *Girl in White,* two "decorations" by Thomas Wilmer Dewing, and landscapes by Impressionist Childe Hassam and Tonalist Dwight W. Tryon. Many of the works Shaw purchased were by living artists, but his choices—primarily examples of American Impressionism and Tonalism—were conservative. The gritty urban images of the Ashcan school that were then the leading style of American painting were excluded, as were American artists' interpretations of avant-garde European styles such as Dada, Fauvism, and Cubism.

A possible motive for Shaw's conservatism could have been his intent, in the mid-1920s, to form "an historical collection of works by important American artists of the post-Civil War period" that would be given to a public gallery.[14] Presumably, the "public gallery" was to be the institute, given Shaw's role in its founding. Yet Shaw's will, written in 1934, was also vague and left his trustees some discretionary power in the disposal of his collection. Of course, that was a bleak time for the institute; its continued existence looked doubtful through most of the 1930s. Shaw died in 1941, but his will was not to be probated until the death of his sister, which occurred in 1955.

The 1942 fire, plus the institute's continued instability, had worried Shaw's executors, but by 1955 board president Keith and director George Culler were able to convince them that the institute was then a stable institution with a fireproof, permanent home and a bright future. Correspondence suggests that Culler and Keith were allowed first pick of Shaw's art for the institute. The remaining works, along with Shaw's household goods, would be disposed of through a house sale. Stella Hall, Pat Dwight, and Bertl Arnstein (head of the accessions committee for seventeen years, from 1952 to 1969) offered to run the sale—provided that the institute would receive the proceeds as well as any remaining art. The sale of furniture and other knickknacks raised over $20,000, but only a few artworks sold, which resulted in a gift to the institute of a second set of Shaw works.

Eleven of the paintings and pastels received from Shaw's collection were deaccessioned in 1965 and traded, along with other works, to the Victor Sparks Gallery in New York for a portrait by the early nineteenth-century American artist Thomas Sully and two seventeenth-century Flemish paintings. A major risk in deaccessioning is that tastes change and histories are rewritten. What seems of little value one year may, even one decade later, find new appreciation and be deemed an important art historical link. This happened with some of the Shaw works. They were disposed of just a few years before America's bicentennial brought new attention and value to American art prior to 1945. Happily, decades later, two other works that Shaw had owned were generously given to the institute to rejoin the rest of his collection. One of them, an elegant Emil Carlsen still life donated by Stella Hall, is illustrated in this book (see pp. 78–79).

During the 1950s and 1960s, other collections yielded turn-of-the-century paintings that would complement those from Shaw's collection. Especially notable are gifts

14. Carr, 28.

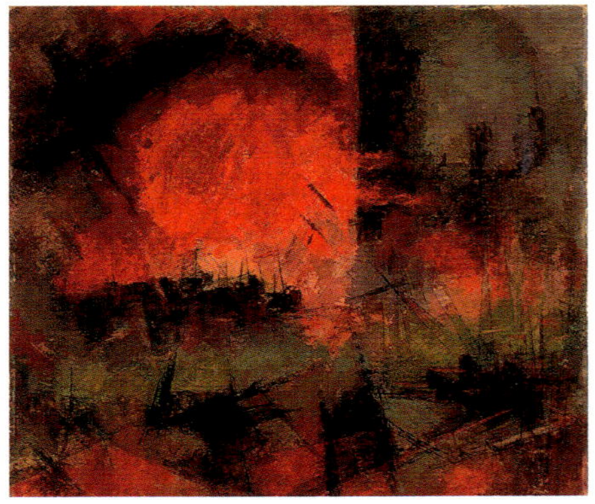
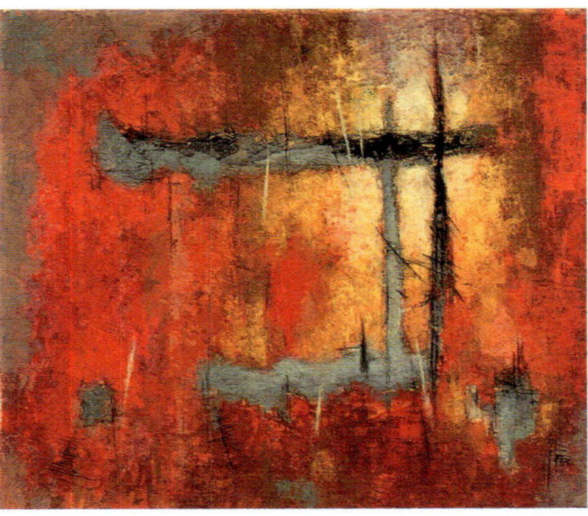
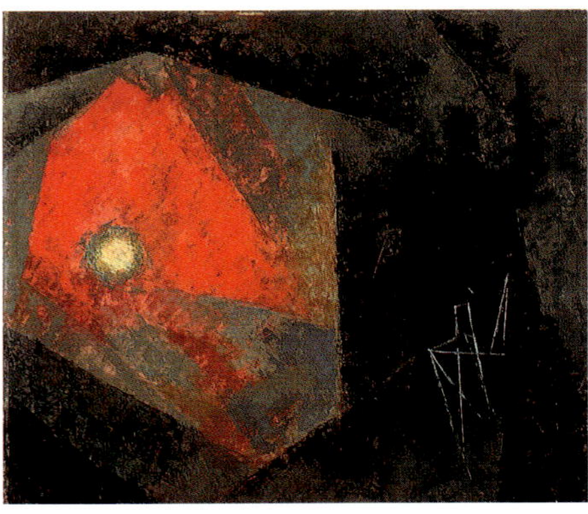

Leroy Flint's *Apocalypse, A Triptych* was purchased in 1953, the year that Flint became curator of education at the institute. He had started there in 1950 as a part-time teacher of painting and art history and in 1956 became director.

from S. G. Carkhuff, a Firestone executive, and Ralph Cortell, a Cleveland businessman, each of whom donated twelve objects. Carkhuff's gift included lusciously painted oils of women by American Impressionists Frederick C. Frieseke and Richard E. Miller. Cortell's included landscapes by Alexander Wyant and William Merritt Chase.

Culler left in 1955 and his successor, Robert Luck, stayed only a year. Leroy Flint, the assistant director, was promoted to director in October 1956, a position he held until 1965. As the second-longest serving director (present director Mitchell Kahan is the longest), Flint presided during a time of relative financial stability and steady growth. Another curatorial position was added, this one full-time. The staff of the school also grew, and accreditation was finally awarded.

Flint felt that the museum's most important role was as a teaching institution. His ambition was to build a comprehensive collection to educate the public and the institute's students. A 1961 description of the exhibition program promised that visitors would have access to "semi-permanent installations of Oriental, Mediaeval, Near Eastern, Egyptian, Pre-Columbian and American Indian art and artifacts, as well as Paintings of the 15th, 16th, 17th, 18th, 19th, and 20th centuries."[15] Flint made it one of his major collecting goals to amass "a group of artifacts and works of art that will eventually make it possible to give…interesting insights into other cultures and life in other periods."[16]

Funds were found to purchase a few historical works of significance for the collection, including Eugene Delacroix's *The Apotheosis of William the Silent,* Cima da Conegliano's *Madonna and Child,* and Hendrick de Clerck's *The Conversion of St. Paul.* Flint, however, felt that not all works needed to be important in order to fulfill their educational purpose. Under Culler and Luck, too, items had been acquired for their instructional rather than historic or aesthetic value. Because these less valuable objects could be handled as well as exhibited, they were used as examples in institute classes and offered to area schools in kits that could be borrowed by teachers. This secondary level of object may have led to the genesis of the "education collection," which in 1978 totaled approximately 385 pieces. The education collection provided a convenient cataloguing classification for craft, ethnographic, and other nonart items: utilitarian objects ranging from furniture and pottery to Inuit boots and a Japanese geisha wig; historic items; toys, puppets, and dolls; and tourist souvenirs such as a sperm-whale tooth, a lion's paw, and a Dutch boy's costume. The education collection

15. Outline of offerings for schoolteachers, summer 1961(?), 1; typescript, Akron Art Museum archives.

16. Description of an exhibition in September 1957 in the newly formed Educational Galleries; Akron Art Museum archives.

also diplomatically solved a curatorial problem: what to do with gifts that were not of sufficient quality to enter the primary or "permanent collection."

Donations of all kinds of art found their way into the two collections. In 1959 the Francis McIntosh Sherwin Collection of lace from a Willoughby, Ohio, couple and European and Asian ceramics, furniture, silver, and prints from the collection of Mr. and Mrs. H. D. Foster were acquired. And in 1965 Mrs. George Oenslager arranged for the gift of a large collection of Egyptian antiquities from the American Research Center at Fustat, Egypt.

One problem with having a comprehensive, two-level collection was that the tiny curatorial staff could not expertly evaluate art from so many different cultures and time periods. In addition, the institute still could not afford to fill in the many gaps in its primary collection with significant works. As a result, the quality of the permanent collection continued to be uneven.

In the hope of raising the number of local collections and their level of quality, Flint initiated a series of exhibitions designed to cultivate collecting. Some of these shows drew attention to local private collections, while others brought affordable, museum-quality art for sale from galleries around the country. Visitors were invited "to take advantage of this opportunity to start or add to your own collection or purchase something as a gift or memorial gift [for] the Art Institute"—and many people did just that.[17] An ulterior motive of the series of course was the hope that local collections would eventually be donated to the institution that fostered their birth and development.

While encouraging individuals to donate art or the money with which to purchase it, the trustees and Flint also sought other types of resources. Beginning in 1955 a brighter financial picture made it possible to allocate some of the funds raised by the annual benefit party, the Masked Ball, to the purchase of art. Then Bertl Arnstein proposed that the entire proceeds of the ball be given over to acquisitions; this policy was approved in 1961. The practice continued for a number of years until the financial picture once again darkened. By then the Masked Ball contributions had been put to good use. When the institute's mission changed and deaccessioning of works dated before 1850 occurred in the early 1980s, the sale of items that had been purchased with Masked Ball contributions yielded over $180,000—the largest amount from any single source.

17. **Description of the exhibition *Collectors' Items* held in spring 1959; Akron Art Museum archives.**

In the mid-1950s and 1960s the institute began applying to private foundations for funding and more actively soliciting acquisition funds from individuals. The Charles E. and Mable M. Ritchie Memorial Foundation awarded grants totaling $15,800 to purchase seventeenth-century European works. When deaccessioned in the early 1980s, the Ritchie works brought over $40,000 into the acquisitions fund. In the late 1960s and early 1970s, funds from the John A. McAlonan Trust Fund were used to match grants from the National Endowment for the Arts, making possible the acquisition of works by eight artists. During this period, there were also a number of individual donors to the acquisitions fund, including several leading supporters who chose to remain anonymous.

Whereas twenty years earlier, the institute owned fewer than a hundred objects, by the end of 1965 the permanent and education collections contained over two thousand works, some of which were of art historical significance. The institute's storage space was now bursting at the seams with objects that still represented just a tiny fraction of what would be necessary for a truly comprehensive collection. One of Flint's reasons for desiring such a collection—to meet the educational needs of art and design students—evaporated in 1965 when the school closed, victim to competition from the burgeoning schools of art at the University of Akron and Kent State University. In addition, the collection's overall level of quality did not meet the expectations of some of the institute's more ambitious supporters. A shortage of space and a desire on the part of the board and staff to upgrade the quality of the collection had once before, in the early 1960s, inspired an assessment and weeding out of holdings under board president Bernard Schulman. Clearly the time had come for another major reassessment.

In 1965 these issues were among the concerns that led the board and its president, Walter P. Keith Sr., to commission a management and development study of the institution. Not surprisingly, the consultants found no clear agreement about the institute's overall role or what type of permanent collection it should have. Their recommendation was that the institute "develop its basic education collection and then select a major area of art (probably contemporary) and endeavor to establish a name for itself in that area."[18]

Flint left shortly after the school closed, and during the search for a new director, the trustees seem to have discussed the importance of the collection. In April 1966, under president Frank M. Whiteman, the constitution was revised. One major change

18. Cresap, McCormick & Paget, "Report on Administration and Future Development," March 1965, III-2 and IV-10.

was the insertion of a phrase stressing the need for quality in the collection: the objective now was "to receive and hold in trust for the benefit of the community significant objects of the highest artistic merit."

The next director, Forrest H. Selvig, also stressed the importance of pursuing the highest professional standards for exhibitions, collections display and care, and acquisitions. He had a very different assessment of the proper focus for the collection than Flint. Since the institute did not have the financial resources to compete with larger museums and would never be able to build a distinguished comprehensive collection, Selvig urged a focus on modern art. He and curator Paul Binai emphasized art of the last few decades in the selections they recommended for purchase, such as René Magritte's *Les Pas perdus*.

Selvig was not the first to question the collection's broad focus. A decade earlier George Culler had hoped to make the acquisition of contemporary American and European art a priority but was not persuasive enough to gain support for his program. Culler's successor, Robert Luck, seems to have had similar aspirations and a similar lack of success during his short tenure. While these directors helped pave the way to a more limited focus, it was Selvig's successor, Orrel Thompson, who ushered in the third phase of the collection's development.

By 1969, the year that Thompson was appointed director, the board was ready to make a change. Selvig's programming, while of extremely high quality, had not appealed to the general public, resulting in several years of low attendance. Thompson and his staff revitalized the institute in the public eye, attracting large audiences with festive openings and innovative, cutting-edge exhibitions.

Thompson and curator Al Radloff also worked with the board and its president, Sam S. McKeel, to bring about the first official steps in transforming the institute from an art center with a general collection to a museum specializing in modern and contemporary art. Just two months after Thompson's arrival, the new director and the accessions committee presented to the board a policy directing future acquisitions "toward the art of the present" as part of "a continuing effort to maintain and add to the Institute's contemporary collection, as well as to supplement the collections of the 19th and 20th centuries." This new policy—a crucial step in shaping the institute's future—was passed unanimously.

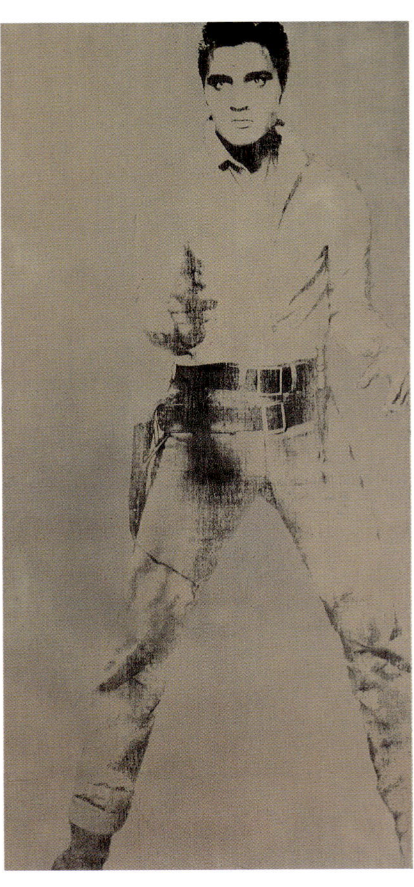

Andy Warhol's *Single Elvis* embodied the new contemporary focus of the institute in 1972, when the painting was purchased with a grant from the National Endowment for the Arts matched by the L. L. Bottsford Estate Fund.

While the policy did not exclude additions to the older segments of the collection "whenever economically feasible and aesthetically practical," purchases of such art became unlikely. Thompson went a step further in 1971–72 and began assessing segments of the collection for deaccessioning. He realized that to expand the modern and contemporary holdings, items no longer relevant to the institute's new focus would have to be sold. Working with the accessions committee and the board, he supervised disposal of segments of the education collection in 1972, but this was called to a halt when it became clear that the practice was offending some of the institute's past donors.

President Louis S. Myers headed the board when it took the second official step toward transforming the institute into a modern art museum in January 1974, the month before Thompson's successor, Robert Doty, started. Programming guidelines were added to the constitution, compelling the institute to "emphasize the best in Regional, National and International Twentieth Century painting, sculpture, and the other visual arts." While acquisitions would be limited primarily to the twentieth century, the board felt that the exhibition program should continue to provide "a cross section of old, new, traditional, and avant-garde."

In reality, twentieth-century art had dominated the institute's exhibitions since its birth because neither funds nor proper facilities were available to host important historical shows. Since the mid-1940s there had been a conscious effort to bring recent national and international art to Akron. This was coupled with a commitment to exhibiting the work of contemporary local artists. In the 1970s exhibitions and acquisitions would finally be in unison and focus on a single, well-articulated goal: a concentration on twentieth-century art.

The 1970s were an especially propitious time for this switch in focus. When Thompson took over as director in 1969, the institute was more financially stable than it had ever been and an endowment fund, though small, was in place. It had been settled into its home at 69 East Market Street for almost twenty years and was approaching its fiftieth anniversary—an occasion for reflection on its history and current mission as well as an opportunity for special fund-raising and significant gifts of art. The institution could afford to direct funds from the Anniversary Gala to the purchase of a sculpture by George Segal, set aside money for art purchases, and consider a serious commitment to future acquisitions.

Between 1968 and 1978 the institute spent over $165,000 on acquisitions and received gifts valued at almost $500,000. The two directors during that period, Thompson and Doty, found that there were donors—local individuals and foundations as well as the National Endowment for the Arts—enthusiastic about helping the institute acquire contemporary art. A number of the most ardent supporters served on the accessions committee: Ruth Roush, Dr. Louis Kacalieff, Dr. George Proskauer, and Mary S. Myers all chaired the committee during this period; also extremely active were committee members Rory O'Neil and Norman Carr. The committee's knowledge of and enthusiasm for contemporary art played a large part in finally beginning to focus the collection. Mary Myers's involvement with public art in Akron and her friendship with Claes Oldenburg led in 1976 to the creation of a work made especially for the city, *Inverted Q*. Mary and her husband, Louis, donated this playful, witty sculpture to the institute, and it still graces the museum's Myers Sculpture Courtyard.

The 1960s and early 1970s were a period of excitement and astonishing growth in the market for contemporary art. With the advent of Pop Art, avant-garde work ceased to be of interest to just a few cognoscenti and entered popular culture, thanks to glitterati such as Andy Warhol. As the market mushroomed, galleries flourished. To reward customers, cement professional friendships, and help establish the reputations of rising stars, some dealers donated works to museums.

To ensure that the institute benefited from this largesse, collectors such as Mary and Louis Myers and Dedee and Rory O'Neil, as well as directors Thompson and Doty, prevailed upon their art world connections. Gifts were received from galleries in New York, Minneapolis, Cleveland, and Cincinnati. O. K. Harris, a New York gallery, not only sent some of

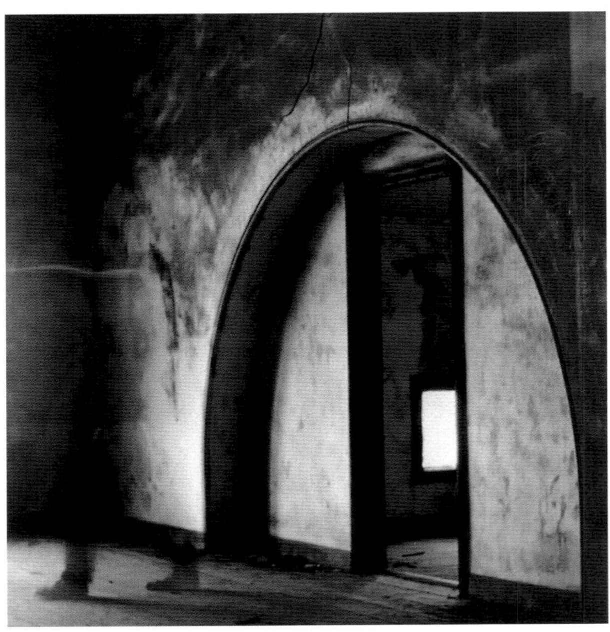

Ralph Eugene Meatyard's untitled 1966 photograph demonstrates a benefit of the exhibition program. When the museum organized a retrospective of the artist's work in 1991, three images from the exhibition were purchased with funds from Anne Alexander and the Museum Acquisition Fund. Five more Meatyard photographs were later donated by Christopher and Diane Meatyard.

its own holdings but also arranged for one of its clients, New York collector Monroe Meyerson, to donate works, including two by Warhol. Art professionals from other organizations also made Akron the subject of their personal generosity, sometimes donating avant-garde works on which the board of trustees might have been leery to expend the institute's limited funds: for example, Yayoi Kusama's *Arm Chair* and Lee Bontecou's untitled sculpture.

Another resource sympathetic to the acquisition of cutting-edge work was the National Endowment for the Arts, which began a grant program to help fund the purchase of works by living artists. Akron took full advantage of this important program. Through grants from the endowment, thirty-five works were purchased between 1972 and 1981, when the program was discontinued. Its brief revival in 1990–91 allowed the acquisition of two additional works. The grants supplied only half the purchase price of the works; matching funds were required. None of the art could have been bought without the generosity of local donors including the L. L. Bottsford Estate Fund, the McAlonan Trust Fund, The Sisler McFawn Foundation, the Elizabeth Firestone Graham Foundation, the Firestone Foundation, and the Mary S. and Louis S. Myers Foundation.

Although a few of the works chosen by the accessions committee and institute staff for the National Endowment for the Arts grants were by acknowledged masters such as Ansel Adams and Joseph Stella, most were by emerging or mid-career artists. Thompson was particularly willing to take chances on younger artists and made several quite astute choices, including a work by Andy Warhol. The artist had been an established painter for less than a decade when his *Single Elvis* was acquired with an endowment grant in 1972. That same grant also brought to Akron a sculpture by Donald Judd, a much riskier selection at the time. Other artists whose works were purchased with endowment support include Robert Morris, Nancy Graves, Frank Stella, and William T. Wiley. The 1990 grant, matched by funds from the Elizabeth Firestone Graham Foundation, was used to acquire works by Robert Arneson and Nancy Spero—mature artists who were working somewhat out of the mainstream.

Despite its newly acquired holdings of contemporary art and its changed focus, the institute remained burdened in the 1970s by its old identity and by its collection. The trustees were aware that the historical works in the collection "were too few in number and insufficient in quality to provide a coherent view of past art" and that it was impossible to compete in that arena with the nearby Cleveland Museum of Art.[19] They also realized that the recent commitment to a twentieth-century focus made Akron unique in the region, since at that time there was no museum devoted to modern art between Buffalo and Chicago. Nonetheless, the permanent collection—which had grown to 3,186 objects in 1978—remained primarily an eclectic assortment of items from different centuries and continents. The 386 items in the education collection were even more far-flung in content and were little used.

The need to bring the collection in line with the institute's stated focus became even more pressing in 1978. It was a terrible year for Akron. Firestone closed one factory; Goodyear shut down most of its Akron tire production. This began almost a decade of high unemployment and troubling economic recession. At the end of it, Akron was no longer the Rubber City. Up to this point, the institute's fortunes had always been tied to those of Akron and the rubber industry. Ironically, Akron's most depressed period, the late 1970s and early 1980s, was a time of prosperity and growth for the institute.

This good fortune was due to the remarkable generosity of an anonymous donor. A devoted patron of the institute, this individual stepped forward with three million dollars to make possible a move across the street to 70 East Market Street, an architecturally significant former post office building that is the museum's current site. The donor also asked that additional funds be raised and set aside to enlarge the endowment so that it could supply a large percentage of the new facility's annual operating expenses. Slightly over two million more dollars were raised from the community in a campaign chaired by Louis Myers. The new site offered more parking, a better gallery configuration, and a loading dock, but not more storage space. If the move across the street was to proceed and the contemporary portion of the collection to continue to grow, then works that did not fit in with the new emphasis on the twentieth century had to be jettisoned.

John Coplans, Doty's successor, was perfectly willing to make such a decisive break with the past. Described in the headline of an *Akron Beacon Journal* profile as "a restless

19. "Current Akron Art Museum Collection Policies," written in 1974 and revised in 1982.

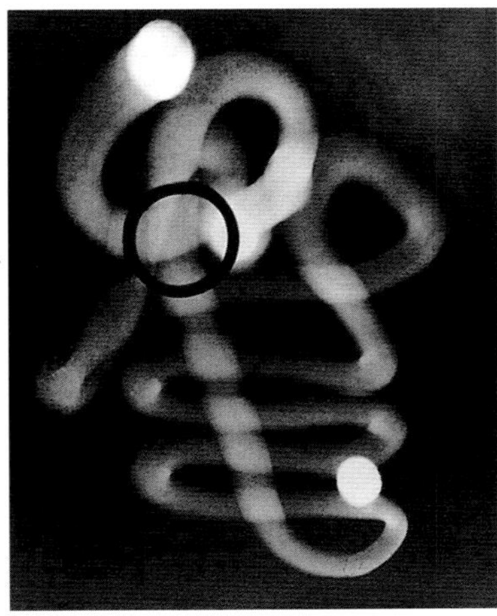

Margaret De Patta's *Positive Form #15, Squiggles with Black*, produced in the 1930s, came to the museum's attention during the organization of the 1996–97 exhibition *A History of Women Photographers*. Funds donated by Mrs. Beatrice K. McDowell allowed three rare works from that show, including the De Patta photogram, to join the collection.

achiever" who "shakes things up," Coplans arrived in Akron in February 1978.[20] His immediate task was to produce a feasibility study for the new site that would determine the future direction of the institute and its collections. Since 1970 the board had periodicially discussed the possibility of a new building for the institute. Several locations, including the old post office building, had been explored. Building on the board's previous deliberations, Coplans added his own thoughts, proposing solutions that were drastic but well reasoned. With a few modifications from the board and later staff, Coplans's ideas shaped the institution's new collection and collecting policies.

It was evident that even with the donor's generosity the institute could not afford the cost of necessary space, either in a new building or in off-site storage—nor did it have a reliable source of funds for future acquisitions. The goal, extant since its founding, that the institute would eventually become a large museum was finally abandoned. Instead, a decision was made to winnow the collection and promote the institution as an exhibition center with small but choice holdings of modern art.

The new plan proposed that exhibitions and collections would both address the slice of art history between 1850 and the present—which was somewhat broader than the earlier focus on the twentieth century. Although the institute would still exhibit regional and European art, its emphasis would be on American art of national significance. Coplans chose 1850 as a starting date because it was when "the essentially agrarian structure of American society was overthrown by the Industrial Revolution" and America, departing from European models, began to develop its own character.[21] Holdings in American art of the last half of the nineteenth century would be complemented by modernist American art since 1945, when American painting and sculpture dominated the art world. "The melding of these two arenas...seems peculiarly suited to...Akron, whose wealth and productivity derives from the American experience of the Industrial Revolution, located as it is in the heart of the American 'Ruhr.'"[22]

Implementing this new mission meant that all American and European art predating 1850 as well as all works from other cultures and the entire education collection

20. Dorothy Shinn, "A Restless Achiever Shakes Things Up at the Art Institute," *Akron Beacon Journal*, July 29, 1979, 6.

21. John Coplans, "Akron Art Institute: Feasibility Study," May 1, 1978, 47; typescript, Akron Art Museum archives.

22. Ibid., 49.

had to be sold. The money from their sale would then be used to "build the nucleus of a first-rate modern collection."[23] New purchases would be concentrated in the areas of photography and recent sculpture. The institute owned few photographic works but had acquired major sculptures by Claes Oldenburg, Donald Judd, and George Segal in the 1970s. Both media were undervalued at the time, so it was possible to purchase important pieces even with limited resources.

The accessions committee and the board approved the plan in May and the lengthy, careful, multistep deaccessioning process began. The requirements were evaluation by outside experts, notification of donors, and approval by the accessions committee and the board for the deaccessioning and method of disposal of each item. As had long been the policy, monies from the sale of artworks could only be used for the purchase of art for the collection. Lauded by *ARTnews* magazine as a model for other institutions, Akron's procedures were in accord with the highest professional standards.[24]

The first works to be sent for auction were seven European paintings; these sold in the winter of 1978–79 at Sotheby Parke-Bernet, fetching around $150,000. These particular items were chosen not only for their value but also because they had been purchased by the institute. There were no donors to offend. Nevertheless, when word spread through town that the institute was getting rid of its old collection to focus on modern art, a furor ensued. Mary Saalfield and other board members and institute supporters worked hard to soothe ruffled feathers, but it took several years for the ferment to subside.

Deaccessioning is an ongoing, normal part of the development of a collection. The institute had deaccessioned groups of works before—in 1949, 1953, 1963, 1965, 1968, and 1972. These previous deaccessioning campaigns had been kept from the public eye for fear of offending past donors. In contrast, the 1978–79 sales were done quite openly, both to adhere to a new code of professional ethics and to help spread the word about the institute's new identity. Since the shift in mission had been a gradual process over the previous decade, the degree of surprise and dismay expressed by the community suggested that previous changes had not been effectively communicated. It also served as a reminder that modern art was, and continues to be, popularly regarded as inaccessible, even irrelevant, to most people's lives.

23. Ibid., 52–54.

24. "Dumping the whole thing," *ARTnews* 78 (May 1979): 10–11.

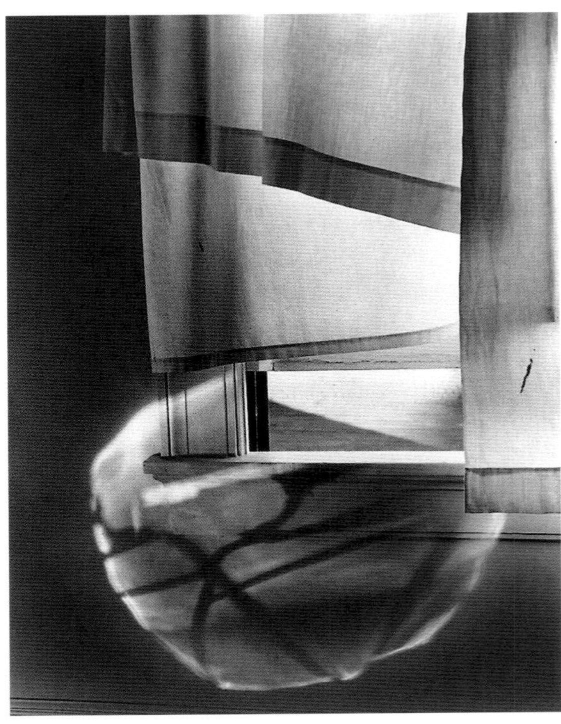

Minor White's *Windowsill Daydreaming* is one of twelve photographs in White's renowned *Jupiter Portfolio,* which was acquired in 1975 with funding from the National Endowment for the Arts and the L. L. Bottsford Estate Fund. For several decades, the museum's goal has been to represent artists in depth rather than by a single work.

One solution was to present art that was relevant to the lives of people in Akron but did not sacrifice the standard of art historical significance called for in the new mission. To this end Coplans involved the institute in a project that would explore Akron's industrial heritage and its present situation. With support from the National Endowment for the Arts and Centran Bank of Akron, he commissioned Lee Friedlander to photograph the industrial landscape in and around Akron. Eighty images from the series entered the collection in 1981. These now-famous photographs, shot in 1979–80 in eastern Ohio and western Pennsylvania, captured the bleak, forlorn mood of what would soon be identified as the "rust belt."

Even as Friedlander was still shooting, plans for a second photographic portrait of the region were initiated. Its subject—the area's natural beauty—would counterbalance the Factory Valleys series' emphasis on industry and decay. This second project began with a suggestion from institute supporter David B. Cooper, who proposed a collaboration with the region's newly created national park, the Cuyahoga Valley National Recreation Area. Cooper, Carolyn Kinder Carr (curator from 1978 to 1983), and two park officials, superintendent William Birdsell and interpreter Ron Thoman, recommended commissioning a fine art photographer working in color to document the park. Despite a number of delays the project was not abandoned. In 1985 director Kathleen Monaghan selected photographer Robert Glenn Ketchum, who completed the project in 1988. A number of donors made possible the acquisition of forty-three of Ketchum's images, so that both views of Akron's environment and history would be available to future generations.

The institute had only a minuscule photography collection before Coplans arrived. Hervey Minns's images, donated in 1924, had burned in the 1942 fire. It was not until 1967, when photographer Vernon Cheek donated eleven of his own works, that the medium again had a place in the collection. In 1975 director Robert Doty, renowned for his expertise in the area of photography, had used funds from the National Endowment for the Arts, matched by local donations, to purchase key works by two masters—Ansel Adams and Minor White.

It was still possible in the late 1970s to start a photography collection worthy of national recognition. While Coplans purchased a few individual pieces ranging from Alfred Stieglitz's masterpiece, *The Steerage*, to works by younger artists Duane Michals, Jan Groover, and Joel Meyerowitz, his principal strategy was to acquire bodies of work by individual artists. During this period, Akron acquired in-depth holdings: 34 scenes by Walker Evans, 44 satirical photomontages by John Heartfield, all 120 gravures from Karl Blossfeldt's *Wundergarten der Natur*, and the complete George N. Barnard album on the Civil War. Generous gifts from Beatrice and C. Blake McDowell Jr. and Mary and Louis Myers made some of these acquisitions possible. Collectors around the country also were solicited, resulting in the donation of works by Elliot Erwitt, Manuel Alvarez Bravo, Margaret Bourke-White, and others. Coplans himself gave a number of items, including twenty-two photographs by Lewis W. Hine, images by Heartfield, Eadweard Muybridge, and Hans Namuth, and sculptures by Man Ray and Marcel Duchamp.

Coplans departed in December 1979, long before the deaccessioning was completed. Purchases during his two years as director amounted to a little over $35,000. The pleasure of spending most of the money from deaccessioning and the responsibility of building a collection of recent painting and sculpture were left to curator Carr and director I. Michael Danoff, Coplans's successor, with the active participation of the accessions committee chaired first by Mary Myers and then by Celeste Roush Myers. Over $880,000 was spent on art between 1978 and 1984. By focusing on nationally recognized mid-career artists, the institution was able to acquire a number of major, large-scale works while hedging its bets on the artists' future significance. Those bets paid off—the choices, many guided by Danoff's collecting acumen, put Akron on the map for its holdings of painting and sculpture since 1960.

A variety of styles was necessary to represent the pluralism of the art scene at the time. The photorealism of Chuck Close and Richard Estes complemented the more traditional realistic approach of Philip Pearlstein's paintings of models done in his studio. Frank Stella's increasingly baroque abstractions contrast sharply with the minimalist, rectilinear aesthetic of sculptures by Sol LeWitt and Jackie Winsor, as well as earlier acquisitions by

Donald Judd and Robert Morris. Gifts from the Myers collection provided examples of lyrical abstraction from the hands of Helen Frankenthaler and Morris Louis. Works by Pop artists Claes Oldenburg, George Segal, and Andy Warhol had already been acquired in the 1970s.

The move into the new building, overseen by Mary Saalfield and her successor as board president, John V. Frank, inspired the acquisition of somewhat massive outdoor sculptures to fill the large courtyard. Claes Oldenburg's *Inverted Q,* a gift of Mary and Louis Myers, was moved from the garden of the old site. They then donated another work—Emile-Antoine Bourdelle's *Figures hurlantes* (Howling Figures)—and a portion of the funds required to match a National Endowment for the Arts grant for the purchase of Nancy Graves's *Variability and Repetition of Similar Forms II.* Monies from the Firestone Foundation and from deaccessioning completed the matching funds. It was also a grant from the National Endowment for the Arts, supplemented by a contribution from The Sisler McFawn Foundation and money from deaccessioning, that made possible the acquisition of Mark di Suvero's *Eagle Wheel.* A fifth sculpture, Bryan Hunt's *Shift Falls,* was acquired with funds from an anonymous donor.

In October 1980 the importance of collecting as part of the institution's mission was sealed by a name change. The Akron Art Institute, which implied an educational focus, became the Akron Art Museum. Danoff worked with the accessions committee and the board to further refine the collecting policy, which was approved at the November board meeting. Primary emphasis was placed on painting, sculpture, photography, and graphics. While holdings of graphics, or works on paper, were included in the policy, these would be expanded primarily by gifts; little money was to be devoted to this area, one of the weakest parts of the collection.

Carolyn Carr worked on a policy to guide photography acquisitions. Coplans had hoped to acquire both recent works and vintage prints of earlier photography. However, by the mid-1980s the photography market had heated up to the point that vintage prints of important nineteenth- and early twentieth-century works were out of Akron's reach. The decision was made to focus on photography since the 1950s, which remained reasonably priced.

Most of the photography acquisitions in the early and mid-1980s were documentary images; among these were donations from Carolyn Carr and her husband Norman of works by Weegee, Walker Evans, Eugene Atget, and others. A few images by Sandy Skoglund and Cindy Sherman, representing the then-new post-modernist approach to photography, were also acquired. The large-scale color prints of these two artists employ a fictional, narrative approach to the medium that is more akin to painting than photography. Their style caught the eye of Michael Danoff, who was among the first museum directors to champion their work.

The next major additions to the photography collection occurred under the brief tenure of Kathleen Monaghan, director from September 1984 to September 1985. Monaghan recommended the acquisition of three important bodies of photography twenty color prints of urban scenes by Harry Callahan, purchased with funds donated by New York collector Arthur Goldberg; sixteen Robert Frank images on the subject of American politics; and ten ironic images from Jim Goldberg's Rich and Poor series.

By this point money from deaccessioning had been exhausted. Local foundations were no longer reliable sources for art purchases. Individual donors have continued, of course, to be a source of acquisition funds and art in recent years. Particularly outstanding in this regard is Beatrice Knapp McDowell. Since 1990 she has generously supported the purchase of works by a number of women artists ranging from those with regional reputations to those of international stature. In addition, Stephen White, a dealer and collector from Los Angeles, has added over a hundred images to the museum's photography collection over the past decade. Nevertheless it was necessary to *ensure* the future growth of the collection. The only way to do this was to establish an endowment devoted to the purchase of art.

This idea had been first proposed by Mary Myers in 1981 at the conclusion of fund-raising for the new museum. Since funds from that campaign had been solicited specifically to support operating costs, one of her highest priorities was to initiate an endowment campaign that would both stabilize the museum's finances in response to the inflation of the 1980s and provide a regular source of acquisition funds. The campaign began under president M. Donald McClusky and continued under three following presidents: Mary Myers, C. Gordon Ewers, and Judith B. Isroff. As an impetus, Mary and Louis Myers created an endowed fund for painting and sculpture which to date has enabled the museum to purchase Richard Deacon's *Cover,* Andy Warhol's *Brillo Box,* Lari Pittman's *Thankfully, I will have had learned to break glass with sound,* and Raoul Hague's *Angel Millbrook Walnut.*

Mitchell Kahan, who came to the museum in the spring of 1986 and would become the institution's longest serving director, worked with the board and development director Arlene Rossen on the endowment campaign. Annual income from sixty percent of the new money raised was earmarked for operating expenses and forty percent for acquisitions.

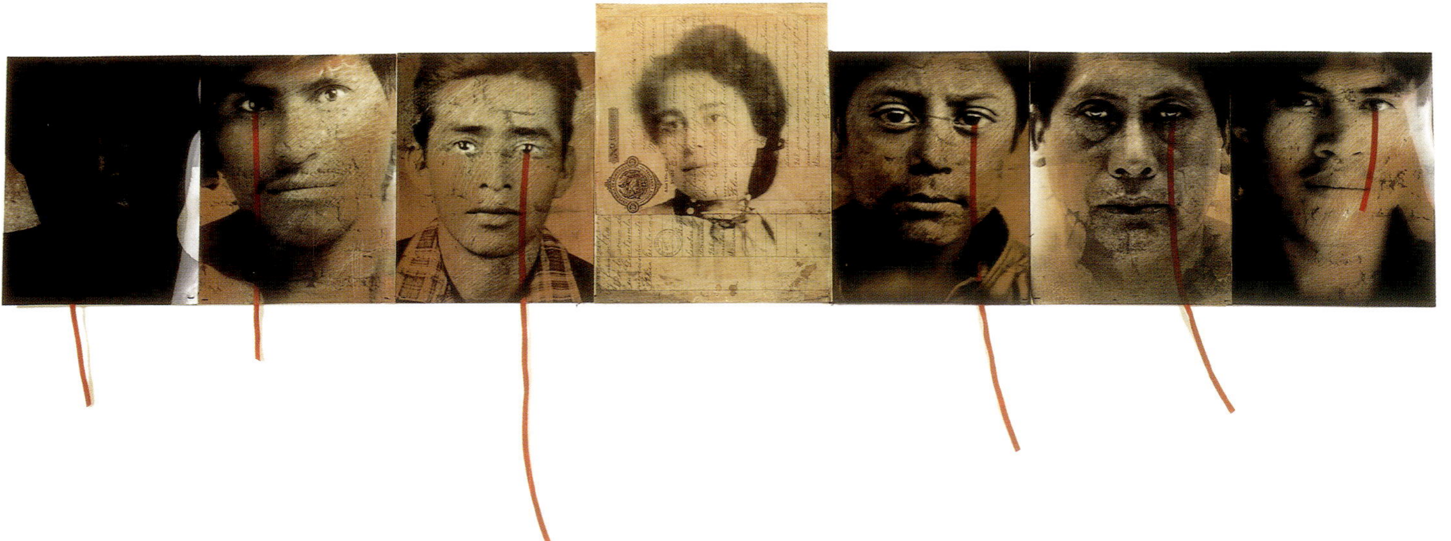

Luis González Palma's *Ella me ha pedido que la olvide* (She Asked Me to Forget Her) approaches the photograph both as an object and an image. This 1993 work by a Guatemalan artist is one of a number of acquisitions in the 1980s and 1990s that reflect the increasing internationalism of the art world.

new money raised was earmarked for operating expenses and forty percent for acquisitions. By 1991 accrued interest, along with money from the Myers Fund, made possible a major purchase—the Deacon sculpture. This income continues to grow.

In 1990 Kahan approached the John S. and James L. Knight Foundation for funds to establish the Knight Purchase Award for Photographic Media. Assisting with this initiative from the outset was David B. Cooper, who at this time was a member of the accessions committee. The foundation generously donated $300,000 to set up an endowment fund that currently generates over $32,000 per year for the purchase of works by living artists using photographically based media. The award guarantees that the photography collection will be able to keep up with new trends and styles over the years, and it continues a tradition dating back to the Friedlander commission—that of museum support for living photographers.

The Knight funds, supplemented with gifts from the artist and funds from former docent Eleanor W. Aggarwal and her husband, S. L. Aggarwal, made possible the acquisition of thirteen classic black-and-white images by the first winner of the prize, Harry Callahan. These complement his color works, which had been purchased earlier. Other acquisitions with Knight Fund income include two Robert Rauschenberg photogravures, Thomas Struth's monumental image of museum-goers, Gilbert & George's irreverent mural-sized self-portrait, and Carrie Mae Weems's explorations of African American folklore and culture. The most recent Knight purchases have been a series of Hiroshi Sugimoto's austere, elegant seascapes and two diptychs by Sophie Calle combining text and photographic images. Both the Knight and Myers endowed funds are key to the continued growth of the collection.

Under Kahan and curator Barbara Tannenbaum (who began as curator in 1985), the museum ventured into two new collecting areas: video art and the work of self-trained artists. The first reflects technological changes in the materials and techniques used by artists; the second is an art historical reappraisal of what types of art merit serious study.

The video collection, while still quite small, includes both single-channel tapes and a video sculpture. The tapes entered the collection through the generosity of the Elizabeth

Firestone Graham Foundation, which has supported many of the museum's most challenging efforts over the past thirteen years. In 1987 and 1989 the foundation funded two exhibitions of single-channel video and the purchase of equipment and tapes ranging from William Wegman's humorous performances with his dog to the meditative works of Bill Viola. The video sculpture by the "father of video art," Korean-born Nam June Paik, was purchased in 1987 with funds donated by trustee Irving Sands and his wife Harriett. It is a baby video robot composed of a metal frame holding thirteen small television sets, all of which simultaneously play the same tape. The video transmissions become the blood and energy coursing through the baby robot's veins. The museum also acquired a single-channel video and a set of etchings by Paik. Whenever economically feasible, Kahan and Tannenbaum prefer to represent the multiple facets of artists who work in more than one medium.

The museum is one of only a handful of modern art museums seriously collecting the work of self-taught (also known as outsider or contemporary folk) artists. Most self-taught artists are blue-collar laborers who began making art out of a personal need. Some are inspired by religious or mystical visions, others by a desire to communicate a political or social message, and others simply by the desire to exercise their creativity. Integrating this type of art into a collection of modern and contemporary art makes sense since it has influenced many twentieth-century academically trained artists. Contemporary folk art can also stand on its own as a powerful visual expression of the concerns of contemporary life. The values it reflects are often those of the working classes rather than the elite groups associated in the past with museums. Because most museums today strive to serve all segments of their community, the fostering of collections that reflect diversity is a logical step.

In the 1970s Robert Doty helped pioneer acceptance of outsider art by organizing and hosting important exhibitions at the institute, but he did not buy any examples for the collection. The museum's first purchase of this type of art came in 1987 under Kahan and Tannenbaum and was made possible by a grant from the Elizabeth Firestone Graham Foundation. The piece was William L. Hawkins's scene of Akron's own landmark, Perkins Mansion. The museum now owns around fifty works, including masterpieces by Ohio woodcarver Elijah Pierce and North Carolina painter Minnie Evans. Two regional artists, W. D. "Crazy Mac" or "Mad Mac" McCaffrey of Akron and Anthony Joseph Salvatore of Youngstown, are represented in depth. The country's leading folk art collector, Herbert Waide Hemphill Jr., and several local collectors donated many of these works.

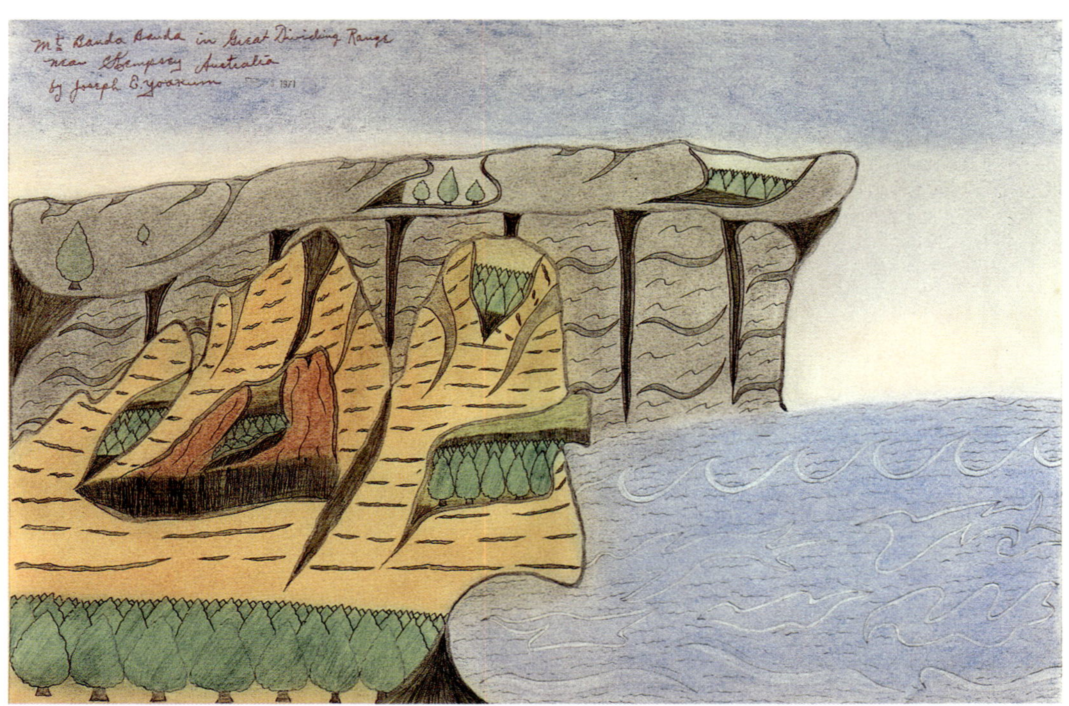

Joseph Yoakum's *Mt. Banda Banda in Great Dividing Range near Kempsey Australia,* 1971, may depict a memory of a real voyage or a flight of the artist's imagination. Donated by Herbert Waide Hemphill Jr. in 1991, this drawing and other works by self-taught artists help broaden the collection to mirror the diversity of the museum's audience.

Contemporary folk art and video art will certainly not be the last new types of work to enter the museum's collection. Just as the Myers, Knight, and general endowment funds guarantee that the collection will continue to grow in size, the open-ended nature of the museum's mission promises that the collection will also change and evolve. A beginning, but not an end date, was set forth in the mission defined in 1978. The board mandated the institution's current and future interest in contemporary art—not just that of the twentieth century but also that of the twenty-first and beyond.

This willingness to acknowledge the importance of the new will endure—perhaps for the rest of the institution's history. For its first quarter century, the institute that hoped to become a museum remained an art center. It owned only a few dozen objects, all of them gifts. In 1945 collecting began in earnest and funds were finally devoted to purchasing art. During this second phase of the collection's history, ambition again exceeded the organization's limited resources. While the goal was to build a comprehensive collection, the result was an eclectic group of objects of widely varying quality.

Half a century after the institute's founding, a focus was finally established—modern and contemporary art. By specializing and by devoting increased energies and funds to acquisitions, the museum was able to develop a sizable core collection of important works. The trustees' commitment to collecting continues to grow. In 1997 the museum marked its seventy-fifth anniversary with an endowment campaign chaired by Judith Isroff. Once again, forty percent of the income from this additional endowment was dedicated to acquisitions, allowing future generations to build upon that core collection. Greatly enlarged gallery space for long-term display of the collection is a high priority in the museum's expansion plans.

When A. H. Marks donated Elliot Torrey's *Surf* to the Akron Art Institute in 1924, he demonstrated his faith that the fledgling organization would be as durable as the rocks of the coastline, not as fleeting as the breaking waves. His faith has been shared by numerous donors of funds and art over the past three-quarters of a century. As the museum moves toward the completion of its first century, this book and the nationally recognized collection represented in it confirm that their faith has not been misplaced.

Dimensions are cited with height preceding width preceding depth. The arrangement of works is generally chronological and also reflects shared aesthetics.

One Hundred Works from the Collection

Jack Becker

Alexander Wyant

Although Alexander Wyant received very little formal instruction in art, by the late nineteenth century he had become one of the nation's most respected landscape painters. The artist's late works are frequently rendered in somber tones with heavily layered paint and expressive brushwork; they are characterized by an introspective and poetic view of nature, which attracted the attention of critics, collectors, and younger artists.

Wyant began working as a saddle maker and a sign maker in his native Ohio. In 1857, on a trip to Cincinnati, his life changed when he saw pictures by George Inness, which so impressed him that he decided to become an artist. Two years later he traveled to New York to meet Inness, who offered advice and encouragement. What training Wyant received, if any, is unclear. In 1863 he settled in New York.

During the early years of his career Wyant followed the practice of the firmly established Hudson River school. As the 1860s progressed, however, he rejected its tight, linear, and finely detailed manner. Following the lead of European art, in particular the works of English landscapist John Constable and the French Barbizon painters, Wyant began to employ a more painterly approach. In 1873, while on a government expedition to Arizona and New Mexico, he suffered a stroke, which partially paralyzed his right side. Unable to paint with his right hand, he trained himself to paint with his left. His physical problems, as well as his penchant for Barbizon landscape, led the artist to develop an even freer and looser style. Wyant's later pictures also generally became smaller in size and more intimate. Rather than fastidiously depicting the details of the natural world, he conveyed poetic impressions of the landscape through the use of somber tones.

Landscape, one of two Wyants in the Akron Art Museum's collection, represents the artist's evolution from a Hudson River style to his later style. In this work Wyant chose to portray not a panoramic, detailed view but a small slice of nature seen from a low viewpoint. The inclusion of framing trees on either side of the composition demonstrates that he has not yet fully rejected Hudson River conventions. His rougher, more expressive later landscapes are devoid of such devices.

Here, giant boulders dominate the view and block the distant landscape. The viewer's attention is drawn to the small pool of water in the right foreground and to the rich colors and surface textures of the rocks, trees, and foreground vegetation where red and green highlights are used to suggest flowers. Thickly layered paint is seen in the tree in the upper right-hand corner, whereas in the broad expanse of the boulders Wyant dragged pigment sparingly across the surface. This picture from midpoint in the artist's career is thus both a backward look to his Hudson River style and a forward look to an expressive handling of paint and the rendering of smaller segments of the natural world.

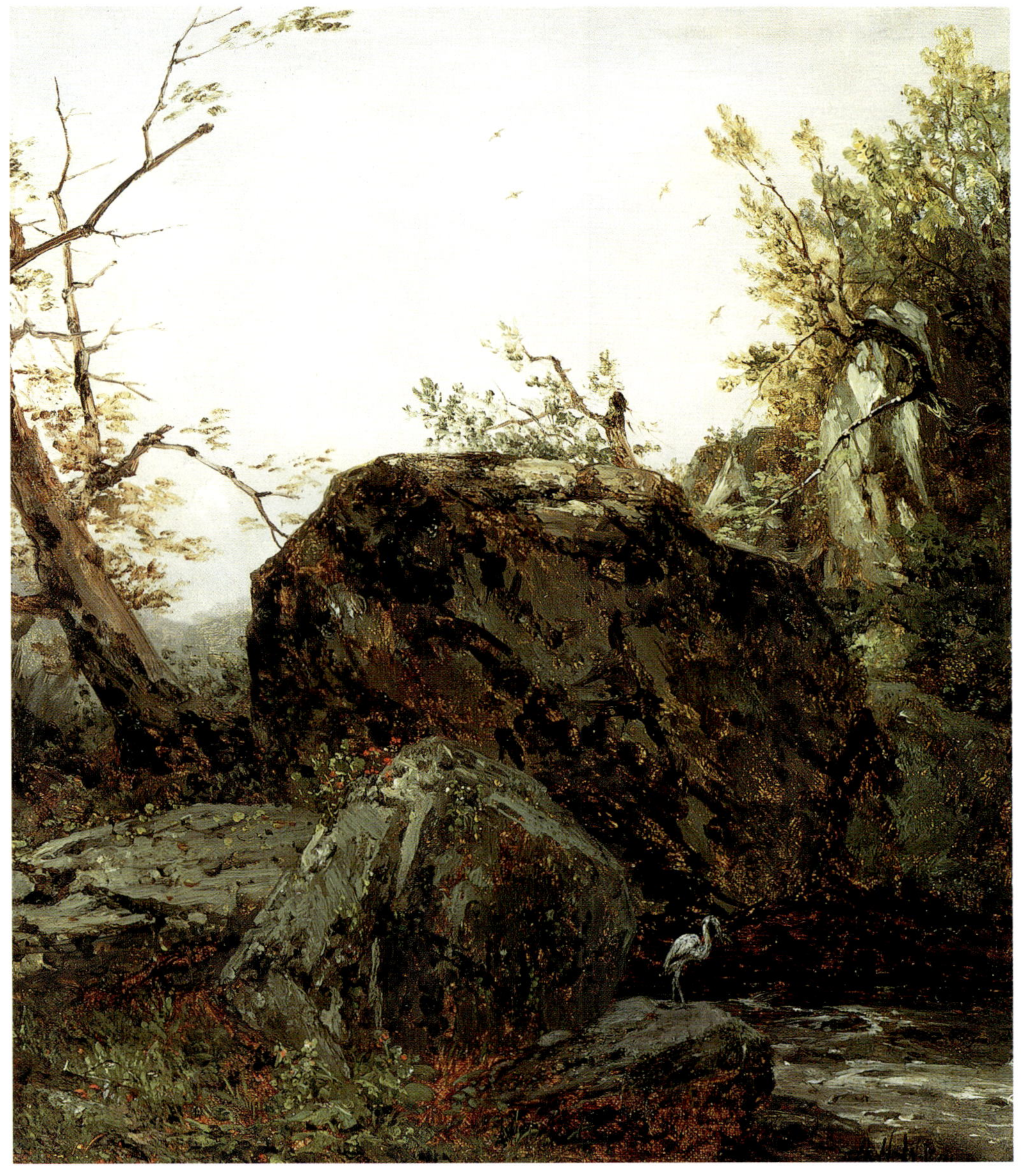

1964.123

Alexander Wyant
Born 1836, Evans Creek, Ohio; died 1892, New York

Landscape, around 1870–80

Oil on canvas mounted on fiberboard; 13 ⅝ x 11 ⅝ in.
Gift of Mr. Ralph Cortell

Keith F. Davis

George N. Barnard

One of the most original and respected photographers in nineteenth-century America, George Barnard entered the profession in 1846 in Oswego, New York, seven years after the invention of photography. He quickly achieved national stature for both the quality of his work and the eloquence of his ideas on the medium's artistic potential. In essays of the early 1850s, Barnard expressed the hope that photography would soon achieve the high artistic status accorded painting and sculpture.

After successfully operating portrait galleries in upstate New York, Barnard worked in New York City with the firms of Edward Anthony and Mathew Brady, and in Washington, D.C., for Alexander Gardner's gallery. Barnard, one of the earliest Civil War photographers, worked in the field in 1861–62. At the end of 1863, he became chief photographer for the Union Army's Military Division of the Mississippi, and accompanied troops in the 1864 occupation of Atlanta and on Sherman's notorious March to the Sea. After the war, he operated galleries in Charleston, Chicago, and Painesville (Ohio).

Today Barnard is best known for his self-published album *Photographic Views of Sherman's Campaign* (1866). Each of its one hundred to one hundred fifty copies contained sixty-one original prints and sold for $100; the albums were aimed at an elite audience of wealthy military men and government officials. While many of the photographs were made during the war in 1864–65, Barnard made a special trip a full year after the war's end to fill gaps in the visual record. The two sets of photographs were combined in a sequence following the Union Army's advance to Atlanta, with concluding views of the decimated cities of Savannah, Columbia, and Charleston.

Sherman's Campaign contains a curious variety of subjects, including scarred battlefields, ruined buildings, scenic landscapes, and bridges, trenches, and forts. Barnard conceived of his pictures as artistic documents that would be both informative *and* beautiful. To this end, he composed his views precisely, later taking the trouble to print clouds into his skies from separate negatives. While these clouds added nothing to the factual value of his views, they were essential to the making of aesthetically satisfying *pictures*.

Since he never recorded actual conflict, Barnard's album is permeated by a mood of melancholy stillness. In fact, these quiet scenes symbolically suggest the overwhelming violence and profound cultural trauma of the war. Mute images of shell-blasted forests, for example, trace the path of a man-made firestorm of desolation.

In *Destruction of Hood's Ordnance Train* the themes of violence and cultural trauma come together in a particularly powerful form. Barnard's photograph shows the remains of an ammunition train that had been ignited several weeks earlier by Confederate troops evacuating Atlanta. The result was a cataclysmic explosion. Here, a ghostly figure stands in the epicenter of the blast, providing a measure of human scale. Incongruously, the sky above is filled with beautiful clouds.

In part, the power of this image stems from what it does not do: it depicts not the violent event but its aftermath, denying in its moody stillness any romantic interpretations of war. Barnard's vision was a product of who he was: a deeply religious northerner who abhorred slavery. While he believed in the Union cause, he had a deep sympathy for the people and the land of the South. Troubled by massive destruction and loss of life, he saw the war as both a political necessity and a cultural tragedy. Through his photographs Barnard sought to document the war and to understand it. His deeply thoughtful images pose a question that haunts us today: how can violence be used as an instrument of justice?

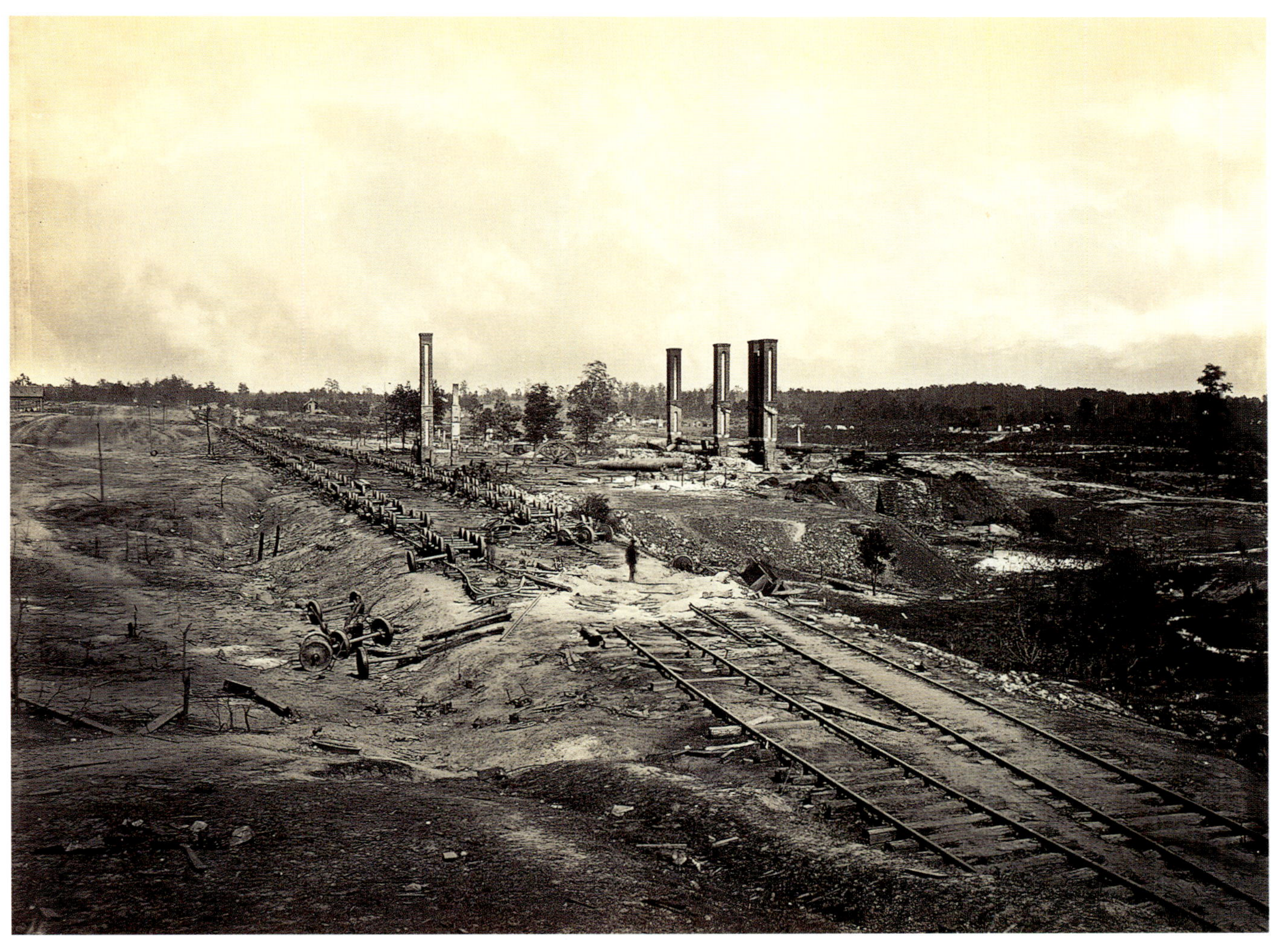

1981.14.44

George N. Barnard
Born 1819, Coventry, Connecticut; died 1902, Cedarvale, New York

Destruction of Hood's Ordnance[1] *Train*, 1864
(Plate 44, *Photographic Views of Sherman's Campaign*, 1866)

Albumen print; 10 x 14 in.
Gift of the Mary S. and Louis S. Myers Family Collection

Jeffrey Grove

Severin Roesen

Although Severin Roesen's life is a mystery and its details are murky, his art could not be more clear nor its details more familiar. He is believed to have emigrated from Germany to settle in New York City around 1848. There he married and began a family that eventually included three children. For unknown reasons, he abandoned his family around 1857 to roam the state of Pennsylvania, settling in the prosperous community of Williamsport in 1862. Roesen left the town in 1872 and is presumed to have died shortly thereafter.

Fewer than four hundred of Roesen's paintings are known to exist, but they have made him one of the best-known nineteenth-century American still-life painters. The qualities that made him a sought-after artist in Pennsylvania a century ago might be decried as commercial today. Roesen was a crowd pleaser: he offered his clients the ultimate embodiment of American optimism. To his wealthy Victorian patrons, paintings such as *Fruit Basket* symbolized the richness and abundance of the land, representing the cornucopia of plenitude their owners had found in the American Eden. To today's viewer, Roesen's paintings may instead recall Dutch still-life painting, which is characterized by painstaking attention to detail and interest in scientific observation. However, the truth suggested by most still-life painting—that it is the permanent replica of an impermanent, natural composition—is not an important factor in paintings by Roesen.

By comparing examples of his work, it becomes clear that Roesen did not work from real objects but from a repertoire of shapes that he kept in his head. These appear time and again in his canvases. Trademark elements include a triangular composition with a horizontal emphasis; a woven or ceramic basket placed on a white or gray marble slab; a water glass—always placed to the left—with lemon rind; and an abundance of grapes, peaches, and plums. Another distinguishing element is the artist's signature spinning out of the grape vine tendrils in the lower right quarter of the composition.

The paradox of presenting an artificially constructed image as the embodiment of natural goodness makes Roesen's work both invigorating and a bit confusing. His manner of constructing a canvas piecemeal may have had less in common with the ideals of fine art than with the pedestrian realities of commercial art. Frequently Roesen's paintings served as bargaining chips or a means of barter to support himself; during one period he traded his paintings for room, board, and beer. (His fondness for the latter may provide insight into his nomadic lifestyle and the abandonment of his family.)

Roesen's paintings were frequently acquired or commissioned for private dining rooms and sometimes for taverns and restaurants. It should not be surprising that his paintings may have appealed to his patrons chiefly for their decorative rather than intrinsically artistic qualities. Roesen, trained in Germany as a decorative artist, supported himself there as a painter of porcelain cups and saucers. His working method—recombining a limited repertoire of forms—may have had its roots in the patterns or formulae often used by china painters.

Roesen's success did not rely primarily on American artistic fashion but on his local popularity, especially during the years he spent in Williamsport. That has changed over the last 150 years, and today Roesen's paintings hang in museums around the country.

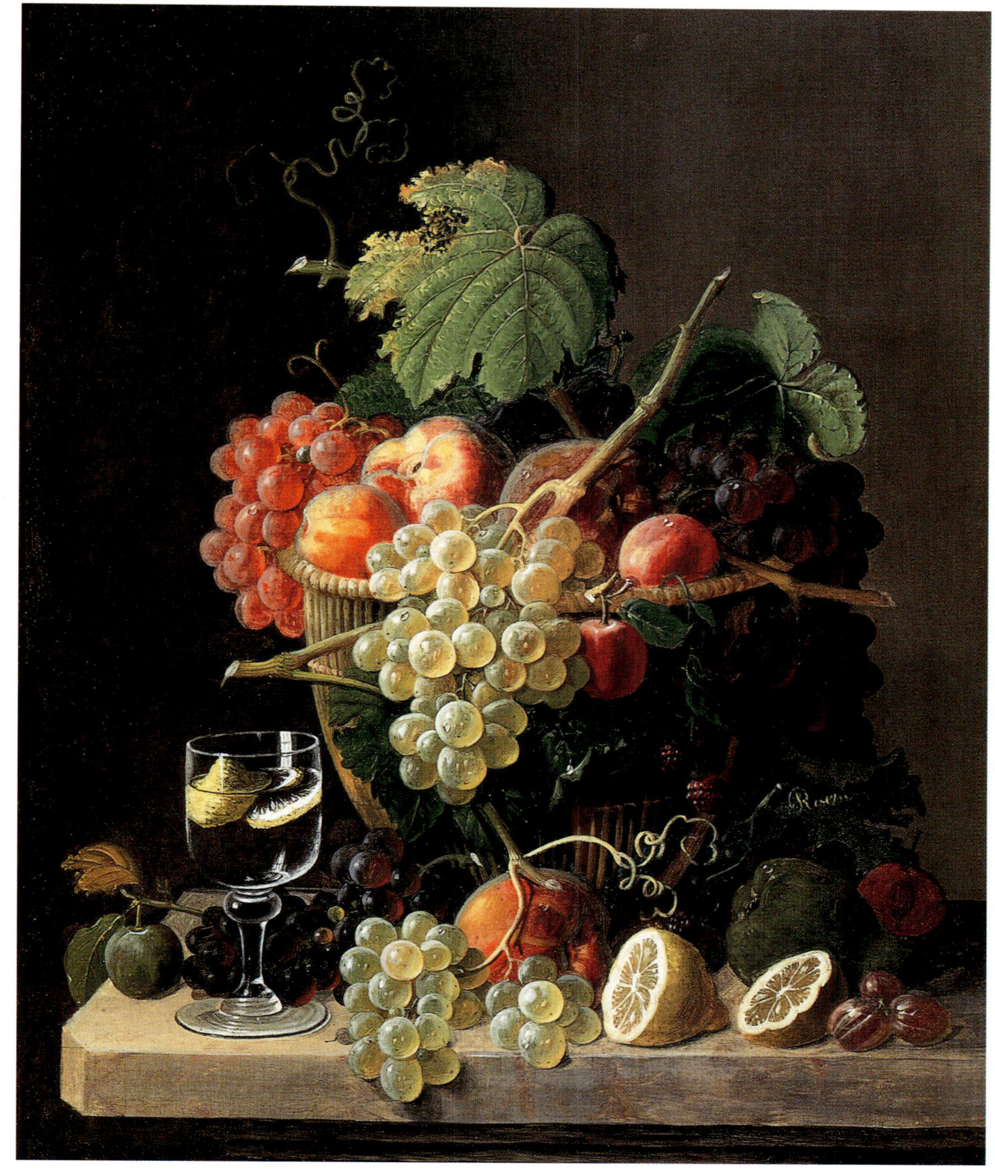

1991.135

Severin Roesen
Born 1815 or 1816, near Cologne, Germany; died around 1872, United States

Fruit Basket, around 1848–60

Oil on canvas; 27 x 22 in.
Gift of Stella B. Hall in memory of her husband, William Curtis Hall Jr.

Jeffrey Grove

Elihu Vedder

One of the few portrait heads that Elihu Vedder painted, *The Sleeping Girl* conveys the same exotic, erotic, and enigmatic aura that distinguishes all of this visionary artist's work. Despite its gentle title suggesting a state of peaceful slumber, this painting alludes to other themes that pervaded Vedder's art: an existential inquiry into the meaning of life and death and an exploration of the schism between sentient and unconscious states.

Though he possessed a great sense of humor and a zest for living, Vedder—who lost two sons to untimely deaths—was haunted by "the hopelessness of man before the immutable laws of nature."[1] Perhaps in reaction to this belief he created an almost metaphysical world in his art, in which allegory, symbolism, mysticism, and the grotesque coexist. Born and raised in Manhattan, Vedder lived primarily in Rome for nearly sixty years. His interest in far-off lands and foreign cultures may have been sparked by the extended periods he spent as a child in Cuba, where his father worked as a dentist. The hot climate, warm colors, exotic fruits, and languorous way of life seems to have had a profound effect on the young artist.

The outcome was a fantastic sensibility atypical for the time. Despite this, or perhaps because of it, Vedder had a distinguished career as a fine artist, illustrator, poet, and designer of decorative arts. His training encompassed both classical and realist influences. He studied briefly in Paris before settling in Florence to study antique and Renaissance art. By the late 1850s he was painting landscapes outdoors with a group of artists known as the Macchiaioli (an Italian equivalent of the French Barbizon school).

Throughout the 1870s, Vedder painted many "ideal heads," as he called his stylized female figures from this period. They did not represent an ideal in the classical sense but rather expressed an otherworldly beauty. *The Sleeping Girl* belongs to a tiny subgroup of these images, one which concentrates more on portraiture than allegorical content. The vast majority were drawn not from a living model but from the artist's imagination.

Many of Vedder's paintings appear to be conjured visions—the products of his tragic and romantic imagination—but it is known that he painted *The Sleeping Girl* from a living model. The artist's daughter recalled: "The girl was a very beautiful young Italian girl called 'Ginditta,' who was living with us as a kind of nursery maid.... Father says she could not pose as she always fell asleep, so he ended by painting her that way."[2]

Even though *The Sleeping Girl* was painted from life, this is not quite a realistic depiction. Vedder chose to garb his subject in a Renaissance costume and give her an ambiguous pose (is she alive or dead?). These few clues hint at some indecipherable allegorical meaning within the painting. Though Vedder was obsessed with death, he did not view it as a negative condition. Rather, he believed that the end of consciousness signals a transition in which the soul is awakened for eternity.

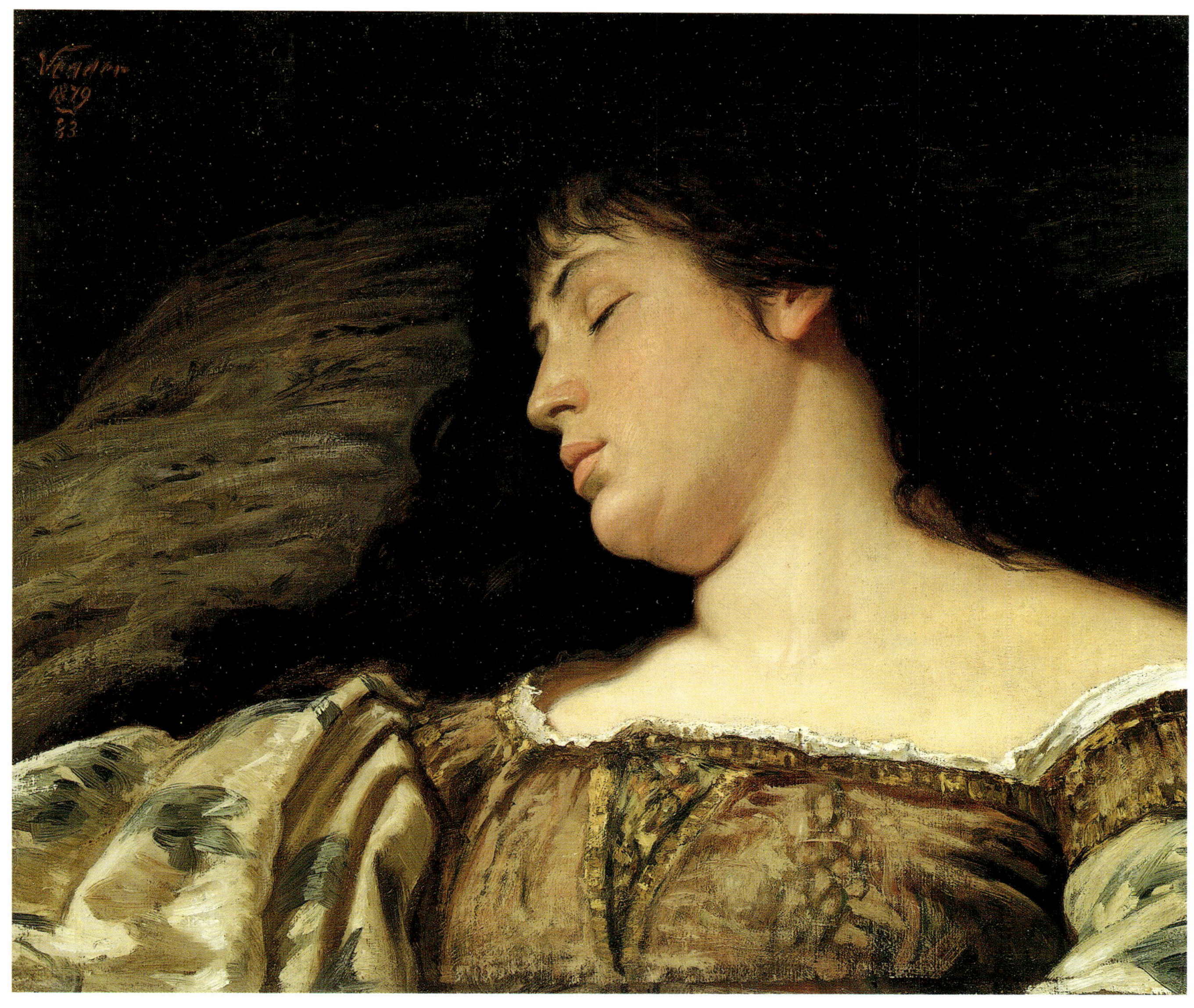

1955.40

Elihu Vedder
Born 1836, New York; died 1923, Rome

The Sleeping Girl, 1879

Oil on canvas; 15 x 18 ¼ in.
Bequest of Edwin C. Shaw

Jeffrey Grove

Emile-Antoine Bourdelle

Exuding passion and violence, *Figures hurlantes* (Howling Figures) is Emile-Antoine Bourdelle's tragic, romantic, and ultimately heroic remembrance of the losses suffered in the Franco-Prussian War of 1870–71. Captured in richly burnished bronze, Bourdelle's contorted figures convey an emotional tenor exceptional in turn-of-the-twentieth-century French commemorative sculpture.

Figures hurlantes repeats three heads modeled by Bourdelle for the full-length figures that appear in his *Monument to the Defenders of 1870–71.* That bronze and granite colossus intended for the town square in Montauban, the artist's birthplace, was a radical update on traditional equestrian war monuments. The banal forms of those representations—somber trumpeters, women with flags, wounded soldiers—were reinterpreted by Bourdelle as passionate, if vaguely abstract, personifications of rage, despair, and brutality.

Born into a working-class family, Bourdelle, at age fifteen, won a scholarship to the Ecole des Beaux-Arts in Toulouse, a region whose expressive early medieval art and architecture inspired him. He soon moved on, however, to the Ecole des Beaux-Arts in Paris, but he found the school's academic focus too rigid and left the following year. A working artist in his own right, Bourdelle simultaneously served as Auguste Rodin's studio assistant from 1893 to 1908.

In 1893, Bourdelle was invited to propose a design for the *Monument to the Defenders of 1870–71.*[1] Although his model was approved in 1894, the commission was not confirmed until 1897, and the monument was not completed until 1902. Altogether, the work consumed nine years of his life. *Figures hurlantes,* first displayed as an independent sculpture in 1899, was cast in an edition of ten; Akron's example was acquired from the artist's widow. It is signed with the artist's symbol, numbered on the base and inscribed "Süsse Fondeur, Paris" (the foundry where it was cast).

Bronze, which even in its cast state maintains something of the violent viscosity it possesses in molten form, was the perfect vehicle for realizing these noble and agonized characters. Bourdelle did not attempt to convey likeness or capture individual personality in these visages: instead he strove to indicate mood and temperament. The heads, tightly compressed and set at odd angles to one another, express different emotions. One defiant warrior faces the viewer, nostrils flared, mouth and eyes wide open, while the other two avert their gaze, resigned to fate. These dramatic distortions recall the explosive rhythms and heated passion of the sibyls in Michelangelo's murals for the Sistine Chapel.

At the time this monument was created, a rapid transition from realism to abstraction was underway in France. Artists like Bourdelle who looked to classical precedents came to be viewed as conservative or even hopelessly retrograde. *Figures hurlantes* may have been daring for its time, but by the early twentieth century Bourdelle was considered among the league of sculptors "who accepted conventional symbols of heroism in styles which modernists felt were sterile falsifications of experience and consciousness."[2] Nonetheless, Bourdelle's Montauban monument provoked a public outcry. The dynamic tension expressed in the rough-hewn figures aroused heated, contradictory emotions not normally elicited by traditional, commemorative monuments.

Bourdelle preferred that his work be installed in public, natural settings. It seems particularly fitting that *Figures hurlantes* presently resides in the museum's Myers Sculpture Courtyard, an oasis of calm in the heart of a bustling downtown.

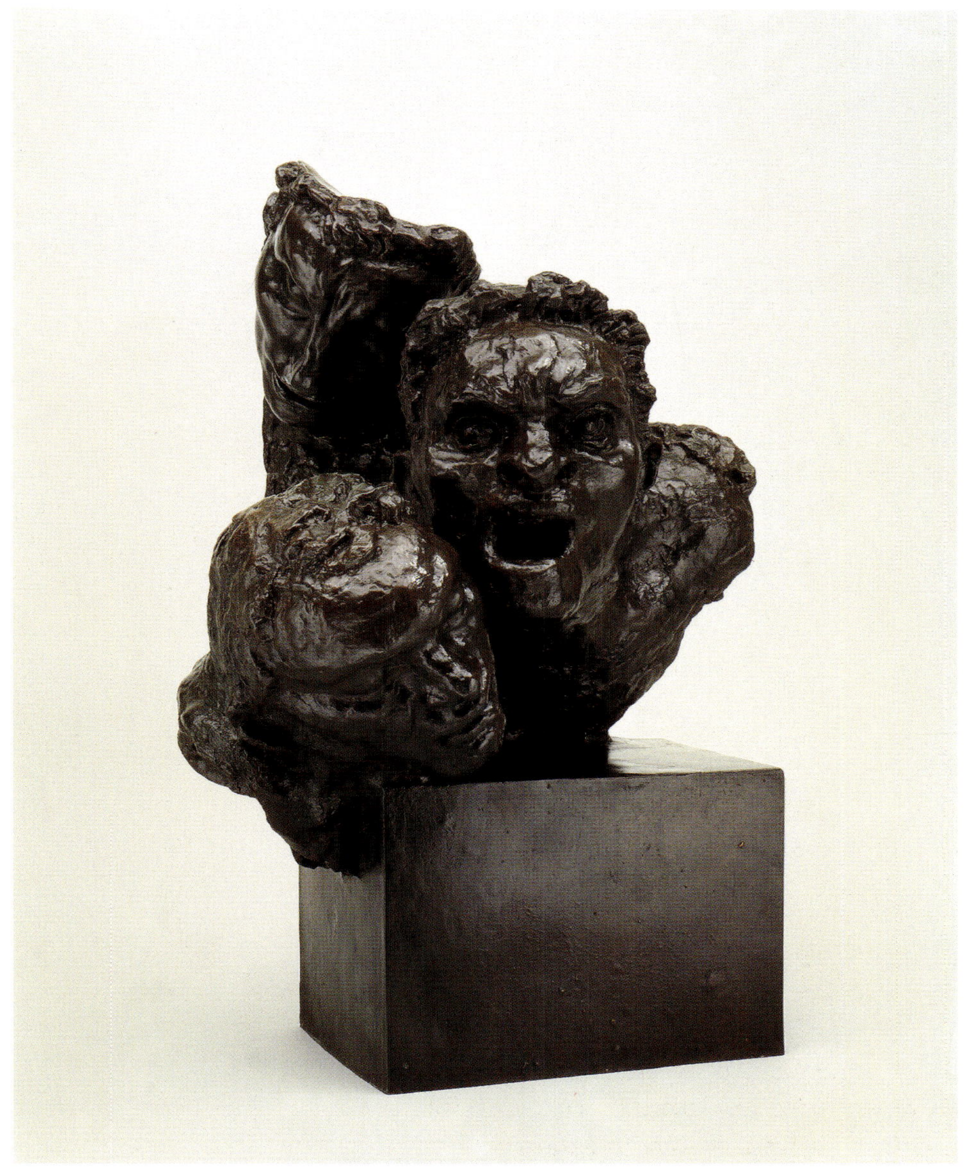

1980.61

Emile-Antoine Bourdelle
Born 1861, Montauban, France; died 1929, Le Vésinet, France

Figures hurlantes (Howling Figures) (Study for *Monument to the Defenders of 1870–71,* of 1902), 1894–99

Bronze; 36 ¾ x 31 ¼ x 25 ¼ in.
Gift of the Mary S. and Louis S. Myers Family Collection

Jack Becker

Ralph Albert Blakelock

Ralph Albert Blakelock's works are synonymous with evocative moonlit scenes. In his *Diana's Mirror,* a dramatic light emanating from a partially hidden silvery moon casts reflections upon the placid water below. A dealer titled the picture *Diana's Mirror* because it evokes mythological associations to the Greek virgin goddess of the hunt, whose symbol was the moon.[1] The painting's original title remains a mystery. This haunting nocturne suggests a response to nature similar to that of nineteenth-century transcendentalists such as Ralph Waldo Emerson, who believed in the possibility of spiritual revelations through the experience of nature. Unrepresentative of any specific place or time, and absent of topographical details and narrative elements, the painting is almost purely a poetic interpretation of the American landscape.

A self-taught artist, Blakelock began to paint in the 1860s in the manner of the Hudson River school and first exhibited at the National Academy of Design in 1867. Unlike his contemporaries who traveled to Europe to study art, Blakelock made a trip to the West that had a lasting influence on the subject matter of his paintings. He frequently depicted the wilderness and scenes of Native American life. Receiving only very unsympathetic criticism until about 1890, Blakelock had great difficulty selling his paintings. Financial and emotional instability led to a mental breakdown in 1891, and in 1899 he had to be hospitalized. Ironically, it was not until after Blakelock was institutionalized that his work began to be appreciated. In 1900 one of his landscapes won an honorable mention at the Universal Exposition in Paris, and he had his first solo exhibition in New York. Afterward his works brought such substantial prices that forgeries flooded the market during the first part of the twentieth century.

Known for his dark palette and roughened surface texture, Blakelock used unconventional techniques and materials in order to achieve the luminous effects of color and light seen in this painting. The ground, or base coat, consists of two layers of opaque white separated by a thin green layer. When the ground was dry, Blakelock worked the surface to create a rough texture. Frequently he flattened the paint with a palette knife and wiped certain areas clean. He was also known to use a pumice stone to grind down a surface. On top of this textured ground, the artist applied several thin, semitransparent layers of oil paint and varnish. This multifaceted process resulted in a textured surface that allows the ground to be seen through the thin top layers—for example, in the flickering highlights and in the milky white areas of the sky.

The artist rarely dated any of his mature works. Because of his unorthodox methods, it is impossible to precisely date his paintings and outline a stylistic or thematic chronology. Blakelock probably painted *Diana's Mirror* during the 1880s or 1890s, when he created his most accomplished works. Here he created a scene that not only evokes the mystical aspect of nature in a time of rapid industrialization and increasing consumerism but also captures the solitude and stillness of night. Blakelock's ability to create a visionary, spiritual image intrigued viewers at the beginning of the twentieth century and continues to do so today.

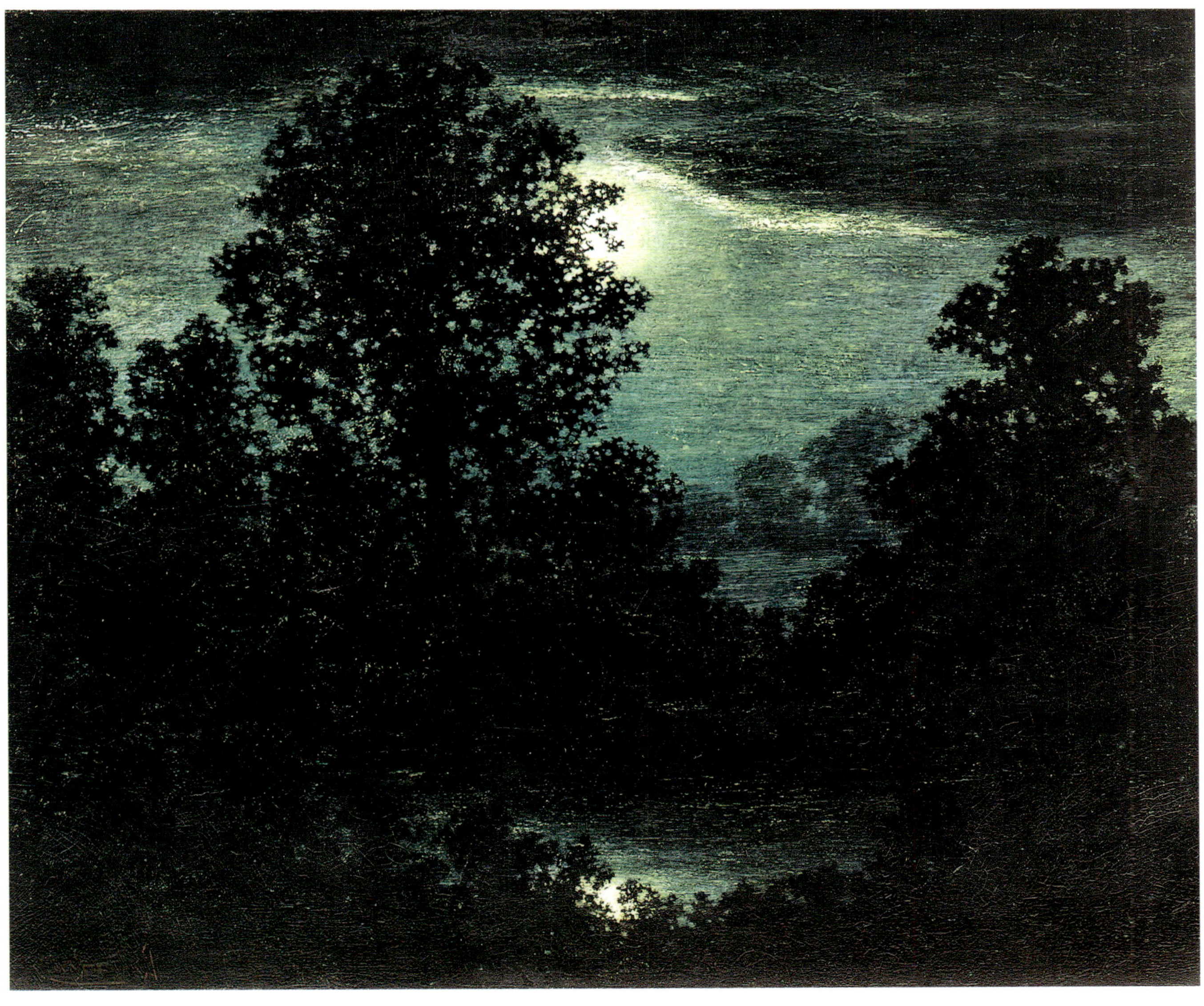

1955.14

Ralph Albert Blakelock
Born 1847, New York; died 1919, Elizabethtown, New York

Diana's Mirror, around 1880–99

Oil on fabric mounted on fiberboard; 24 ¼ x 30 ¼ in.
Bequest of Edwin C. Shaw

Mitchell D. Kahan

Lawrence Alma-Tadema

By the time he had completed several years of study at the Antwerp Academy, Dutch-born Laurens Alma-Tadema had received a thorough grounding in academic practice, especially the techniques of Dutch and Flemish old masters. Before the age of thirty he was elected to the Amsterdam Academy and won a gold medal at the Paris Salon for a historical painting depicting ancient Egypt. After living in Brussels and Paris, he settled in London to avoid the 1870 Franco-Prussian War. He was knighted by Queen Victoria and enjoyed widespread popularity, particularly for his perfectionist renderings of life at the end of the Roman Empire. Such visions of the past were intended as a tonic for stampeding industrialization and urbanization during Queen Victoria's reign.

In most of his work Alma-Tadema depicted the leisure activities of the ancient world's upper class, but oddly Caligula's assassination drew his repeated attention. *Ave, Caesar! Io, Saturnalia!* is the artist's third version of the subject. The scene combines what were probably three distinct episodes: the assassination of the debauched emperor and his family in A.D. 41; a spirited celebration of the festival of Saturnalia; and the guard Gratus's discovery of Claudius, Caligula's respected uncle. Claudius is horrified by the events and hides, assuming he too will be killed, while ironically he is being hailed as the new emperor. Among the carved portrait heads depicting Caligula's and Claudius's noble predecessors is one of their common ancestor, the great Augustus Caesar. Against such a past this scene appears even more pathetic.

The two earlier and much larger versions were completed in 1867 and 1871. The second painting is almost a reversal of Akron's. It was reported that the artist was not satisfied with the composition and wanted to give more emphasis to the Praetorian Guard in the small, third version.[1] Akron's work also shows Claudius in deeper shadow and includes live snakes at the foot of the household altar, adding a further note of theatricality and menace. In 1906 the *Journal of the Institute of British Architects* found Akron's painting imposing but less tragic than the large, second version. More recently, scholar Jennifer Gordon Lovett found Akron's painting "by far the most dramatic" of the three.[2]

Of Alma-Tadema's attraction to the subject, his contemporary, Percy Cross Standing, reported: "It had always appeared to him that this election of an Emperor by the army in opposition to the Senate—in utter contradistinction to all that had gone before—actively foreshadowed the ultimate downfall of Rome."[3] Lovett speculates that "Claudius may have been a character that Alma-Tadema found sympathetic. Sickly in his youth (as was Alma-Tadema) and physically awkward, he was considered an embarrassment by the imperial family. Consequently left to his own devices, Claudius developed into an avid scholar and historian."[4] Claudius also distinguished himself as a leader. "That Claudius was responsible for connecting Britain to the Roman Empire may have had special appeal to the Anglophile Alma-Tadema."[5]

It was not uncommon for Alma-Tadema to create elongated compositions bustling with activity. This work takes that practice to an extreme and is further reinforced by the title. "Hail, Caesar" contrasts almost humorously with "Hurrah, Saturnalia." Triumph, anguish, and fear offer a greater variety of mood than is typical of Alma-Tadema's images, making this small painting a rich example of his work.

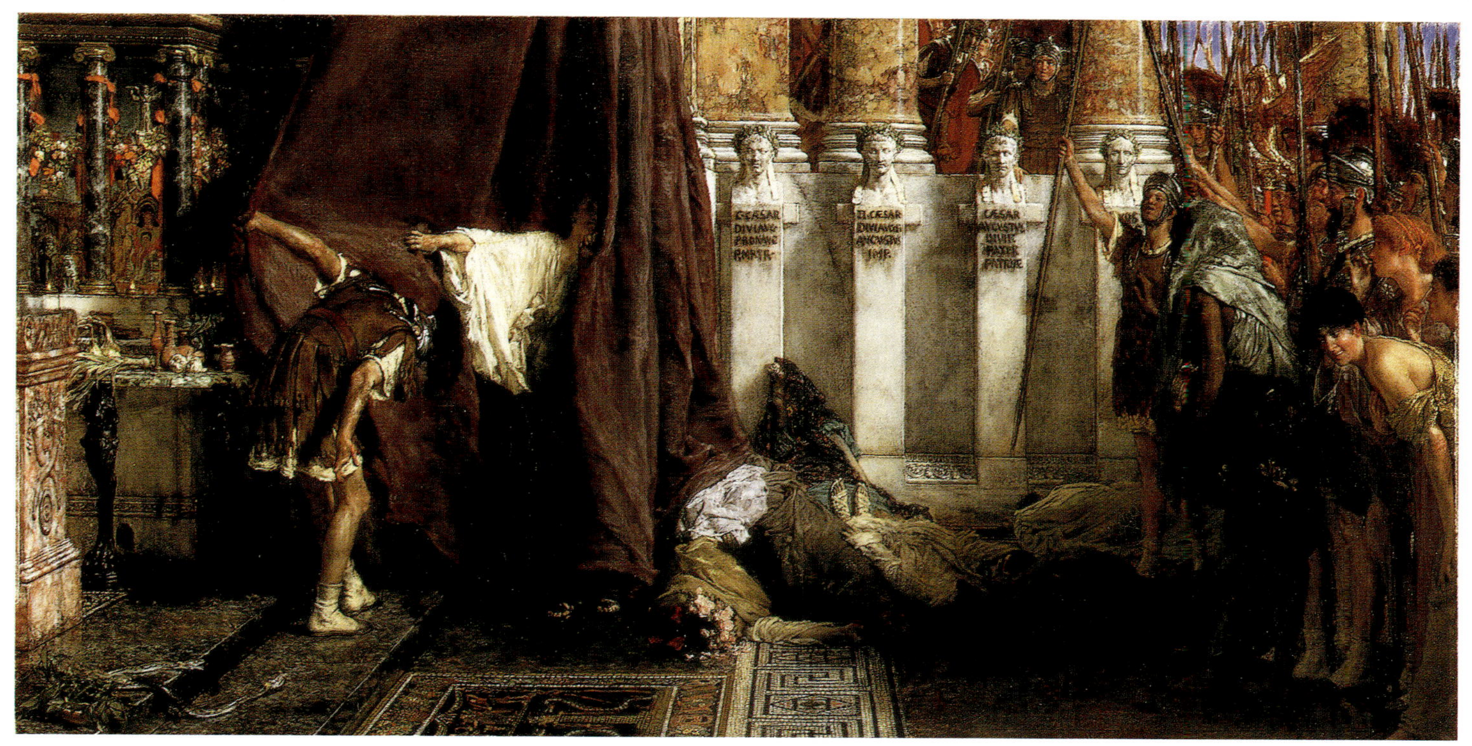

1968.13

Lawrence Alma-Tadema
Born 1836, Dronrijp, Friesland, Holland; died 1912, London

Ave, Caesar! Io, Saturnalia!, Opus CCXVII, 1880

Oil on panel; 8 ¾ x 17 ¾ in.
Gift of Mr. Ralph Cortell

Jeffrey Grove

Frank Duveneck

Frank Duveneck—popular painter, respected teacher, and a distinguished Ohio artist—has been praised as "one of the most talented artists America had ever produced."[1] Yet the critic who conferred that honor in 1926 chose to title his essay "The Problem of Frank Duveneck," in part because only seven years following his death, the artist was already nearly forgotten. One of the reasons for Duveneck's lack of renown may have been his choice to live a quiet life in Cincinnati, away from the world's art centers. It was to that city, rather than New York, that he returned following extended periods of studying and teaching in Europe.

As a teenager in Covington (just across the river from Cincinnati), Duveneck worked as an assistant to a German church decorator from whom he learned carving, gilding, and the rudiments of painting. He first went to Germany to study at the Royal Academy. Following a brief time back in Ohio, he returned to Europe to teach painting in Germany and Italy. In the 1870s Duveneck established his reputation through portraits and figure studies. Like his friend William Merritt Chase (see pp. 62–63), he was a leading exponent of a realist painting style developed in Munich that was characterized by quick, bravura brushwork and transparent, spontaneous color.

In the early 1880s a neoclassical, or Italianate, style began to emerge in Duveneck's art, distinguished from his earlier work by the appearance of brighter color, more thinly applied paint, and carefully blended brushwork. Figures were defined with crisp, linear silhouettes, and the jarring color combinations of his Munich style were replaced with creamy, delicately hued modeling.

The portrait *Miss Molly Duveneck* is a masterful amalgamation of the lessons Duveneck had learned. From a distance the canvas reflects his later, smoothly applied, Italian style, but a closer inspection also reveals the quickness of handling typical of his Munich period. Through these distinct qualities the artist captures the simple beauty and psychological complexity of his subject.

Duveneck's sister Mary (known as Molly) was one of the youngest children in a brood of ten. Frank, as the eldest, assumed a protective role when their father died. Molly was a vivacious, free-spirited woman who never married. She flaunted social convention, causing a social scandal in the 1890s through her affair with a married man. This portrait was painted around the time Molly was twenty years old; already she was projecting a powerful fire and an icy attitude. The veil of innocent childhood is still there, yet the determination of a strong-willed young woman shines through. Following the deaths of Duveneck's wife and his mother, Molly became the artist's constant companion and devoted housekeeper. Less than forty years old when he died in 1919, she became stricken with grief and died twelve days later.

In recent years Duveneck's "problematic" omission from the histories of American art has begun to be corrected. For its compelling beauty and astonishing technical virtuosity, *Miss Molly Duveneck* makes a powerful argument for the artist's inclusion.

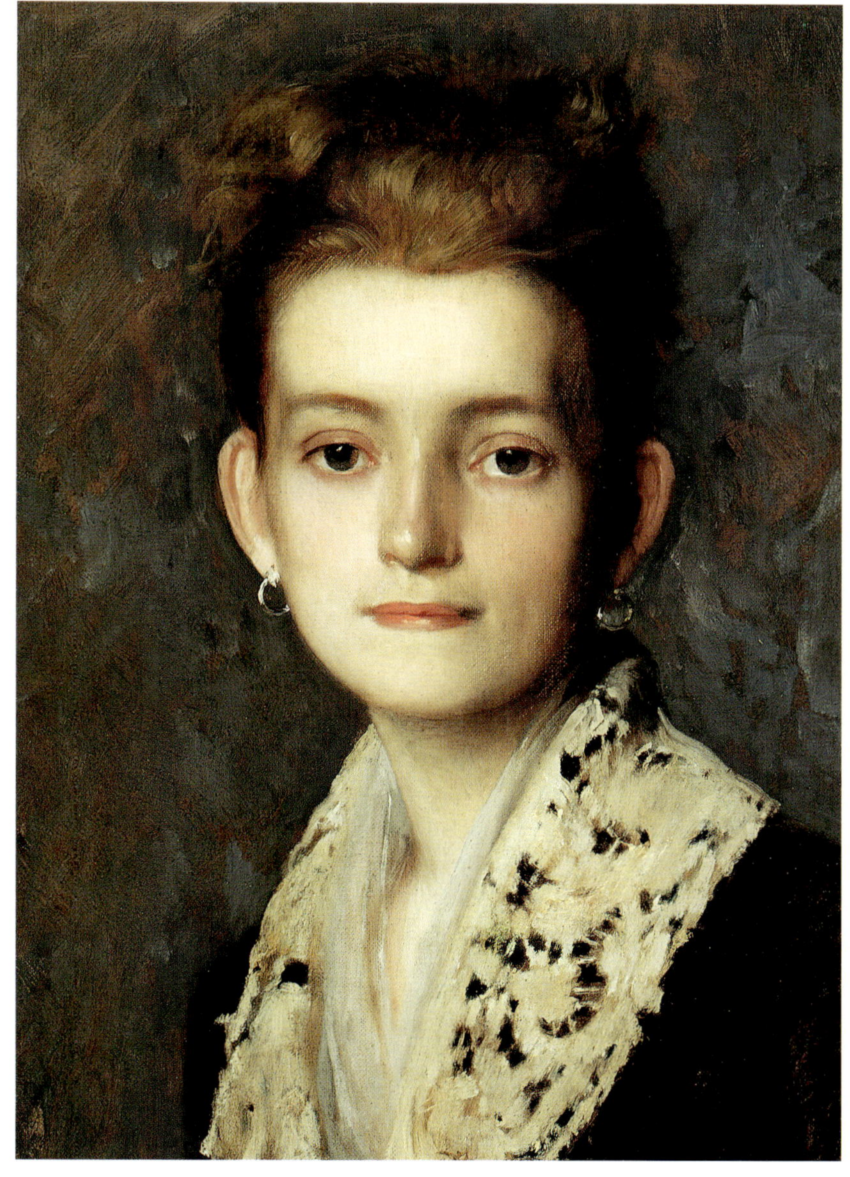

1955.26

Frank Duveneck
Born 1848, Covington, Kentucky; died 1919, Cincinnati

Miss Molly Duveneck, around 1888–90

Oil on fabric; 17 x 12 ⅛ in.
Bequest of Edwin C. Shaw

Carolyn Kinder Carr

William Merritt Chase

The late nineteenth and early twentieth century was a period of immense social and economic change in the United States. As this country's industrial base grew and vast personal fortunes were made, many of the newly prosperous turned to the arts to signify their status. Portraits found new favor among the affluent, particularly imposing likenesses in the grand manner that had long been the mark of wealth and class in Europe. When around 1901 the well-established Hartford silk merchant Ira Dimock commissioned William Merritt Chase to paint a large formal portrait of his daughter Florence Irene (1888–1962) to adorn the staircase of his stately Connecticut residence, his decision was not unusual for a man of his means.[1]

Dimock chose wisely. The fifty-two-year-old artist was a formidable figure in the art world, with a reputation matched by few of his contemporaries. Chase's exceptional talent was recognized when he was still a young man. In 1871, after studying briefly in New York at the National Academy of Design, he returned to his family, then living in St. Louis. Several local businessmen sensed his unusual ability and gave him the funds to study at the Royal Academy of Art in Munich. While a student there, he won a medal at the 1876 Centennial Exhibition in Philadelphia. Success followed success. During the 1880s and 1890s there were few important art exhibitions in which Chase was not invited to participate and few in which he was not singled out for critical praise.

An ebullient personality who was well-liked by his fellow artists, Chase was an integral part of the social and political milieu fundamental to the art world of the time. He was a pivotal figure in numerous artists' organizations, including the Society of American Artists, formed in the late 1870s to show art that was more avant-garde than that displayed at the annual National Academy of Design exhibitions. A frequent traveler abroad, Chase also established friendships with expatriates John Singer Sargent and James McNeill Whistler as well as numerous distinguished European artists. Chase taught, too—at the Art Students League, the Brooklyn Art Association, the Pennsylvania Academy of the Fine Arts, and at his own schools in New York City in the winter and on Long Island at Shinnecock during the summer. He earned the admiration of a large number of his students. It was through classes taken with Chase that Irene's older sister and the Dimock family first came to know the renowned artist.[2]

Girl in White brings together numerous characteristics of Chase's mature painting style. Beginning in the mid-1880s, he repeatedly and with great success filled his canvas with a full-length standing figure set against a subtly modulated background. Whistler's influence is evident in Chase's composition and his concern with tonal nuances. His sensuous, free-flowing brushstrokes reflect his longstanding admiration for the technique of Franz Hals, a seventeenth-century Dutch painter, and Diego Velázquez, Hals's Spanish peer. Chase loved the elegant and the beautiful: his studio was known for its abundance of luxurious textiles, metal objects, and elaborate furniture. The care and attention he gave to Irene Dimock's white silk and lace dress and black feather hat attest to his fascination with luscious and sumptuous objects.

A nephew subsequently claimed that the formality of Chase's portrait of Irene belied his aunt's "madcap" nature. The subject and her family, however, seem to have understood that Chase selected the rather fanciful and theatrical pose "with an idea of its ultimate value as a work of art, rather than a portrait."[3]

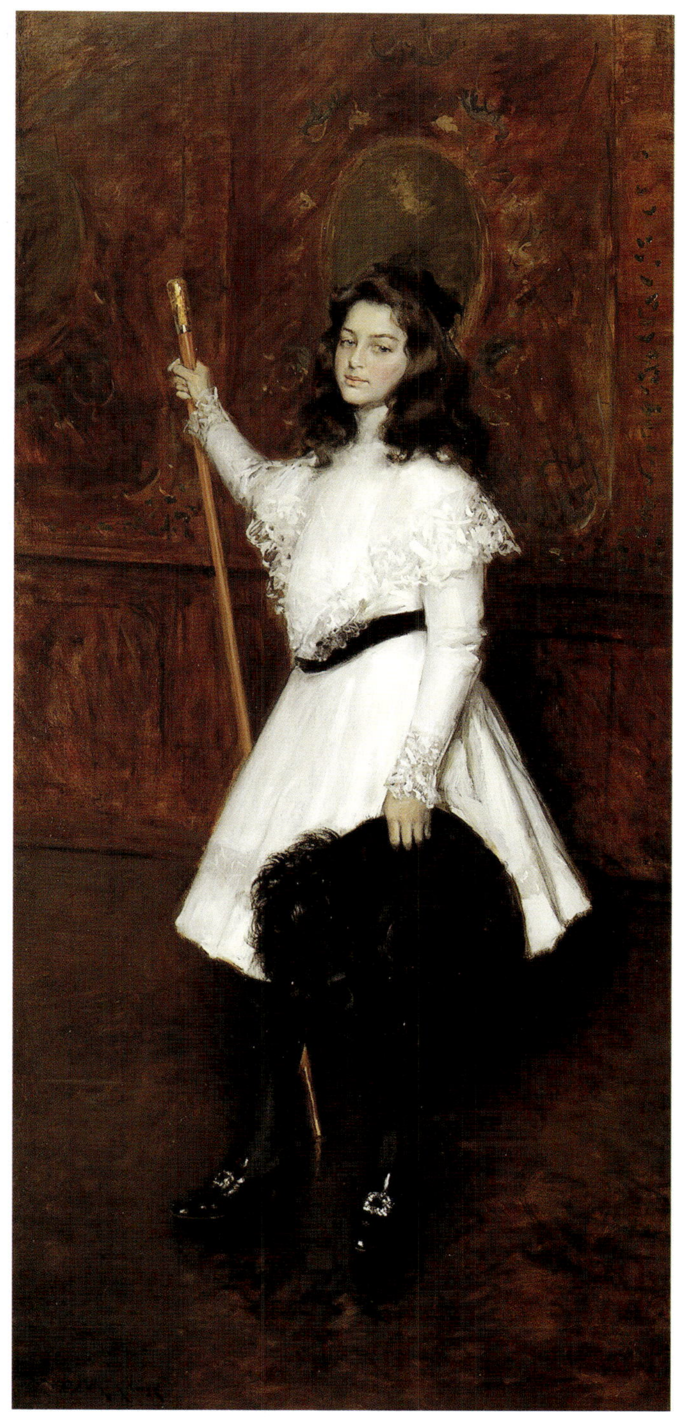

1955.16

William Merritt Chase
Born 1849, Williamsburg (now Nineveh), Indiana; died 1916, New York

Girl in White, around 1901

Oil on fabric; 84 ⅜ x 40 in.
Bequest of Edwin C. Shaw

Jack Becker

Childe Hassam

Bedford Hills exemplifies the Impressionist style of Childe Hassam. In 1886 the young painter traveled to Paris to study at the Académie Julian; while in France he was introduced to Impressionism. One of the earliest proponents of this movement in America, Hassam fused its technique and palette with his interest in American subject matter, both urban and rural. Returning from Europe in 1889, Hassam depicted the dynamic energy of New York in brightly colored canvases. During the summers he traveled regularly to the Isle of Shoals, where he painted some of his most memorable works in the gardens of Celia Thaxter.

In 1903 Hassam began to search for subject matter in New England, having discovered the charms of its rural landscape and colonial architecture. He became the acclaimed leader of the art colony at Old Lyme, Connecticut, and directly influenced the careers of a number of American painters. *Bedford Hills* may have been painted on the way to Ridgefield, Connecticut, where the artist and his wife went to visit the illustrator and painter Frederic Remington.[1]

Focusing upon several large elements in the composition—the river, a few trees, and a distant hill—Hassam fashioned a quiet rustic scene flooded with sunlight. He squeezed the paint directly from the tube, applying short, staccato brush strokes onto a grayish-white ground, or base coat, which occasionally shows through. In the river, for example, one can see the ground between individual slashes of bright blue pigment. Hassam interwove strokes of yellow, green, and violet with the blue of the water in order to suggest the reflection from the bushes and trees along the riverbank. When seen from a distance, these single brush strokes of different hues mix in the viewer's eye to create colored shadows on the water. While Hassam's painting depicts the landscape around the old town of Bedford in Westchester County, New York, the work is as much about the transitory effects of sunlight as it is about a specific location.

Like other American painters working in an Impressionist idiom, Hassam did not fully abandon traditional methods. Instead he merged Impressionist technique and color with a structured composition. For example, he rendered the distant hill on the right as a three-dimensional solid form. By painting the hill a dull gray-blue instead of the bright blue in the foreground, he represented a traditional recession into space, showing how the hill was affected by distance and atmosphere.

Hassam's rural images, such as *Bedford Hills,* convey the beauty of rustic areas as well as his own deep feelings for the land. Along with his friends Julian Alden Weir (see pp. 68–69), Theodore Robinson, and John Twachtman, Hassam is credited for bringing Impressionism to America and transforming it into a unique pictorial style suitable for native subjects and American audiences.

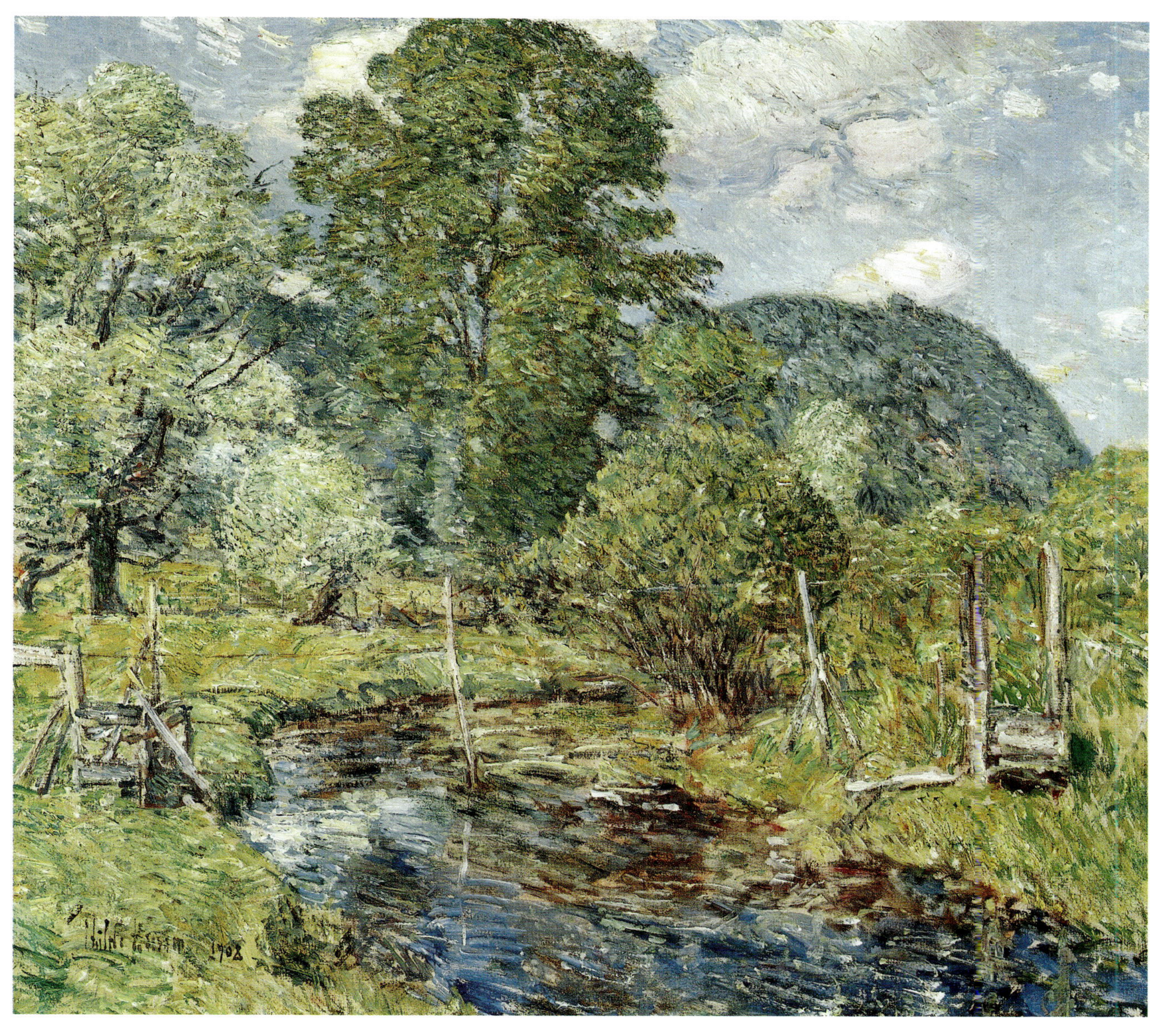

1955.30

Childe Hassam
Born 1859, Dorchester, Massachusetts; died 1935, Easthampton, New York

***Bedford Hills*, 1908**

Oil on canvas; 21 ⅞ x 25 ⅞ in.
Bequest of Edwin C. Shaw

Nicholas Kilmer

Frederick C. Frieseke

The little river Epte runs through Giverny, stroking the underside of Monet's water lilies. In 1908 the river still supported enough fish to tempt Monet's neighbor, Frederick Frieseke, to occasionally leave his painting in favor of a less risky activity. Frieseke had visited Giverny earlier and was surely working there in the summer of 1905, when he wrote from the local Hotel Baudy to Sarah O'Bryan in Paris. The artist married O'Bryan in October of that year, and in the summer of 1906 the couple began renting a house near Monet's. In the months of good weather they, like many among the summer colony of American artists, lived in Giverny. There Frieseke could expand his experiment of working directly from the figure in moving sunlight.

Frieseke's had been the standard painter's training, prescribing the use of the regulated light that falls into the studio from the north. This exposure was chosen because the shifts in cast shadow were minimized, allowing the student to consider the three-dimensionality of a figure for many daylight hours while, now and then, a passing instructor complained about the harshness of a line, or the weight of a rendered volume. Under the north light, color also tended to remain muted and harmonious, and seldom shocked.

By 1903 when Frieseke began painting out of doors, plein-air painting was already a well-established and highly visible tradition in Paris. He knew it well, but even so the change occurring in his work when he took his tools into the world outdoors was like being swept into a revolution.

What first stands out when we look at *Through the Vines* is its vibrant, almost vicious color. Just two years earlier Frieseke had installed the murals of beach scenes he had painted for the Hotel Shelburne in Atlantic City. Although he painted the murals in his Paris studio, their scale—and their purpose as decoration—had finally weaned him from the obedient harmonies fostered by his academic training. In the murals Frieseke experimented with the color of the Fauves and of Edvard Munch and Joaquin Sorolla. The dazzling rush of color threatens but, with Frieseke, can never conquer the accuracy of his line.

To paint outdoors is to wrestle with defiantly independent elements, including viscous and expensive materials, the plan of the painting, the changes to that plan caused by the act of painting, the wind, the threat of rain. In addition, the artist's wife, in a boat, on the river, may at any moment complain that if she doesn't get out of that costume and to the bakery before noon, lunch is going to be a problem. Or does someone else want to go? Likely enough Lawton Parker or Guy Rose may be on the bank and painting from this frantic idyll at the same time. Meanwhile, at 11:03:17 A.M., the painter, holding the canvas steady with one hand, has just caught sight of the transparent double disks of red light cast by the sun through the parasol onto the model's cheek and chin—and he must have them. At 11:03:18 A.M. they will exist no longer. Their color and shape are as precious and fugitive as the illuminations on the skin of the neck, which are a different color since they have not passed through the parasol.

Everyone and everything here is working. If the image presented should be read as one of leisure, the viewer might do well to remember the old show biz line, "Never let 'em see you sweat."

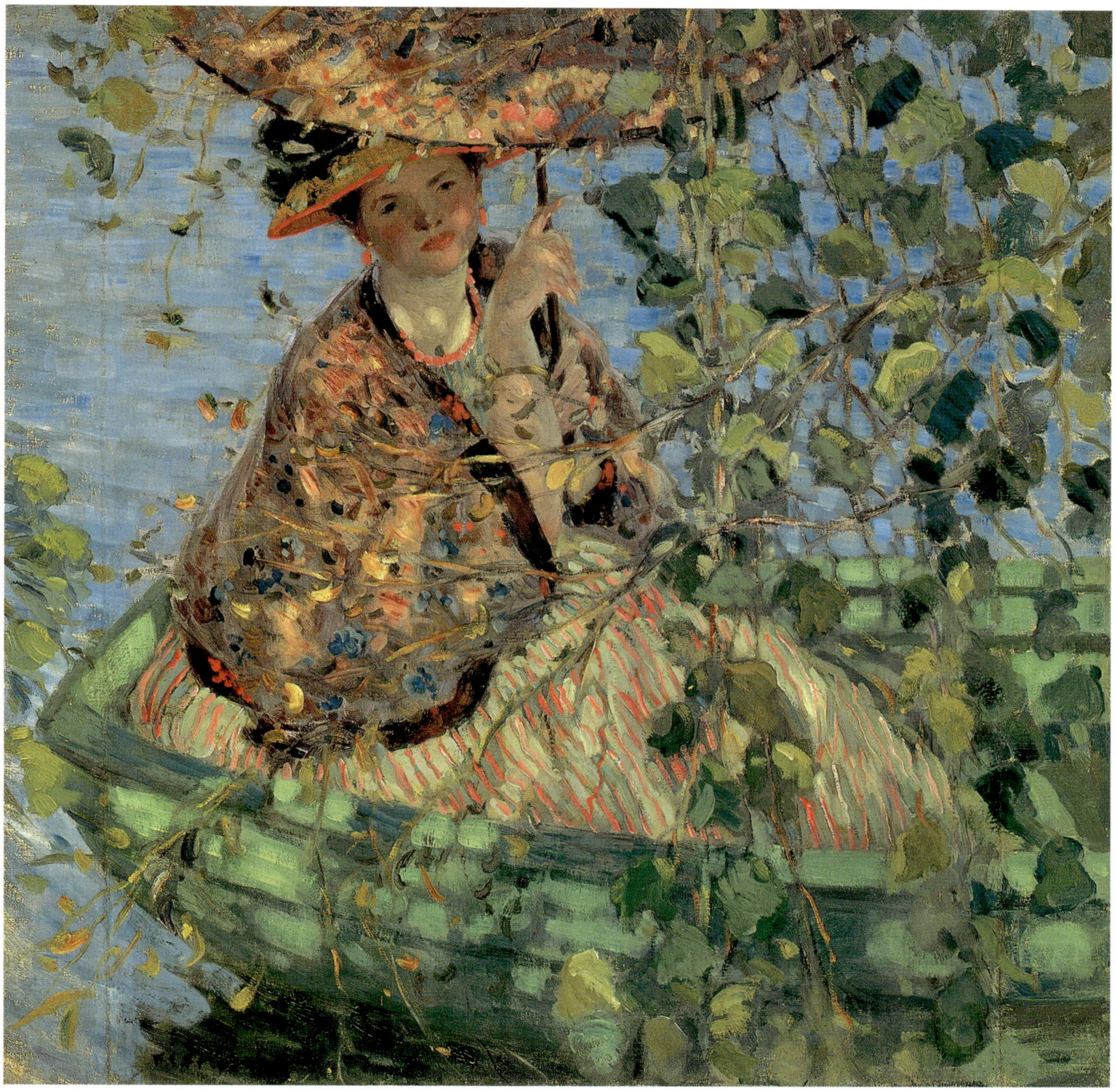

1954.38

Frederick C. Frieseke
Born 1874, Owosso, Michigan; died 1939, Le Mesnil-sur-Blangy, France

Through the Vines, around 1908

Oil on canvas; 32 x 32 in.
Gift of Mr. S. G. Carkhuff

Jack Becker

Julian Alden Weir

Julian Alden Weir's poetic rendering of a woodland scene exemplifies the artist's nearly forty-year interest in the Connecticut landscape. After his 1883 marriage Weir purchased a farm near Branchville, Connecticut, which would be his summer home until his death in 1919. New York artists such as Albert Pinkham Ryder, John Twachtman, and others were also attracted to the area, and the countryside around Weir's farm inspired some of the most memorable images in turn-of-the-twentieth-century American painting.

White Oaks portrays the Connecticut landscape on a late autumn day.[1] A dirt path in the foreground quickly disappears from view in the dense woods. Tall slender trees, absent of leaves, create a pattern of vertical forms against a blue sky speckled with small round clouds. A giant oak tree, which retains some of its leaves, occupies a dominant spot in the right foreground of the composition. Weir chose not to present the traditional view of autumn—a forest rendered in bright golds, oranges, and reds—but rather to portray a clear day in late autumn when the leaves have fallen from the trees and the blue sky can be seen through what is usually dense with foliage. His unconventional approach focuses upon the intimate qualities of the rural landscape rather than the drama of bold color changes associated with the season.

Painted during the last decade of his life, *White Oaks* conveys Weir's fascination with the American landscape and with creating his own Impressionist style in order to capture the transient beauties of the countryside and the passing seasons. He applied paint directly onto the canvas with a rapid wet-in-wet technique so that the creamy whites of the clouds behind the central oak tree mix with the delicate pink and rust colors of the leaves. Using varied brushstrokes, Weir produced thick creamy areas of impasto (thickly layered paint). Contrasting with these heavily painted areas are places such as the foreground, where the light gray ground (the first layer of paint covering the canvas) shows through. Although Weir adopted the Impressionist practice of creating shadows with blues and light gray-violets rather than blacks or browns, he emphasized the contours of individual forms and did not entirely dissolve objects in an Impressionist manner. The year that *White Oaks* was painted Weir suffered a heart attack. Perhaps as a consequence, in his later works, including *White Oaks*, he shunned the pure hues and brighter colors of his earlier paintings, preferring a delicate pastel palette.[2]

Descended from a family of distinguished artists, Weir mastered figure drawing and traditional methods through study at the National Academy of Design in New York and the Ecole des Beaux-Arts in Paris. Friendships with French realist painter Jules Bastien-Lepage and American expatriate James McNeill Whistler influenced the direction Weir would take as a painter. Although he embraced French Impressionism later than many of his colleagues, he made a significant contribution to the style's acceptance by American audiences. *White Oaks* reveals how Weir merged a subdued Impressionistic palette and technique with his interest in the rural countryside to create a unique and vital American landscape art.

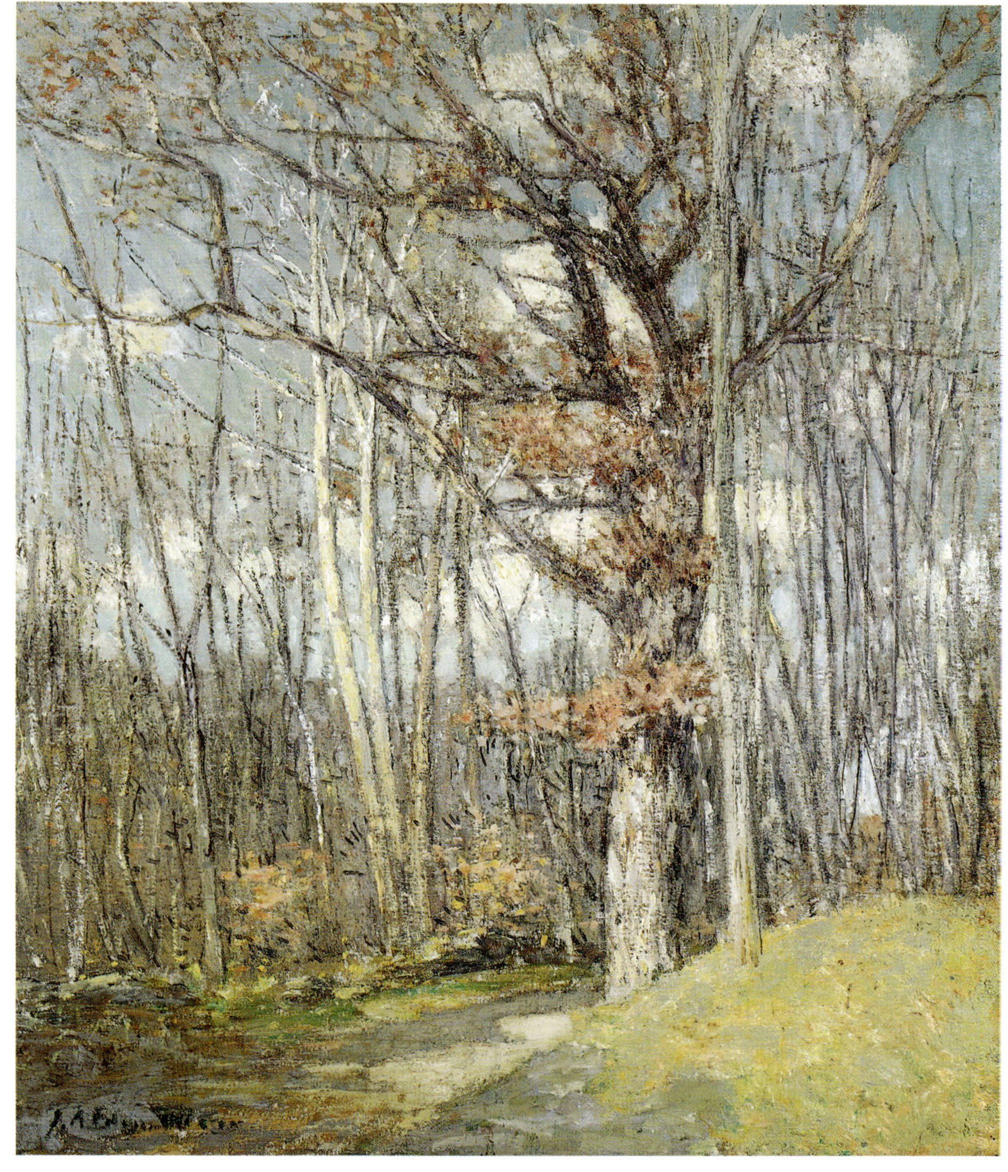

1955.42

Julian Alden Weir
Born 1852, West Point, New York; died 1919, New York

White Oaks, 1913

Oil on fabric; 30 x 25 ¼ in.
Bequest of Edwin C. Shaw

Jack Becker

Willard L. Metcalf

Maytime, wrote Willard Metcalf, "was painted at Leete's Island, Connecticut, in the spring of 1909.... This canvas has always been a favorite of mine, in as much as I felt that I had succeeded in getting some of the elusiveness of that beautiful spring morning."[1] Begun six years after the artist gave up a career as a New York illustrator to pursue plein-air painting, *Maytime* exemplifies Metcalf's ability to render the character of the individual seasons. Tacking holes in the canvas reveal that he probably painted the work while out of doors, where he would have been able to observe firsthand the transitory effects of light and color. The artist's facility in rendering the essence of spring in this work earned him the praise of critics when he first exhibited it in January 1910 at the Montross Gallery in New York. One critic claimed that "*Maytime* is one of the most poetic interpretations of the swift, tense mood of the New England spring that I have ever seen."[2]

Metcalf's broken brushwork and bright palette reflect the influence of French Impressionism, which the artist had absorbed as a student in Paris in the 1880s. Blues and yellows predominate; shadows are rendered in violet and other hues preferred by the Impressionists over the black and gray shadows of academic painting. However, like other American artists, Metcalf merged this foreign style with a more traditional, realist approach in which the forms of objects do not dissolve and spatial relationships are clearly defined.

In *Maytime* Metcalf produced a highly ordered composition using the square format for which he is known. Dividing the canvas in half by a center horizontal line, he employed a series of diagonals to lead the viewer back into space. For example, a strategically placed opening in the center of the canvas reveals a view across a marsh and beyond to a yellow house perched on a distant hill.

Having successfully captured the color of foliage and the quality of light associated with a spring morning in *Maytime*, Metcalf later that year began a series of snow scenes exploring the traits of color, light, and mood associated with winter. He was not alone in his interest in the New England countryside, for at the turn of the century a number of other artists also found the region to be rich in subject matter. Metcalf, however, was singled out from his fellow painters as the artist who could best celebrate nature; one critic wrote of his ability to render the "truth to the very soul of the American landscape."[3]

Metcalf painted *Maytime* in the spring of 1909 and made changes to the work in 1914, covering large portions of the light gray-blue sky with a brighter cerulean blue while adding greenish grays to the foreground. He also altered the date in the lower left-hand corner from 1909 to 1914. Why he made these modifications is unclear. He painted few pictures in 1914 and, despite earlier critical acclaim, his sales were extremely low. Perhaps in an effort to make *Maytime* more saleable Metcalf reworked the canvas. These alterations seem to have been successful: the painting went to a Milwaukee art dealer in 1917 and was sold that same year to Akron collector Edwin C. Shaw.

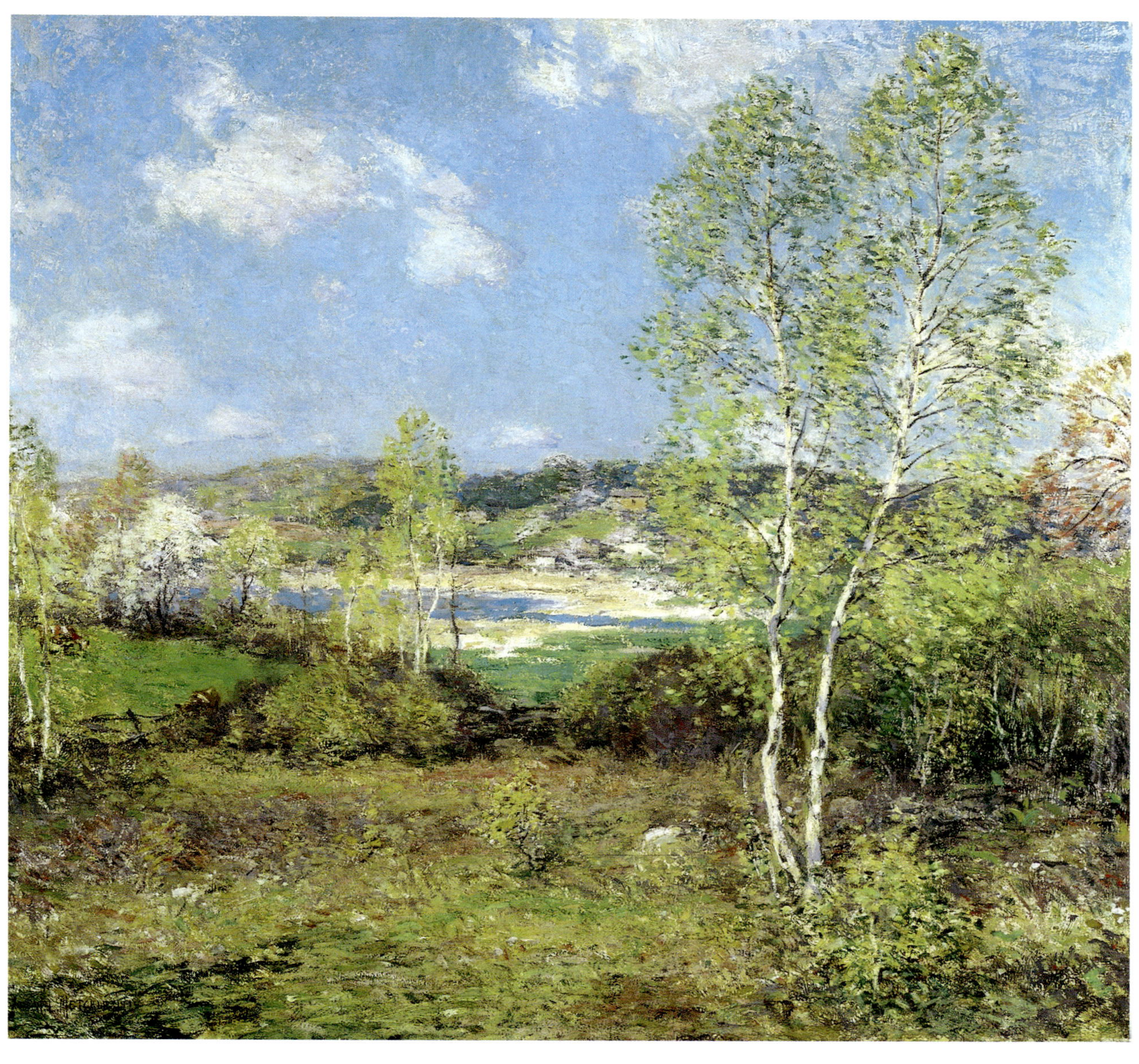

1955.35

Willard L. Metcalf
Born 1858, Lowell, Massachusetts; died 1925, New York

Maytime, 1909–14

Oil on fabric; 25 ⅞ x 29 ¼ in.
Bequest of Edwin C. Shaw

Jack Becker

Dwight W. Tryon

The New Moon, Dwight Tryon wrote,

> is more or less a culmination of my efforts in previous pictures to portray the pensive beauty of the twilight hour.... As my aim in art is [to depict] some mood and special phase of nature rather than to depict some local spot the name does not so much matter. Good art is like good music or a beautiful flower—its name is only secondary—its beauty should be all sufficient—its appeal direct to the mind.[1]

Using intense hues, tonal effects, and expressive brushwork and applying paint vigorously onto a panel, Tryon rendered both the transient effects of twilight and the mood of an evening landscape in this painting. Skillfully he varied his brushwork from thin, fluid strokes in the sky to intense scrubbing and scraping in the center hills. A screen of trees across the middle of the composition mediates the viewer's interaction between the foreground and the distant landscape.

"The time of year is early autumn," wrote Tryon, "when some of the verdure is still green and some of the warm colors are felt in the leaves."[2] The fall theme combined with the crescent moon in the upper left corner and a poetic twilight sky evoke not only the passage of time but perhaps also the inevitability of death. In any case, the simplified composition, dramatic tonal effects, and expressive brushwork convey a highly personalized response to nature. Uninterested in transcribing a specific location or narrative structure, the artist portrays the spiritual aspects not just of nature but also of the act of painting.

Having adopted a painterly approach while a student in France in the late 1870s, around 1885 Tryon began working in a tonal style, restricting his palette in order to create harmonious gradations of color. He claimed that *The New Moon* of 1921 represented the culmination of three years of experimentation with smaller pictures. During this time he learned new techniques: "drying of undertones, tone over tone, and color over color are required for the qualities I [am] after."[3] In order to create an aesthetic ensemble, Tryon even toned the frame to harmonize with the colors in the picture. Close examination of *The New Moon* confirms that Tryon probably spent several years on the picture, repainting portions as he progressed. Pentimenti (earlier forms that have been painted over) reveal that he changed the position of the trees and repainted the right side of the picture. The artist even signed the panel three times, perhaps indicating three separate stages of completion.

The New Moon held special significance for Tryon, who painted very few large pictures and had been deeply involved with this one over a period of time. He considered it one of his most important works, agreeing to sell it only when he heard that it was to end up in a public gallery. "'The New Moon' is one of my exceptional pictures. Now I am not in the least anxious to dispose of this work but as your man [Akron art collector Edwin C. Shaw, see pp. 16, 24–25] destines his pictures for a public gallery, I will let it go. From now on I do not intend letting any of my pictures of this size go for private collections."[4] Shaw acquired the painting in 1922; after his death it came to the Akron Art Museum, which he helped found.

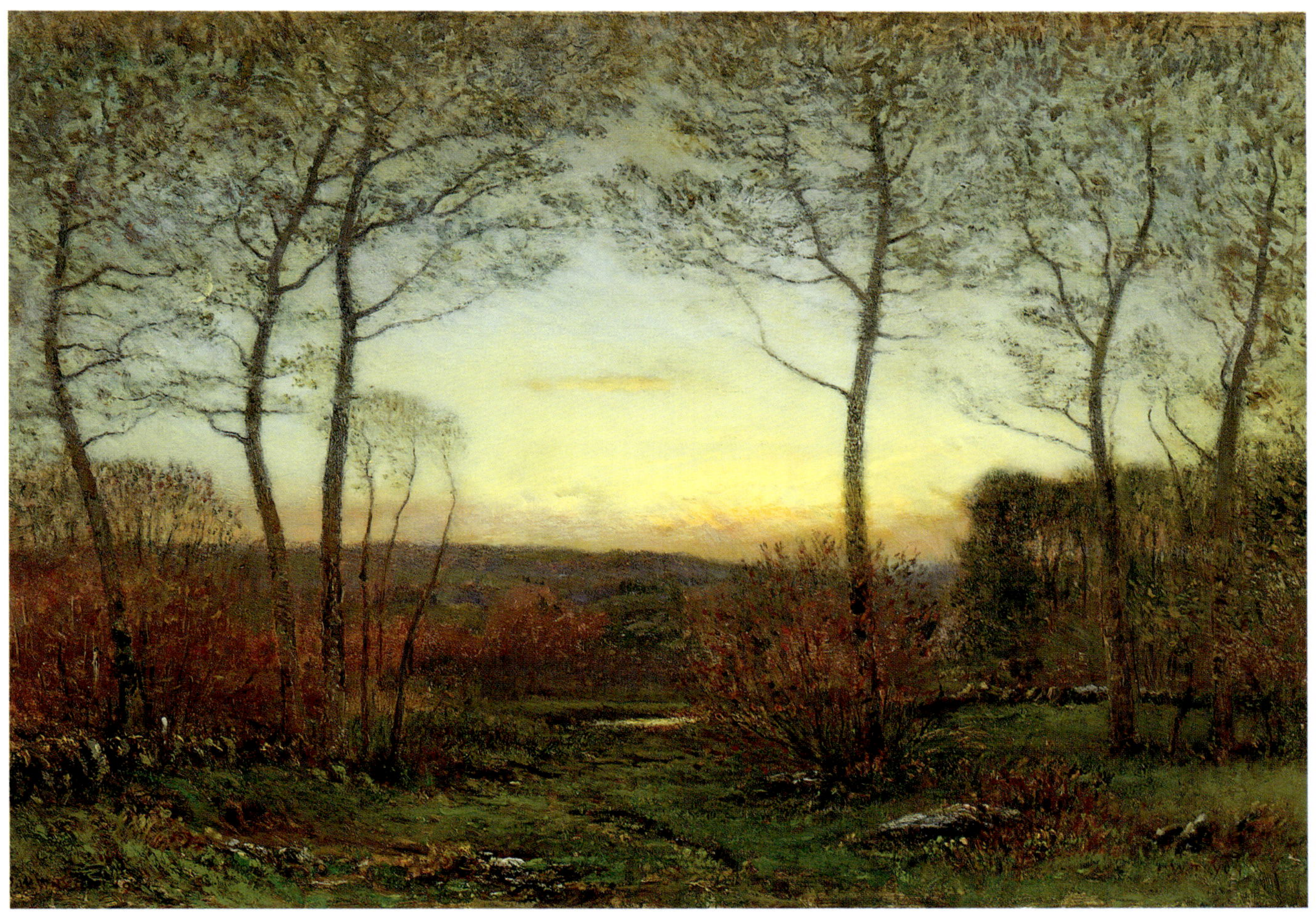

1955.38

Dwight W. Tryon
Born 1849, Hartford, Connecticut; died 1925, South Dartmouth, Massachusetts

The New Moon, 1921

Oil on panel; 20 x 30 in.
Bequest of Edwin C. Shaw

Mitchell D. Kahan

Charles W. Hawthorne

Today the figure paintings of Charles Hawthorne seem predictably traditional, even to the point of being stilted and sentimental. Why then did the renowned abstract painter Hans Hofmann, a confirmed modernist, write a laudatory essay for a Hawthorne catalogue in 1952? The answer is that Charles Hawthorne, now almost forgotten, was once regarded as one of the country's greatest art teachers.

Growing up near the Maine coast, Hawthorne moved to New York in 1890, performing manual labor by day and painting at night at the Art Students League. In 1896, he studied with William Merritt Chase (see pp. 62–63) and the following summer became his teaching assistant. After Chase closed his famed summer school on Long Island, Hawthorne established his own summer school in Provincetown, Massachusetts, in 1899. For three decades art students from across the country repaired there for summer instruction and camaraderie.

In Europe Hawthorne fell in love with the art of the old masters, in particular sixteenth-century Venetian painting and the atmospheric works of Titian. In *Mother and Child,* Titian's influence is felt in the deep greens and moody brown of the background and especially in the carefully applied layers of glaze (an old master technique) that meld the colors, gently fusing the foreground and background into one sensuous surface of delicately modulated tones. Hawthorne commented that what collector Duncan Phillips termed the "lustrous mellow paste" of his surfaces may have come less from the old masters than from "Italy itself—the familiar look of it as I lived there day after day, the texture of the stone and of old fresco."[1]

Hawthorne's devotion to the Italian Renaissance is clearly reflected in his choice of a wooden panel as the painting's support rather than canvas, which supplanted panel as the choice of artists in the seventeenth century. Equally indebted to the old masters is the subject of mother and child, which directly recalls the myriad versions of the Madonna and child that pervade Renaissance and Baroque art. The artist consciously thought of himself as an heir to those traditions, which he hoped to modernize by portraying the inhabitants of his beloved New England.

The fishermen of Cape Cod and their families were Hawthorne's most frequent subjects, but after 1908, when his only child, Joseph, was born, images of mother and child became common. This theme allowed the artist to combine an emotional, personal subject with a motif central to the history of Western painting. He decided to paint the clothing with few details, resulting in timeless images at once ancient and modern. Although the museum's painting depicts the artist's wife and son, it is less a portrait than a symbol of the sanctity of motherhood.[2] In fact, the words "Motherhood," "Adoration," and "Madonna" appear frequently in the titles of similar paintings by Hawthorne.

The artist's goal was not to repeat the old masters but to use their lessons to "express something about the humanity of my time that will live."[3] While there is a lack of emotional variety in Hawthorne's pensive figures, his sincerity is irreproachable. The painter, Hawthorne wrote, "must show people more—more than they already see, and he must show them with so much human sympathy and understanding that they will recognize it was as if they themselves had seen the beauty and the glory."[4]

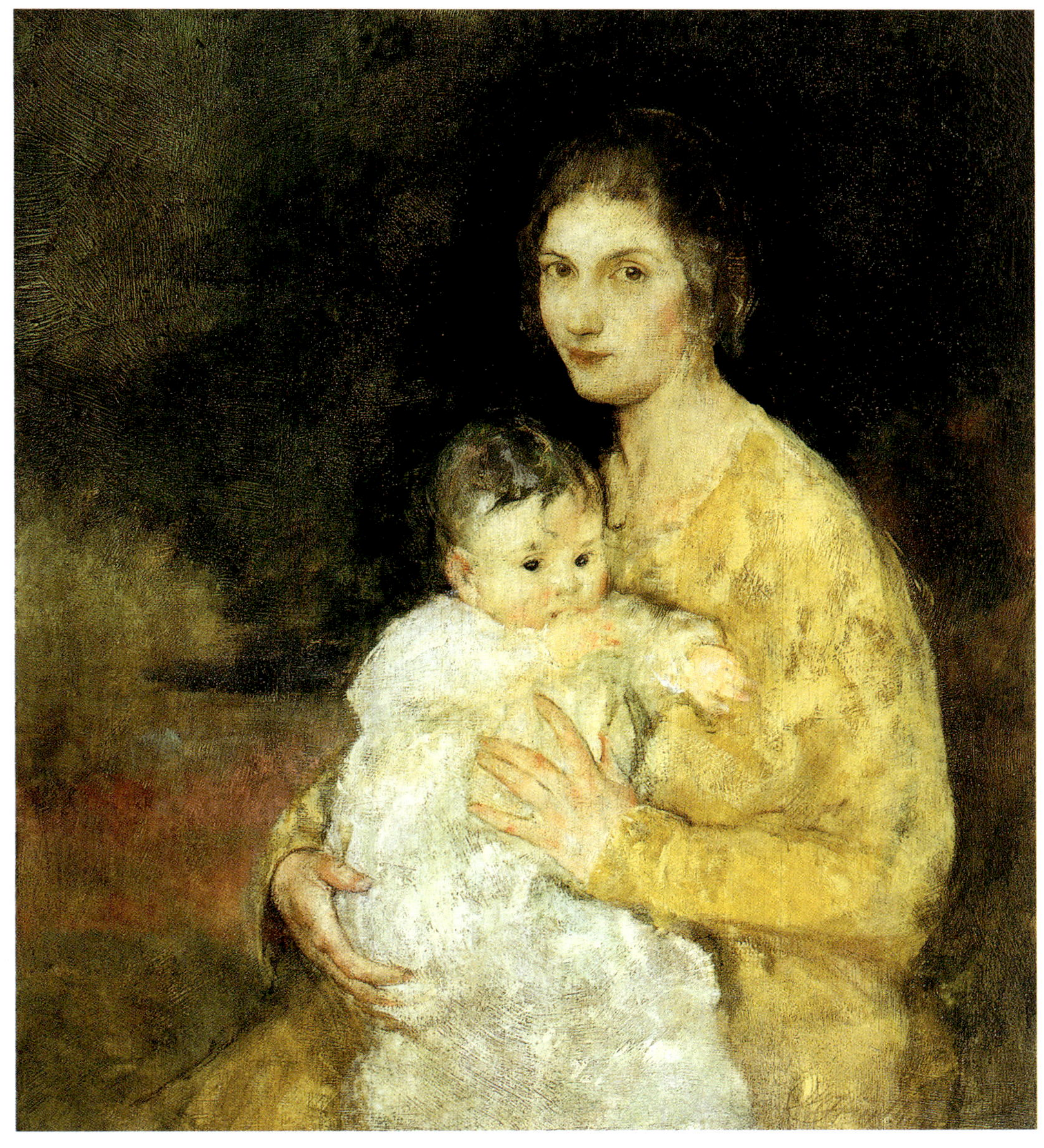

1955.31

Charles W. Hawthorne
Born 1872, Lodi, Illinois; died 1930, Baltimore, Maryland

Mother and Child, around 1908–9

Oil on panel; 33 ⅞ x 30 in.
Bequest of Edwin C. Shaw

Susan A. Hobbs

Thomas Wilmer Dewing

Symphony in Green and Gold belongs to a group of landscape "decorations" that Thomas Dewing painted during his summers at the renowned artists' colony of Cornish, New Hampshire. Dewing valued these outdoor themes because they were less easily understood than his interiors, and because they appealed to those "choice spirits," as he termed them, who were his most discerning clientele.[1] When Akron art collector Edwin C. Shaw purchased this painting, Dewing wrote him, "the Green and Gold that you bought...is as fine as anything of my decorations."[2]

The lush Cornish terrain, reached after a day's journey by train from New York, offered its inhabitants a respite from the city where they spent most of the year painting. In Cornish, Dewing and his friends created an environment for themselves inspired by the art of the past. They built Italianate villas with vine-draped porches and planted formal gardens, which they furnished with high-backed, semicircular wooden benches reminiscent of ancient Greek and Roman seating. Dewing introduced gardening and elegant dinner parties. He also staged theatricals with Greek and Roman themes similar to the one he depicted here. While the Cornish colonists enjoyed dressing up in "greek costume," as Dewing put it, they also may have found another source of inspiration in third-century Tanagra figures.[3] Discovered during the 1870s in archaeological digs near Athens, these tiny statuettes with their elegant drapery and dainty poses captured the imagination of many artists.

Symphony in Green and Gold is related to a series of screens that Dewing executed in Cornish. The wooded environment surrounding the chiton-clad figures in the first of these, *The Four Sylvan Sounds,* was inspired by that of the art colony. A subsequent commission, *Classical Figures,* depicts this landscape as a mere billowing mist. The jewel-toned background in *Symphony* is even more abstracted, its emerald curtain of color referring perhaps to the ravines that punctuated the Cornish terrain.

As in Dewing's earlier *Classical Figures,* the model for this painting was probably Mollie E. Chatfield, whose likeness can be recognized in the distinctive high cheekbones of the finely modeled head. Her pose recalls other works of the same year—as for example the figure at the right in *The Garland,* painted just before Dewing worked on *Symphony.* At that time the artist wrote that he considered his latest picture "new" and "better," a reference perhaps to the increased size of the figures.[4]

Accordingly the artist featured a single large image in *Symphony,* balancing its verticality with a horizontal bamboo pole and lantern. This lantern had appeared earlier in Dewing's landscape decoration *Before Sunrise.* Here, however, it is central to the composition, seeming to emanate from within the primed wood panel itself. The glow signals the picture's Cornish theme, for after late-night dinner parties the artists sometimes walked home along a pathway illuminated by lanterns such as this.

For Thomas Dewing the purpose of art was to evoke memory and imagination. With its classical theme and clear reference to the exotic aspects of Cornish, *Symphony* pays homage to the cultivated and fanciful world of the art colony that had inspired his art for more than two decades.

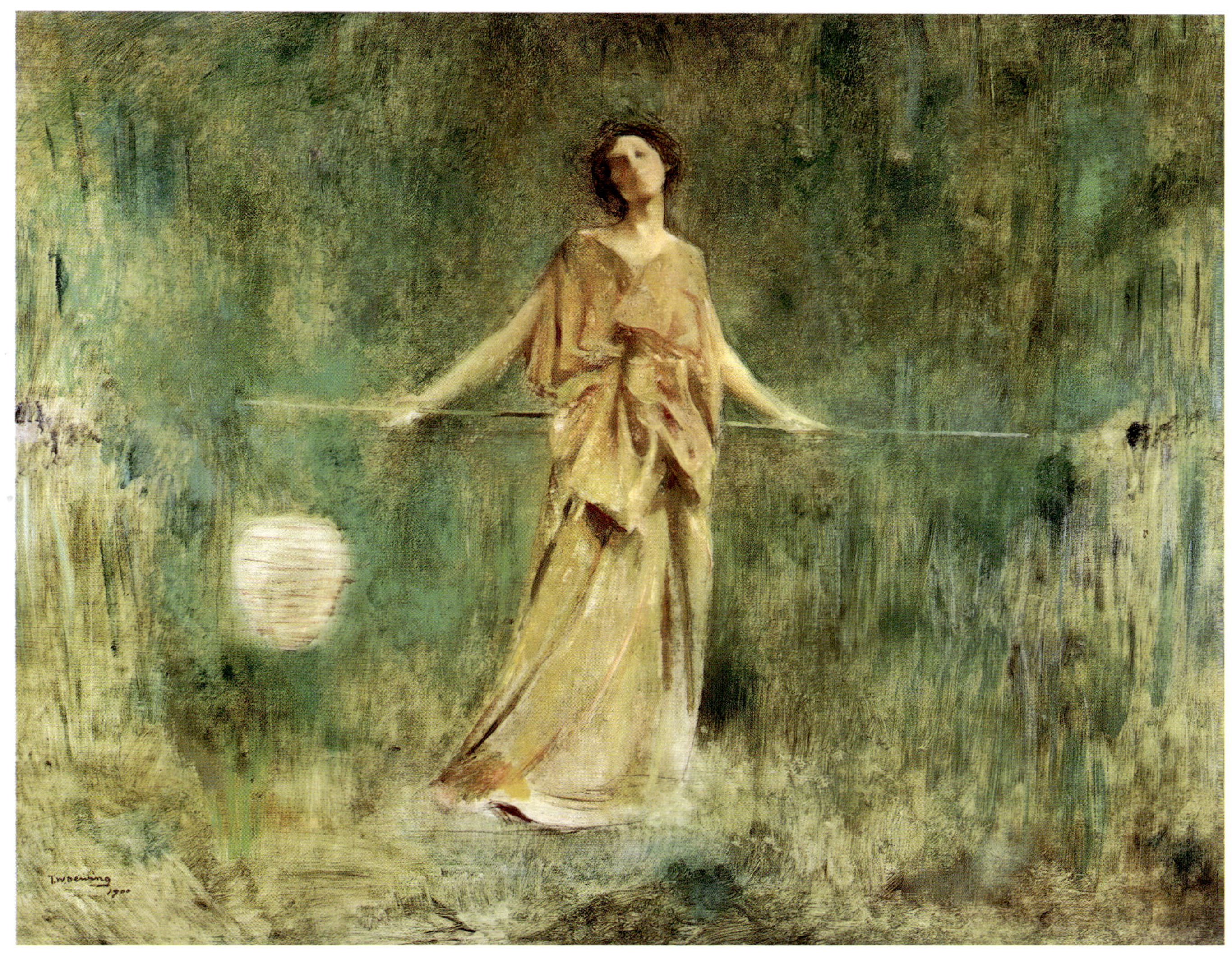

1955.25

Thomas Wilmer Dewing
Born 1851, Boston; died 1938, New York

Symphony in Green and Gold, 1900

Oil on panel; 36 x 48 in.
Bequest of Edwin C. Shaw

Mitchell D. Kahan

Emil Carlsen

Before immigrating to the United States, Sören Emil Carlsen learned painting from a cousin and studied architecture at Copenhagen's Royal Academy. In Chicago he worked in both painting and architectural studios. Relocating several times, Carlsen had difficulty establishing a reputation. He was director of the fledgling California School of Design (now the San Francisco Art Institute) from 1887 to 1891. Returning east to New York, Carlsen finally achieved success and was elected to both the National Institute of Arts and Letters and the National Academy of Design, where he also taught. In his later years Carlsen concentrated on landscapes and seascapes which were widely exhibited, but he is remembered today mostly for his still-life paintings, which initially found few buyers.

On trips to France Carlsen was exposed to the still-life paintings of eighteenth-century French master Jean-Baptiste Siméon Chardin, which were enjoying a revival. Carlsen called Chardin "the very greatest still-life painter" and was inspired by his renderings of a few simple objects "limited in their color scheme" and viewed from a fairly close vantage point.[1] Initially Carlsen's canvases repeated Chardin's darker tonalities, but gradually Carlsen's palette lightened, as in *Rhages Jar.* He was also probably influenced by James McNeill Whistler, the American expatriate whose interest in tonal painting and all things Japanese inspired many artists. The precise draftsmanship and delicately applied paint of *Rhages Jar* recalls works by the seventeenth-century Dutch painter Jan Vermeer. Not surprisingly, a reproduction of a Vermeer painting hung in Carlsen's studio. The author of a 1921 book on still-life painting characterized Vermeer's art as "perfect balance, hence perfect rest, perfect satisfaction. And this is Carlsen's art—perfect balance of form—perfect proportion—completeness."[2] The same writer proclaimed Carlsen "unquestionably the most accomplished master of still-life painting in America today."

While Carlsen's better-known canvases depict the prosaic copper pots and rustic kitchenware typical of Chardin, the artist also created a group of canvases similar to *Rhages Jar,* with an Asian theme and objects from a more refined world. The painting was one of at least two Carlsen works owned by Edwin C. Shaw (see pp. 16, 24–25). Once dated to the 1880s, *Rhages Jar* was more likely painted later. Its title refers to the Persian city of Rhages, known today as Rayy in Iran. However, the low bowl appears to be a common Japanese form adapted from earlier Korean tea bowls. The two taller objects in the picture—also inspired by Asian prototypes—may be American art pottery from around 1900. Whatever their origin, the ceramic objects and title poetically allude to the East and reflect American interest in Asian aesthetics around the turn of the century.

Carlsen has made careful choices in composition and technique. The edge of the table melds into the background. The porcelain is almost translucent; the colors are muted and their range fairly limited, with cream, white, gray, and touches of blue and green. The warm background has the texture of soft linen. And most noticeably the flowers are at the end of their bloom. Together these effects impart a contemplative, symbolic mood, reminding us that beauty fades with time.

Critic and collector Duncan Phillips thought Carlsen's still lifes had the ability to lull viewers into a trance, as if "nature exerts at times an influence curiously hypnotic."[3] Carlsen portrays a luminous world where beauty can be delicately savored.

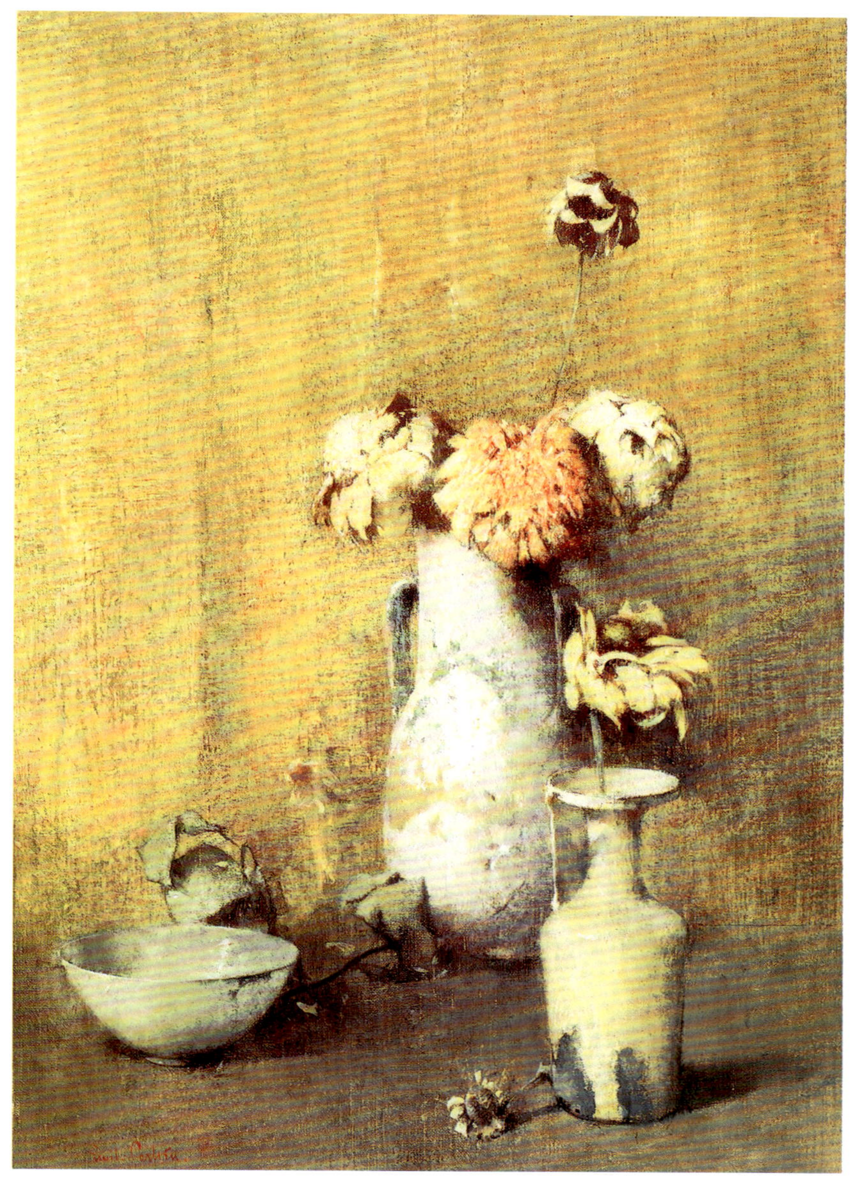

1991.133

Emil Carlsen
Born 1853, Copenhagen; died 1932, New York

Rhages Jar, date unknown

Oil on canvas; 23 ½ x 16 ¾ in.
Gift of Stella B. Hall in memory of her husband, William Curtis Hall Jr.

Naomi Rosenblum

Edward S. Curtis

"The longer I work at this collection of pictures the more certain I feel of their great value."[1] When Edward S. Curtis wrote these words in 1907 he had just started a wildly ambitious project to document Native American life in the United States and Alaska. His aim was to introduce more recently arrived Americans to a much older native culture through beautifully realized photographs and reliable texts.

During the next twenty-three years, Curtis traveled widely and photographed avidly, eventually producing twenty volumes of *The North American Indian*. He wished to create, in his own words, "a broad and luminous picture" of the customs, traditions, and environments of what at the time was referred to as "the vanishing race."[2] Ironically, by 1950 Curtis's grand endeavor had itself more or less vanished from view. It is only within the past twenty-five or so years that his efforts to bridge the gap between art and documentation and between past and present have been recognized and reappraised.

Curtis came of age and started in the photography business in Seattle, Washington, during a troubled period in American history: great individual fortunes were being made, corruption was rampant, and periodic financial panic was a fact of life. His desire to evoke a vanished culture was eminently suited to the nation's state of mind as turn-of-the-twentieth-century Americans looked to the past as a more spiritually pure time.

The culture of Native American tribespeople, who by then had been moved onto reservations, was also changing. Choosing not to picture the actual acculturation taking place, Curtis adopted a more romantic outlook, which as might be expected appealed to a number of powerful figures in business and government—notably Junius P. Morgan, Edward Harriman, and Theodore Roosevelt. Morgan in particular provided financial help with the enormous expenses involved in producing the elegant volumes.[3]

The Fisherman—Wishham is one of many photographs taken by Curtis along the banks of the Columbia and Willamette Rivers. Depicting a lone figure fishing for salmon with net and pole in the Columbia River, it suggests the concordance between Native Americans and the natural world that traditionally provided their sustenance. Like many of Curtis's images, it was made with a soft-focus lens and from a vantage point that ignored all that might be ugly or disturbing in the environment. While this approach may be ethnographically flawed, the Native American subjects appear beautiful and proud, just as Curtis wished them to be perceived.[4]

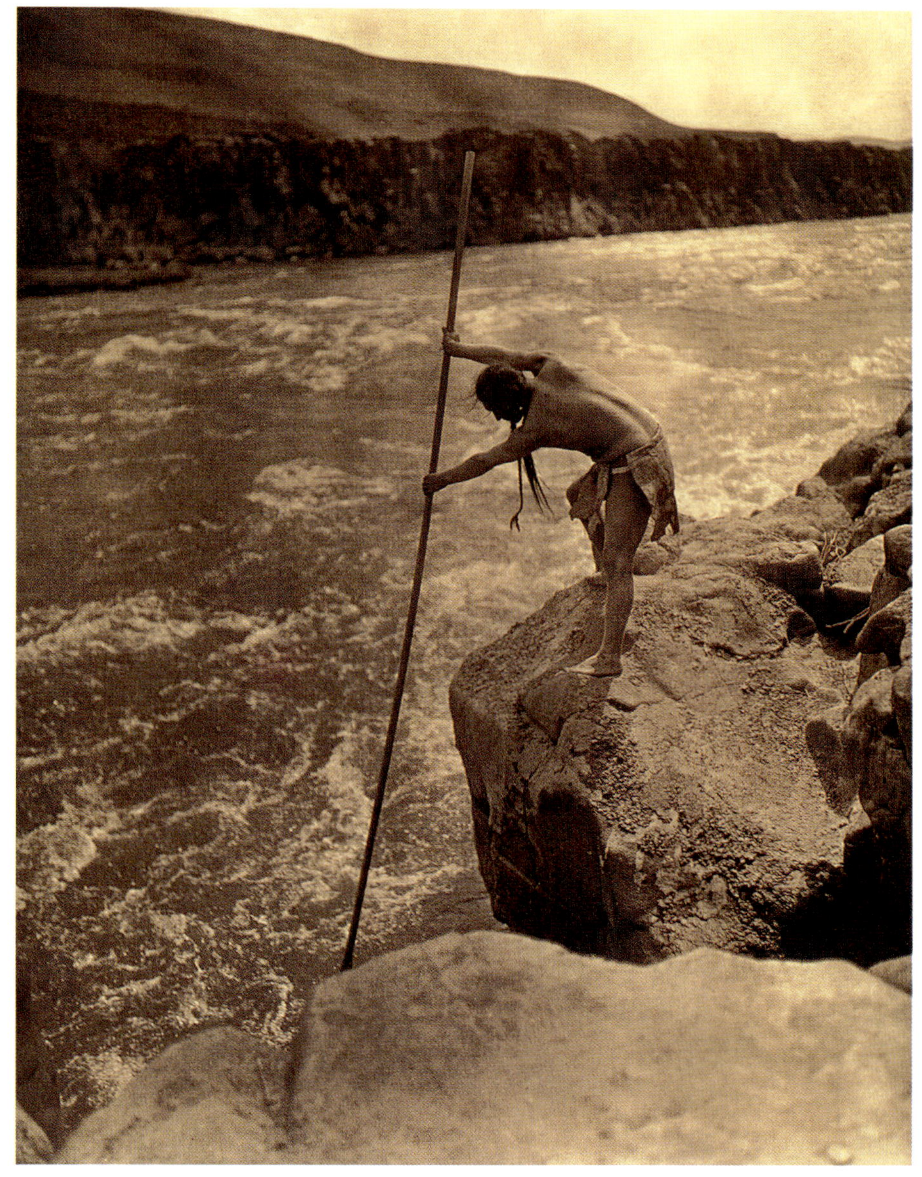

1992.44 s

Edward S. Curtis
Born 1868, probably Madison, Wisconsin; died 1952, Los Angeles

The Fisherman — Wishham, 1909, from *The North American Indian,* Portfolio VIII

Photogravure; 15 ½ x 11 ¾ in.
Gift of Nancy and Robert F. Meyerson

Naomi Rosenblum

Alfred Stieglitz

"I raced to the main stairway of the steamer, chased down to my cabin, picked up my Graflex, raced back again, worrying." So wrote Alfred Stieglitz about the circumstances surrounding the photograph he titled *The Steerage.*[1]

This image was made on the ocean liner *Kaiser Wilhelm II* during Stieglitz's 1907 voyage to Europe with his wife Emmeline and daughter Kitty. The photographer, who was unhappy with his domestic situation and bored with the milieu in first class, let his eyes fall upon the several forward decks that held steerage passengers. The vitality of the scene that presented itself seemed to express exactly his conviction that the less well-off showed greater warmth in their relationships than his fellow upper-class travelers.

Stieglitz processed the negative when he arrived in Paris but was unable to make a print until he returned to New York four months later. The photograph was not published until 1911, when it appeared in gravure reproduction in the Photo-Secession journal *Camera Work* along with fourteen other images by Stieglitz of New York, its people, and its structures.

A complex arrangement of a "round straw hat, the funnel leaning left, the stairway leaning right, the white drawbridge,...white suspenders,..." *The Steerage* lent itself to the avant-garde ideas entering artistic discourse in the United States after 1908.[2] Stieglitz, who was an intuitive artist himself, generally paid little attention to aesthetic theory in his own work, but in his role as a gallery director and publisher he became a strong supporter of new ideas in art, in particular those propounded by American painter Max Weber and the European Cubists. With its intricate arrangement of curves and angles and its edges cutting and flattening the various structural elements, this photograph makes elegant use of the vocabulary of Cubism while still expressing the artist's personal reaction to the scene.

As Cubist art had become more acceptable to American viewers following the 1913 Armory Show, Stieglitz was encouraged to make larger gravure prints on Japanese tissue in 1915.[3] The Akron Art Museum print is one of these. Stieglitz took exceptional care with the printing of his photogravures; they are considered original prints, not reproductions.

In its crowded, complex composition and its balance of formal organization and emotional sensibility, *The Steerage* is unique in Stieglitz's work. The photographer himself recognized this when later in his life he wrote: "If...I were represented only by *The Steerage,* that would be all right."[4]

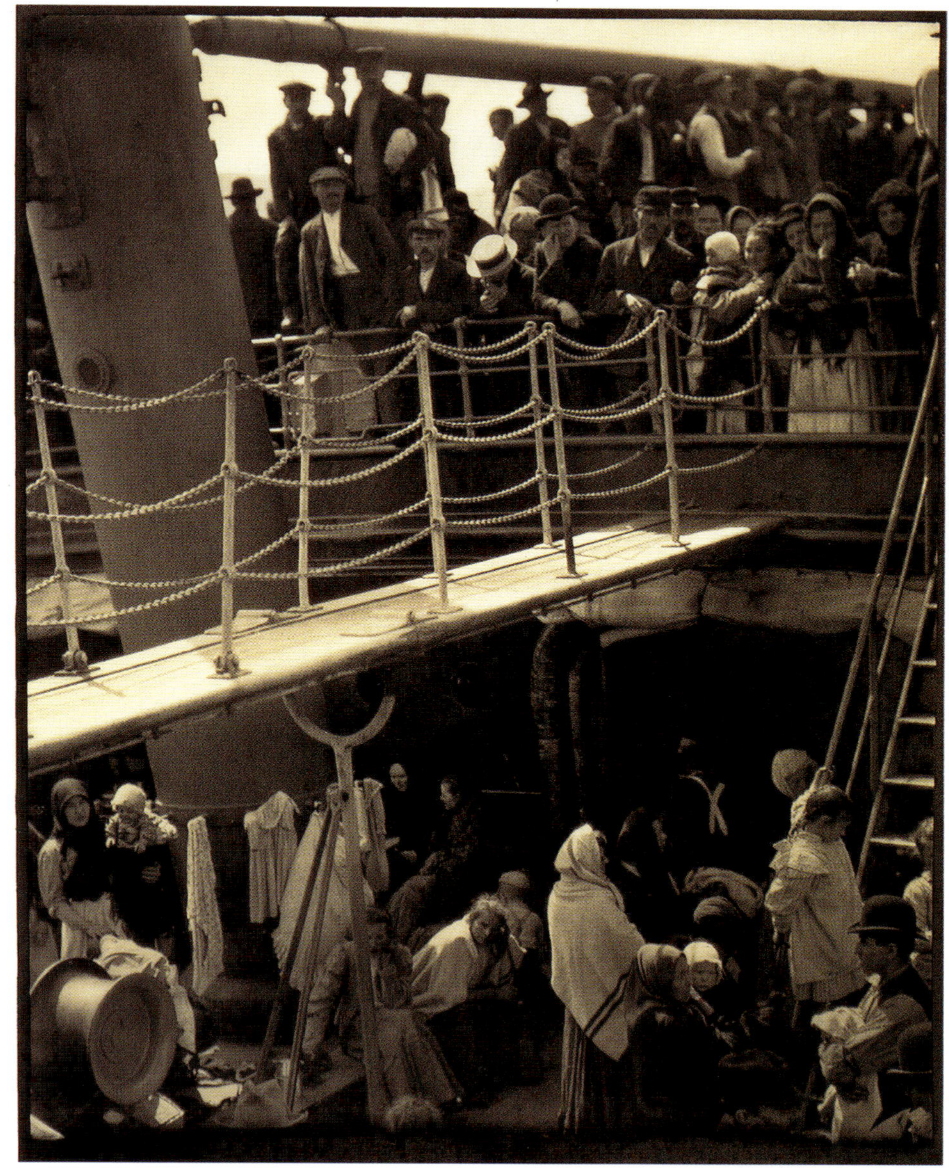

1978.25

Alfred Stieglitz
Born 1864, Hoboken, New Jersey; died 1946, New York

The Steerage, 1907 (printed 1915)

Photogravure; 13 ⅛ x 10 ½ in.
Museum Acquisition Fund

Wendy Kendall-Hess

Raphael Gleitsmann

This scene of a downtown Akron intersection, bustling with activity on a snowy winter's evening, captures the feel of the city's Main Street in the 1930s. Now seen as a glimpse into a vanished past, *Winter Evening* represents an ambitious young artist's effort to show the city he knew best.

Raphael Gleitsmann moved to Akron with his family at age six.[1] His father, Louis, an architectural engineer and amateur painter, inspired Raphael to pursue art as a career. After graduating from high school, Gleitsmann studied art with Katherine Calvin, an Akron painter, and Paul Travis, an instructor at the Cleveland School of Art.[2] Gleitsmann remained essentially self-taught, however, exploring new ideas and materials on his own. Although he favored oil painting, he also worked in watercolor, photography, and other media.

Gleitsmann developed his style by looking to those artists he most admired. His strongest early influences were Edward Hopper, famed for his stark scenes from American life, and American Scene painters such as Thomas Hart Benton and Grant Wood, who depicted realistic images rooted in midwestern rural life. *Winter Evening* also appears to have been influenced by the loose brushwork of an earlier generation of urban scene painters, such as John Sloan and George Bellows. These sources are apparent in many of Gleitsmann's paintings from the early to mid-1930s depicting slightly stylized rolling landscapes, factories, and cityscapes characteristic of Akron and eastern Ohio. Gleitsmann's decision to paint what he knew best was not an effort to reject a larger world. Rather, it was the choice of a young man who had seen little beyond his home state.

Winter Evening typifies such works. A mostly straightforward cityscape, it is rendered clearly but without sharp detail.[3] The artist's youth and inexperience show in the rough handling of the figures and structures, but the painting's ambitious scope, sophisticated composition, and overall cohesion transcend its limitations. Working with a palette emphasizing blues and grays, Gleitsmann ably handled the challenge posed by the muted colors of a nighttime scene. He also gave Akron an active, cosmopolitan feeling: the play of indoor and outdoor lights and the almost palpable movement of cars, trams, and people lend the scene a feeling of energy and excitement. Yet such telltale signs as the single tall building—Akron's first skyscraper, built in 1929-30—and the modest crowds serve as reminders of Akron's true character, that of a small city.

By the late 1930s Gleitsmann's art took on a sleeker, more sophisticated look as he embraced new influences, integrating elements ranging from the hard edges of modernism to surrealist imagery. In 1943 his career was interrupted by World War II and active service in Western Europe. An injury in March 1945 ended his military service, but the violence and devastation of the war continued to haunt him.

After returning to Akron, Gleitsmann struggled to put his new feelings and thoughts into visual form. He started painting images of Europe in his prewar style but gradually shifted to expressionistic depictions of imaginary ruins inspired by destroyed buildings he had seen during the war. He achieved significant professional successes with his postwar art, the most notable being first prize at the Carnegie Museum Invitational in 1948, in which he competed against an array of nationally and internationally noted artists. Sadly, however, Abstract Expressionism and other new movements had gained momentum, and as a result Gleitsmann's more traditional work fell out of favor. He virtually stopped producing art after 1954. The Akron Art Museum owns six oil paintings and seventy-nine watercolors, drawings, and photographs by Gleitsmann.

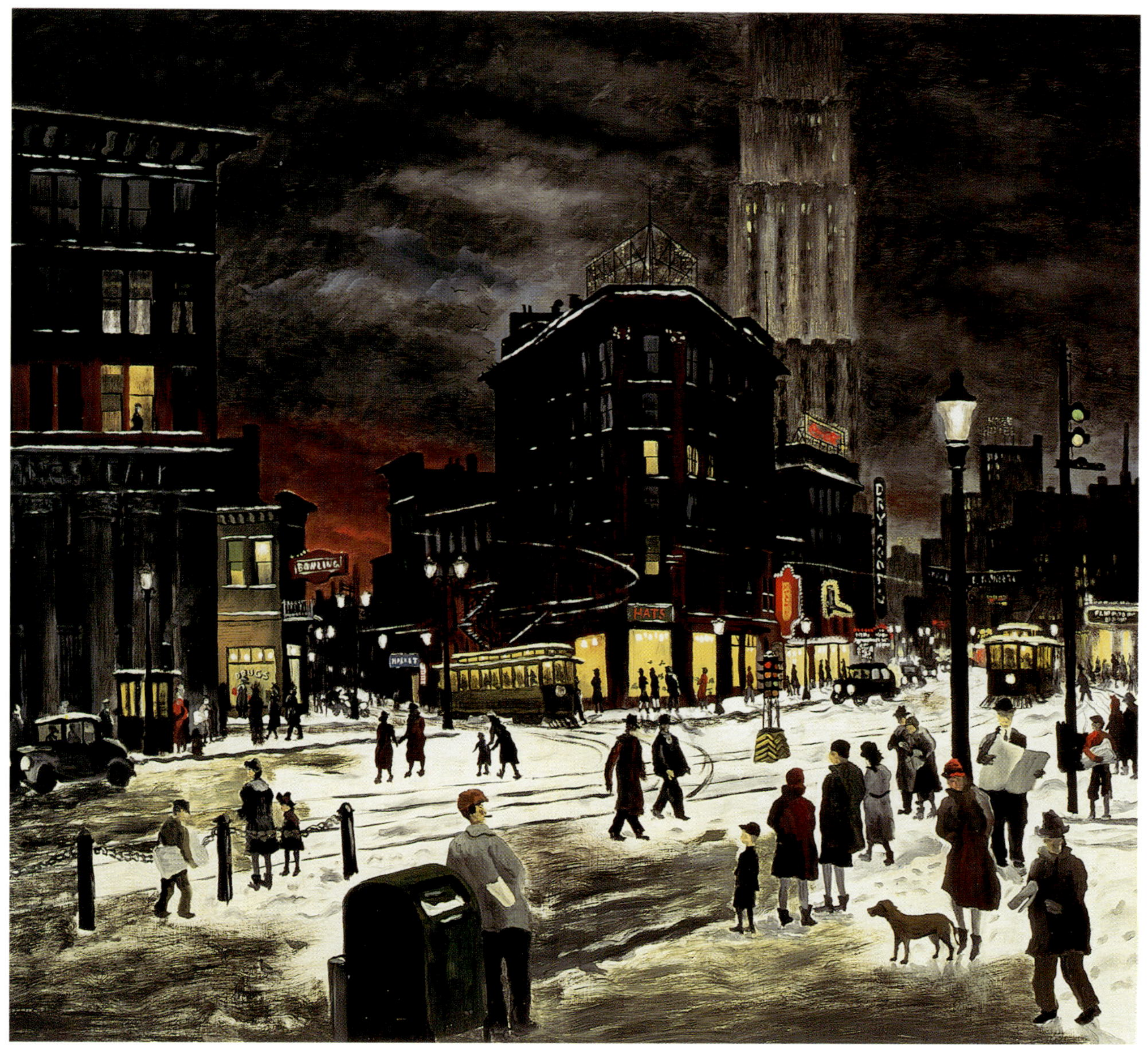

1981.25

Raphael Gleitsmann
Born 1910, Dayton, Ohio; died 1995, Akron, Ohio

Winter Evening, around 1932

Oil on fiberboard; 39 x 44 in.
Gift of Joseph M. Erdelac

Judith Keller

Walker Evans

The photographs of Walker Evans have shaped the way we view the Great Depression and the American South. His close association with these two areas of the American psyche is a surprising achievement for the son of an affluent Chicago businessman. Evans himself spent most of his adult life in New York. He had been a photographer for about eight years when he was commissioned in July 1935 by the Farm Security Administration (FSA) to document federal subsistence housing in Pennsylvania and West Virginia.[1] By that time his photographs of Victorian New England architecture had been exhibited at the Museum of Modern Art, and his published works had ranged from illustrations for poet Hart Crane's *The Bridge* to photographs of Havana for the book *The Crime of Cuba.*[2]

All of these experiences contributed to the evolution of a style that continued to mature as Evans traveled through the South in the employ of the FSA—first to West Virginia and then in the next eighteen months to Alabama, Arkansas, the Carolinas, Florida, Georgia, Kentucky, Louisiana, Mississippi, Tennessee, and Virginia. On his forays into the southern states he made photographs of roadside stores, rural churches, Victorian houses, steel mills, "company" houses, outdoor signs, and the modest buildings that lined the main streets of America's small towns. Although as a U.S. information specialist Evans was supposed to follow a firm itinerary, he was happiest making his own record of vernacular (as opposed to what he called "educated") architecture.

In the summer of 1935, during his first trip for the FSA, Evans photographed two rare interior views, one of which is Akron's *Interior Detail, West Virginia Coal Miner's House.* This seemingly straightforward picture, simply composed with an 8 x 10-inch view camera, is in fact cluttered with contradictions. The most obvious paradox is the sense of emptiness and the jarring presence of a specterlike hand of a woman at the extreme left of the picture. This fragmentary image injects a feeling of motion at the edge of the frame rather than in the center, where a rocking chair might lead the viewer to expect it. In addition, the handcrafted bentwood rocker contrasts sharply with the mass-produced signs that serve as both decoration and insulation in this poor household.

Signage, with its varied typography, was a favorite motif for Evans. Here signs enhance the collage effect seen elsewhere in the crudely tacked-together interior walls and the well-worn rug resting on rough floor slats. The signage also dramatizes the discrepancy between the smiling face of corporate American advertising and the desperate bleakness of the human condition in the rural South. It is appropriate that Coca-Cola, a southern invention, is featured so prominently in one of these signs. Ironically, Santa Claus, shown here promoting the product, has become as successful a consumer commodity as the soft drink, thanks in large part to advertising men like Evans's father, Walker Evans Sr.

Among other incongruities in the picture's iconography is the Rexall drug store sign celebrating a high school or college graduation, a luxury denied to a family for whom work rather than education had to be the priority. A globe in this same sign hints at world travel, but the tenants of this home are severely isolated by their poverty. "BUY GRADUATION GIFTS HERE" is the sales pitch, effectively transforming domestic into commercial space and ordinary objects such as a chair, a broom, and a crowbar into potential purchases.

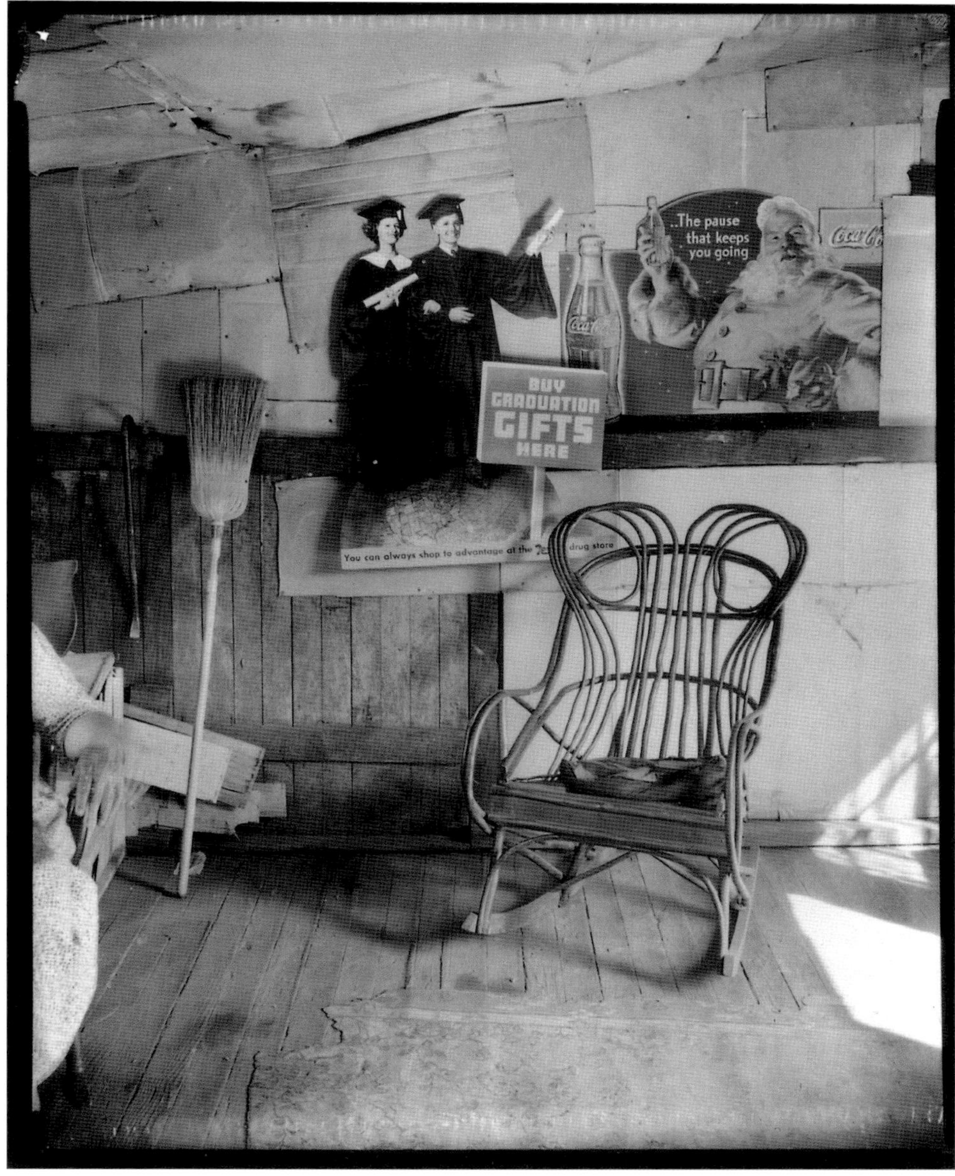

1980.12

Walker Evans
Born 1903, St. Louis, Missouri; died 1975, New Haven, Connecticut

Interior Detail, West Virginia Coal Miner's House, 1935

Gelatin silver print; 10 x 8 in.
Gift of Mr. and Mrs. C. Blake McDowell Jr.

Mitchell D. Kahan

Harvey R. Griffiths

Harvey Griffiths was a key figure in the Akron art scene during the 1930s and 1940s. He was one of fourteen artists who joined together in 1931 to create the Akron Society of Artists, for which he later served as president. In 1936 he was elected to the institute's board of trustees for a five-year term, which appears to have inaugurated the longtime practice of installing a representative from the Akron Society of Artists on the institute's governing board.

Griffiths's career as an artist included commercial work and fine art. He served an apprenticeship in a glass painting studio in Pennsylvania, then in his late teens worked in Chicago decorating fine china and glass. During World War I he served in the Marine Corps and was able to spend some leave time exploring France's art treasures. Upon discharge in 1919, he returned to Akron and enrolled for several years in night classes at the Cleveland School of Art (now the Cleveland Institute of Art) taught by Sandor Vago, a painter prominent in Cleveland in the period between the two world wars.

Griffiths earned his living as a commercial artist, working both independently and for several of Akron's major rubber companies. But it was his fine art that brought him some national recognition—acceptance in the 1936 annual exhibition of the American Water-Color Society in New York. In 1938 and 1939 he toured Europe for eleven months and undertook further studies in Florence and Milan. The watercolors he produced during that excursion were exhibited in a large show at the Akron Art Institute. In addition to watercolor, Griffiths also worked in oils and produced figure studies, flower paintings, and landscapes. He was given a memorial exhibition at the Akron Art Institute in 1953.

His watercolor *Arrangement with Billboard* is undated but was likely produced in 1938 or 1939, shortly before its inclusion in the *1940 New Year Show* at the Butler Art Institute in Youngstown. The scene, presumably of Akron, depicts a commercial building and a billboard with a bus stop in the background.[1] The subject clearly identifies Griffiths's work with the American Scene movement of the 1930s in its commitment to regional themes and local color.

The watercolor makes an interesting comparison with Raphael Gleitsmann's *Winter Evening*, painted almost a decade earlier (see pp. 84–85). While Gleitsmann depicts Main Street and the dramatic, recently constructed Art Deco bank topping Akron's skyline, Griffiths gives us a fairly anonymous scene that could be from any one of several cities across the state. In addition, Griffiths's modernity is more subtle than Gleitsmann's. He contrasts the dark, dilapidated building (probably a Shell service station) and the brand new, brightly illuminated billboard.[2] The parked car in the foreground is also fairly new, from the mid-1930s. The shift from old to new and dark to bright offers visual interest but also adds a subtle political dimension. If the times are prosperous enough for an illuminated billboard, they are still not far removed from the worst years of the Great Depression. The appeal to buy Ohio apples has more than a hint of economic necessity; it exhorts city folk to support local farmers.

Griffiths preferred painting landscapes on the spot and often worked in the company of other artists, mostly in the immediate area but also on longer trips, including one to the New England coast. *Arrangement with Billboard*, in his traditional watercolor technique, is a slice of northeast Ohio city life that is affectionate, intimate, and sincere.

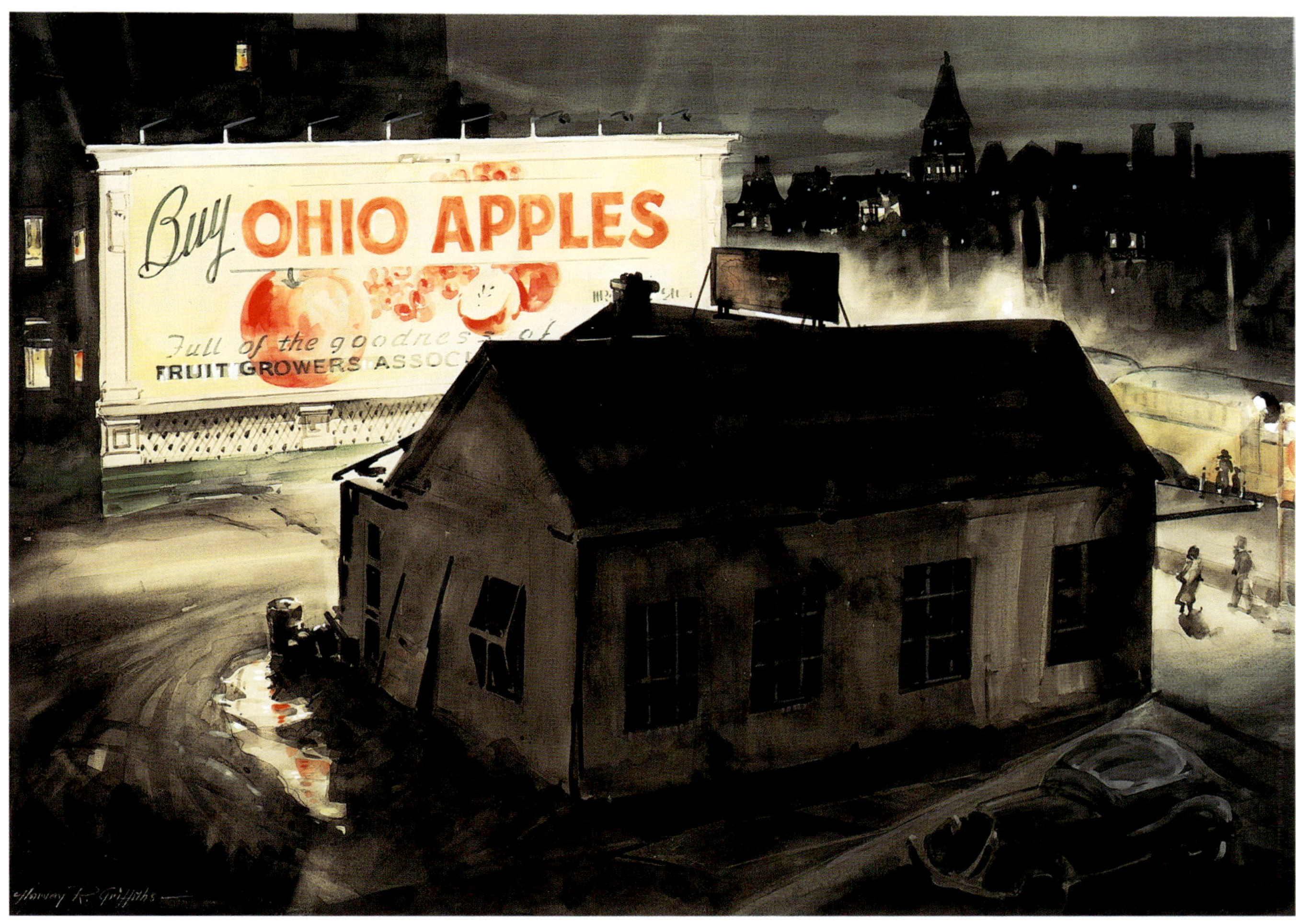

1958 13

Harvey R. Griffiths
Born 1883, Akron, Ohio; died 1952, Akron, Ohio

Arrangement with Billboard, late 1930s

Watercolor and graphite on illustration board; 19 7/8 x 29 in.
Anonymous Gift

Naomi Rosenblum

Lewis W. Hine

In *Topping the Mast, Empire State Building* two construction workers stand at the highest point of what became the world's tallest building on its completion in 1931.[1] As the photograph shows, the building was set among a dense array of already existing structures, all with the same purpose: to provide office space in midtown Manhattan. The irony of erecting an office building of exceptional height that would remain more than half empty for years during the Great Depression could not have been lost on Hine. Like the moment captured in this image, Hine's documentation of the skyscraper's construction represented a pinnacle in his career; but like the building's fate in subsequent years, his was disappointing in the extreme as fewer and fewer commissions came his way.

Hine's interest in working people and what they produced had begun early in the century. Leaving a teaching position in New York, he chose instead to transfer his "educational efforts from the classroom to the world."[2] His early projects depicted immigrants and their young children doing piecework in crowded tenement apartments and the unhealthy living and working conditions in the quintessential American industrial city of Pittsburgh. Between 1908 and 1916, for the National Child Labor Committee, Hine photographed children working at difficult and tedious jobs in mines and mills and on farms and city streets. His extensive documentation succeeded in making photography a significant element in campaigns for social change.[3] Twenty-two of these poignant photographs are in the collection of the Akron Art Museum.

Photographing conditions among refugees in the Balkans and France after World War I changed Hine's perspective. He now wished to photograph skilled workers doing jobs that needed celebrating, in order, he wrote, to counter the prevailing idea that the nation's "material assets" were "the product of a bunch of impersonal machines."[4] The commission to photograph the construction of the Empire State Building was well-suited to his outlook because this monumental project was one of the last to utilize the contributions of individual craftsmen.[5] Between July and April of 1930, Hine, assisted at times by his son Corydon, was "pushed and pulled up onto the *Peak*,...the highest point yet reached on a man-made structure." He also described being "swung out in a box from the hundredth floor...to get some shots of the tower."[6] *Topping the Mast* is a tribute not only to the workers but to this intrepid and gifted photographer whose only wish throughout a lifetime of photography was to create "a human document."

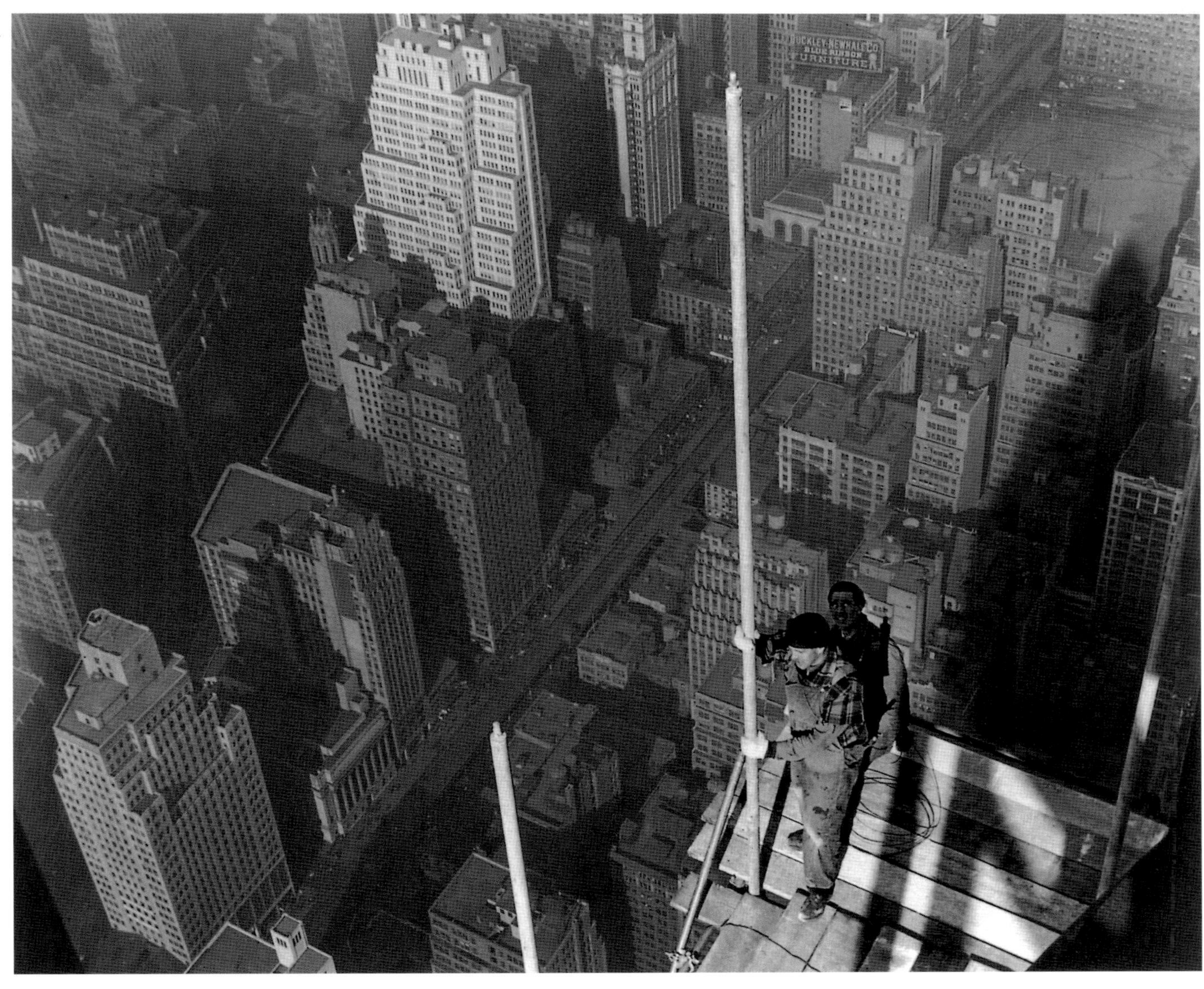

1995.10

Lewis W. Hine
Born 1874, Oshkosh, Wisconsin; died 1940, Dobbs Ferry, New York

Topping the Mast, Empire State Building, 1931 (printed later)

Gelatin silver print; 10 ¾ x 13 ¾ in.
Gift of Naomi and Walter Rosenblum

Luc Sante

Weegee

Weegee (Arthur H. Fellig) was a rough-and-tumble tabloid street photographer, the first of his species to be recognized by the art establishment. His family immigrated to the United States in 1910; he left school in his teens and lived awhile in Bowery flophouses. After a decade as a darkroom technician at a photography agency, he became a freelance photographer in 1935, contributing principally to the *New York Mirror.* Weegee employed a Speed Graphic camera, the standard press photographer's tool of the day, but his secret weapon was the police radio he had installed in his car. He was the only paparazzo so authorized. His amazing ability to arrive on the scene even before the police got there earned him his nickname, a phonetic spelling of "Ouija."

Weegee is usually described as a "primitive." While not inaccurate, this label merits a closer look. He was self-taught and not overly cultured, but then so were nearly all of his colleagues in that era, when only art photography inspired by the Pictorialists of several decades earlier held any sort of cachet. He always went for the big, crude effect. He hardly gauged his compositions—but how could he, when speed was of the essence, his camera was bulky, and mobs surrounded him? His darkroom work was never terribly subtle, but subtlety had no chance in the tabloid printing process, which rendered the entire midrange as mud. Likewise his venue demanded broadly iconic images for an immediate impact upon the preoccupied reader who was hastily leafing through the paper on the subway.

For all of that, Weegee's eye—and personality—rapidly made him known in very disparate quarters. Only ten years separate the beginning of his freelance career from the 1945 publication of his first book, *Naked City,* an unheard-of accomplishment for any sort of photographer then. He was just one of the herd of news photographers out covering murders and fires, but even today, when our respect for their trade has increased, he remains the only one whose name we are likely to know. This reflects on his genius for publicity, but it is also due to his uncannily consistent ability to make photographs that convey a narrative simply and dramatically, that are visual slogans or epigrams—or, more to the point, headlines. His pictures do not depend on any knowledge of the circumstances of their making; they are reduced to essentials and so are effortlessly timeless.

Anthony Esposito, Accused "Cop Killer" is a case in point. We are not looking at just any hood who murdered a policeman while trying to escape arrest, but—so the picture says—at *the* cop killer, the only one we need ever look at to recognize the breed. He has been worked over by the boys downstairs, hastily patched up, and then fingerprinted (which accounts for the right hand he seems to still be deploying in self-justification). Now he is being shoved over to the wall to be photographed. We get a sense of frozen turbulence. The killer looks small next to the broad back of the cop who is manhandling him, which takes up a full quarter of the frame, and who is given further height by the yardstick apparently growing out of his head. The flashbulb lights up the killer's face and sprays onto the cop's shoulder. The wall is neutral; the figures might be cut-outs glued to its surface. And they are, forever: two unindividuated blocklike representatives of the law and one small cop killer who will never be anything else.

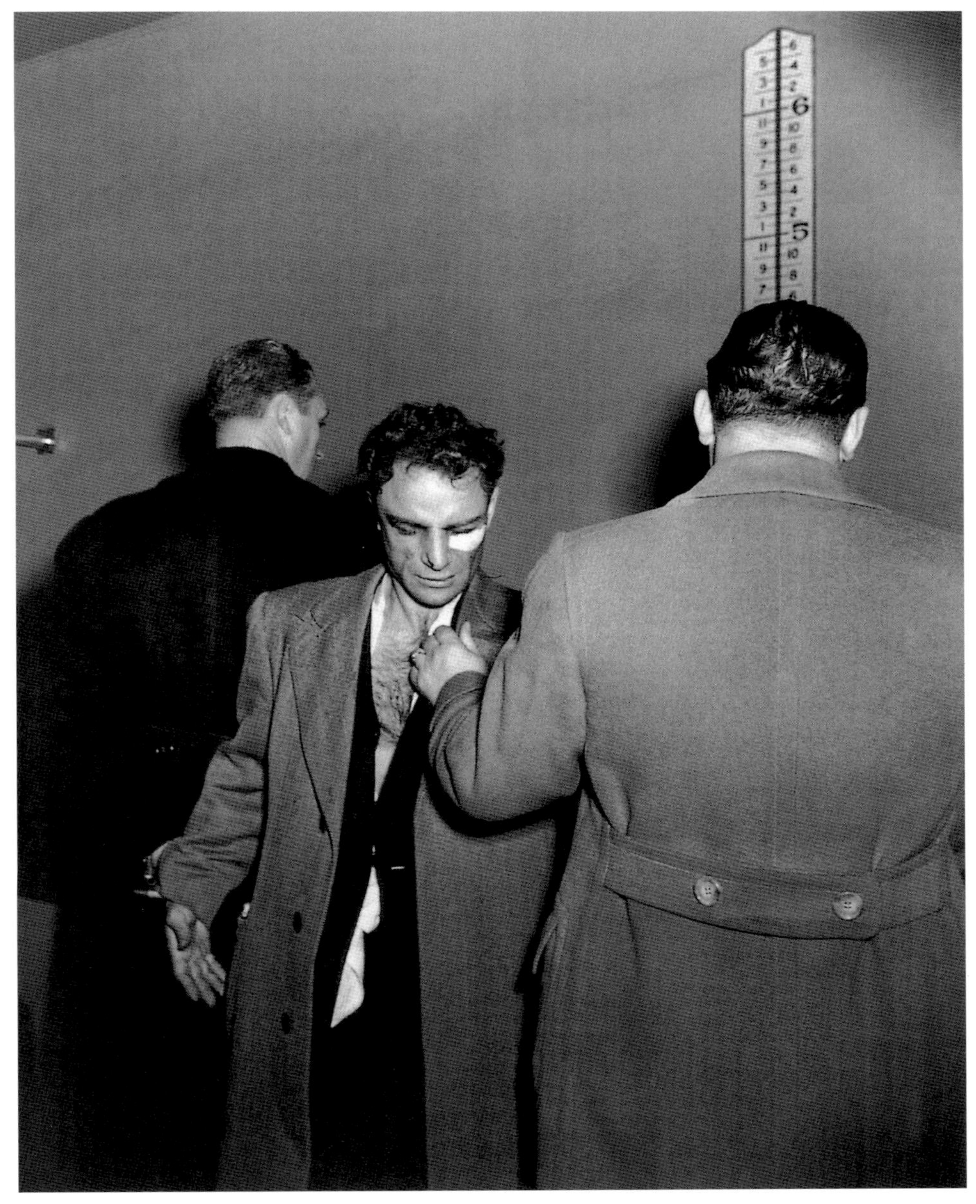

1982.7

Weegee
Born 1899, Zloczew, Austria (now Poland); died 1968, New York

Anthony Esposito, Accused "Cop Killer," 1941

Gelatin silver print; 13 $\frac{1}{4}$ x 10 $\frac{3}{8}$ in.
Gift of Norman and Carolyn Carr

Naomi Rosenblum

Vera Jackson

Until she took a photography class at a Los Angeles recreation center in the early 1930s, Vera Jackson found life somewhat boring. She had been brought to California with her siblings shortly after the death of her mother in the influenza epidemic of 1918. In her photography class, she became so taken with the basic skills of the medium—the darkroom work as well as the picture taking—that she vowed "to go into photography in a big way."[1] Using a neighbor's child as a model, she produced a prize-winning picture that was used on the cover of an educational magazine published by the Los Angeles school system.

Jackson's professional career began shortly thereafter when she was employed by the *California Eagle,* an important West Coast newspaper owned and edited by black activist Carlotta Bass. An early warrior in the struggle for equal rights, Bass became the first African American woman to run for vice-president of the United States (on the Progressive Party ticket in 1952). Jackson covered picket lines, rallies, and strikes. *Picketing in Los Angeles* was taken at 35th and Central Avenue during one of the many demonstrations organized in the 1940s against Jim Crow laws (restricted housing covenants for African Americans). The young boy in the lower right-hand corner of the picture is the artist's son, who accompanied her on this assignment. With its high contrasts and crisp patterning, this image suggests the energy and excitement felt by those engaged in civil rights activities in those days.

As the only full-time photographer on the staff, Jackson was afforded the opportunity—unusual for a black woman at that time—to photograph a wide range of events and personages besides those related to civil agitation. She depicted sporting meets, church and community affairs, and also photographed many of the African American celebrities who came to Los Angeles, among them Duke Ellington, Dorothy Dandridge, Paul Robeson, and Jackie Robinson.

Jackson's experiences on the *California Eagle* prompted her to return to school to earn a master's degree in education and to keep improving her camera skills. Although her next career was as an elementary school teacher, she continued to photograph for a number of West Coast publications. "Photography," she has written, "enriched my life in many ways. It taught me to see, and to understand myself and others...and to enjoy the wonders of the beauty on this planet."[2]

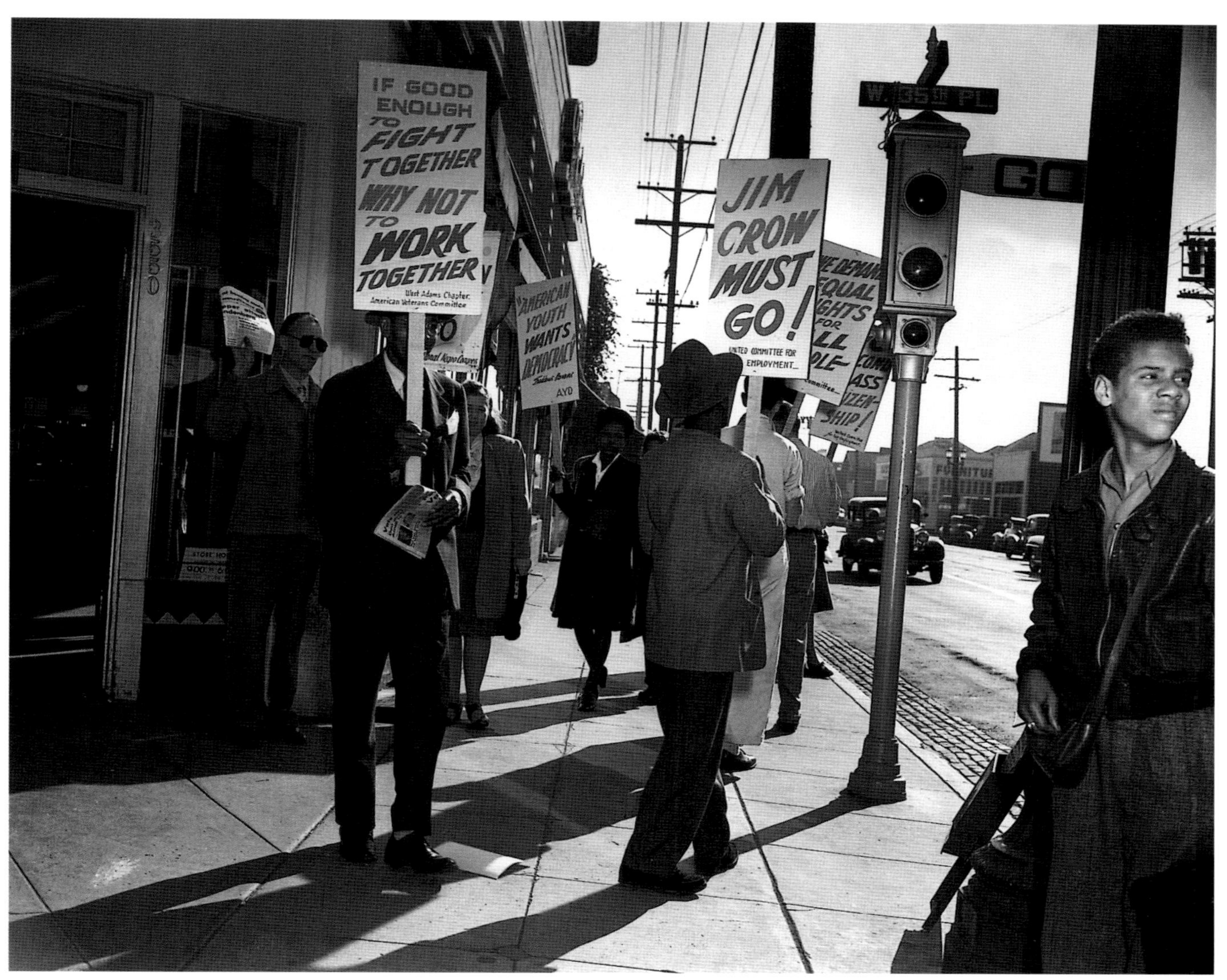

1996.7

Vera Jackson

Born 1911, Wichita, Kansas; lives Corona, California

Picketing in Los Angeles, 1948 (printed 1996)

Gelatin silver print; $6\frac{3}{4} \times 8\frac{3}{4}$ in.
Gift of the artist

Mitchell D. Kahan

Elmer Novotny

A portrait and landscape painter, Elmer Ladislaw Novotny remained a traditional realist throughout his career, resisting the revival of abstraction after World War II. Though they possess only a regional reputation, his emotionally powerful and technically superb paintings from the 1930s deserve a wider audience.

Novotny's first paintings were done under the direction of his father, an amateur artist. At age thirteen, the precocious son completed the first of over three hundred portrait commissions created throughout his career. He attended the Cleveland School of Art (now Cleveland Institute of Art) on scholarship and, with awards and support from Cleveland patrons, traveled to London and Zagreb for further study. After receiving degrees from Western Reserve College and Kent State University, he obtained a teaching position at Kent. He remained there for four decades, retiring as chairman of the School of Art in 1974. Both the Akron Art Institute and the Butler Institute of American Art mounted solo exhibitions of his work.

"I've always considered portraiture a fine art and not a commercial venture," Novotny explained, citing the vast number of old master portraits hanging in museums. "I truly hope my portraiture is still a high art form."[1] *Citizen of Onsted* fulfills Novotny's ambitions. An arresting profile of a worker in a Michigan logging town, it also serves as an icon of America during the Depression. The mill was painted on site, which partially accounts for the modest size of the painting. The figure, however, was added in Novotny's studio in Ohio, a practice recalling that of earlier landscape painters who combined various outdoor sketches into finished compositions in the studio.

The rural subject and the tightly rendered naturalism of the painting ally Novotny with the American Scene movement. This artistic development, which had its heyday in the 1930s, was a reaction against the currents of technology, modernism, and abstraction typically identified with major cities on the East Coast and in Europe. American Scene painting's relationship with European art, however, was complicated. Like Grant Wood's famous *American Gothic,* Novotny's subject is identifiably American and rural, but the European old masters hover in the background. Novotny's realism recalls Dutch and Flemish naturalism; his unusual choice of casein (similar to tempera in using egg as a base instead of oil) points to an interest in the centuries-old practice of handmade paint. A revival of such esoteric painting techniques was common among American realists in the 1930s and 1940s as an antidote to mechanization and mass production. Updating older European practices into an American dialect was not merely a technical choice. It suggested an artist's identification with traditional values—that is, individualism and capitalism as opposed to communism or socialism, and sometimes a preference for isolationism as opposed to internationalism.

Nevertheless, a close look at Akron's painting reveals the impact of modern art. The close-up cropping of the farmer's figure recalls both the compositions of modernist photography and the dynamic angularity of certain images by Toulouse-Lautrec and Degas (who were also influenced by photography). Regardless of its artistic antecedents, *Citizen of Onsted* is most notable for its emotional appeal. In the dignity and determination of his subject, Novotny, an artist raised in the city, has created a paean to America's heartland.

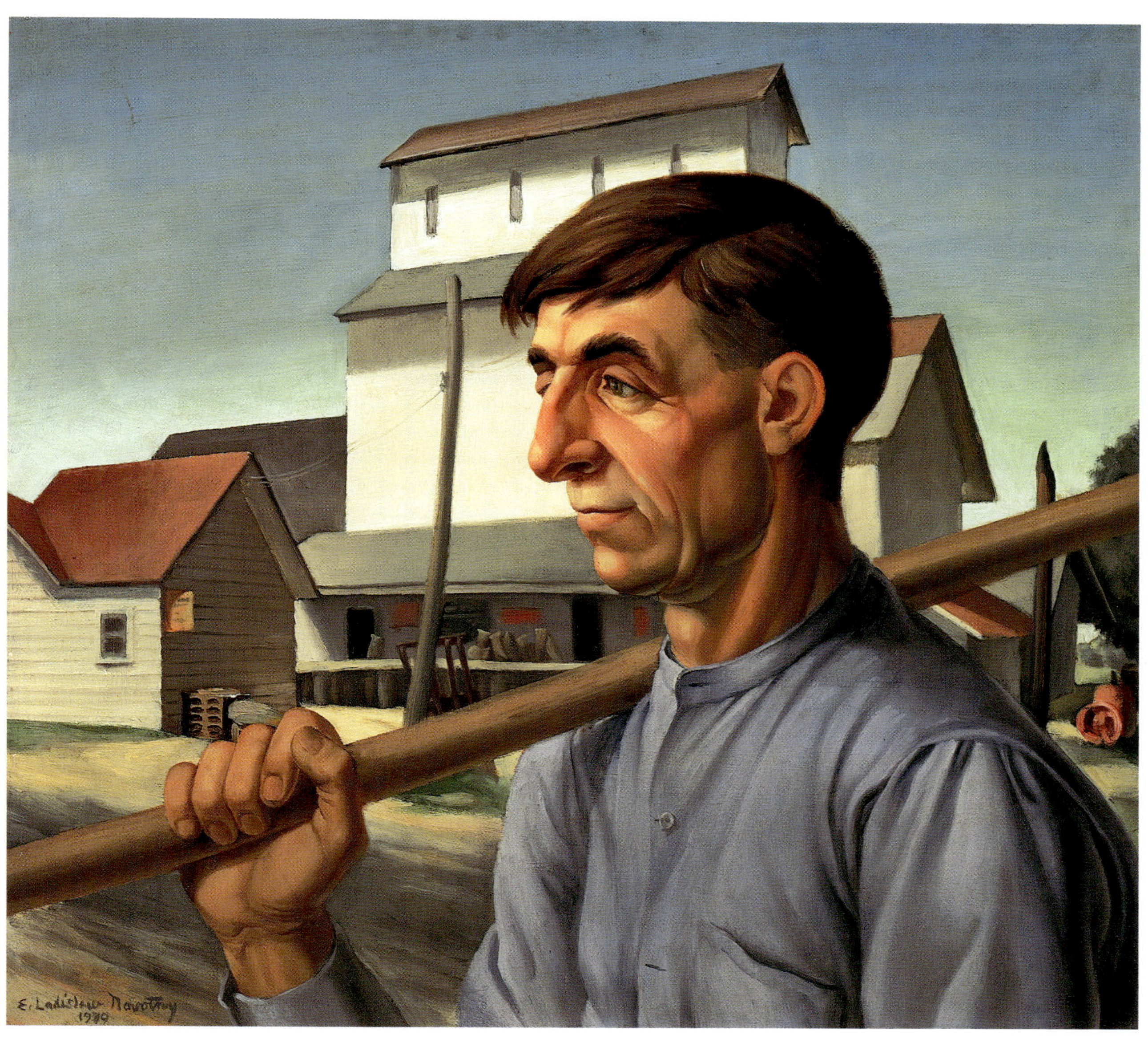

1962.74

Elmer Novotny
Born 1909, Cleveland; died 1997, Walnut Creek, California

Citizen of Onsted, 1939

Casein on fiberboard; 22 x 25 $\frac{1}{4}$ in.
Gift of the artist in memory of Mrs. Janet Schulman

Wendy Kendall-Hess

William Sommer

As a commissioned piece, the *Bordner Mural* may not be William Sommer's most daring work, but it exemplifies his style, his favorite subject matter, and his greatest gift: a fanciful, innovative approach that enabled him to transform his everyday northeastern Ohio surroundings into a transcendent vision of the world. The *Bordner Mural* is one of thirty-seven paintings, watercolors, prints, and drawings by Sommer in the collection of the Akron Art Museum.

Sommer was born in Detroit to German immigrant parents. His artistic skills were apparent at an early age, but pursuing a fine art career was out of the question for someone of little means. Consequently, Sommer left school at the age of fourteen to learn commercial lithography. After completing an apprenticeship in 1888, he worked on the East Coast and in England, all the while harboring a desire to create fine art. In February 1890 a generous friend took Sommer to Munich, where he studied painting through March 1891. During his year in Munich he obtained a solid conservative education.

Upon his return Sommer resumed his career in lithography. Settling in New York, he married, had three sons, ventured into the fine arts community to socialize with other artists, and produced earthen-hued portraits. In 1907 he joined the Otis Lithograph Company in Cleveland, where he met William Zorach, Abel Warshawsky, and other innovative artists and was introduced to Impressionism and Post-Impressionism. A quick learner, he mastered each one in turn, and then progressed through several phases of modern art in just a few years.[1]

In 1914 Sommer moved to a country home between Cleveland and Akron. This shift from a crowded urban setting to a hilly, wooded, four-acre lot energized the artist, spurring him to new levels of creativity. In an abandoned schoolhouse-turned-studio, he started experimenting more, adding watercolor to his repertoire and finding new inspiration in music and literature. The influence of Vorticism—a British variant of Cubism—was discernible by the early 1920s in Sommer's use of more angular, denser forms. His subjects, however, came directly from his rustic surroundings: landscapes, livestock, neighborhood children, and still lifes.

Despite heavy drinking, financial woes, and periodic bouts with depression, Sommer continued to grow artistically. By the late 1920s his own unique style emerged. The *Bordner Mural*, which is also signed by the artist's middle son, Edwin,[2] exemplifies that style: a combination of the innovations of European modernism with rural midwestern imagery. The work was probably commissioned by Ruth Bordner as a birthday gift for her husband Robert, a Sommers family friend. This scene, which hung over the Bordners' mantel for some thirty years, is believed to depict their home and land.[3]

The overall composition is a product of the artist's eye more than reality. Characteristically, Sommer stylized the components of the scene using a range of hues; some images are simplified, others are adorned with decorative flourishes. The sky is filled with dramatic sun rays, and clouds appear as bold organic shapes. While the details of the painting—from the vague slope of the land to the two buildings—relay a sense of the site, personal expression is more important than accuracy of representation. The ground has been broken into a number of different color fields defined by curves and angles. Sommer's neat arrangement of cows, horses, and chickens certainly owes more to his quest for balance than to the animals' cooperation. Even inclusion of the seated boy was probably the artist's idea, for the Bordners were childless.

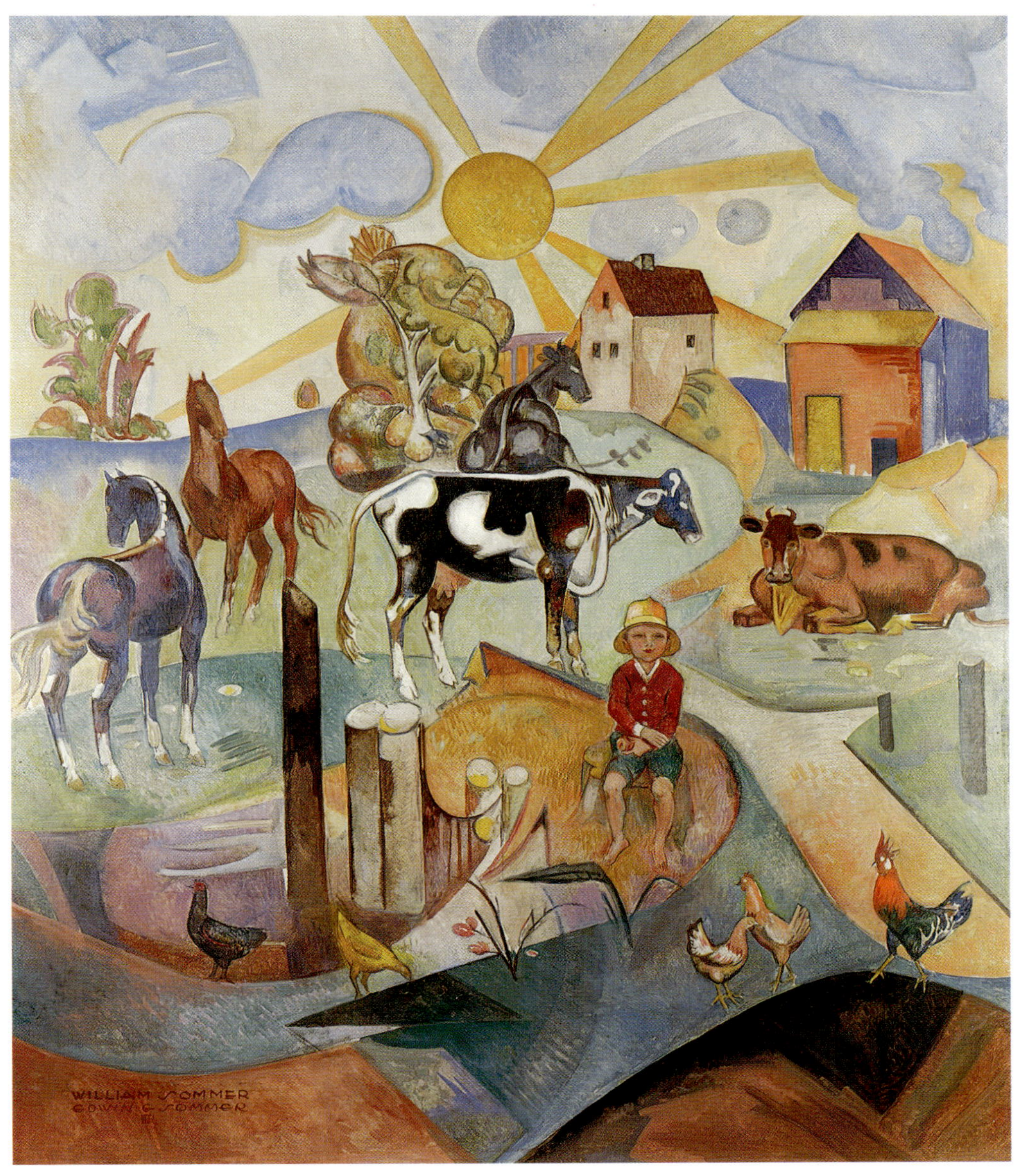

1973.17

William Sommer
Born 1867, Detroit; died 1949, Northfield, Ohio

Edwin Sommer
Born 1899, New York; died 1957, Sacramento, California

Bordner Mural, around 1936–37

Oil on fiberboard; 55 x 47 in.
Gift of Robert Bordner

Barbara Tannenbaum

Karl Blossfeldt

For thirty-five years Karl Blossfeldt had been producing photographs of plants for use as teaching aids. Around 1925, these were suddenly designated works of art by an art dealer. Blossfeldt was then a sixty-year-old professor of drawing and sculpture at a Berlin college of fine and applied arts. His first exhibition, held in 1926, was followed two years later by the publication of *Urformen der Kunst* (issued in English as *Art Forms in Nature*). The popularity of this book led to the production of a second volume, *Wundergarten der Natur* (Nature's Garden of Wonders), which contains *Blumenbachia Hieronymi (Loasaceae)*. These books of photogravures of Blossfeldt's images were the primary means by which his work was disseminated.[1]

The professor deemed his images to be documentation, not art. "My flower documents," he wrote, "should...reawaken a sense for nature, pointing out its teeming richness of form, and prompt the viewer to observe for himself the local plant world."[2] Blossfeldt made regular excursions to the countryside and occasionally took trips abroad to harvest botanical specimens for the six thousand images he photographed in his studio between 1890 and his death in 1932. The format of his images is always the same: sharply focused, shot at extremely close range, and usually only a detail of the plant. Occasionally he included several examples of the same plant to form a pattern. The cleaned and trimmed specimen was photographed against a gray cardboard. Blossfeldt used a camera he had built himself, to which he added a special lens to magnify the object between three and forty-five times.

The purpose of his "flower documents" was to teach future architects and designers that the best engineering and aesthetic solutions to design problems could be found in nature. He instructed them that "the plant...developed according to the same structural rules which every architect must observe...[but it] never reverts to mere functionality: it...is compelled, by an elemental force, toward the highest artistic form."[3] This philosophy, first espoused in mid-nineteenth-century Germany, was put into wide practice by the Art Nouveau and Arts and Crafts movements. It still influenced German design education in the 1920s.

Even though Blossfeldt's theories had been long established, his work was acclaimed for its modernity. His technique exemplified a new German style known as the New Objectivity (Die Neue Sachlichkeit). Its hallmarks were careful naturalistic observation, extreme detail, crystalline clarity, and above all a (supposedly) neutral stance toward the subject—all qualities evident in *Blumenbachia Hieronymi (Loasaceae)*.[4]

The *Blumenbachia hieronymi* is a flowering plant native to Argentina but cultivated elsewhere. Blossfeldt photographed it not for its botanical value but for its visual interest. Its spiraling closed seed capsule, seen here magnified eighteen times, is said to resemble the top of an Asian mosque. While Blossfeldt's presentation of it is factual, a surreal aspect is added through magnification, lighting, and angle of view. Unnatural scale transforms the viewer into a Lilliputian gaping at biology gone mad. Each hair could be a menacing thorn, each leaf a pincer. Little wonder that Blossfeldt was compared to the surrealists as early as 1927.

Blossfeldt's impersonal study of the variations within one subject has influenced contemporary German photographers such as Bernd and Hilla Becher and Thomas Struth (see pp. 238–39). Irving Penn, Harry Callahan (see pp. 118–19), and Robert Mapplethorpe are among the many photographers who employ similar techniques, using isolation and magnification to glorify humble objects. Like much photography that was never intended as art, Blossfeldt's plant pictures have had a profound effect on the medium.

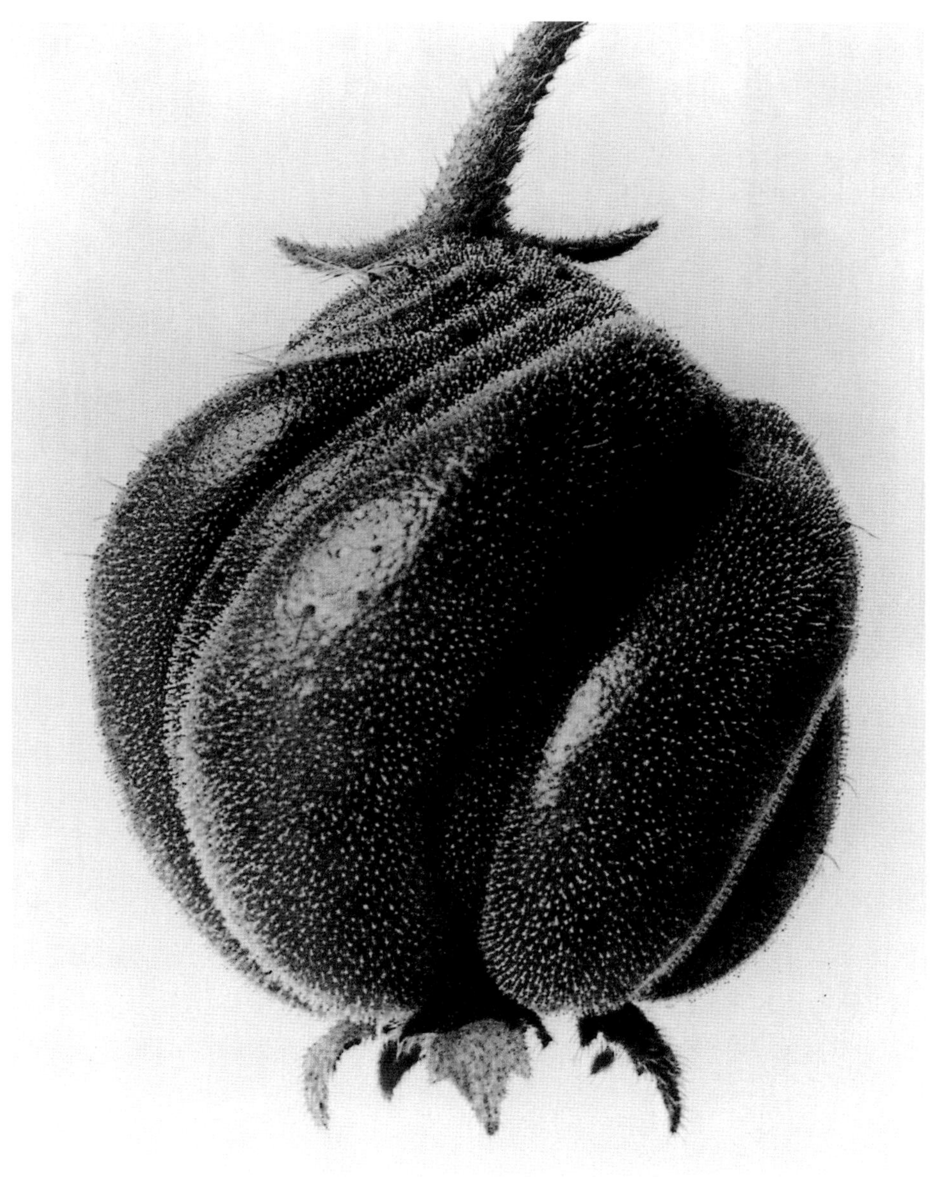

1979.27.103

Karl Blossfeldt
Born 1865, Schielo (in the Harz Mountains), Germany; died 1932, Berlin

Blumenbachia Hieronymi (Loasaceae), date unknown,
from *Wundergarten der Natur* (Nature's Garden of Wonders), 1932

Photogravure; 11 x 8 ½ in.
Museum Acquisition Fund

Jeffrey Grove

Man Ray

Man Ray, a pioneer of Dada and Surrealism, was the only American artist to play a major role in developing those influential early twentieth-century movements. He was born in Philadelphia and raised in New York, but the artist's unusual name—changed from his birth name Emmanuel Radnitzky—and the years he spent living overseas led many to assume he was European. As Marcel Duchamp's close friend and a founder of the Société Anonyme (one of the first American organizations to promote and collect avant-garde art), Man Ray was a vital link between European and American artists from the 1920s to the 1940s.

Man Ray began his career as a commercial artist, then worked extensively with collage and painting before turning to photography. His contributions to abstract and fashion photography and portraiture eventually overshadowed his work in other media. Man Ray was forever irritated that he was considered primarily a photographer, an aggravation that was not unwarranted. In 1923 he produced *Indestructible Object,* a metronome with a photograph of an eye attached. It became one of the most recognized ready-mades in history.

Ready-mades consist of everyday, mass-produced objects that attain status as a work of art through selection, slight alteration, and designation by an artist. This common Dada and Surrealist practice, popularized by Marcel Duchamp (see pp. 104–5), often involved investing an object with sexual, autobiographical, or violent significance. *Indestructible Object* was, in different versions, informed by all of these impulses. Originally titled *Object to be Destroyed* or *Object of Destruction,* it has also been known as *Lost Object* (1945), *Indestructible Object* (1958), and *Perpetual Motif* (1971).

Regarding the first metronome's genesis, the artist remembered: "A painter needs an audience, so I also clipped the photo of an eye to the metronome's swinging arm to create the illusion of being watched. One day...the silence was unbearable and...I smashed it to pieces."[1] His next interpretation was motivated by the ending of his love affair with Lee Miller, a former fashion model and fellow photographer. In 1932 he replaced the photograph on his metronome with one of Miller's eye. On the back of a drawing of that object, titled *Object to be Destroyed,* he inscribed: "Cut out the eye from the photograph of one who has been loved but is seen no more. Attach the eye to the pendulum of a metronome and regulate the weight to suit the tempo desired. Keep going to the limit of endurance. With a hammer well-aimed, try to destroy the whole at a single blow."[2]

The inner rage that propelled Man Ray to imbue this object with intense personal meaning evoked an especially strong audience reaction in 1957 at the Exposition Dada in Paris. There, students demonstrating against Dada and Surrealism attacked and destroyed the sculpture. The artist, in true Dadaist fashion, refused to prosecute the vandals. The insurance company covered the damage despite its suspicion that he might use the money to buy a whole stock of metronomes. The artist recalled: "That was my intention.... However, I assured [them]...I'd change the title."[3]

Consequently, in 1958 Man Ray made another version of *Indestructible Object.* He authorized its production in a limited edition, and the work soon became an icon of modern art. Further editions were issued in the 1960s and 1970s. Akron's metronome, from the final version authorized by the artist, is the classic example. Bearing a photograph of Lee Miller's eye and again titled *Indestructible Object,* it represents the ultimate, surreal synthesis of Man Ray's artistic and emotional history.

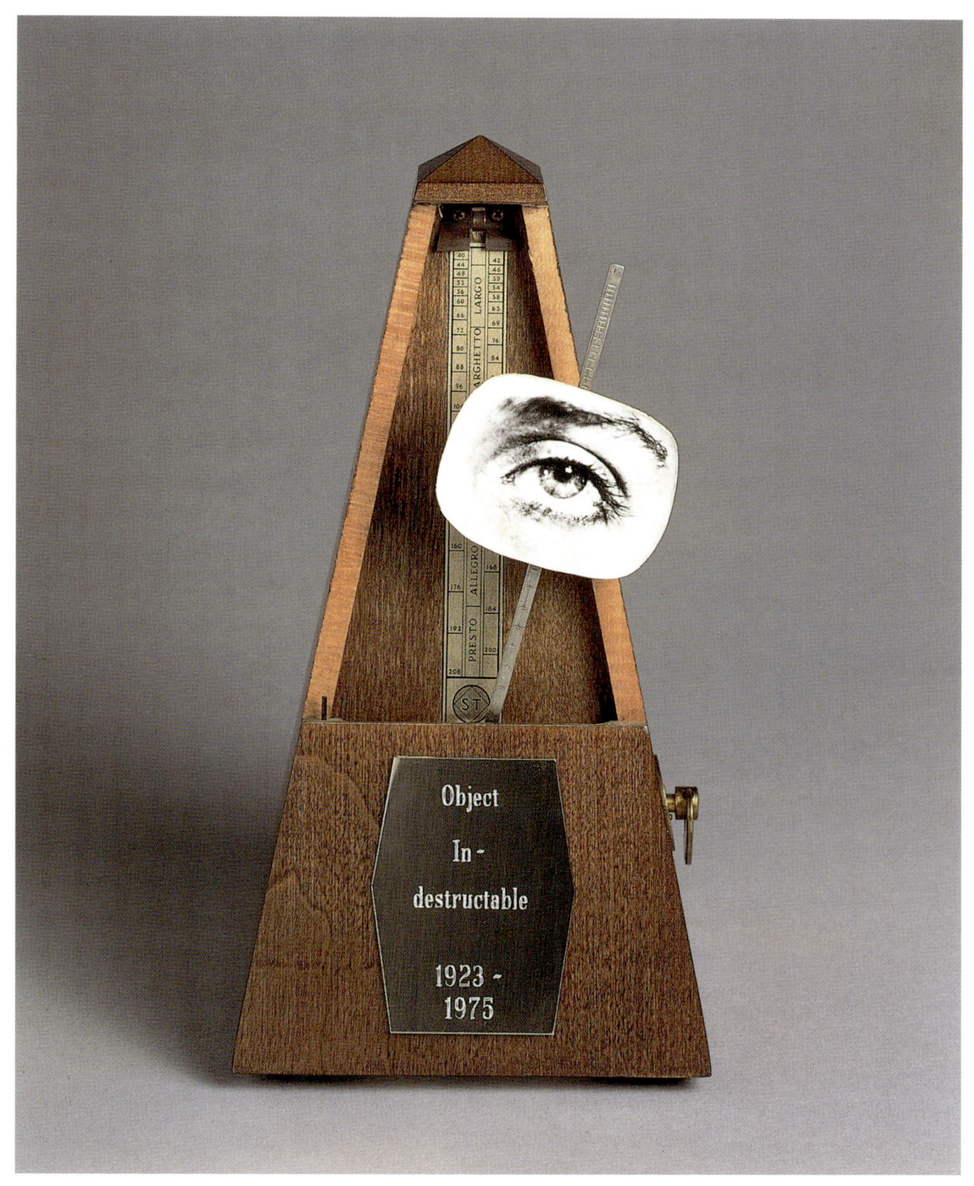

1979.10

Man Ray
Born 1890, Philadelphia; died 1976, Paris

Indestructible Object, 1923 (1975 edition)

Metronome with cardboard; 8 ¾ x 4 ½ x 4 ½ in.
Gift of John Coplans

Jeffrey Grove

Marcel Duchamp

Henri-Robert-Marcel Duchamp claimed to be shy, lazy, and lacking ambition. Nonetheless, this master of irony and understatement emerged as one of modern art's pivotal figures. He did not develop a recognizable style or exhibit his work regularly, yet Duchamp's legacy has profoundly influenced subsequent generations of artists. He believed art could be made out of anything, from air and bottle racks to physics and geometry, for he was convinced that the concept behind an artwork was more important than its physical presence. His view decisively altered notions of what constitutes an aesthetic object.

Duchamp produced an imposing number of the twentieth century's masterpieces. They include *Nude Descending a Staircase No. 2,* 1912, a Cubist-inspired painting that led the artist to abandon traditional artmaking tools; *The Bride Stripped Bare by Her Bachelors, Even,* 1915–23, a complex web of mechanical imagery, sexual themes, and mathematical references sandwiched between two sheets of glass; and *Fountain,* 1917, an ordinary urinal Duchamp inverted, signed "R. Mutt," and declared art. *From or by Marcel Duchamp or Rrose Sélavy (The Box in a Valise)* contains a diminutive replica of each of these, plus facsimiles of nearly eighty other works produced by the artist between 1910 and 1954.

Declared "a portable museum" by Duchamp,[1] *The Box in a Valise* (as it is called) is a fascinating mini-retrospective that anticipates future developments in art and technology. His condensation of vast amounts of visual information into a compact form presaged ideas behind the CD ROM and the Internet, and his decision to have miniature versions of his work commercially manufactured was a radical notion. Duchamp began the initial six-year project of assembling his mass-produced reproductions around 1935. In 1940–41, as World War II raged, he smuggled these components out of occupied France and shipped them to New York, where he immigrated in 1942. The first series of twenty boxes were produced in the spring of 1941. Subsequently, between 1941 and 1968, he produced six series totalling approximately three hundred boxes. Akron's example, from the final series, contains twelve items more than the first box. It is stamped, posthumously, with Duchamp's signature and is signed by the artist's wife, Teeny.

The Box in a Valise may be the quintessential Duchampian object: as serious as quantum theory and as entertaining as a child's toy. Duchamp delighted in the union of opposites and reconciliation of apparent contradictions. Nowhere was this tendency more clear than in his creation of Rrose Sélavy, the feminine alter ego mentioned in the work's title as its co-creator. This fictional character materialized in 1920, when Duchamp began to sign his work occasionally with her name. In 1921 Rrose's identity was revealed when the artist donned makeup and a woman's hat and fur and posed for two memorable photographs by Man Ray (see pp. 102–3). "Rrose Sélavy" pronounced phonetically sounds like *"Eros, c'est la vie,"* or "Eros, that is life," a motto combining the wit, amusing word play, and themes of sexuality that informed much of the artist's work.

Duchamp's fusion of autobiographical, intellectual, and sexual elements in his work effected a seismic shift in attitudes toward art that still resonates. His denigration of the purely visual—"retinal," as he phrased it—qualities of art influenced the formation of Minimal and Conceptual art in the 1960s. His creation of Rrose Sélavy foreshadowed two primary concerns of artists in the 1980s and 1990s: gender and identity. His willingness, even desire, to make his artistic legacy and personal history immediately accessible through reproductions, as in *The Box in a Valise,* anticipated the blurring between original and copy and the confessional approach of many contemporary artists. Ultimately, Duchamp's importance must be measured not only in terms of his artistic influence but as a harbinger of social and philosophical changes in contemporary culture.

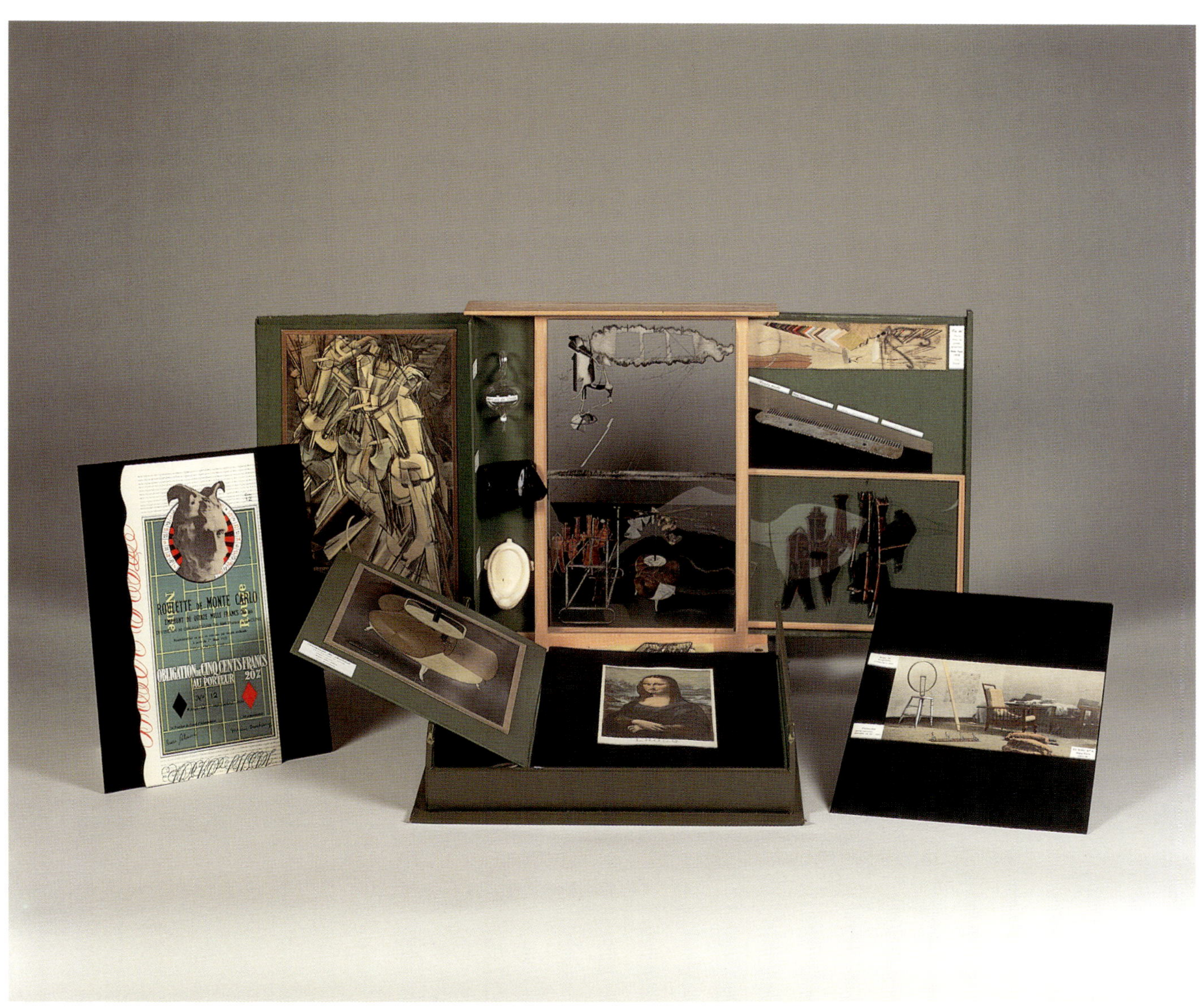

1973.2

Marcel Duchamp
Born 1887, Blainville, France; died 1968, Neuilly-sur-Seine, France

From or by Marcel Duchamp or Rrose Sélavy (The Box in a Valise),
1941 (1968 edition)

Green leather box with mixed media; 16¼ x 15⅛ x 3⅞ in. (closed)
Purchased with funds from the Walter P. and Fama Keith Foundation in memory of Walter P. Keith, the Arts Council, and John Coplans

Naomi Rosenblum

Laure Albin Guillot

"Photography," claimed Laure Albin Guillot, "must be true to life and sincere; it must likewise be beautiful."[1] Working in Paris in the years when the New Realism (also called the New Vision) was replacing the Pictorialist style, Albin Guillot maintained an unabashedly romantic outlook, which can be seen in *Narcisse.*

The image is based on the Greek myth of a beautiful male youth who spurned the love of a young girl, Echo, who then pined away until only her voice remained. In retribution, the goddess Nemesis caused Narcissus to gaze with everlasting love at his own reflected image until finally he was transformed into a flower. In the softness of the swirling forms and the languor of the pose, Albin Guillot created a dreamlike atmosphere that evokes beauty, love, and longing. *Narcisse* is one of a series of nudes and landscape photographs inspired by French author Paul Valéry s book of poems, *Charmes.* These images are not so much illustrations of the texts as they are poetic creations in themselves.[2] Valéry, who was initially skeptical, praised Albin Guillot for having produced poetry equal to his own.

The artist's feeling for beauty remained constant during thirty years as a professional photographer, but her style showed considerable diversity, sometimes glorying in the blurred forms of *Narcisse* and other times assuming the crispness associated with the New Realism. Albin Guillot was active at a time when photography was only just becoming "the queen of illustration" both in Europe and the United States.[3] With the perfection of halftone printing and the improvement in magazine paper stock, camera images became much more desirable as product illustration. Albin Guillot specialized in publicity portraits of well-known figures in French society, many of which appeared in periodicals, but she also did product photography for Omega, Renault, and the department store Bon Marché.

For her own aesthetic satisfaction she produced landscapes, studies of nudes, narrative tableaux using dolls and figurines, and scientific images. The latter derived from her interest in microscopy, which she shared with her physician husband. The images were published under the title *Micrographie décorative*—a portfolio of twenty prints in a variety of colors and on unusual papers as well as metallic foil. The photographs appear to be abstract patterns but are in reality views of natural substances seen through a microscope.[4]

Unlike many of her contemporaries, for whom the image as seen through the camera lens was the single important aspect of the work, Albin Guillot regarded the mastery of photographic printing techniques as an integral part of the endeavor. "Few other photographers," it was said of her, "possess the knowledge and mastery...[and] take the same care with the execution of a work...as with the taking of the view."[5] The sensual matte surface and unusual green hue of *Narcisse* are the result of Fresson printing, invented around 1899 by Théodore-Henri Fresson. The process was first employed by Pictorialists at the turn of the century and carried on by the inventor's descendants and others. In Fresson printing the use of pigment and carbon rather than silver provides greater permanence than gelatin silver printing and allows maximum control of effect in the print. Albin Guillot worked with Pierre Fresson (a descendant of Théodore-Henri) to master this relatively rare process, which she used primarily in her personal, rather than commercial, work.

Despite her illustrious career in the forefront of French photography in the 1920s and 1930s, Albin Guillot's work was entirely forgotten very soon after her death. Only now is it receiving a deserved reappraisal.

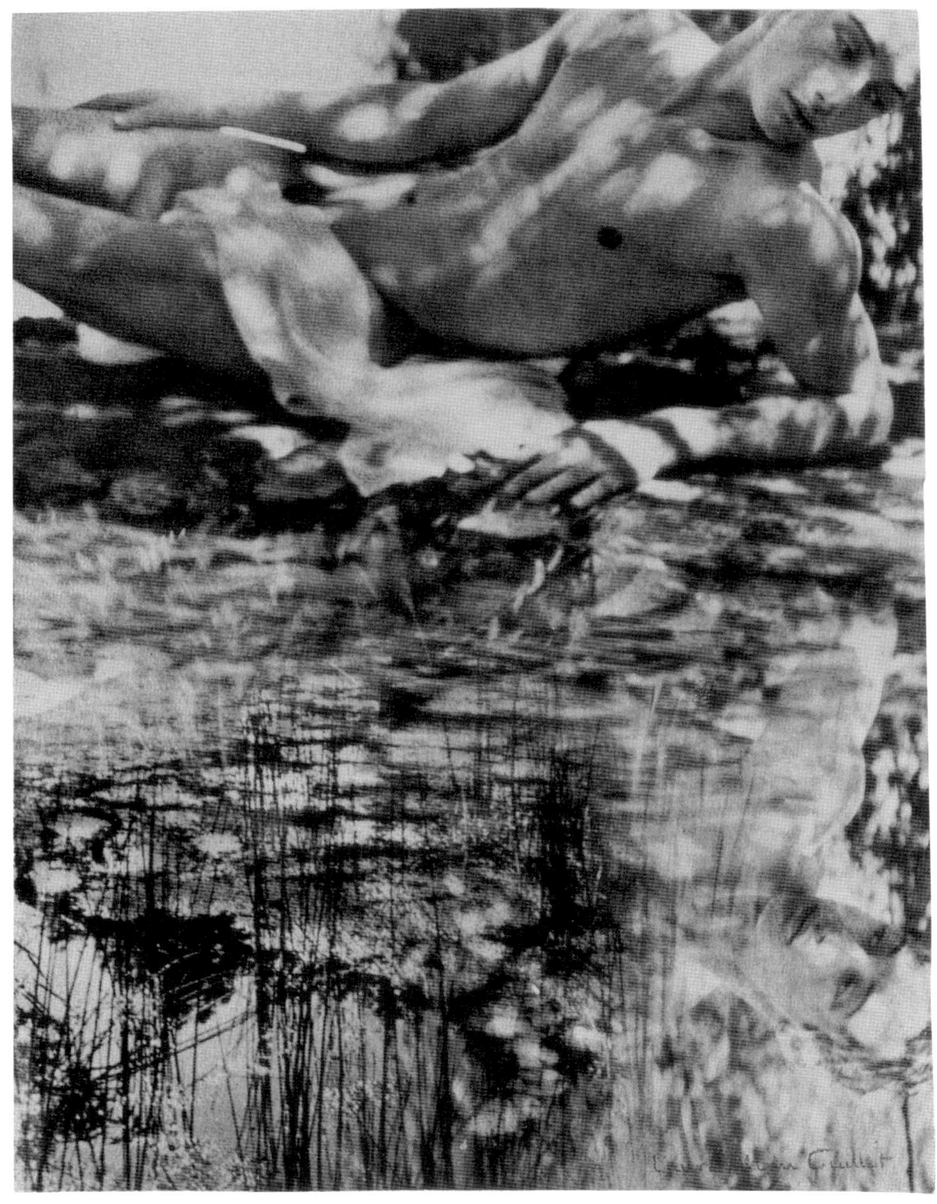

1996.11

Laure Albin Guillot
Born 1879, Paris; died 1962, Nogent-sur-Marne, France

Narcisse (Narcissus), 1934

Fresson print; 13 ⅜ x 10 ⅛ in.
Purchase with funds donated by Mrs. Beatrice K. McDowell

Naomi Rosenblum

Ansel Adams

Driving in the Chama River Valley toward Santa Fe at the end of an unproductive day, Ansel Adams observed an extraordinary vista off to the east. Unable to find his exposure meter and eager to capture the scene before it disappeared, he quickly calculated the footcandle power of the moon's rays and exposed the film for one second at f/32. He later wrote that he had tried for another exposure, but as he "pulled out the slide the sunlight left the crosses and the magical moment was gone forever."[1]

Moonrise, Hernandez, New Mexico is arguably one of the best-known images of the American landscape. The photograph shows a small village on a plain beneath an expanse of darkened sky. The moon has just risen over distant snow-capped peaks, which are topped by a bank of clouds. But what gives the scene its extraordinary brilliance are the rays of the late afternoon sun illuminating the cloud bank and turning the crosses in the church cemetery a blazing white. Adams reprinted this popular image over the years, at first allowing random clouds to appear in the sky. It was not until the 1970s, when he printed the sky as an almost cloudless dark-toned expanse, that he felt he had achieved an effect equal to his original visualization of the scene.

Adams's passion for spectacular landscape had begun in his youth, when he spent summers in Yosemite National Park, and continued throughout the 1920s and 1930s when he returned there and to the Sierra Nevadas to photograph the majestic lakes and peaks of these western ranges. In his early years he was equally devoted to music and photography, but a 1930 meeting with Paul Strand settled his indecision about which of the two would become his profession. In 1941 his expertise in landscape photography drew the attention of Harold Ickes, Secretary of the Department of the Interior, who employed him to document other American national parks; he made *Moonrise* while fulfilling this commission.[2]

Like many artists and photographers, Adams was often inexact in the dating of his pictures. An astronomer friend, Dr. David Elmore, finally came to the rescue. By studying astronomical data, Elmore determined that *Moonrise* had been taken between 4:00 and 4:05 P.M. on October 31, 1941. Whatever its specific date or time of day, this image remains a timeless metaphor of the stillness of the American landscape and the magical character of its light.

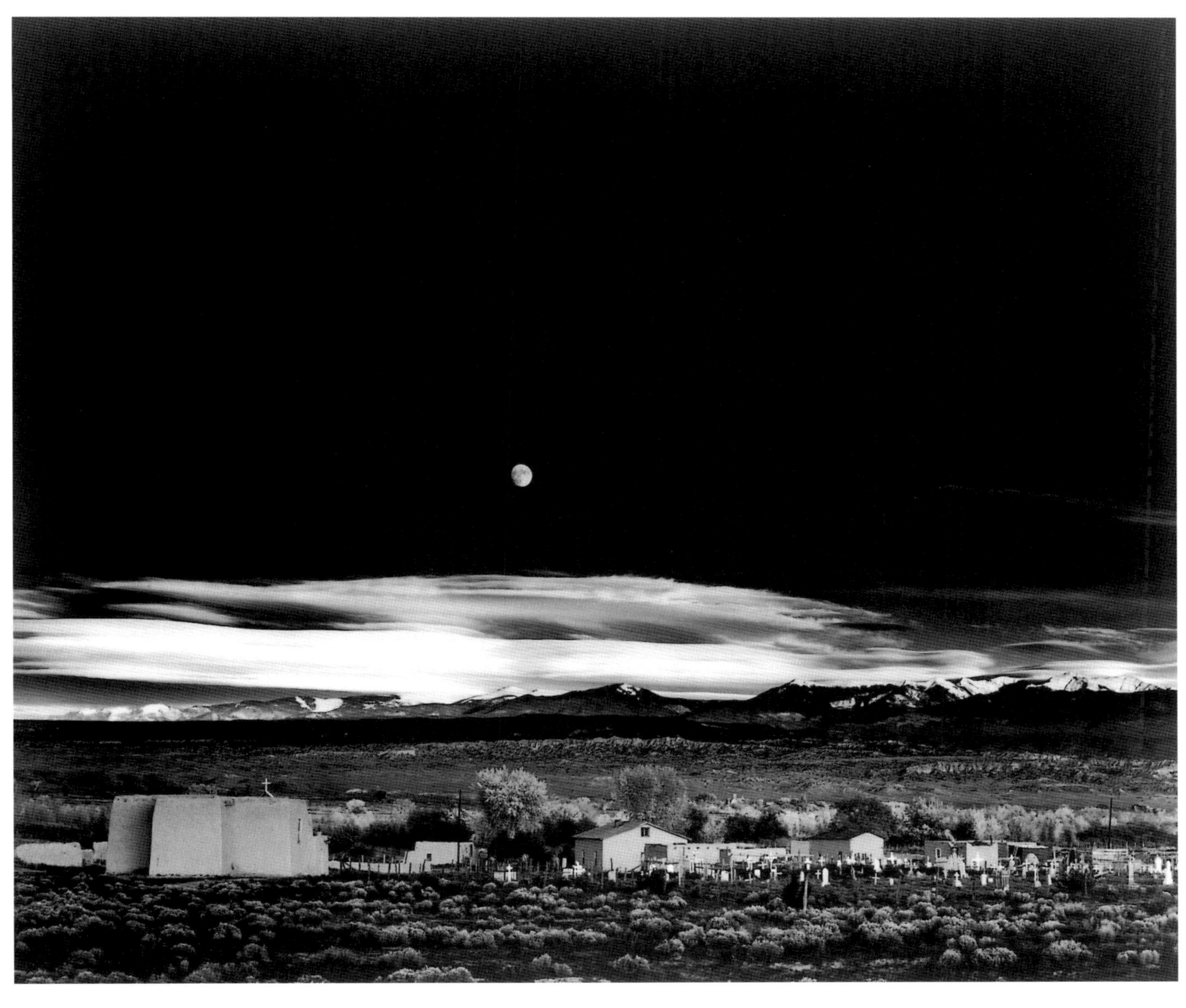

1975.1

Ansel Adams
Born 1902, San Francisco; died 1984, Carmel, California

Moonrise, Hernandez, New Mexico, 1941 (printed early 1970s)

Gelatin silver print; 15 ½ x 19 ½ in.
Purchased with funds from the National Endowment for the Arts and the John A. McAlonan Trust Fund

Mitchell D. Kahan

René Magritte

The family of René-François-Ghislain Magritte relocated numerous times during his childhood, but by far the most traumatic event of his youth was his mother's drowning when he was thirteen. Perhaps these events added to his sense of the inexplicable and his preoccupation with the inconstancy of meaning. After studies at the Academy of Fine Arts in Brussels, Magritte married and worked for many years in advertising and commercial art. From 1927 to 1930 he lived outside Paris and was a key participant in the salons, publications, exhibitions, and intellectual life that centered around the new literary and artistic movement Surrealism. His canvases, however, are not voyages into Surrealism's world of irrational dreams but are instead conscious subversions of reality that aim to reveal the mystery behind what is seen.

Magritte explored *le mystère* with calm deliberation. Returning to Brussels, he cut the image of a bourgeois banker rather than an artist, dressing in the dark suit, tie, and bowler hat that appear in so many of his paintings. The man who painted methodically at a small easel placed on an oriental rug in his wife's sitting room was preoccupied with images of the implausible and an often frustrated or violent eroticism. His paintings demonstrate that language is arbitrary and descriptions of reality are merely conventions with no basis in truth.

Les Pas perdus dates from the latter part of Magritte's career, when some of his most famous images were produced—the bowler-hatted men falling like raindrops, the giant rock suspended above the sea. Although these were fertile years for the artist, the title of Akron's painting suggests a mood of melancholy and self-doubt. Perhaps it is relevant that Magritte had recently abandoned an experimental phase which was very poorly received by his wife and friends as well as critics. The title can be translated colloquially as a waiting room, and indeed the eagle appears to be waiting or guarding the vertiginous peaks surrounding some enchanted domain.

Magritte frequently recycled his images into new configurations. Barren alpine vistas and petrified imagery appear throughout his later work. The stone eagle reappears often, most notably in the numerous versions of *Le Domaine d'Arnheim,* where a rocky mountain ridge takes the form of an eagle's head. In another work, the eagle's profile crowns a granite marker bearing the name of Coblenz, a German city that was bombed in World War II. In Magritte's petrified world, both animate and inanimate objects can be transformed into stone, poignantly heightening awareness of the passage from life to death and from usefulness to uselessness.

Magritte's titles were chosen after his canvases were completed. Sometimes suggested by writer friends, the titles do not directly describe what is seen but offer a poetic perspective on the image. *Les Pas perdus* was also the title of a collection of writings published in 1924 by Surrealist leader André Breton. One wonders whether the painting somehow refers to Breton, whom Magritte greatly respected but who had once asked Magritte's wife to remove the cross from around her neck when visiting his house, prompting the couple to leave.

Despite these stabs at meaning, interpretation is always frustrated in Magritte's work. He sought what he called "the poetic title," not a descriptive title that "has nothing to teach us; instead, it should surprise and enchant us."[1] "What I think about constantly and strikingly, is the mystery of life. That, you cannot represent. You can only evoke it."[2]

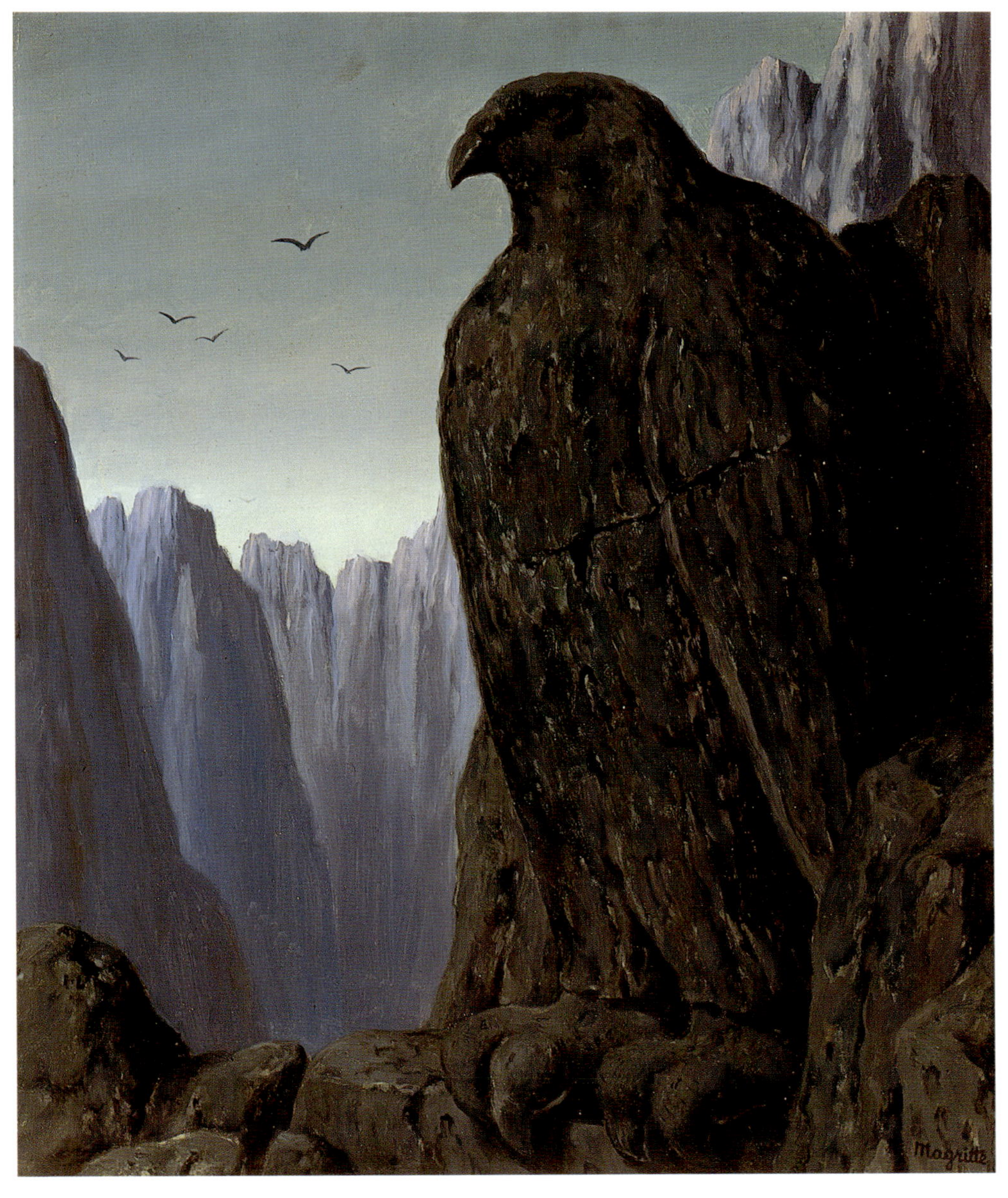

1966.2

René Magritte
Born 1898, Lessine, Belgium; died 1967, Brussels

Les Pas perdus (The Wasted Footsteps), 1950

Oil on canvas; 22 x 18 ¼ in.
Purchased with funds provided by anonymous donors

Mona Hadler

Jean Dubuffet

The postwar era in Europe and America witnessed heated debates about the viability of abstraction for a world in conflict. Abstraction dominated in the United States, but many in Europe adopted a humanism marked by the expressive presence of the human figure. The issue was memorably stated by Nathan Rapoport, the creator of the 1947 Warsaw Monument commemorating Jewish resistance to Nazism: "Could I have made a stone with a hole in it and said, 'Voilà the heroism of the Jews'?"[1]

In this charged atmosphere Jean Dubuffet, a prosperous forty-one-year-old wine-merchant-turned-artist, began to exhibit his art. His purposefully crude, figural paintings received notoriety in the press while being championed by a wide circle of intellectuals and artists. Dubuffet's 1947 exhibition of over seventy portraits was greeted by dozens of articles in the French press, in part due to the role many of his sitters had played in the postwar controversy over resistance and collaboration.[2] One critic noted the irony of needing guards in an exhibition featuring portraits of writers dedicated to notions of freedom. The identity of the sitters aside, the human face bore witness to the validity of figural works in an era of abstraction. *Tête aux quatre râclages* was painted several years after this show but at a time when Dubuffet was still producing portraits of controversial authors. By 1950 his figures were more generalized and interchangeable, as in *Tête*.

Critics, however, condemned Dubuffet's rough use of materials and crude, childlike drawing, which conjured up the graffiti adorning the walls of Paris. His encrusted, inscribed, earth-colored surfaces and compositions lacking in perspectival space, as in *Tête,* scorned Western notions of beauty. Furthermore, Dubuffet linked children's and naive art as forms of proletarian art, which is accessible to all. In his quest for an alternative artistic vision, Dubuffet became a proponent of what is now sometimes referred to as "outsider art" (a number of examples of such works are in the Akron Art Museum's collection).[3] Also at this time he was amassing and exhibiting his large collection of Art Brut (raw art), a combination of schizophrenic and naive art. Rather than treating the works he collected in psychiatric hospitals as illustrative of disease, Dubuffet presented them as art and the patients as artists. Indeed, parallels between Art Brut and the harsh lines and flat spaces of Dubuffet's art are readily apparent.

The artist's attitude toward materials and process are perhaps most significant in *Tête.* In his childlike drawing style, layered impasto, and especially in the "four scrapings"—arguably the subject of the painting—the artist suggests notions of art as an encounter with materials and sets forth his belief that the finished work should retain the marks of that encounter. In this regard Dubuffet's painting recalls the importance of the existential act popularized in the writings of Jean-Paul Sartre in the postwar era. While the painting is about the artist's struggle with materials, it is also a strong testimony to the humanism of postwar European art in its subject, the expressive figure, and in its style, the expressive surface.

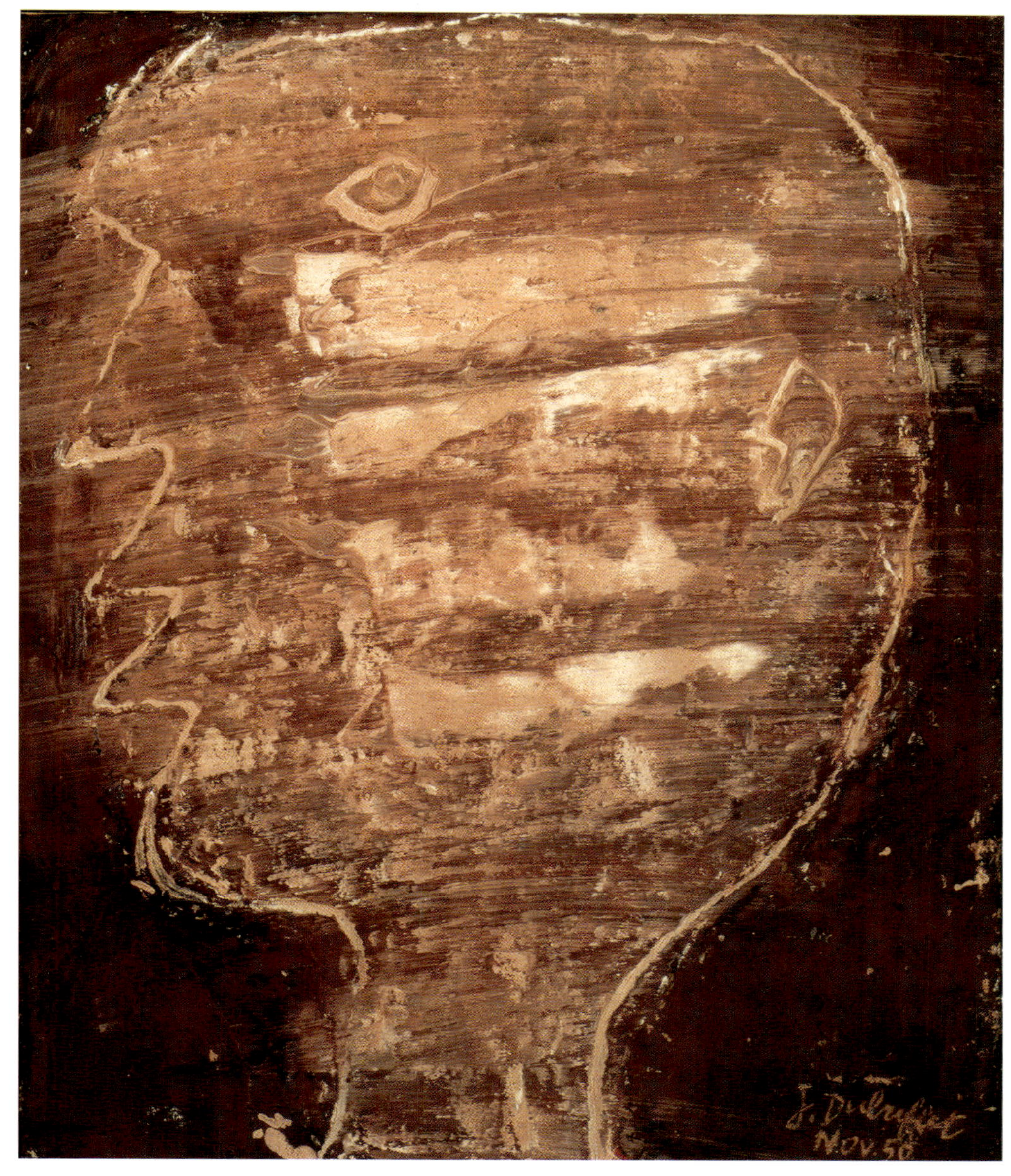

1975.6

Jean Dubuffet
Born 1901, Le Havre, France; died 1985, Paris

Tête aux quatre râclages (Head with Four Scrapings), 1950

Oil and plaster on fiberboard; 21 ¾ x 18 in.
Gift of Mr. and Mrs. Jerrold Mirman

Mitchell D. Kahan

Charles Burchfield

Charles Burchfield's one great inspiration was nature. Unlike the French and American Impressionists who preceded him, Burchfield made it his goal not simply to record nature but to invest each image with a resounding emotional and visceral impact.

Raised in Salem, Ohio, by his widowed mother, Burchfield was already producing watercolors of flowers and trees in high school. Graduating as valedictorian in 1911, he secured a scholarship to study at the Cleveland School (now Institute) of Art. Only a year after graduating from art school, and while working full-time in Salem, he was producing watercolors that qualify him as one of the century's finest practitioners of the medium.

Burchfield moved to Buffalo in 1921 to work as a designer for a wallpaper company. He married and later moved to the suburb of Gardenville, where he raised a family and remained until his death. By 1929 Burchfield was able to devote his energies entirely to art. He occasionally taught, including two summer appointments at Ohio University in the 1950s. Eventually he achieved the status of a senior American artist, with numerous awards and major surveys of his work.

Except for a middle period of moody realism, Burchfield's art consisted of evocative, abstracted watercolors of nature. *Spring Thunderstorm* is typical of his later work, which tended to be large in size and fashioned from several sheets of paper pasted down side by side. This method allowed the artist to expand his working surface according to compositional needs, independent of the standard sizes of watercolor paper. Such works were often preceded by numerous pencil sketches, but during the mid-1950s, when *Spring Thunderstorm* was painted, Burchfield was often overwhelmed with ideas and began painting without preparatory studies.

Spring Thunderstorm is almost certainly one of Burchfield's many depictions of his backyard in Gardenville, a prosaic place that nevertheless excited the artist's imagination repeatedly during the last twenty years of his life:

> This tiny corner of the earth that is ours gives a feeling of deep content and security; this is the base to which we can always come back, and be ourselves, alone, completely free from the outside world. There is the sky, above the village housetops, so vast and mysterious.... Through it I have access to infinity. And down below, very tangible, is the yard and the garden and how good all the things in it seem.[1]

Like the literary romantics of the nineteenth century, Burchfield found in nature a manifestation of God's divinity.

External reality was inspirational to Burchfield but limited: "While I feel strongly the personality of a given scene, its '*genius loci*' as it were, my chief aim in painting is the expression of a completely personal mood."[2] He was devoted to the turn-of-the-century concept of "synesthesia," a belief that there are equivalents between the different senses. For example, colors, lines, or shapes could suggest specific emotions, states of mind, even sounds. He had special interests in storms, snow, and the passage from winter to spring, when nature's sounds, visual effects, and physical sensations are the strongest.

"It almost seems as if the thunder-clap caused the peach tree to burst into bloom," Burchfield wrote about this painting, in which he transforms a few daffodils, an awkwardly blossoming tree, and the naked branches of early spring into a celebration of life's renewal.[3] He seems to say that those white blossoms will ultimately drive away the rain clouds and the last blast of winter. Living on the outskirts of an industrial city in the harsh snowbelt of western New York State, Burchfield was at one with nature when extolling its evocative drama.

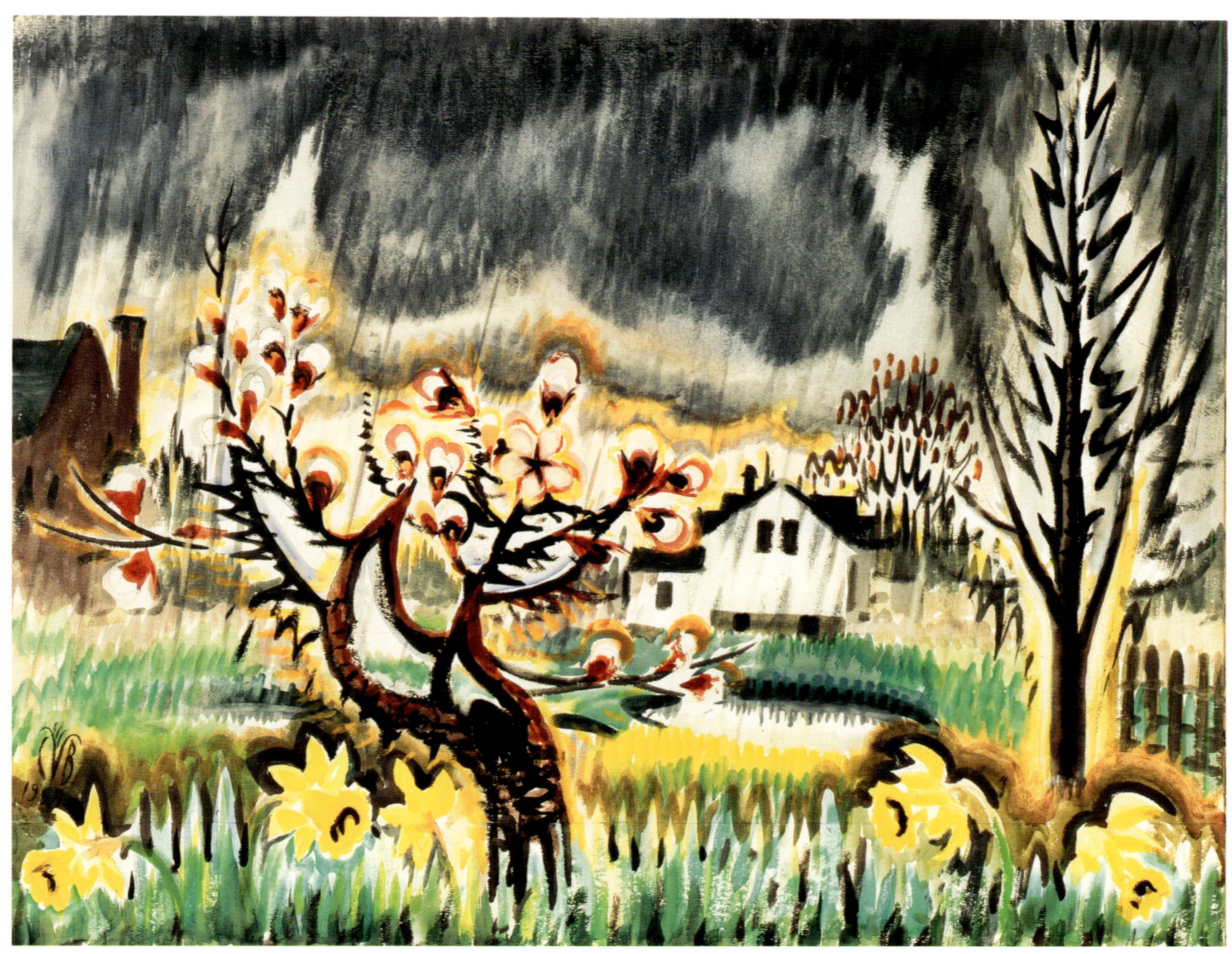

1964.11

Charles Burchfield
Born 1893, Ashtabula Harbor, Ohio; died 1967, Buffalo, New York

Spring Thunderstorm, 1955

Watercolor on paper; 29 7/8 x 40 1/8 in.
Gift of Mrs. Mary S. Huhn, Mrs. Dorothy S. Steinberg, and Mr. John F. Seiberling Jr. in memory of their father, Mr. J. Frederick Seiberling

Barbara Tannenbaum

Eugene Von Bruenchenhein

"Create and be recognized" was one of the mottoes adorning Eugene Von Bruenchenhein's humble, eccentrically decorated Milwaukee home.[1] Indeed, it was through his art that this self-taught artist and writer finally gained recognition, but unfortunately not until after his death.[2] In addition to paintings, this Milwaukee Leonardo also created poetry and scientific treatises; fanciful, touchingly erotic photographs of his wife; ceramic and cement sculptures; and miniature chairs and towers made from chicken and turkey bones (the remnants of numerous poultry dinners eaten by the impoverished artist and his wife).

Von Bruenchenhein left high school before graduation and was employed by a florist until 1944, one year after his marriage. He then changed to a job in a large bakery, where he worked until 1959. Health problems and the company's closing forced him into early retirement but freed him for artistic and intellectual pursuits. His mentor in these areas had been his stepmother, a chiropractor and amateur painter who had authored pamphlets on evolution and reincarnation.

His stepmother's interests may have inspired the artist's pseudo-scientific flights of fancy about the geological history of the earth and the evolution of its life forms—possibly the subject of *No. 534*. According to researcher Joanne Cubbs, "one of the artist's earliest and most frequently recurring protagonists is a snakelike monster with bulging eyes, sharp whiskers, a long pointed beak, and a glowing mane"[3]—almost certainly the creature portrayed here. Perhaps the monster is one of the inhabitants of the "First World," noted by Von Bruenchenhein in his treatises as the mother planet from which the earth was torn by an explosion. Or perhaps it stems from the artist's exploration of life's beginnings, inspired partly by his views of ordinary materials through a microscope and partly by a large collection of *National Geographic* magazines.

The creature's mythological status is echoed in the way it is painted; here Von Bruenchenhein exalted in the lusciousness of paint and the drama of gestures while eschewing anatomical detail and biological accuracy. His typical working method was to pour white enamel over a fiberboard panel to form a smooth ground (base coat); then he squeezed oil pigments directly on the painting and used his fingers, along with sticks, cardboard, leaves, burlap, combs, and crumpled paper, to spontaneously create shapes, textures, and spatial illusions.[4] His expressionistic style coincides with the heyday of Abstract Expressionism and shares with Surrealism of the 1930s and 1940s an interest in abstract biological imagery and "automatic" painting (letting the image flow directly from the unconscious onto the canvas). Von Bruenchenhein could have become aware of these mainstream art movements through articles in popular magazines.[5]

The popular press also provided Von Bruenchenhein with another source of inspiration. He began painting seriously in 1954 in reaction to news reports, complete with color photographs, of the first hydrogen bomb tests in the Pacific. His earliest images—painted with a brush which he soon abandoned—were vividly colored mushroom clouds billowing over scorched landscapes. By the end of 1956, he had created over five hundred paintings.

The serpent in *No. 534* coils at the center of a maelstrom of green and reddish-brown forms (lines of explosive force or vegetal matter in the primordial sea?). Is this creature a progenitor of human life or a snake who tempted modern man with the forbidden knowledge of how to destroy the earth? In the awesome power of both creation and destruction, of nature and science, there is a terrible beauty and a terrifying energy. Von Bruenchenhein eloquently captures this duality in *No. 534*.

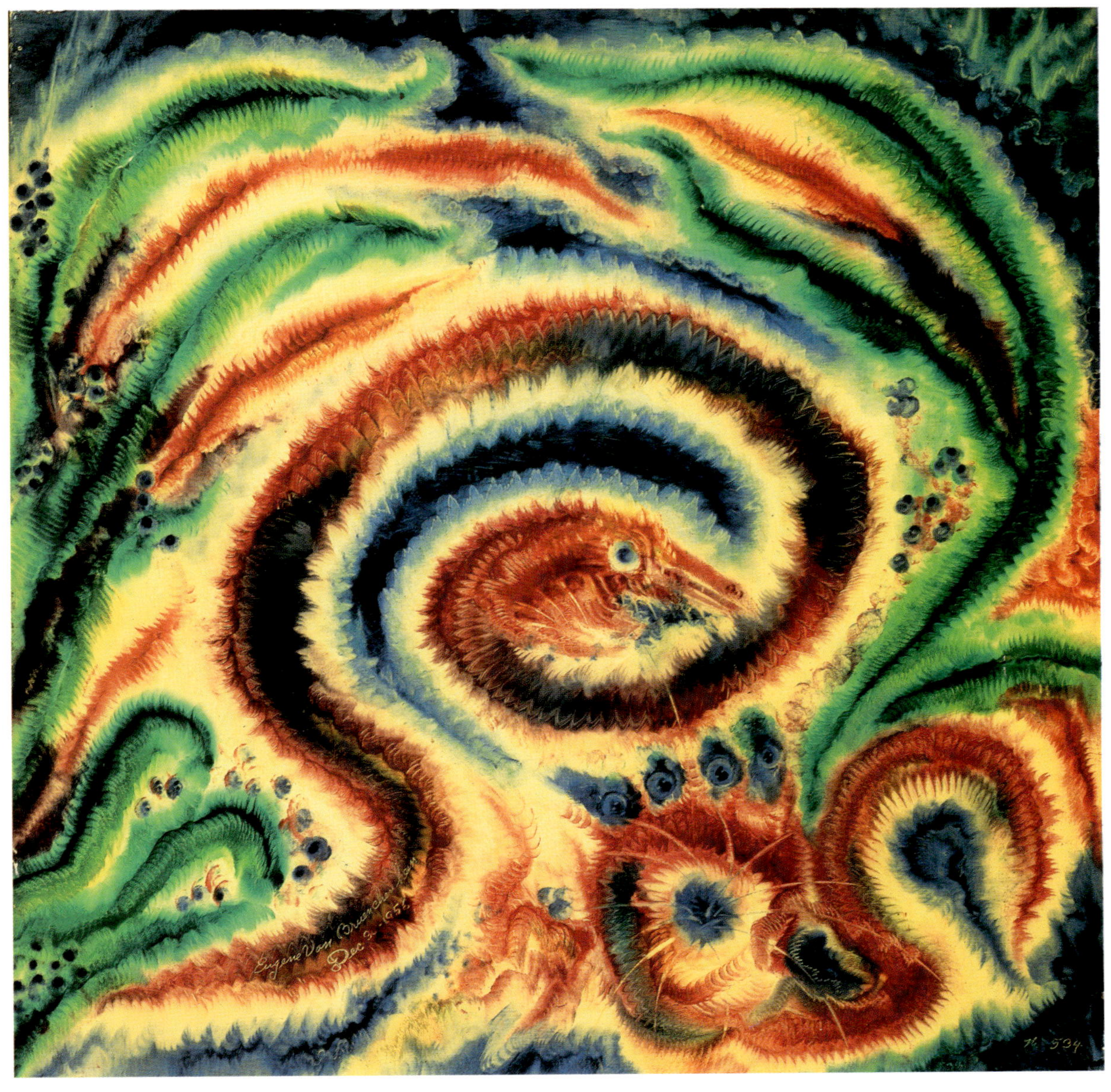

1990.24

Eugene Von Bruenchenhein
Born 1910, Marinette, Wisconsin; died 1983, Milwaukee

No. 534, December 30, 1956

Oil on fiberboard; 24 x 24 in.
Museum Acquisition Fund

Barbara Tannenbaum

Harry Callahan

"It wasn't enough just to photograph a nude," explained Harry Callahan. "I hired a model once and it didn't work. I wanted to photograph the person for whom I had feeling."[1] That person was Eleanor Knapp, whom he met on a blind date in 1933 and married three years later. In the mid-1940s Callahan began regularly photographing his wife—clothed and nude. Being photographed by her husband "was part of our daily lives for 25 years," recalled Eleanor. "He took pictures wherever we happened to be."[2] These sessions, often occurring in the most mundane of domestic surroundings, resulted in the creation of some of Callahan's best-known images from a career spanning over half a century.

Callahan was working as a clerk for the Chrysler Motor Parts Corporation when he took up photography as a hobby in 1938. A 1941 workshop conducted by Ansel Adams (see pp. 108–9) gave Callahan his first glimpse of the medium's full expressive possibilities and inspired him to begin a serious study of photography. Four years later he quit Chrysler and, the following year, was hired to teach at Chicago's Institute of Design. He went on to become one of the most influential photographers and teachers of the late twentieth century, winning numerous honors for both activities. Among the prizes for his work was the first Knight Purchase Award, presented annually since 1991 by the Akron Art Museum to a key figure on the international art scene working with photographic media.

A major source of this renown has been Callahan's ability to combine emotion and metaphorical content with formal exploration. None of his series shows that trait better than his photographs of Eleanor. Callahan used his wife to represent woman in all her roles—but especially as beloved, mother, and symbol of nature. The first of those three roles is seen in *Eleanor,* one of thirty-four works by the artist in the museum's collection. While the image is sensual and adoring, it does not idealize or glamorize. Eleanor wears no makeup or clothes in this close-up view; the natural folds and wrinkles of her body are emphasized rather than hidden. The directness and openness of her gaze and pose reveal that Callahan's love is returned. The deep affection, intimacy, and trust so evident in this photograph are the fruit of eleven years of married life.

Eleanor's body and her stare press forward not just toward the photographer/viewer but also against the flatness of the paper. This visual pressure reflects the physical process of producing this artwork, a contact print in which photosensitized paper is pressed against the negative, then exposed to a light source. Other clues remind the viewer that this, and all photographs, are but the miraculous illusion of three-dimensional reality on a flat surface. Callahan left visible the film identification lettering and the edges of the film, which form a black border around the entire image and echo the way Eleanor's arms surround her face. He also heightened the contrast in large areas of skin just enough to subtly flatten out Eleanor's limbs, emphasizing the strong abstract composition that underlies their positioning.

These references to composing, shooting, and processing a photograph complete the work, unifying its form and content while also joining the artist to his lover. Callahan's presence, and his response to Eleanor's gaze, are indelibly marked on the print in these signs of his art.

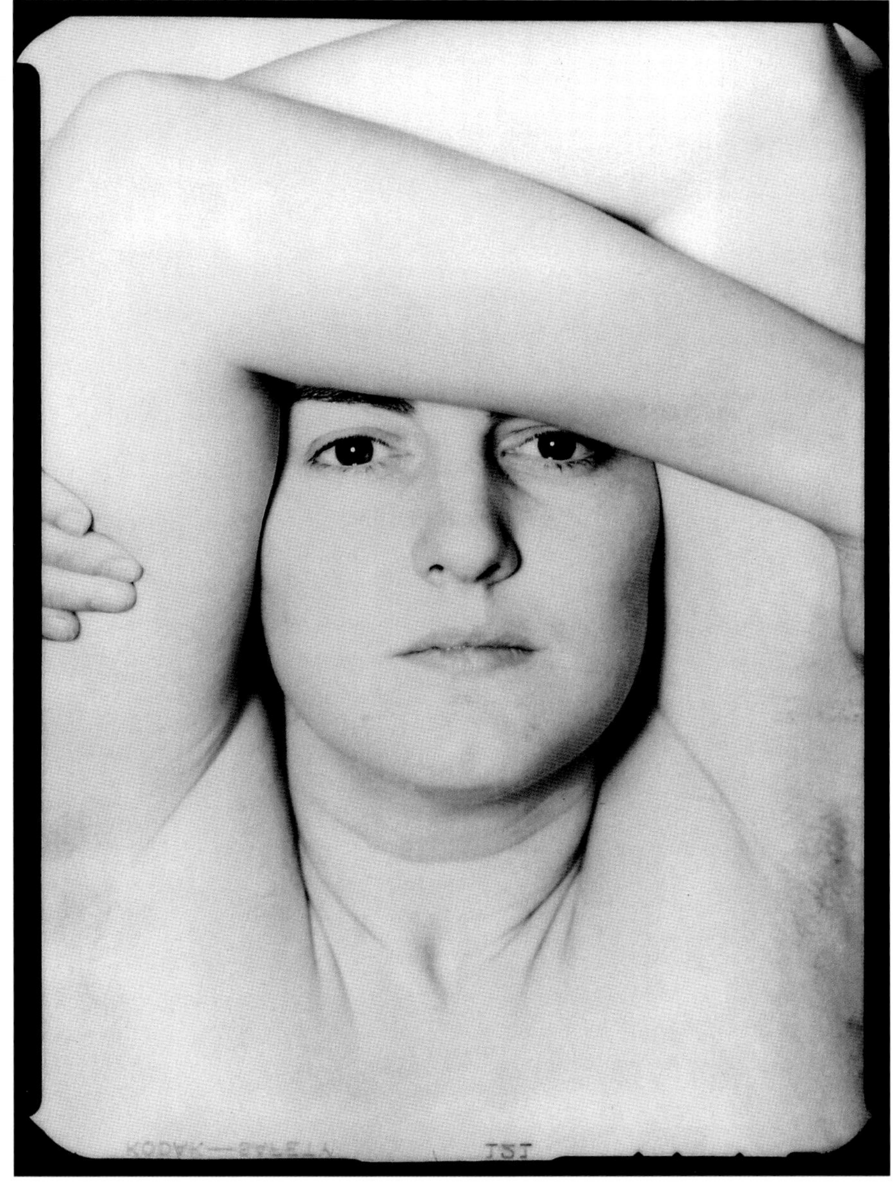

1991.53

Harry Callahan
Born 1912, Detroit; died 1999, Atlanta

Eleanor, around 1947 (printed later)

Gelatin silver print; $4\frac{1}{2}$ x $3\frac{3}{8}$ in.
Purchased with funds donated by Eleanor W. Aggarwal

Jeffrey Grove

Larry Rivers

Larry Rivers, a notoriously nonconformist painter, poet, printmaker, and sculptor, is one of the art world's true iconoclasts. A successful artist for over forty years, Rivers's critical reception has fluctuated between acceptance and rejection, perhaps more a comment on the artist's rocky personal history than a fair assessment of his art. Born Yitzroch Loiza Grossberg, the artist raised his two sons with the help of his ex-wife's mother; won $32,000 on the scandal-wracked television program *The $64,000 Dollar Question*; and in the conservative 1950s, publicly discussed his suicidal tendencies, addiction to heroin, and homosexual relationships.

Describing Rivers's persona in the 1950s, poet Frank O'Hara wrote that he was "rather like a demented telephone...nobody knew whether they wanted it in the library, the kitchen or the toilet, but it was electric."[1] Despite his unconventional stance and remarkable aptitude for agitating his critics, Rivers built an important bridge between 1950s Abstract Expressionists and Pop artists of the early 1960s. His loose, expressionistic style echoed the painterly touch of Abstract Expressionism, but his inclusion of mass media imagery and recognizable forms, especially the human figure, was viewed as a radical (and by some as a regressive) departure from the avant-garde. *Lady from Panama Street,* with its calligraphic surface, is a striking example of Rivers's unusual technique developed in the 1950s of merging painting and drawing.

Rivers's interdisciplinary approach has also made him difficult to pigeonhole. Clearly, his involvement with other disciplines has informed his approach to making art. Rivers collaborated with poets O'Hara, Kenneth Koch, and John Ashberry; wrote articles on contemporary art; experimented with film and video; and remains a dedicated jazz saxophonist. His wide-ranging interests and ability to synthesize elements from the visual, literary, and performing arts contribute to his distinctive style.

In *Lady from Panama Street,* the figure, both in finished and unfinished form, appears tentative, dissolving almost before it begins, not unlike a time-lapse exposure in film. Pencil-like markings, visible under alternately thin and dense washes of pigment, form the composition's foundation. Translucent passages of color, delicately painted, suggest a lyrical, musical structure. Indeed jazz, with its "anti-establishment ideology, inventive variations on well-known themes and firm rhythmic structure supporting daring improvisation," is an apt analogy for Rivers's style.[2]

Primarily a portrait painter, the artist traditionally focuses on familiar surroundings, using friends, family, and acquaintances as models. As his reputation escalated in the 1950s, Rivers was increasingly solicited for his talents as a portraitist. *Lady from Panama Street,* despite its nonspecific title, is one such example. Claude Rains, star of 1940s and 1950s motion picture classics including *Casablanca* and *Notorious,* commissioned Rivers to paint this portrait as a gift for his fourth wife. Upon receiving it, the actor's spouse rejected her portrait, claiming it resembled her sister more than herself. As Rivers blithely recalled, "she returned it to my dealer and took something else. Because you can't sell a portrait of one person to someone else, we changed the name to *Lady from Panama Street.*"[3]

Lady from Panama Street, with its staccato-painted surface, is at once specific and generic, a painting and a sketch. It possesses an ephemeral quality that echoes in the artist's refusal to commit to absolutes. Anchoring all of his work, however, and integral to *Lady from Panama Street,* has been Rivers's commitment to draftsmanship. As he affirmed in a 1954 conversation with fellow artist Fairfield Porter, "Drawing, which ties everything into a picture, [is] the most thrilling part of painting and one which I feel most sure about."[4]

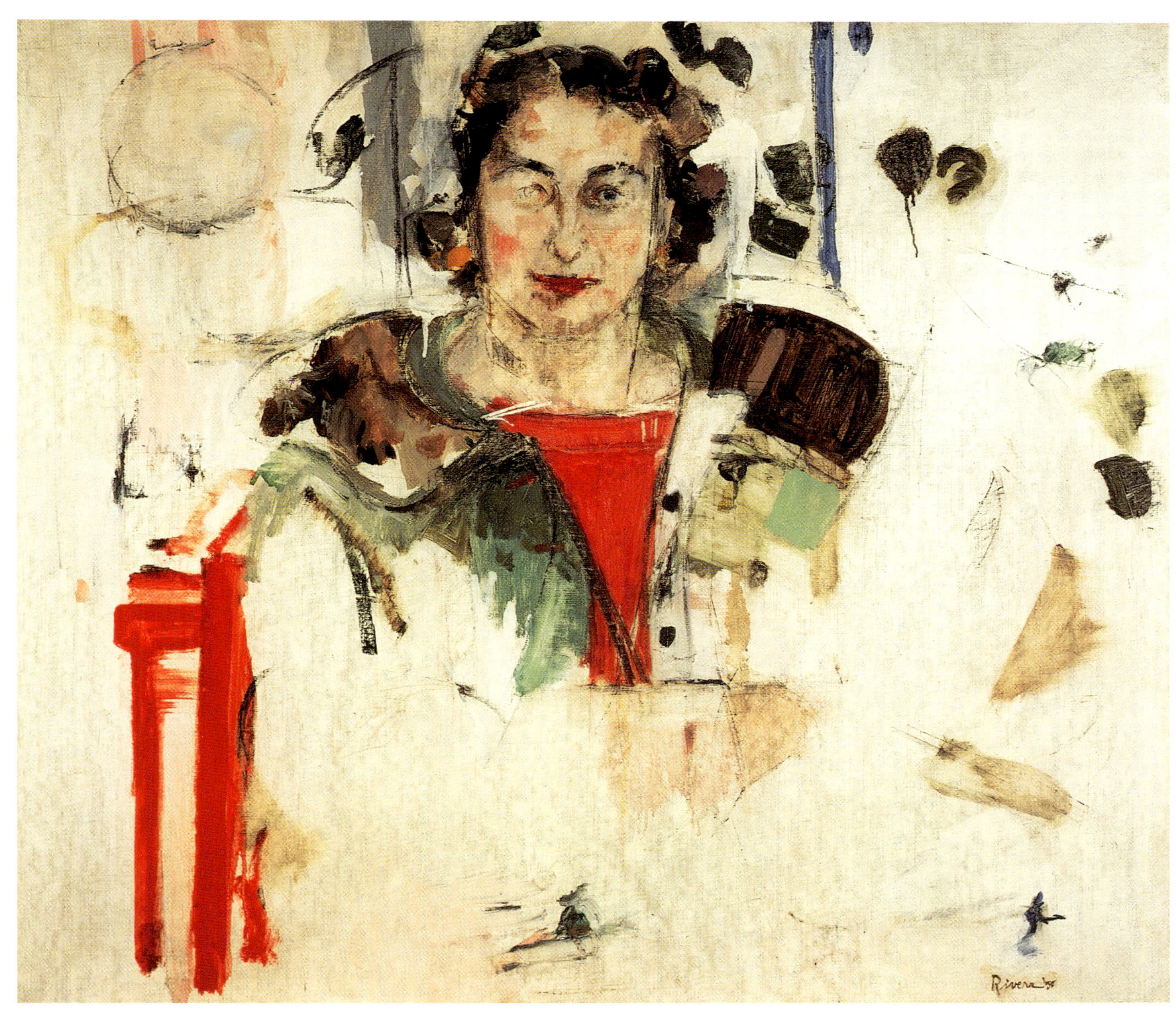

1977.12

Larry Rivers
Born 1925, New York; lives Southampton, New York

Lady from Panama Street, 1958

Oil on linen; 27 $\frac{3}{4}$ x 33 $\frac{1}{2}$ in.
Purchased with the aid of funds from the National Endowment for the Arts, The Sisler McFawn Foundation, and the L. L. Bottsford Estate Fund

Jeffrey Grove

Milton Resnick

"I worked day and night.... I never stopped. I never laid down.... I was haunted by art."[1]

The last surviving member of the acclaimed first generation American Abstract Expressionist painters, Milton Resnick—unlike other members of that celebrated group, including Jackson Pollock, Mark Rothko, and Willem de Kooning—toiled in obscurity for years. Also unlike them, Resnick alone maintained an unwavering dedication to creating strictly nonfigural abstractions, at least until the mid-1990s. In 1994 Resnick stated: "I never thought I'd be painting goddesses in my old age."[2] "The figure happened out of need."[3] That need, expressed by an artist who had always adamantly maintained his painting's independence from landscape or figural traditions, may have been a surprise to him alone.

Looking at *Abstract Expression,* painted in 1959, the viewer could hardly be faulted for suspecting that more personal, emotional elements were present in Resnick's painting all along, surreptitiously revealed in both landscape and figural elements. The Resnick family emigrated from Russia to Cuba before settling in New York when the artist was six. Resnick, whose birth name was Rachmiel and whose nickname was Milya, was renamed Milton, an issue he finds troubling to this day. He confesses that he spent much of his life feeling unmoored. Childless and married only later in life, Resnick was often depressed and seems to have used painting as a way to work through personal conflicts at significant junctures in his life. *Abstract Expression,* for instance, was painted in the year Resnick was diagnosed with and operated on for stomach cancer.

Wealthy, well-educated, and cultured, Resnick learned technical drafting, drawing, and lettering at Pratt Institute. After a stint in the army in World War II, followed by a three-year sojourn in Paris, he settled back into New York and life as an abstract painter. He did not have his first solo exhibition until 1955, when he was thirty-eight. The late date of his first New York show led many critics to place him erroneously among the younger generation of the so-called New York school painters, including Larry Rivers (see pp. 120–21) and Helen Frankenthaler (see pp. 174–75), rather than with the earlier, pioneering group of Abstract Expressionists, where he truly belongs.

Abstract Expression is one of a group of paintings created between 1957 and 1959, when Resnick revolutionized his style by concentrating on its smallest element—the brushstroke. *Abstract Expression,* with its vivid palette and nervous brushwork, is one of Resnick's finest—and final—paintings where the sensuous physicality and emotionalism of his application of paint can be clearly discerned. In 1959 he began to paint huge, monochromatic canvases in which his brushstrokes became completely invisible.

While the use of color gives *Abstract Expression* a fresh, even joyful presence, it is the application of paint—here, thin and watery, with a quicksilver stroke; there, thicker and more belabored—that lends the painting its unique suggestive quality. Its lyrical passages of color and shimmering overall effect are reminiscent of the French Impressionists, especially Claude Monet. Resnick once claimed—perhaps unconvincingly—"I am not the follower of Monet [and] I am not an Abstract Expressionist."[4] *Abstract Expression*—despite its title—is a clear statement that the artist's primary interests lay not in art historical associations but in exploring the evocative qualities of paint and in producing powerful art.

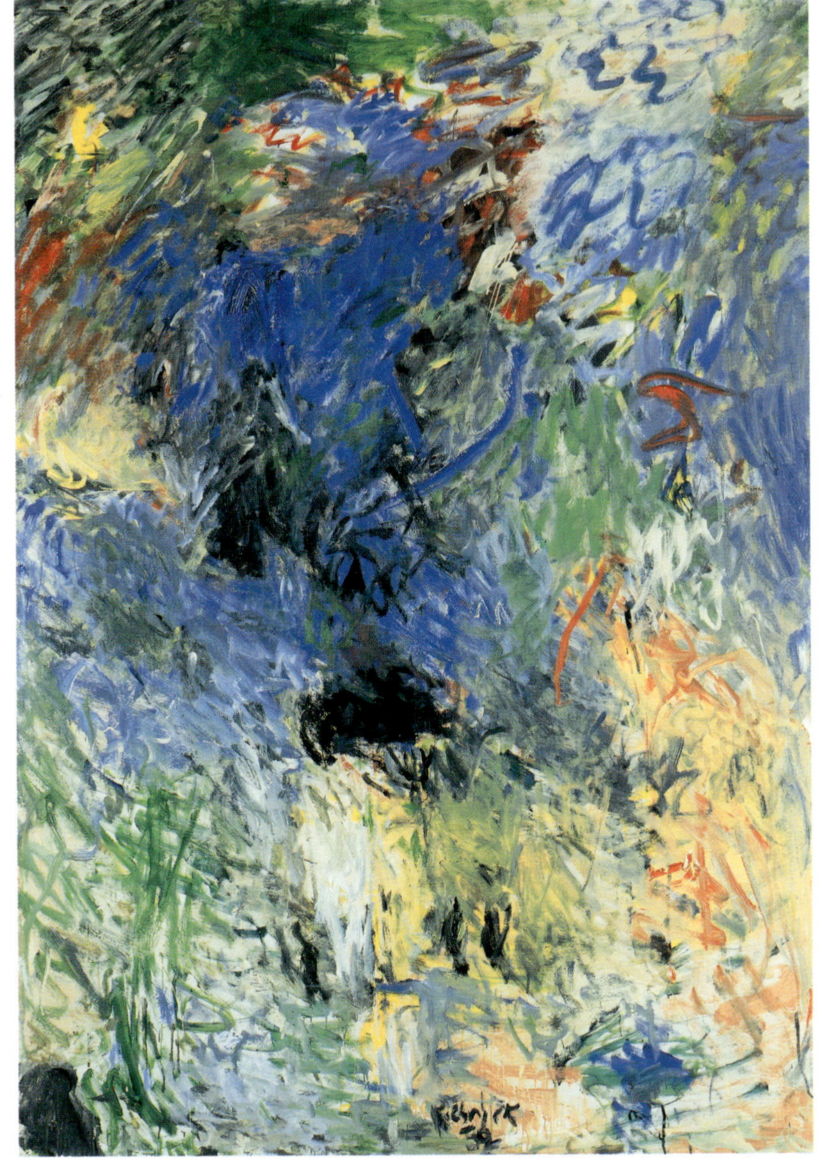

1964.14

Milton Resnick
Born 1917, Bratislav, Russia; lives New York

Abstract Expression, 1959

Oil on linen; 78 ⅛ x 53 in.
Gift of Mrs. Mary S. Huhn, Mrs. Dorothy S. Steinberg, and Mr. John F. Seiberling Jr. in memory of their father, Mr. J. Frederick Seiberling

Sheryl Conkelton

Aaron Siskind

Aaron Siskind, elementary schoolteacher turned photographer and college professor, was an important influence on generations of American photographers, both as exemplar and mentor. His photographic abstractions achieved a deep level of conceptualization while retaining a humanistic concern for meaning. His teaching at the Institute of Design in Chicago from 1951 to 1971 and the Rhode Island School of Design from 1971 to 1976 inspired and informed hundreds of students of the medium.

Siskind began his photographic career as an amateur but very quickly became seriously committed to the documentary mode. He was active in the Film & Photo League in New York throughout the 1930s and founded their Feature Group, which produced several photographic series on life in the city, including Siskind's own Harlem Document in 1936. The league, which presented an alternative to government-sponsored documentation projects, emphasized stories of individual rather than societal scale and consequence.

In the early 1940s Siskind discovered a means to express his humanist ideas in more abstract images. Photographing the graceful lines of seaweed and isolated bits of flotsam on the beach at Martha's Vineyard gave him the opportunity to express himself without narrative. In the often-quoted 1945 essay titled "The Drama of Objects," Siskind wrote about this new kind of personal seeing: "For the first time in my life subject matter had ceased to be of primary importance. Instead, I found myself involved in the relationships of these objects, so much so that these pictures turned out to be deeply moving and personal experiences."[1]

Siskind's consistent project from then until his death was the search for forms that communicated emotion and created a resonant excitement by both reinforcing the picture plane and transforming it. He photographed worn signage, crumbling walls, calligraphic streaks of tar—even lava formations. Sometimes language fragments communicated meaning; more often tonal contrasts and compositional rhythms expressed an idea or emotion. During the 1940s and 1950s Siskind was the only photographer affiliated with the community of Abstract Expressionist painters, which included Willem de Kooning, Jackson Pollock, and Franz Kline, and the only photographer to exhibit with them.

Siskind's photography paralleled their painting in its emotive intensity and discovery of primitive forms in gestural marks. His marks, of course, were framed by the camera and excerpted from the world of real things, but his powerful, animated compositions and the encrusted surfaces of his subjects were as compelling as those created in paint. In *New York, 1951,* made early in that year, Siskind focused closely on a section of rusted metal sign, capturing not only the decay in the aging enamel surface but also the strange calligraphy of the rusted parts. An important work for Siskind, the image served as the cover to the brochure accompanying his one-person exhibition at the Art Institute of Chicago in 1956 and has been published many times since.

Throughout his life Siskind experimented with the formal conventions found in *New York*. He characteristically eschewed any sense of location or space and usually kept his lens parallel and close to the surface or object he was photographing. His use of a large-format camera insured accurate rendering of a full range of black to white tones. All pictorial activity was contained and energized by the framing edge, creating a strong sense of picture plane. He believed that the combination of material subject and his own private intention created a rich ambiguity that activated the image. For almost fifty years Siskind worked to promote the idea of personal vision in photography and photographic abstraction as compelling art making.

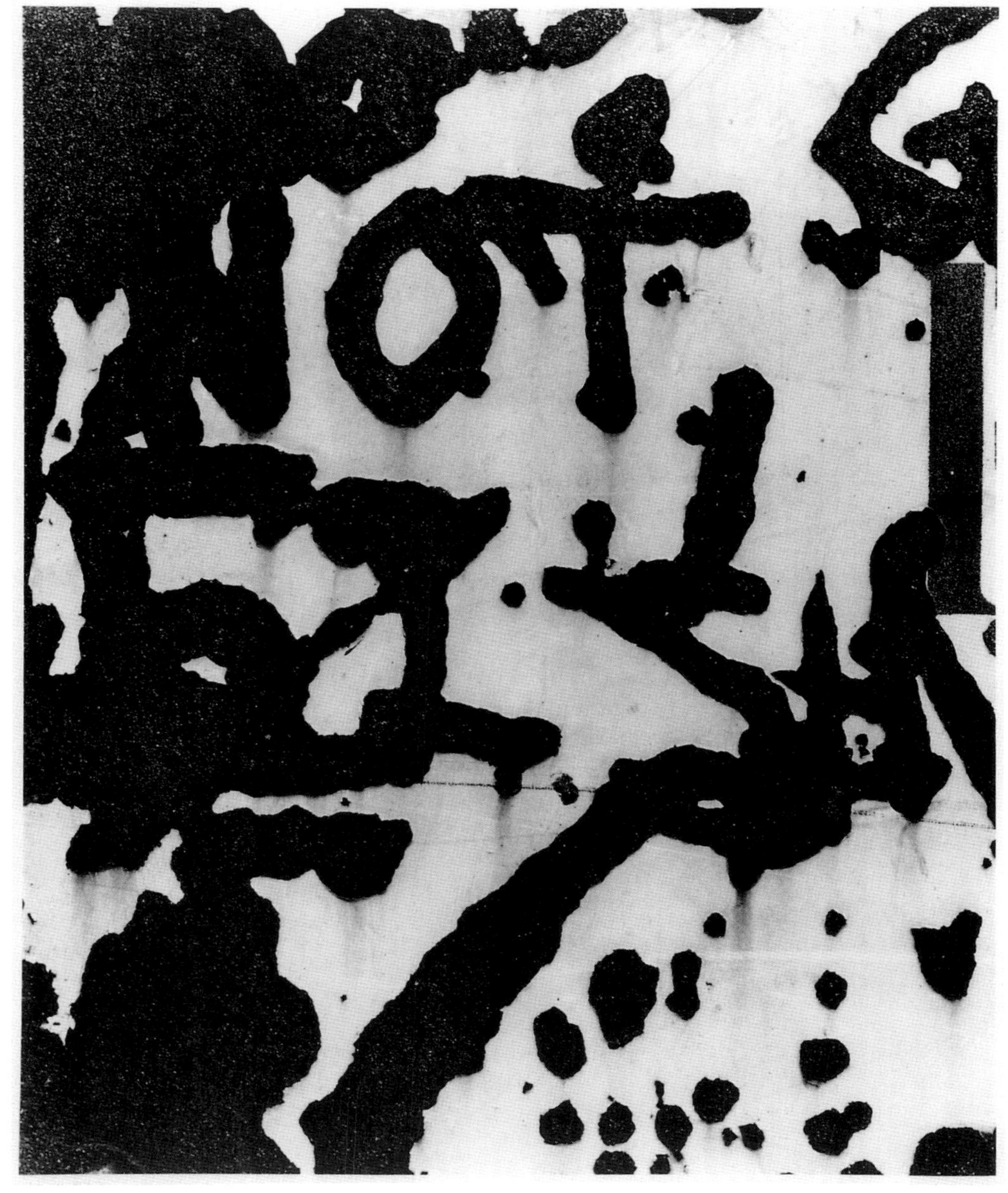

1994.9

Aaron Siskind
Born 1903, New York; died 1991, Providence, Rhode Island

New York, 1951, 1951 (printed in mid- or late 1960s)

Gelatin silver print; 21 ½ x 17 ⅞ in.
Museum Acquisition Fund

Barbara Tannenbaum

Morris Louis

One April weekend in 1953, Morris Louis traveled from his Washington, D.C., home to New York, where he saw paintings that radically changed his own art. Born Morris Louis Bernstein, he had been a practicing painter since graduating from the Maryland Institute of Fine and Applied Arts in 1932.[1] After twenty years, aside from a brief stint working on an art project sponsored by the federal Works Progress Administration, Louis had yet to make a living as an artist. He began as a figurative painter, but around 1951 he became interested in abstraction.

On his visit to New York in 1953 Louis experienced in person the openness, energy, and expansive scale of abstract works by Franz Kline and Jackson Pollock. Most important was a visit to the studio of Helen Frankenthaler (see pp. 174–75), where he learned about her technique of pouring paint onto unprimed canvas and manipulating it as it was absorbed into the fabric. Shortly thereafter, Louis used this stain technique to arrive at his first unique style and vocabulary of forms. Dubbed the "Veils" by curator William Rubin, these large canvases from 1954 and 1958–59 finally launched him toward national recognition.[2]

In the Veils, Louis strove to make shape derive from color, which meant abandoning line and edge for a subtler relationship between the figure (a flow of paint) and ground (in Louis's case the unprimed white cotton of the canvas). He produced delicate bands of translucent yet brilliant color which were then "veiled," or covered over, with layers of diluted black paint. New technology—Magna acrylic paint—made this possible. Composed exclusively of pigment and Acryloid F-10, an exceedingly transparent acrylic resin, Magna gave "a quality of light reflection and refraction...that provides a luminosity and a sense of depth unattainable in any other medium."[3]

Untitled has been categorized as one of the "split" Veils, which consist of separate sections.[4] The artist would have begun this painting by loosely tacking canvas over an 8 x 12-foot work stretcher leaning against the wall.

> Louis prepared the paint...by thinning Magna first with acrylic medium and then with large quantities of turpentine. This produced a diluted paint that poured easily. He poured it from the top edge or along the braces and directed it to the bottom of the canvas.... He probably achieved internal variations in the tapering or swelling of the color planes by manipulating the angle of the stretcher and by varying the surface tautness.... Louis almost always began the veils with bright colors. In 1958 and early 1959, he used dark washes to unify the surface, which then glows with the warmth of the underlying layers.[5]

When the canvas was dry, he would decide on and mark its edges and roll it up for storage. The canvases were permanently attached to wooden stretchers only when they were sent out for exhibition.

Unlike Jackson Pollock's all-over, horizonless compositions, *Untitled* relates to the natural world in its emphasis on the orderliness of gravity. The clear downward flow of the separate streams of paint form a single pool along the canvas's bottom edge. This dense pool contrasts with the almost immaterial lightness of the painting's color. At first glance the dominant hue is brownish-gray; a closer look reveals the multitude of colors underneath. With no evidence of a brush or direct contact with the artist's hand, color seems to float on top of the canvas yet also appears to be part of it.[6] That effect, coupled with the canvas's monumental scale, evokes nature's power and inevitability, its grandeur and subtlety, and its sense of mystery.

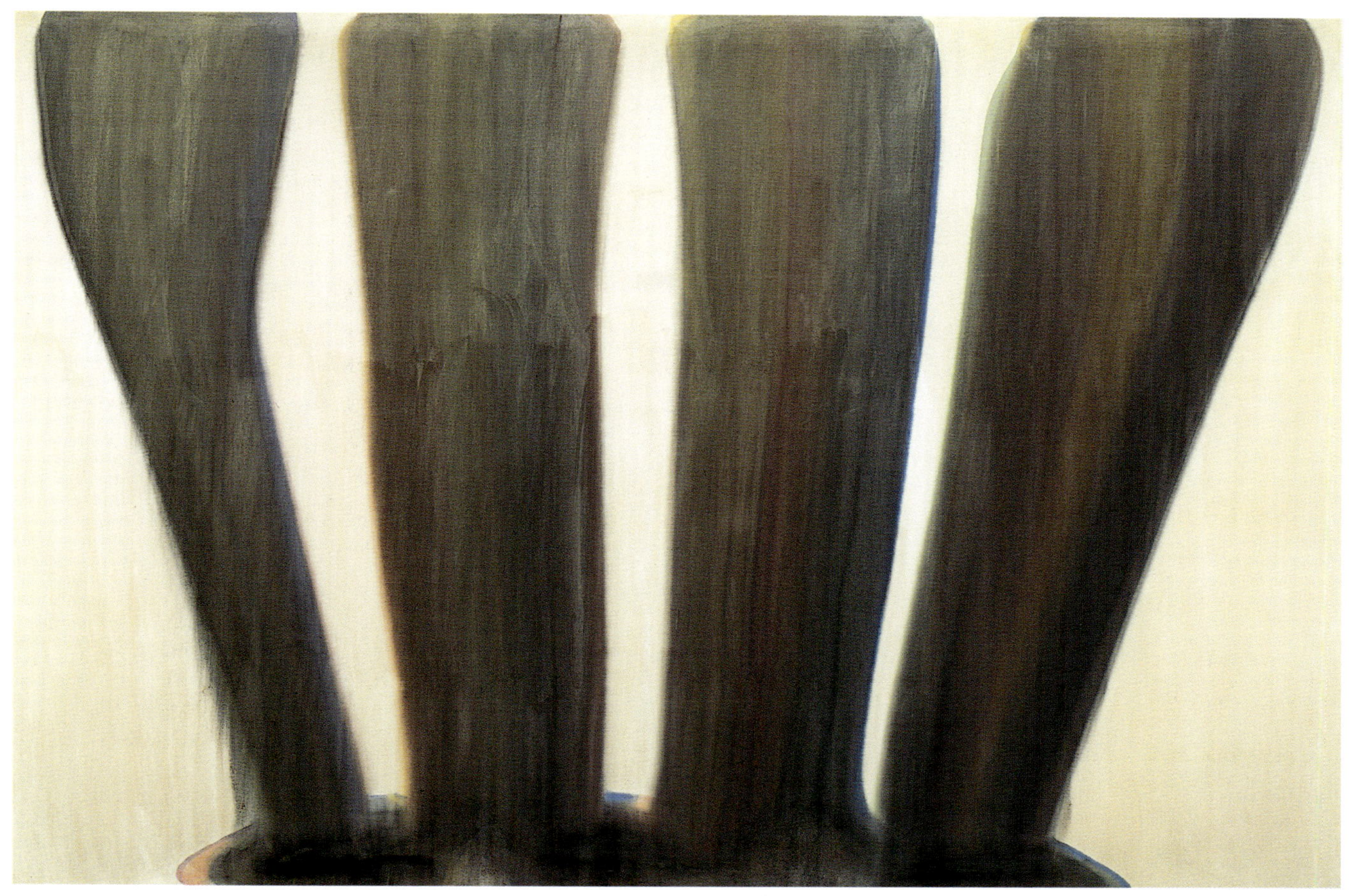

1982.10

Morris Louis
Born 1912, Baltimore; died 1962, Washington, D.C.

Untitled, 1958

Acrylic on canvas; 91 ½ x 142 ⅝ in.
Gift of the Mary S. and Louis S. Myers Family Collection

Gerald Nordland

Raoul Hague

Angel Millbrook Walnut was carved more than forty years after Raoul Hague left Turkey to study art in the United States. Hague attended Iowa State University, then transferred to the School of the Art Institute of Chicago. While in Chicago he formed a vaudeville act with a young Italian dancer who prevailed upon him to change his name for the sake of the act: Haig Heukelekian, of Armenian descent, became Raoul Hague, of indeterminate origin. In New York in 1925, he studied at the Beaux-Arts Institute of Design and the Art Students League.

Around 1925, Hague met John Flannagan (1895–1942), a self-taught stone sculptor who espoused direct carving rather than the traditional Beaux-Arts system in which the artist first models the piece in clay, then translates it into stone through the mechanical practice of "pointing." In direct carving, the resulting work is uncompromised by intermediate steps. Flannagan associated the technique with pantheistic urges to reveal the sleeping subject within the rock by stripping away excess material.

Hague became a practiced hand at direct carving in stone and wood in the 1930s, creating portrait heads, upright and reclining female torsos, standing figures, and primitivistic totems. After World War II he settled into a cabin in Woodstock, New York. Because the local rock (bluestone) was unpredictable and difficult to carve, he became committed to working exclusively in wood.

He carved local woods including chestnut, poplar, cottonwood, butternut, and walnut, and named each sculpture for the wood and the place of its origin.[1] Initially he used found wood, dragging logs and fallen trees from swamps and forests. Later, when timber in the area was being harvested, Hague would reserve a tree, then rush off by motorbike to confirm a preferred chunk for purchase.

He chose his wood for mass, density, and weight: "I've got to have...girth. At least 42 inches in diameter. I'm interested in height also. I can't handle more than six foot four and one-half inches in height [in my studio]. I'll take...either [a] drum shape or a crotch.... In spite of what people think, I do not see the graining at all. I am not choosing the wood because of its graining."[2] He favored walnut because "it doesn't check very much and it cuts evenly.... You can make space in the wood; go in.... I cut the mass into fragments and I move in it. One can orchestrate in the wood.... You make a cut. From then on it follows. Like the jazz musician, music comes out of you."

Until the late 1950s critics insisted on finding female torsos, reclining figures, and references to classical sculpture in his work, but Hague's forms became increasingly independent of figuration. He cut into 800-pound chunks to find abstract forms and relationships. He balanced negative (cut away) spaces by undercutting and shaping opposing positive faces of the wood. *Angel Millbrook Walnut* is a "crotch shape" that has been upended. From one side it reads as a balanced composition of three closely related forms, and from its opposite side, as a downward-thrusting monolith.

As Hague grew more knowing, he carved his sumptuous woods into ever more seductive abstract forms by rhyming elements, pooling shadows, and shaping reflecting bosses to cast light on complex forms. Hague's sculpture embraces wood's nature and its natural references. It is profoundly handmade, deeply felt, and enduring.

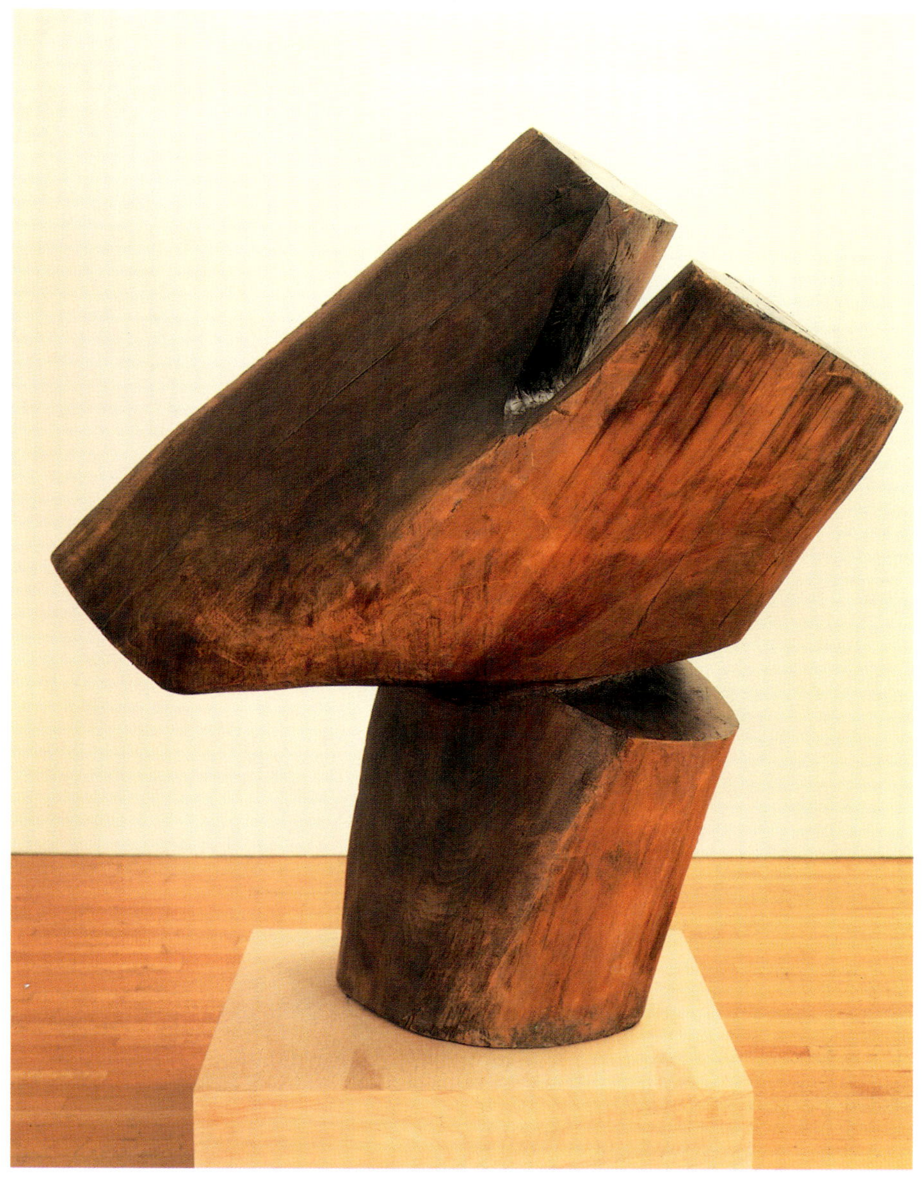

2000.3

Raoul Hague
Born 1905, Constantinople, Turkey; died 1993, Woodstock, New York

Angel Millbrook Walnut, 1964

Walnut; 57 x 57 x 29 in.
The Mary S. and Louis S. Myers Endowment Fund for Painting and Sculpture

Naomi Rosenblum

Ruth Bernhard

Couched in a quintessentially modernist style that emphasizes clarity and simplicity, *Two Forms* nevertheless exemplifies Ruth Bernhard's profound belief that camera images should be enigmatic rather than documentary. This photograph depicting two human torsos—one dark-skinned and one white, one facing forward and one backward—does more than merely record the shapes of two elegant human bodies. It suggests, in the photographer's words, "mysteries that lie behind our limited human perceptions."[1]

Paradoxically the two bodies bring to mind both classical marble sculpture and sentient living entities. Indeed, when working with models, Bernhard sometimes thinks of herself as a sculptor desirous of creating beautiful form through the agency of light, and at other times has considered light to be "the pencil that draws the picture I'm trying to create."[2] Despite its economy of information, the image also hints at tender relationships among women and among people of different racial backgrounds, and it seeks to arouse all-embracing rather than particularized sensations.

Following training in Berlin at the Academy of Art and immigration to the United States, Bernhard began a career in 1930 as an advertising photographer in New York. Through contacts with prominent industrial designers, she photographed a wide variety of handmade and manufactured objects and eventually produced tasteful images for Macy's and Sloane's department stores and for the magazine *Advertising Age*.

A chance meeting with Edward Weston during a visit to California in 1935 proved to be a defining experience for Bernhard. Inspired by his example and precept, she began to consider photography a medium of artistic expression rather than just a means of livelihood. After relocating to the West Coast permanently in 1949, she was introduced to the work of Ansel Adams and Minor White, whose approaches to clarity in one case and ambiguity in the other also exerted a telling influence on her vision.

Bernhard works with ordinary materials—shells, leaves, the nude human form—which she composes and lights to reveal elusive meanings. Her images express her keen conviction that photography is, in her words, "a gift...[that] reaches into dimensions that words cannot touch."[3]

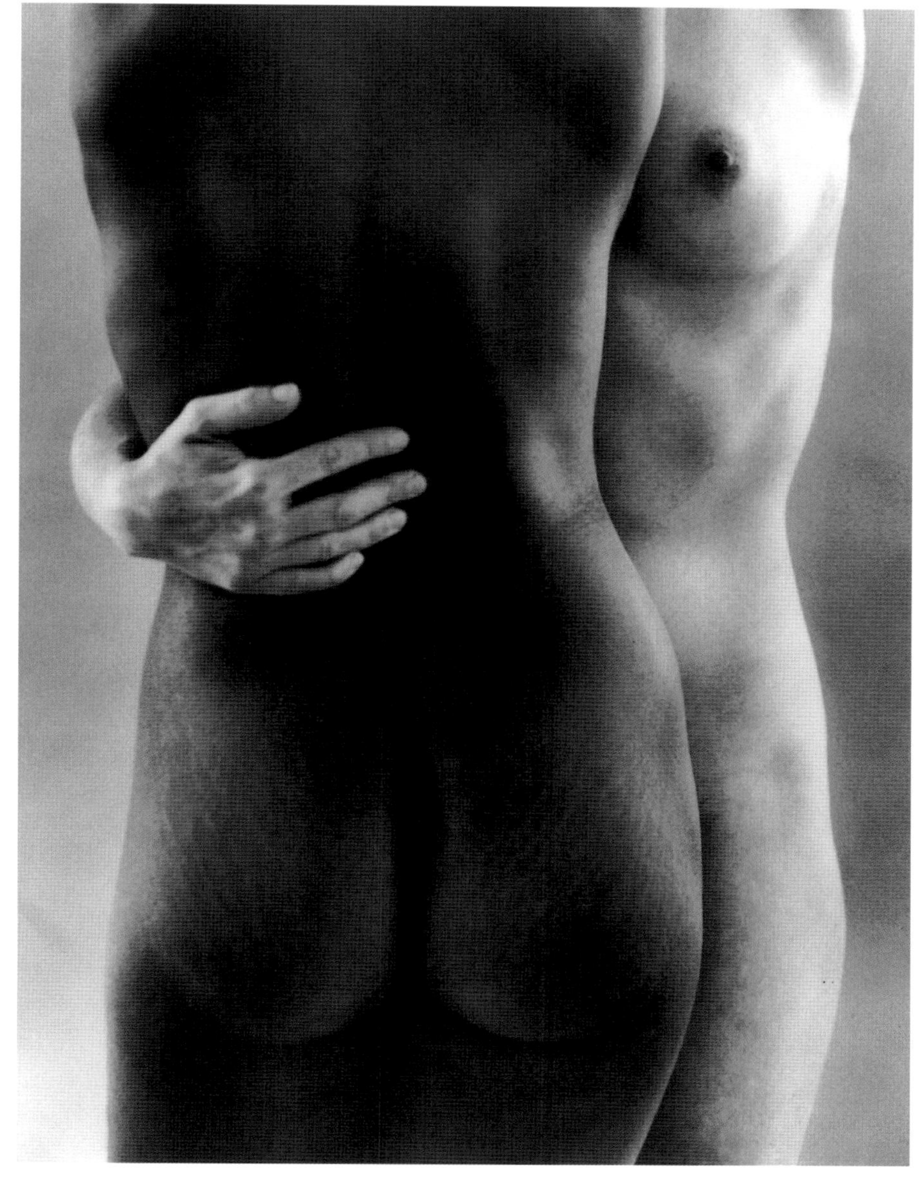

1996.10

Ruth Bernhard
Born 1905, Berlin; lives San Francisco

Two Forms, 1963

Gelatin silver print; $13\frac{3}{8}$ x $10\frac{1}{4}$ in.
Purchase with funds donated by Mrs. Beatrice K. McDowell

Barbara Tannenbaum

O. Winston Link

In *Hot Shot Eastbound, Iaeger, West Virginia,* Ogle Winston Link, it seems, was lucky to have captured one of those rare moments that photographers dream about: in this case, the simultaneous presence of a steam locomotive and the two modes of transportation that by 1956 were clearly its successors, the automobile and the airplane. In fact, Link carefully planned this and other photographs of steam locomotives in the Norfolk and Western Railway system.[1]

The project was a labor of love for Link, a freelance commercial photographer in New York whose clients included the BFGoodrich Company and Texaco. Although he never considered himself a rail fan, he was intrigued by trains as a child and renewed that interest during World War II. In the 1950s Link became concerned about the demise of the steam engine. An assignment in January 1955 took him near the tracks of the Norfolk and Western, the last main line in America to operate with steam equipment. He photographed a train on its run and, thrilled with the results, went on to take around 2,500 photographs of the company's steam locomotives, personnel, and facilities between 1955 and 1960.

Hot Shot, one of four works by Link owned by the museum, is one of his best-known images. As a commercial photographer, Link could create a photograph that was candid in appearance but in reality was contrived to promote an idea or product. In *Hot Shot,* a young couple cuddles at a drive-in movie; they were locals posing in Link's convertible in exchange for their admissions.[2] *Battle Taxi* was showing that night; on the screen is a jet in flight.[3] Like the car and the plane, the film is a dream machine that can transport the young couple to a world far away from this small coal town isolated in the hills of southern West Virginia. Link juxtaposes the jet with the Hot Shot, a freight train pulled by a Class A 1200 coal-fired steam locomotive—to Link's mind, "the most beautiful engine ever built."[4]

Night photography of trains had been attempted only rarely before Link because it presented a myriad of technical difficulties. He quickly became a virtuoso with the flash. *Hot Shot* required forty-three bulbs placed to illuminate the train, its smoke, the cars, and the couple. Bulbs and camera had to be synchronized to go off at the split second when the train was in the right place. Calculations and set-up had to be done in daylight, long before the arrival of the Hot Shot. Just before the photograph was taken, Link recalled, "I could only see the headlight of the locomotive in total darkness."[5]

Since the light required to photograph the train wiped out the image on the film screen, *Hot Shot* is made from two negatives: one of the film and a second of the rest of the scene. These were then combined during printing, at first by simple collage, later by using two enlargers and a pin registration system, and finally, for the last dozen years, by printing from a copy negative of the combined image.[6]

Hot Shot is Link's carefully composed hymn to an idealized 1950s America, an era of innocence, prosperity, optimism, and leisure but also nostalgia for a vanishing America. Ironically, his Norfolk and Western photographs would not be widely exhibited or published until the early 1980s, when they were discovered by the art world. The Akron Art Museum played an important part in this process: Link's first solo museum show was held at the Akron Art Museum in June 1983.

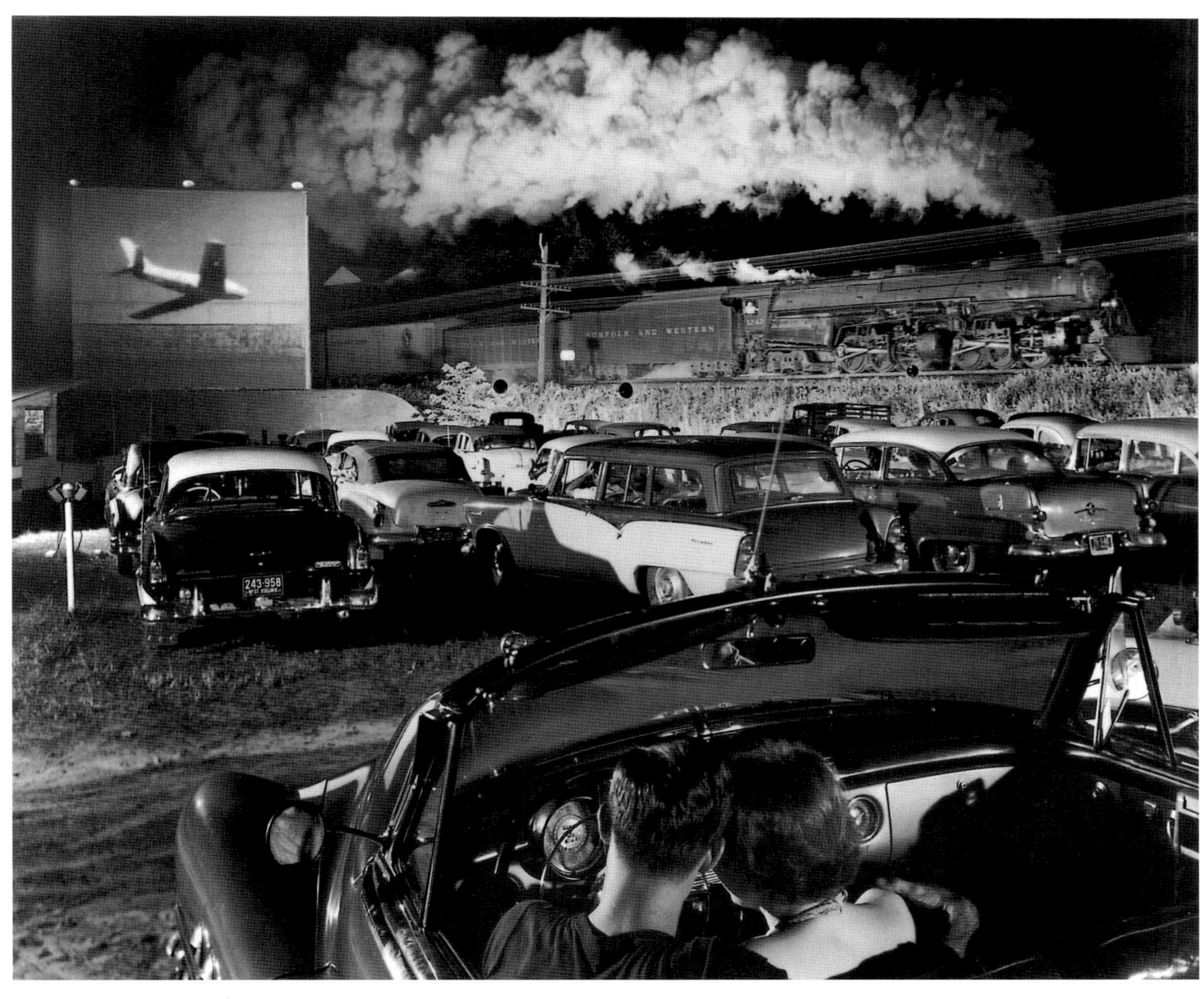

1984.1

O. Winston Link
Born 1914, Brooklyn; died 2001, South Salem, New York

Hot Shot Eastbound, Iaeger, West Virginia, August 2, 1956 (printed 1983 or earlier)

Gelatin silver print; 15 $\frac{1}{2}$ x 19 $\frac{1}{2}$ in.
Museum Acquisition Fund

Naomi Rosenblum

Robert Frank

"Life here is very different," Robert Frank wrote his parents soon after his arrival in the United States in 1947.[1] Having been involved in conventional photographic documentation in his native Switzerland, Frank must have been hugely unprepared for the diverse cultural scene he experienced on his first photojournalistic assignments in the United States. By 1955, however, when a Guggenheim grant made possible a more focused project involving "a spontaneous record of a man seeing this country for the first time," he was comfortable enough to intuitively react to and capture the chaotic and volatile elements in post-World War II American culture.[2] The images, made with a Leica camera, were published in 1958 in France and a year later in the United States as *The Americans.*[3] The book, which was meant to be seen as one person's view of American social culture, evoked an outcry from those who felt that its focus on alienated, lonely people, graceless buildings, and barren landscape presented a distressing and untrue picture of life in this country.

Frank found the American political process to be an especially engaging aspect of his odyssey to understand his adopted country. At the suggestion of a magazine editor but without a specific assignment, Frank covered the 1956 Democratic convention.[4] He went on to photograph the inauguration in January 1957 of President Eisenhower and Vice-President Nixon, producing a series of images of American political activities and conventions. Many at the time held these events to be the mark of the nation's most significant democratic right, but in Frank's work they are revealed as bombastic and empty charades, full of sound but not of much significance. *Chicago,* one of twenty-three works by Frank owned by the museum, is a particularly ironic work that resonates on several levels.[5] The empty seats, distant crowd, and upside-down poster may suggest that John F. Kennedy's failure to win the nomination at the 1956 convention was no great cause for regret. However, in light of his subsequent election to the presidency, his assassination in 1963, the aura of glamour surrounding his administration, and the later revelations about him, the image has taken on added meaning over the years.

Other works by Frank also have gained new meaning as time passed, as if the photographer somehow could foresee the cultural topography of the future. The photographer's trips through the American South, for example, resulted in images that subtly but unmistakably signaled the problematic relationships between African Americans and whites—relationships that a few years later were to erupt into civil disturbance. Similarly, his focus on road travel and the icons of popular culture foreshadowed the explosion of artistic and popular interest in these aspects of American life in succeeding decades.

Following the publication of *The Americans,* Frank's involvement in still photography waned and for some ten years he was engaged in making films. Later, he returned to photography, combining portions of individual still images and motion picture film in collage compositions. He believed this would better express his sense of life's flux than would single straight images. Whatever means Frank has used, however, his aim always has been to capture a bit of the truth, even though truth, in his words, is "a bit like a slippery fish escaping from your hands."[6]

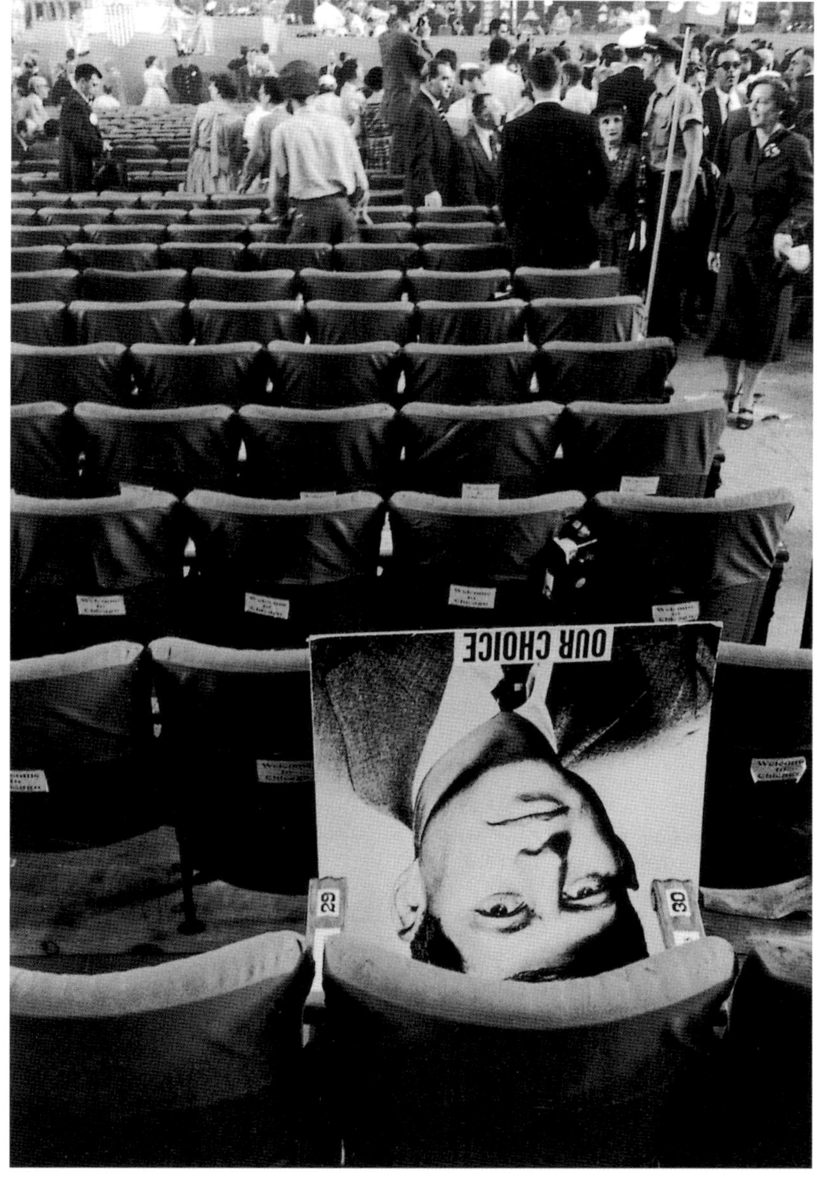

1985.16

Robert Frank
Born 1924, Zurich, Switzerland; lives Mabou, Nova Scotia

Chicago, 1956

Gelatin silver print; 13 ¾ x 9 ⅜ in.
Museum Acquisition Fund

Barbara Tannenbaum

Elijah Pierce

Elijah Pierce, one of Ohio's most important twentieth-century artists, was the son of a former slave. Although he never received academic art training, he became a master carver, able to bend the wood's will to his personal expression.

In addition to woodcarving, Pierce had two other vocations—barber and lay preacher. All three intermingled in a relationship unique to African American communities, where the barber shop is a place to receive news and wisdom along with haircuts. Whether preaching in church or offering counsel in his barber shop, Pierce often used his carvings to illustrate his points. Even though he is gone, his art continues to inspire and to preach. "Every piece of work I carve is a message, a sermon," said Pierce.[1]

The Wise and Foolish Virgins and Four Other Scenes, one of Pierce's masterpieces, combines five carvings in a single frame, arranged in three horizontal rows, one atop the other like a comic strip. This charming sculpture presents serious messages about forgiveness and the rewards of virtue, vigilance, and faith.

The top third of the work illustrates the parable of the wise and foolish virgins (Matt. 25:1–13), who were to escort a bridegroom through the night to his wedding. Five, shown at the left with unlit lamps, foolishly brought no oil for their lamps, so left to purchase some as the groom approached. Meanwhile, the five wise virgins, lamps lit, led the groom to his wedding. Pierce shows the wise virgins twice: at the top, reclining but remaining vigilant, and at the bottom, in an orderly line ready to march off the right side of the carving. The moral is that one must always be ready, for "ye know neither the day nor the hour wherein the Son of man cometh."

The left half of the second row describes a tale of forgiveness (John 8:1–11). A woman taken in adultery kneels before Jesus, who exhorts the crowd that he who is without sin must cast the first stone; when no one does, he tells the woman to "go, and sin no more." The story suggests that no one is entirely virtuous and that we are able to choose between rectitude and sin. The latter concept is exemplified by the man in the right half of the second row who holds two hearts, one clean, the other soiled.[2]

On the left half of the bottom row is a courtroom scene showing two men presenting a case or testifying. Both look toward the highest figure, probably the judge, and point at a lower figure, probably the accused. The inspiration for the carving may have been John 8:17: "It is also written in your [the Pharisees'] law, that the testimony of two men is true." Perhaps the requirement of two witnesses had personal meaning for Pierce, who around 1913 was falsely accused of murdering a white man.[3]

Following these cautionary tales is Pierce's final panel, the story of a miracle which is told in each of the Gospels (Matt. 9:1–8, Mark 2:1–12, Luke 5:17–26, and John 5:1–18).[4] The scene shows a "man sick with palsy, lying on a bed." Above, to the right, the man, cured of his illness and forgiven his sins, has been told by Christ to "arise, take up thy bed, and go unto thine house."

Pierce's "sermons in wood" were seen mostly by the African American community until 1970, when he was discovered by the art world. National recognition and honors soon followed. Pierce enjoyed this success, but for him, carving remained first and foremost a spiritual mission.

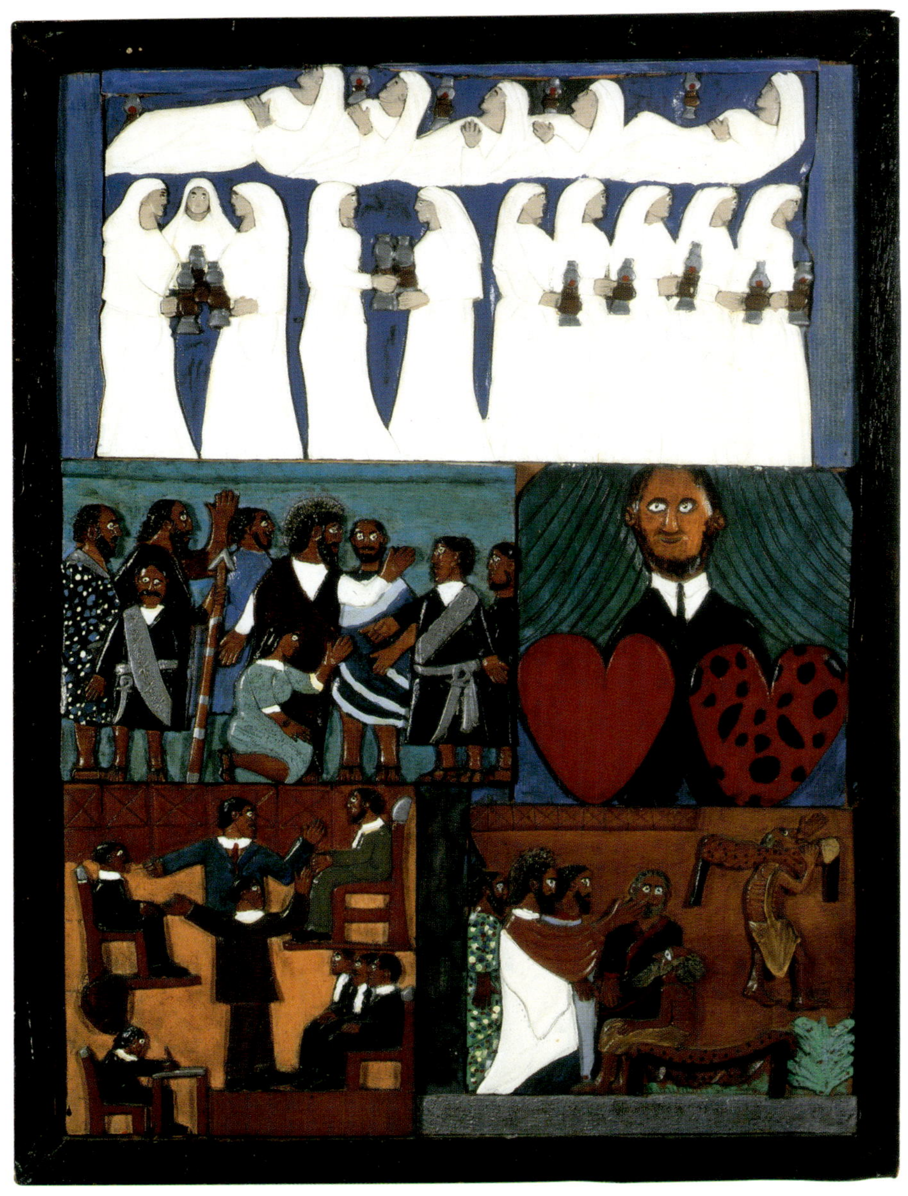

1993.13

Elijah Pierce
Born 1892, Baldwyn, Mississippi; died 1984, Columbus, Ohio

The Wise and Foolish Virgins and Four Other Scenes, around 1942[5]

Carved and painted wood relief with glitter; 39 $\frac{3}{8}$ x 29 $\frac{3}{4}$ x 1 $\frac{1}{2}$ in.
Museum Acquisition Fund and funds donated by Beatrice K. McDowell and the Graves Foundation

Mitchell D. Kahan

Minnie Evans

From childhood on, Minnie Evans was plagued by visions. On Good Friday 1935, a particularly intense vision instructed her to draw. Her first crude pencil marks ignited the career of an artist who brought together religion, history, and nature in compelling and passionate images.

Born to a mother who was barely a teenager, Minnie Jones was raised in Wilmington by three generations of women. Though she left school after fifth grade to help support her family, she became a devoted reader, especially favoring the Bible and Edith Hamilton's book on mythology. In 1908 she married Julius Evans and worked with him on an estate in nearby Wrightsville Beach. Later, when their widowed employer married Henry Walters, a leading art collector, Evans was exposed to a world far removed from her humble origins. When a new owner opened the estate—Airlie Gardens—to the public, Evans worked there as gatekeeper, occasionally selling her drawings and paintings to interested visitors. Local and eventually national recognition followed.

In her work Evans explored two stylistic approaches: abstracted, symmetrical designs involving floral motifs and figures; and more traditional scenes using a simplified two-point perspective. The untitled work in the Akron Art Museum collection is a hybrid. It is colorful, flattened, and symmetrical in the upper portion, representing the heavenly realm, and asymmetrical with shallow space in the darker, earthly sphere below. This dual structure suggests the symbolic message that faith accompanies beauty and harmony. Created with simple art supplies bought at a local store, the painting is small and portable, allowing it to be worked on at home or at the gatehouse.

Divine presence is a central subject in Evans's art. Her optimistic vision presumes that the kingdom of God exists everywhere. In the museum's painting, the devil, who is shown grasping a snake, is certainly a traditional image of evil; but he and his fellow creatures are in no way triumphant. In fact, they seem to be under the spell of the angels above, some of whom smile as they march toward the light that spills through the break in the cliffs. It is possible that this hallucinatory image is inspired by the Book of Revelation, Evans's favorite biblical text. On the other hand, it might be a unique interpretation of a common religious theme, one depicted by Evans in more conventional renderings: the Peaceable Kingdom, where the wild and the tame dwell together.

Evans admired exotic cultures and all races, purposely bringing them together in her work. Her long-haired, blonde angels are always white, the color of purity and of the afterlife in many cultures (including that of the Yoruba, possibly Evans's ancestors). The facial features of these pale angels appear to be African American. The godlike divinities, so frequent in her work, are varied in gender and race; sometimes a Caucasian Christ appears, at other times a Mayan God. The obviously Chinese face in the museum's work transforms an Asian stereotype, reminiscent of Fu Manchu movies, into an exotic God surrounded by rainbows in heaven.

Among the most memorable elements of Evans's art are the haunting eyes that so often stare at the viewer. Whether attached to figures, or emerging from abstract designs, or peering out from the heavens, they accentuate the unearthly quality of her vision. They also draw the viewer to the image, intensifying his or her passage into the artist's spiritual realm. These eerie eyes testify to Evans's belief that God is everywhere—in plants and animals, water and air. For indeed, Evans is almost a pantheist, who finds God in all earthly creation and in every dream.

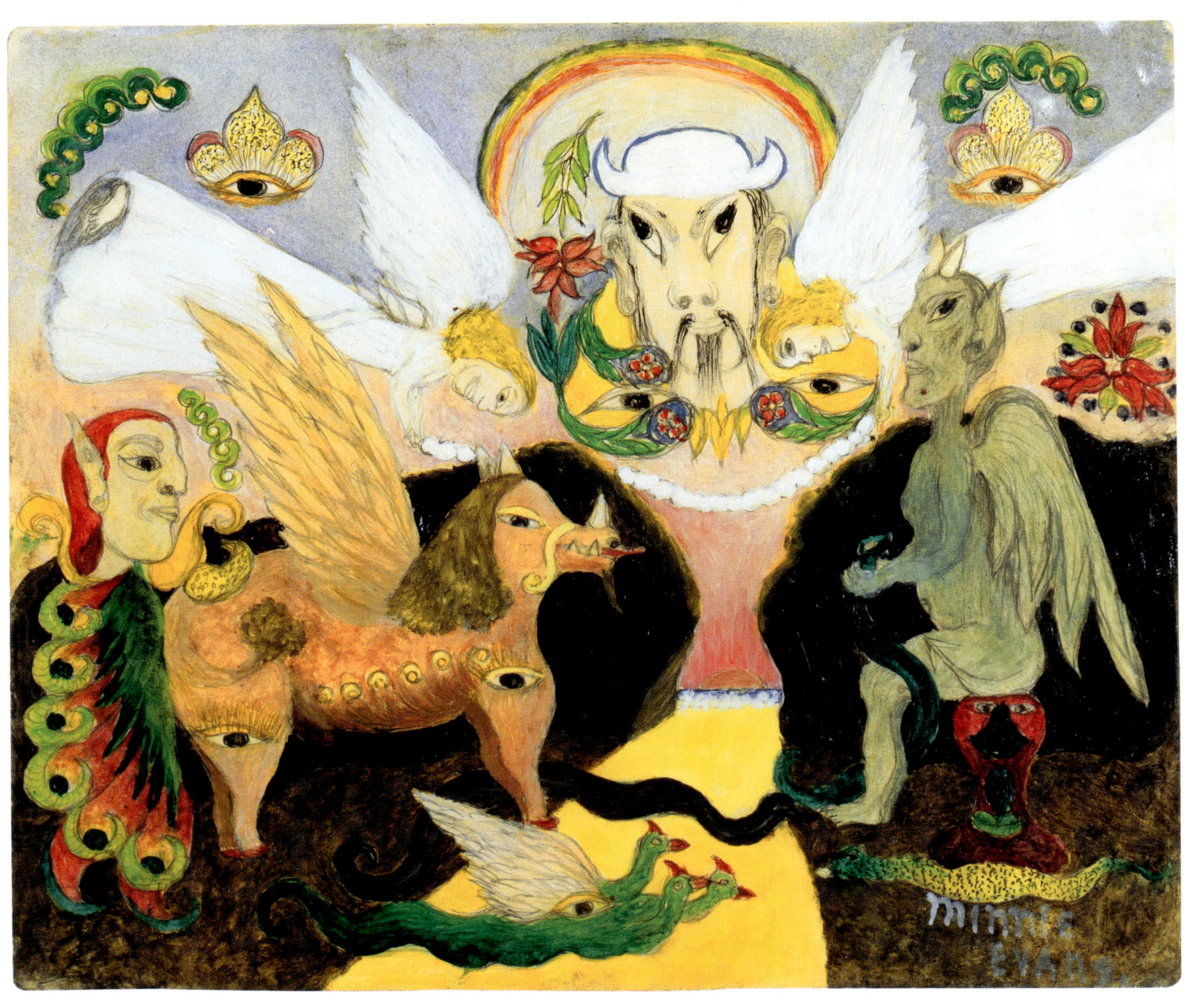

1993.7

Minnie Evans
Born 1892, Pender County, North Carolina; died 1987, Wilmington, North Carolina

Untitled, 1966

Oil, graphite, and ink on paper; 11 x 13 ¾ in.
Museum Acquisition Fund in memory of Honorary Trustee Jean Palmer Wade

Barbara Tannenbaum

Ralph Eugene Meatyard

A few ounces of rubber mask add the weight of the world to the boy in Ralph Eugene Meatyard's untitled photograph about the difficult transition between childhood and adulthood. Although Meatyard made several bodies of abstract photography, it was staged, figurative scenes like this, which he produced regularly throughout his career, that brought him international acclaim.

Taking family and friends to meadows, woods, and abandoned houses, Meatyard provided them with props and asked them to stand or move a certain way as he snapped their picture. The resulting images are hardly portraits or snapshots. They are fictions. Like a wizard, Meatyard transmuted the drab banality of ruined houses, rubber masks, and hooded sweatshirts into disturbing surrealist dramas that reveal truths about the human condition.

An optician by trade, Meatyard was living in Lexington, Kentucky, in 1950 when he bought a camera to document his firstborn child. He quickly became serious about the medium and began studying with Van Deren Coke at the Lexington Camera Club. He also attended a three-week workshop at Indiana University taught by Henry Holmes Smith, Minor White, and Aaron Siskind (see pp. 124–25).

Meatyard soon turned away from the documentary aspects of photography. He wanted not merely to photograph what he found but to transform it, either through the camera's unique qualities of vision or through the fabrication of a scene at a found location. Masks were among his most frequently used props. Plastic or rubber, from a dime store or magic store, neither elaborate nor precious, these false faces bear idiotic grins, physical deformities, flayed skin, or exaggerated features. On a child at Halloween they might be scary or mocking. In Meatyard's photographs they assume a melancholy yet compassionate air, as in *Untitled*.

The boy sits patiently on a rock in front of some trees or bushes, tilting his oversized pumpkin-like head in a reflective posture. His enormous hands would be folded in his lap, but they are too big, so they hang over onto the rock. His pose brings to mind the physical awkwardness of a teenage boy whose limbs have grown too quickly for the rest of his body to adjust. The wrinkled mask and gnarled hands prophesy his further aging, inevitably to be accompanied by suffering and sadness. Growing old is a morbid joke indeed. This Frankenstein made of mismatched parts—a creature tamed and sadly aware of his own grotesqueness—elicits the viewer's sympathy, not horror. Like many of Meatyard's images, it is ambiguous, combining humor and tragedy to reveal truth rather than mere fact.

During his lifetime a number of Meatyard's colleagues were highly critical of his use of posed tableaux and his cultivation of multiple readings. Ironically, these same traits make his work especially relevant to current art practice, including that of Cindy Sherman (see pp. 216–17) and Carrie Mae Weems (see pp. 240–41). While the approach of these younger artists usually derives from social and political concerns, Meatyard's preference for fiction and his belief in the legitimacy of ambiguity stemmed from strongly personal sources: his adherence to the Asian philosophy of Zen (with its respect for paradox) and his own innate personality. The masked boy in *Untitled* is awful to look at but draws our curious gaze; he is at once humorous and sad, a joke and the most serious of statements.

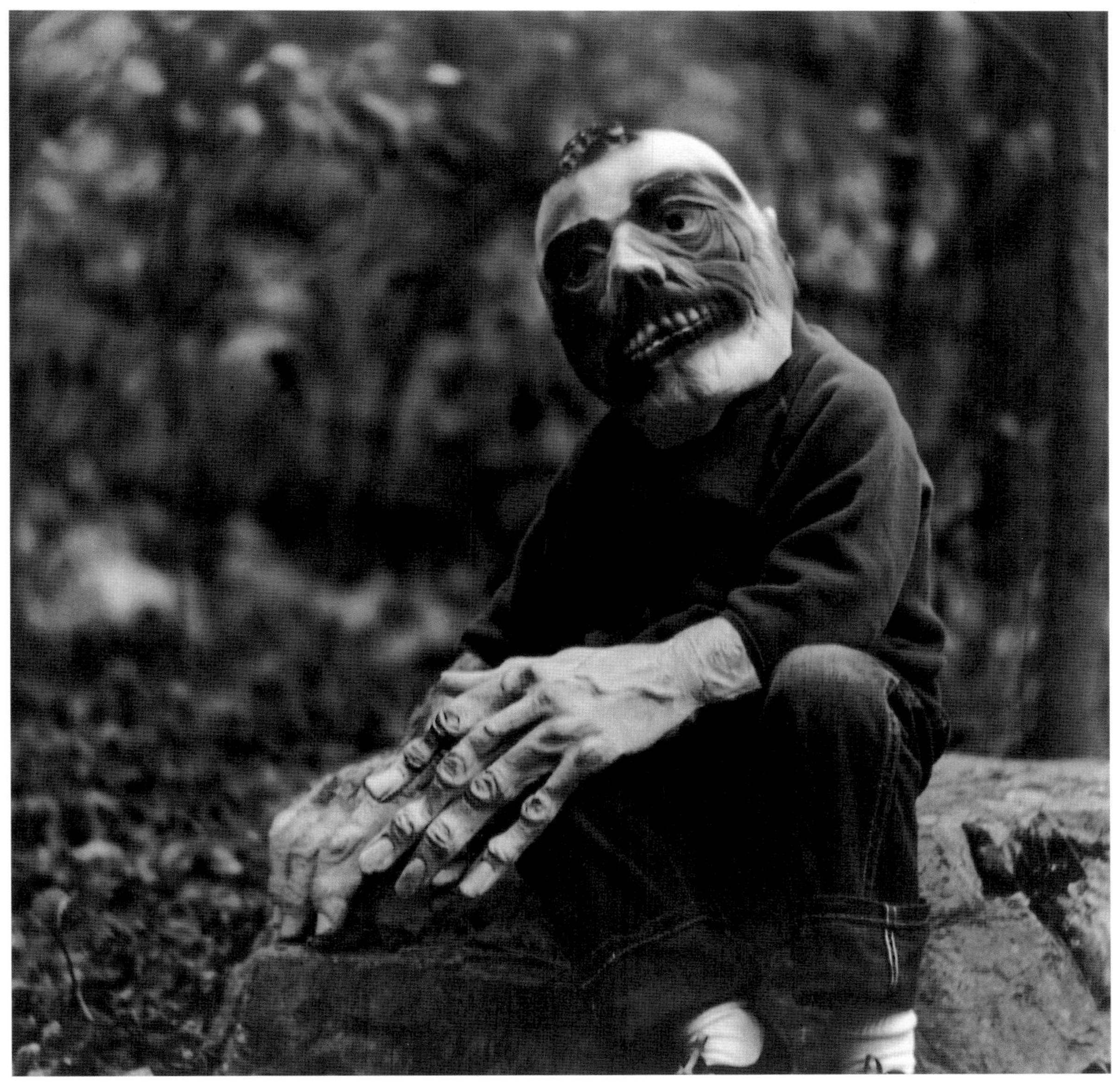

1992.48

Ralph Eugene Meatyard
Born 1925, Normal, Illinois; died 1972, Lexington, Kentucky

Untitled, 1960

Gelatin silver print; 7 3/8 x 7 3/4 in.
Purchased with funds from Anne Alexander and the Museum Acquisition Fund

Mona Hadler

Lee Bontecou

"Is it a pterodactyl? A Flash Gordon spaceship? An outsize artichoke or a monstrous whorl of giant flower corollas?" asked one critic in the mid-1960s of Lee Bontecou's dramatic constructions on exhibit at the Leo Castelli Gallery in New York.[1] Though the show drew a barrage of criticism, Bontecou was quickly lionized by Americans and Europeans alike. By 1964 she was exhibiting in Paris and Germany and at the Museum of Modern Art in New York. Her pioneering direct metal sculpture, incorporating such varied materials as canvas, denim, tarpaulin, epoxy, and fiberglass, has influenced generations of process artists.[2] Rife with associations, her work has engendered a multiplicity of responses.

Bontecou was born in Providence, and shortly afterward her family moved to Westchester County, New York. She began her art education in the mid-1950s, studying at the Art Students League in New York City. By 1959 she had moved to the Lower East Side. Living over a laundry, Bontecou rescued discarded canvas conveyor belts from the garbage and fastened them with pieces of wire to monumental metal frames she had welded together. In so doing she produced her most characteristic work, which, like the assemblage art of the time, incorporates a broad array of materials. These range from garment district racks to washers and bits and pieces of Canal Street to bullets, Nazi helmets, and gas masks.

Bontecou was profoundly affected by World War II and has poignant memories of her mother wiring submarine parts in a factory during the war. These early experiences awakened a lifelong political awareness in Bontecou that fueled the intensity of much of her work.

> I was angry. I used to work with the United Nations program on the short-wave radio in my studio. I used it like background music, and in a way, the anger became part of the process. During World War II we'd been too young. But at that later time [the 1950s and 1960s], all the feelings I'd had back then came to me again.... Africa was in trouble and we were so negative. Then I remembered the killings, the Holocaust, the political scene.[3]

Bontecou's indignation deepened with the outbreak of the war in Korea. Her persistent angry feelings are expressed clearly in *Prisons,* a series of small rectangular metal works executed in the early 1960s. Many of the images from this series, she maintains, reappear in larger works.[4] Indeed, *Untitled* of 1966 closely resembles these smaller works. Like them, it is rectangular and marked by entrapping geometry, sharp toothy elements, and—most prominently—the striations that recall prison suits. The piece, a characteristic mixture of materials, incorporates garment racks; trapped behind a horizontal grid of bars lurks a figure with a threatening grin.

It is in her formal language, above all, that Bontecou most effectively expresses her social concerns: the grid of entrapment, the sharp edges that appear in most of her work and "mentally scrape the viewer," the ominous black openings and expressive play of light and dark. In *Untitled,* as in her other works, she speaks with an oppositional language that she feels reflects the dualities in society. Here she has achieved a formal elegance through the image's stark rectangular shape and carefully rendered horizontal bands while contrasting these with subtle tonal variations and a careful asymmetrical geometry. Here and elsewhere Bontecou combines the aggressive and the beautiful—in her words, "the balance of what we are up to."

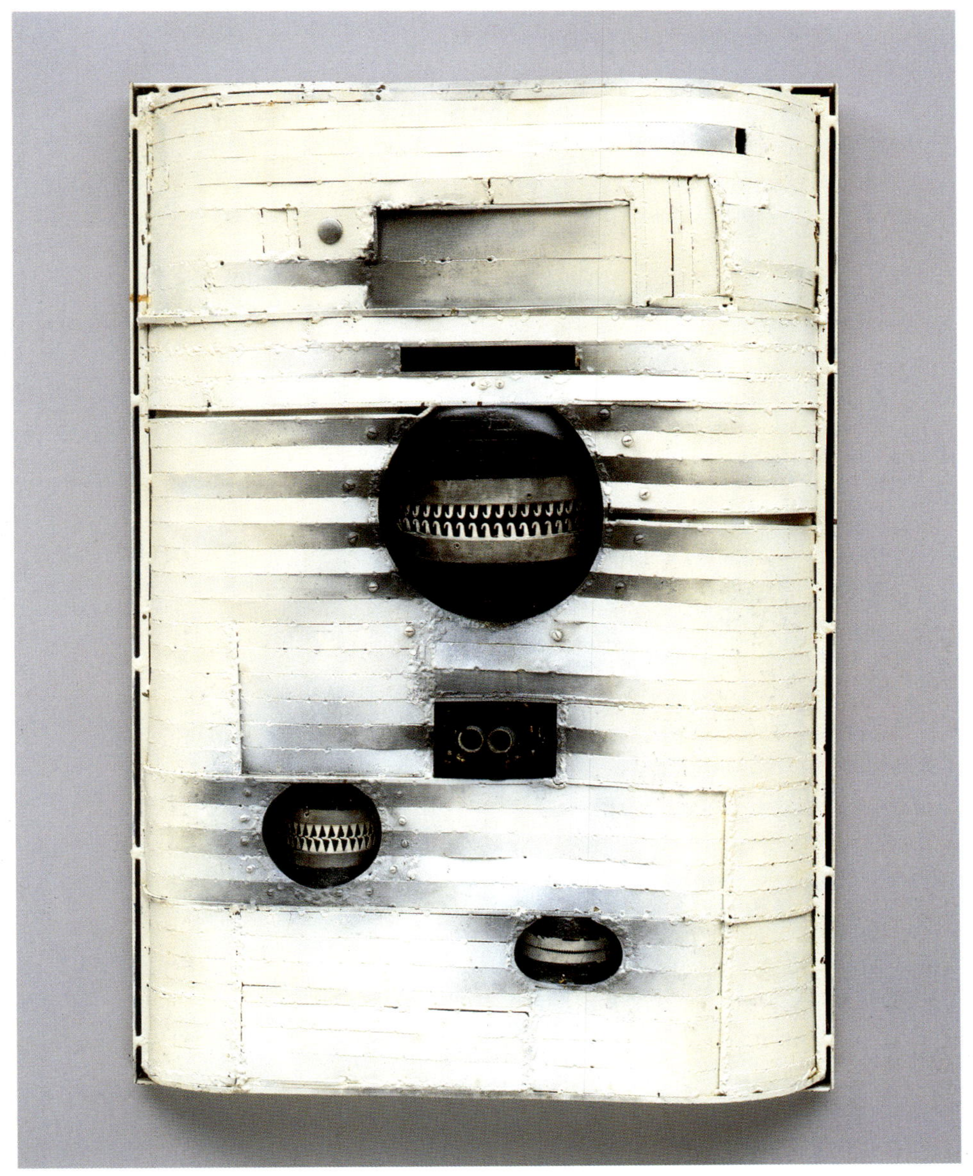

1974.122

Lee Bontecou
Born 1931, Providence, Rhode Island; lives Pennsylvania

Untitled, 1966

Painted iron, fiberglass, and fabric; 41 x 29 x 8 in.
Gift of Leo Castelli, Castelli Galleries

Barbara Tannenbaum

Philadelphia Wireman

One dark night in 1982 an artist was driving through the streets of Philadelphia when his headlights caught a glittery lump of metallic objects spilling onto the street from decaying cardboard cartons. Stopping his car, he picked up one of the objects and realized it was a piece of sculpture. Thus was the work of the sculptor now known as the Philadelphia Wireman discovered. Approximately 625 pieces ranging in height from one inch to over two feet were rescued from oblivion. Their acquisition by numerous art professionals and several museums suggests that others share their finder's belief that these objects should be considered artworks.

The Wireman's sculptures are accumulations of urban detritus—from small vials of over-the-counter medicines and crumpled radio antennas to soap wrappers and even a museum-admission button—compressed inside wire that has been wrapped around them to form anthropomorphic, zoomorphic, and other metaphorical forms. To persons with art-school training these works are reminiscent of the scavenger tradition of American folk art and the found-object aesthetic of twentieth-century European artists like Kurt Schwitters and Pablo Picasso.

Whether their maker, whose identity remains a mystery, was aware of these traditions is unknown, but several other assumptions can be made about the artist. Because great pressure was required to bend the heavy wire, yet few tool marks are present, their creator is presumed to have been male. Given the volume of work and the failure of efforts to locate the artist, it is assumed that the works were discarded because of his death. They were found in one of Philadelphia's oldest, continually black neighborhoods, suggesting that their maker was African American.

Another argument for African roots is the works' resemblance to *minkisi* (things that do things). These are power objects that were made by the Kongo people of Central Africa, who today inhabit the Republic of Congo, Angola, and the Democratic Republic of Congo.[1] The Kongo believed that these charms, which often involved binding or wrapping found objects (medicines), were inhabited by spirits with powers for healing and other phenomena. Just as each piece by the Wireman is individual, so each charm was made for a specific situation and person. The Wireman's works seem to have a distinct front, top, and back, but none stand readily on their own; they may have been intended to hang or to be handled in a ritual rather than to be on permanent display.

Over the past few decades, there has been a spread of underground, African-based religions in American urban centers including Philadelphia.[2] Art dealer and scholar John Ollman assumes that the Wireman was a "medicine man or shaman within the old black community.... Somebody came to the Wireman to be healed, or for some similar purpose, and...he would create a piece specific to that individual."[3] If this was the case, the problems addressed were often universal: about one-tenth of the sculptures contain money; several have hypodermic needles; and the smallest sculpture in the museum's collection resembles a human heart.

Some people are skeptical about the origin of these sculptures, finding them too artful and too perfect a link between modernist aesthetics and folk and ethnographic traditions. Others see them as just so much rubbish. There will probably never be any confirmation of the Wireman's intentions and sincerity. His works, like the many anonymous pieces that dominate the first millennium of art, will have to rely on their own aesthetic worth, and perhaps magical power, to attract viewers.

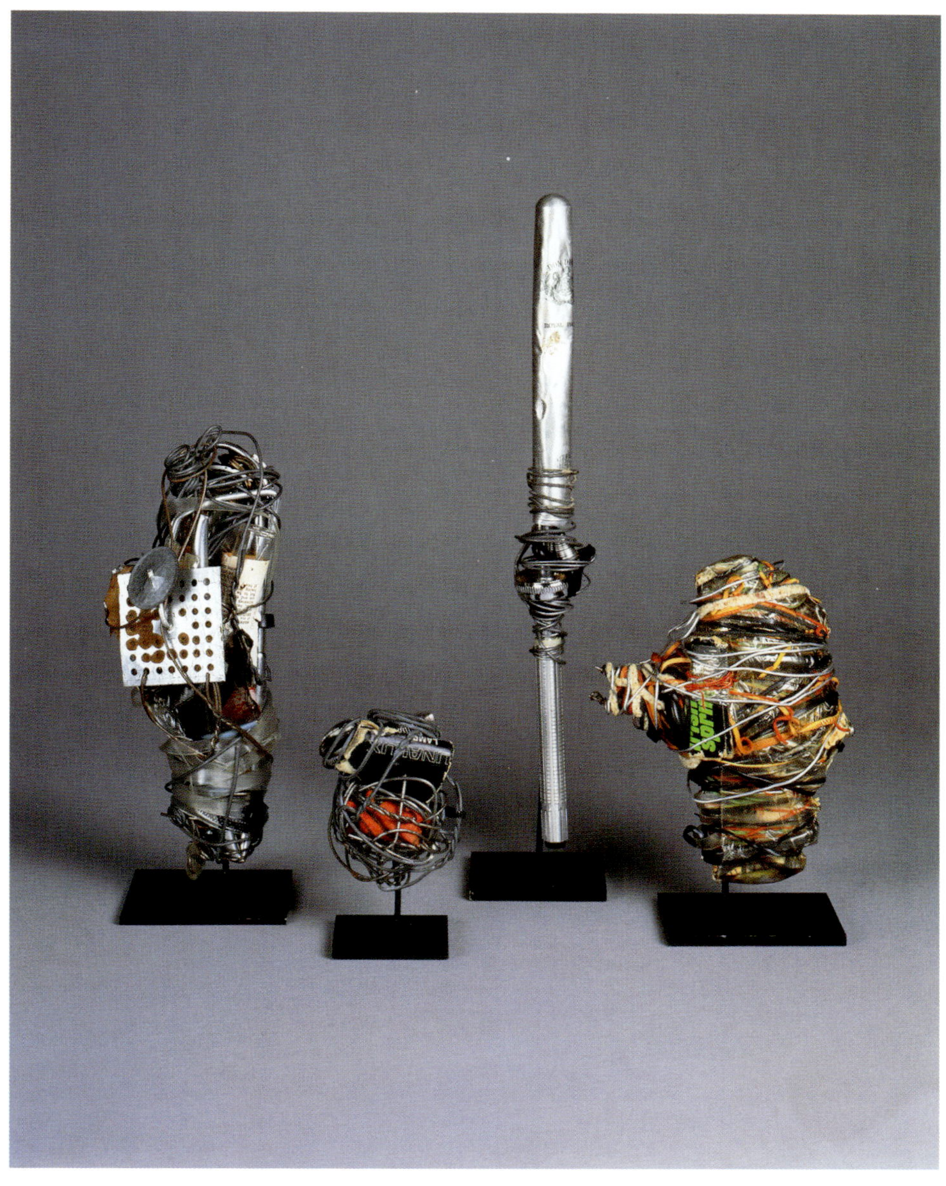

1992.1–1992.4

Philadelphia Wireman
Dates and places of birth and death unknown; lived Philadelphia

Untitled, around 1967–75

Wire and found objects; left to right, 8 x 3 1/4 x 3 1/2 in., 3 x 2 1/2 x 2 in., 12 x 1 3/4 x 1 1/2 in., 6 x 4 3/4 x 2 in.
Museum Acquisition Fund

Mitchell D. Kahan

Yayoi Kusama

Yayoi Kusama has had an erratic but distinguished career. She spent eighteen years in the United States, The Netherlands, and Germany, energetically seeking artistic recognition as well as freedom from Japanese constraints on women. Even more disruptive than her sojourns abroad have been her continuing struggles with physical and mental illness, to the point that she lives and works mostly at Seiwa Hospital, where she has her own studio. Besides making paintings and sculptures, Kusama also writes poetry and fiction. In 1992 she was chosen to represent Japan at the Venice Biennale.

British critic Herbert Read describes Kusama's works as "images of strange beauty that press on our organs of perception with terrifying persistence."[1] Her long obsession with repeated forms and grotesque eroticism is well illustrated in *Arm Chair*. This work is from her first significant body of sculpture, which she originally called "accumulations." These consist of common household items—chairs, strollers, suitcases, sofas—upon which masses of stuffed and sewn cloth protrusions have accumulated. Akron's chair is painted a soft white. Many other works are silver; some have brightly colored stripes or polka dots. The use of repeated elements is a key ingredient of Kusama's intense art. *Arm Chair* is smothered with phallic forms like metastasizing tumors, creating a visual equivalent of Kusama's obsessive-compulsive disorder. She accentuates the psychological edge by choosing a domestic object often associated with femininity and security and invading it with aggressive male forms. Paradoxically, these uncontrollable phalluses have been created through sewing, a traditional female craft.

Arm Chair updates the precepts of Surrealism, particularly in its revelation of subconscious sexual associations. Kusama's phallic protrusions, however, are more than personal fetishes. They recall the 1960s fascination with sexual titillation that was an ingredient of Pop Art (especially the soft sculpture of Claes Oldenburg [see pp. 184–85]) and much experimental theater. In New York, Kusama created numerous counterculture "happenings" involving nudity. However, she eschews Pop Art's frequent references to media and popular culture. Instead, she locates her work in the home, introducing a distinctive feminist vocabulary into the overwhelmingly male world of Pop Art. Baby carriages, strollers, arm chairs, sofas, all produce a nightmarish vision of domesticity gone awry. Tumescent sexuality invades what should be soft, innocent, or comforting.

Kusama has said that her formal vocabulary derives from her psychological conditions. She even refers to her work as "psychosomatic art." Of the phalluses, she explains that she was terrified of men as a teenager yet was also obsessed by sex and thus developed an extreme fear of anything phallic. "As a way of either freeing myself from my obsession or neutralizing it, I obliterate the surface of my works with protruding phallic objects."[2] While Kusama's art certainly reflects her illness, she orders and channels her compulsions into something that is consciously art, not therapy.

If her obsessiveness is offputting, Kusama's exploration of fear and desire is cleverly tempered by humor. In *Arm Chair* the shoes resting on the arms of the chair create a visual pun. Kusama exploits the classic alternation between attraction and repulsion: soft materials seem ready to attack; chairs would be destroyed if sat upon; silliness is mixed with sexual threat. She clearly enjoys the opportunity to scandalize.

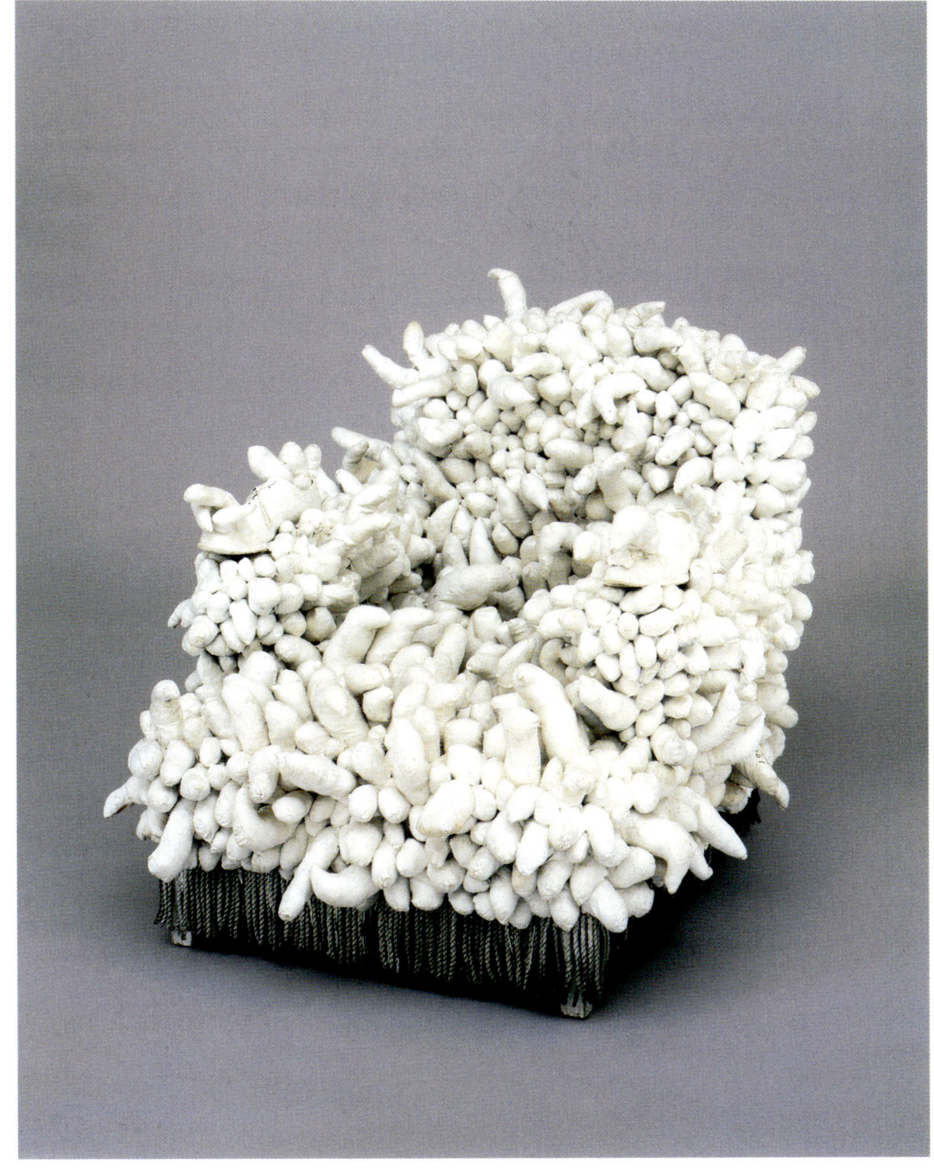

1970.54

Yayoi Kusama
Born 1929, Matsumoto City, Nagano, Japan; lives Tokyo

Arm Chair, 1963

Acrylic on chair, shoes, and sewn cloth and canvas pouches (stuffed with various fillings); 38 x 38 x 50 in.
Gift of Mr. Gordon Locksley and Mr. George Shea

Mitchell D. Kahan

Andy Warhol

Whether as artist, filmmaker, or publisher of celebrity gossip, Andy Warhol lampooned fame and success even as he eagerly sought it. Along with other Pop artists of the early 1960s, he brought popular culture into the realm of fine art, turning banal items and images into lasting icons of their time. In addition to the Brillo boxes, the Akron Art Museum owns two paintings by Warhol, *Single Elvis* and *Jackie;* two portfolios of prints, *Electric Chairs* and *Mao Tse Tung;* and four other prints.

After majoring in art at the Carnegie Institute of Technology, the young Andrew Warhola moved to New York in 1949 and became Andy Warhol. Over the next decade he became a highly successful commercial artist and illustrator. In 1960 he began his first fine art paintings. Within two years his witty images of celebrities and mundane commodities had helped usurp Abstract Expressionism's ambition for a spiritual, timeless art. Rebelliously calling his succession of studios "The Factory," Warhol celebrated the commonplace with a commercialism unprecedented in the realm of fine art.

Primarily a painter and printmaker, Warhol rarely produced sculpture. His first attempt was a silkscreened rendering of stacked soup cans on a wooden box, which he found unsuccessful. He then sent an assistant to the supermarket to bring back rectangular cartons that could be duplicated convincingly. The ones chosen were too "arty," so Warhol himself went to the store to seek the most banal examples: cartons of Brillo soap pads, Heinz ketchup, Campbell's tomato juice, and Del Monte peaches. "Plywood boxes were made to order in large numbers to the specified sizes, painted to match the color of the cardboard used for each, and then printed by hand from separate sets of screens" copied from the original boxes.[1] The total number of boxes produced may number as many as four hundred, with the largest number depicting cartons of Brillo soap pads.

When first exhibited in 1964, these revolutionary and humorous works destroyed the illusion of art's sacred mission and obliterated the distinction between mass-produced items and unique, handcrafted works of art. Warhol's boxes dramatically proclaimed that anything could become art and that art was infinitely reproducible, not rare or refined.

Warhol wholeheartedly embraced photo-silkscreening, a method of mechanical reproduction used at the time for advertising purposes. This repetitive process was perfectly suited for an artist whose self-mocking ambition was "to be a machine" and who claimed, "I like things to be exactly the same over and over again."[2] Paradoxically, photo-silkscreening also depended on messy handwork to squeegee the images onto wood or canvas. The results were not exactly identical because of the uneven pressure of forcing the paint through the screen, errors in registration, and other slips. Unlike contemporary Minimalist sculptors, Warhol did not have his objects entirely made by industrial fabricators. Instead, he combined methods from the factory, the artist's studio and the craft workshop. He constantly explored ambiguities between originality and reproduction, repetition and variation, choice and accident.

The artist who said that everyone would be famous for fifteen minutes was as well known as the celebrities he chronicled. Warhol fulfilled his belief that "being good in business is the most fascinating kind of art."[3] He left an extensive legacy that includes a charitable foundation to support the visual arts and the Andy Warhol Museum in Pittsburgh, the largest museum in the world devoted to a single artist.

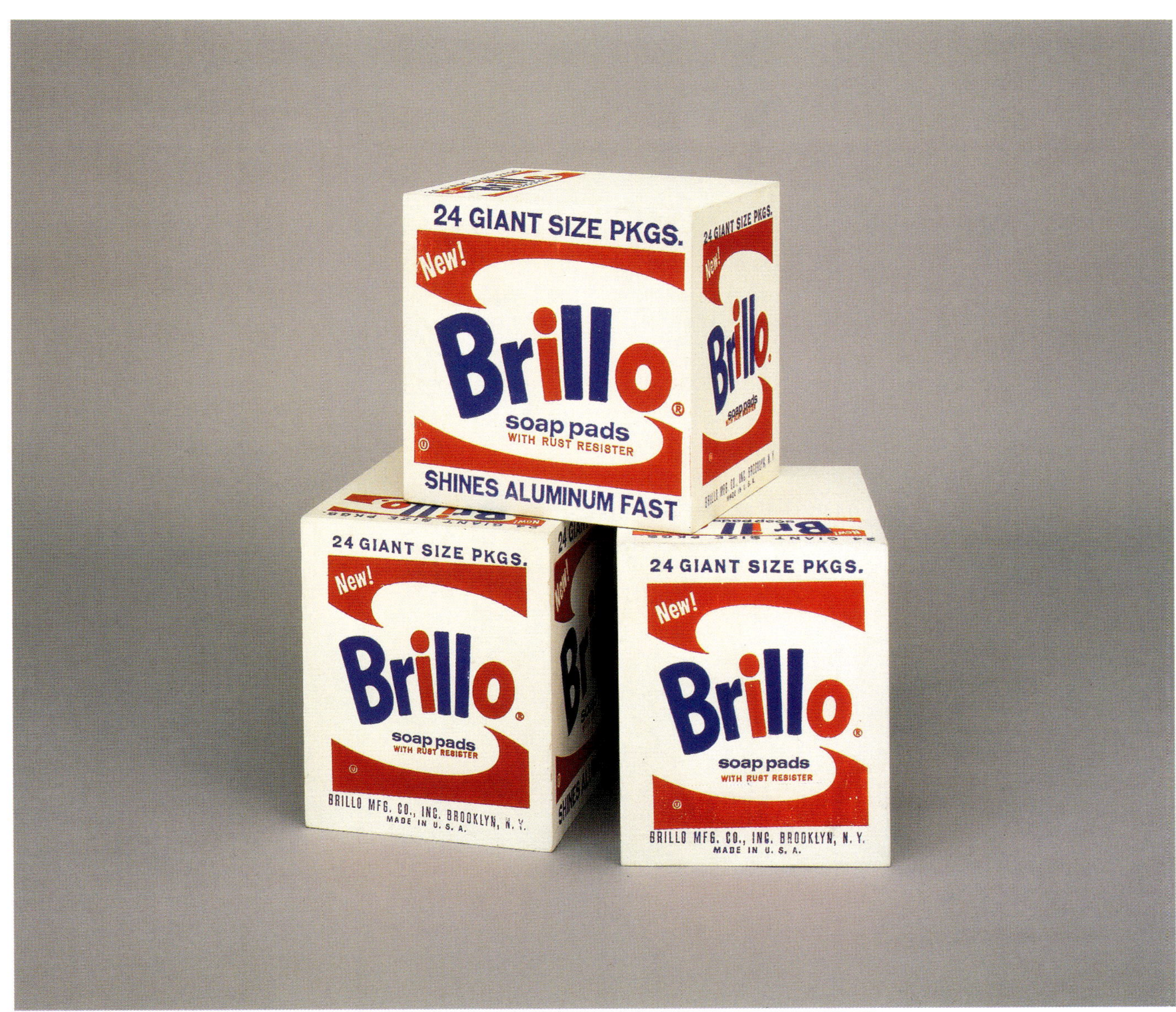

1972.51; 1994.1; 1994 2

Andy Warhol
Born 1928, Pittsburgh; died 1987, New York

Brillo Box, 1964 (three works)

Synthetic polymer paint and silkscreen on wood; each 17 x 17 x 14 in. Gift of Monroe Meyerson; Museum Acquisition Fund in honor of the eightieth birthday of Louis S. Myers and partial gift of The Andy Warhol Foundation for the Visual Arts, Inc.; The Mary S. and Louis S. Myers Endowment Fund for Painting and Sculpture and partial gift of The Andy Warhol Foundation for the Visual Arts, Inc.

Mitchell D. Kahan

Donald Judd

Donald Judd's use of industrial materials and fabrication initially struck viewers as a rejection of aesthetics. In retrospect, his rigorous proportions and elegantly spare surfaces establish a radical new vision of classical order.

After army service during the Korean War, Judd received undergraduate and graduate degrees from Columbia University, where he studied philosophy and art history. In New York in the early 1960s he painted, taught, and became well known as an art critic. By 1963 he was working almost exclusively with three-dimensional boxlike structures. Two years later he began exhibiting internationally. His most unusual legacy is the Chinati Foundation in desolate west Texas. In a former army base, Judd presented his art and that of selected colleagues in ideal environments that they painstakingly designed.

One of the major sculptors of the twentieth century, Judd rejected Abstract Expressionism's gestural, emotional approach to painting and sculpture. Along with Frank Stella (see pp. 202–3), Judd became a key proponent of an analytical emphasis on art's basic visual properties. In this approach, painting might investigate flatness and color; sculpture would seek to define structure, volume, and edge. Like Stella, Judd was committed to forms and shapes that made no allusion whatsoever to nature. He insisted that an artist's ambition to create metaphorical meaning could only lead to a dead end. Instead, in his geometric forms Judd tried to concentrate attention on perception and structure, issues that reflect his philosophical study of empiricism.

In 1964 Judd turned to outside industrial fabrication rather than hand construction in the studio. Metals, plastic, concrete, and plywood became his favored materials. His rejection of the artist's individual touch became widely influential. "Minimalism" became the commonly accepted term for this new aesthetic, which was also championed by Robert Morris (see pp. 152–53) and Sol LeWitt (see pp. 180–81).

A key work in Judd's career, *Untitled* is a rectangular box with open ends. Its pristine exterior is clear anodized aluminum, and its sleek interior is sheathed in a one-eighth-inch layer of green Plexiglas. Judd also created a second, identical version of *Untitled.* In addition he designed other boxes of the same dimensions with blue and violet Plexiglas, as well as versions in brass and steel without interior plastic.

The box was Judd's favorite format; he employed it throughout his career in different dimensions with openings variously at the ends, sides, and tops. He often arranged boxes in series, either horizontally or stacked vertically. His use of different materials for exterior and interior breaks a primary unit into two parts, even as the eye sees one basic form. As Judd explained, "The whole's it. The big problem is to maintain the sense of the whole thing."[1] By also focusing attention on the green interior of *Untitled,* Judd challenges the expectation that a sculpture's interest resides solely in its external surface. The play of reflections is almost baroque by Judd's austere standards, introducing complexity to an apparently simple structure.

Judd declined to title his work because he did not want to allude to anything beyond the object itself. To discuss a piece demands uttering a physical description of its dimensions and materials. Experiencing the work is based on facts and observation, not touch or a psychological reaction.

Judd decried the pretension that art reveals "some larger order" in the universe, but great art by definition deals with metaphor and refers to ideas and feelings beyond what the eye can see. One of the paradoxes of Judd's aesthetic is that his insistence on clarity and the integrity of unadorned materials often results in an experience of elation and purity for the viewer. Inevitably, his immaculate and refined structures extol the mind's capacity for comprehension, control, and order.

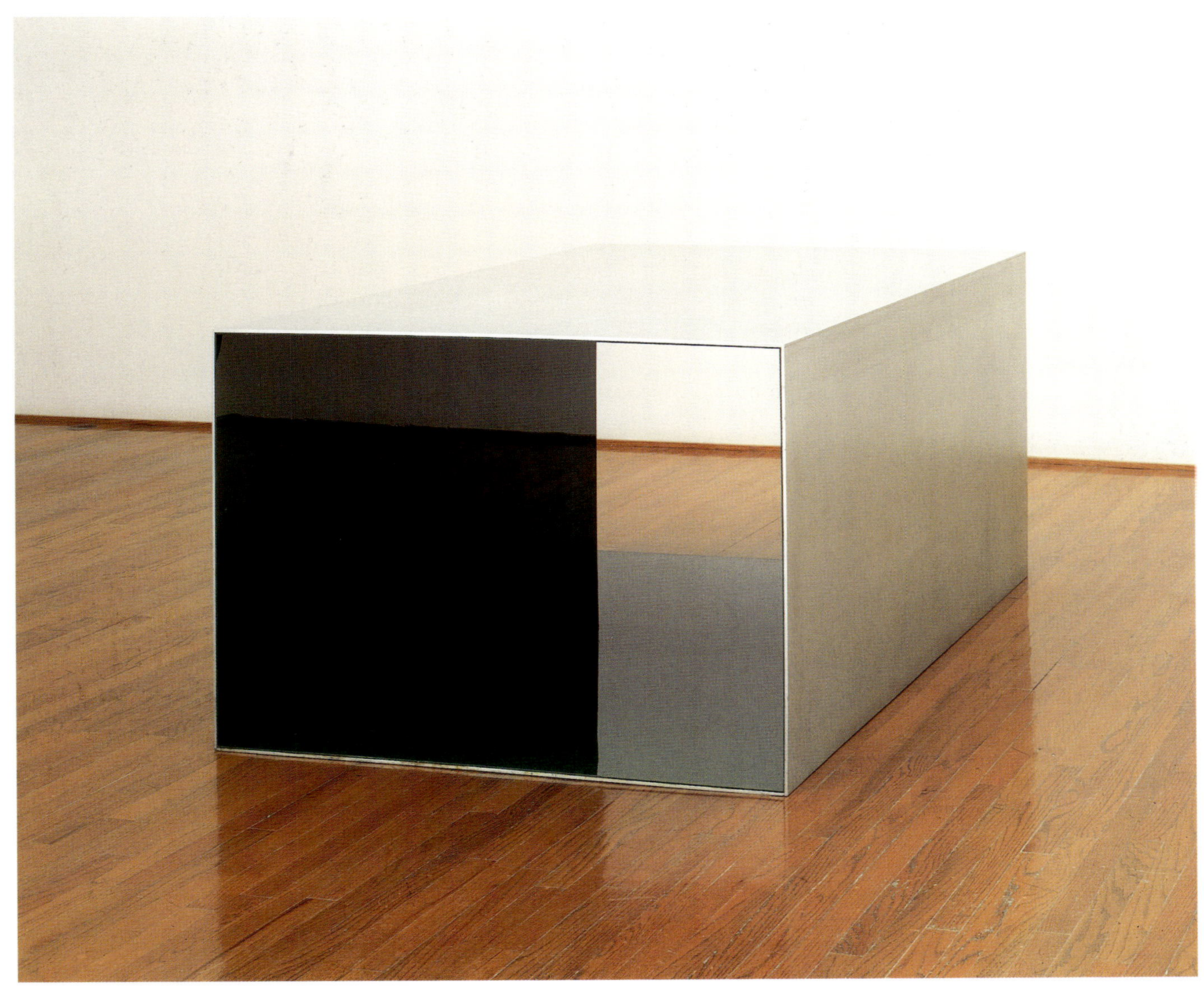

1972.19

Donald Judd
Born 1928, Excelsior Springs, Missouri; died 1994, New York

Untitled, 1969

Anodized aluminum and Plexiglas; 33 x 48 x 68 in.
Purchased with funds from the National Endowment for the Arts and the Museum Acquisition Fund

Mitchell D. Kahan

Robert Morris

As a youth Robert Morris attended Saturday morning art classes at his hometown museum; later he studied engineering in college and then art at the Kansas City Art Institute. Following army service in Korea, he painted and worked with theater and film on the West Coast in the 1950s before turning to sculpture in 1959. In 1961 Morris moved to New York, where he earned a master's degree in art history.

Throughout the 1960s and 1970s Morris made a major impact as a teacher, an artist, and an art critic as well as an activist on political issues ranging from artists' rights to the Vietnam War. He was a key theorist for the Minimalist movement (see Donald Judd, pp. 150–51, and Sol LeWitt, pp. 180–81), but after a few years' involvement with Minimalism, Morris restlessly moved on to new approaches, including outdoor environmental art and, much later, political paintings.

In late 1964 the first version of *Untitled* was exhibited in a solo show at New York's Green Gallery. It was one of seven geometric painted plywood forms suspended from the ceiling, leaning against walls, or set freestanding in the gallery. Morris's exhibition became a manifesto for Minimalism, one of the key international developments of the time. Although the exhibition was criticized for lacking aesthetic interest, the overall installation was subtly theatrical, like a Minimalist stage set, reflecting Morris's involvement with dance and performance art.

That first version of *Untitled* was destroyed. Another plywood version, now also destroyed, was exhibited at the Akron Art Institute in 1978, at which time the decision was made to acquire the work if it could be produced in a more durable material. In 1979, following the artist's specifications, the piece was reconstructed in aluminum by Lippincott Inc., an industrial fabricator. On arrival at the institute it was painted light gray.[1] At that time Morris also created for Akron's Federal Building an outdoor work: a series of mammoth stone blocks that recall Stonehenge, but arranged in a straight line instead of a circle.

The history of Akron's *Untitled* points to a primary characteristic of Minimalism: the artist's thought processes take precedence over personal touch or technical skill. The plywood versions were replaceable, easily refabricated for each new exhibition. The aluminum version was made at a factory. Thus, *Untitled* rejects the notion of art as a handmade treasure and celebrates its new status as a manufactured item.

Although *Untitled*, when leaning against the wall at its prescribed angle, is about the height of a man, it hardly exudes intimacy. Instead, it offers an imposing physical encounter that invites visual examination rather than touching. In a widely discussed article from 1966, Morris memorably proclaimed: "The sensuous object...has had to be rejected."[2] Sculpture would not represent things we know from life but would investigate aesthetic issues such as scale and the relation of the object to the viewer and to surrounding space. An art object would be seen as a single unit, a whole or Gestalt, that would explore basic elements such as volume, gravity, and shape. Multipart complex arrangements were to be banished.

In Akron's sculpture, the emphasis on concept and theory reflects a moment when art gazed not at life outside the studio but at itself. While some critics have extolled Morris's intellectual vision for sculpture, others have chided him for advancing such an austere and intimidating vision of art.

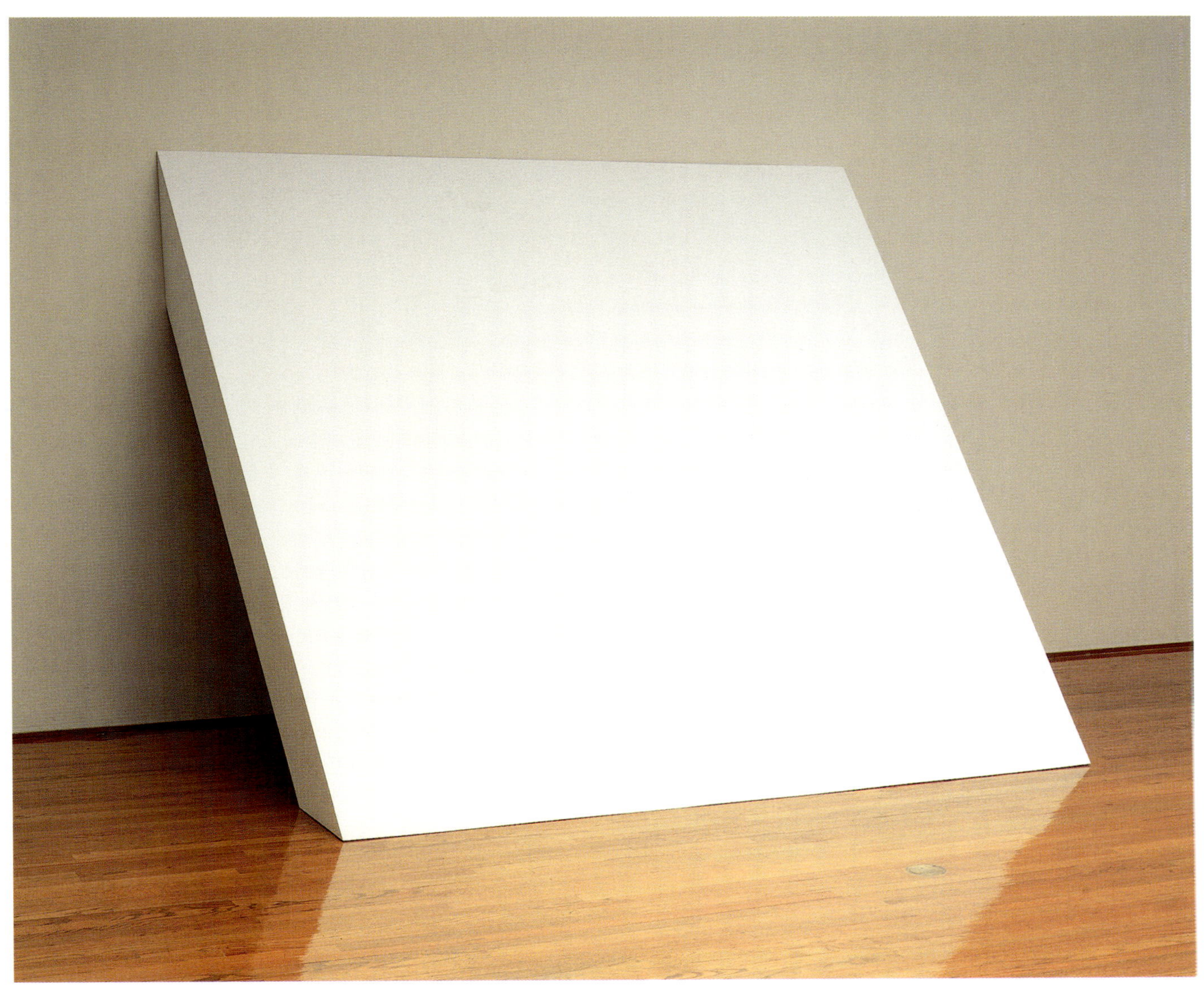

1978.43

Robert Morris
Born 1931, Kansas City, Missouri; lives New York and Gardiner, New York

Untitled, 1964 and 1979

Painted aluminum; 96 x 96 x 12 in.
Purchased with funds from the National Endowment for the Arts and the Museum Acquisition Fund

Mitchell D. Kahan

Richard Estes

Applying modern technology to the traditional realist practice of making studies on site, Richard Estes uses photographs as his source instead of charcoal, ink, or pencil sketches. He first used photographic aids upon leaving art school, having lost easy access to models. By the early 1970s, after working as a commercial artist in Chicago and New York, he had become highly successful—a key figure in Photorealism, a new wave of realist painting derived from photography.

Critics interpreted Photorealism as an outgrowth of Pop Art, sharing its interests in consumerism and media. Photorealism acknowledged that information today rarely comes from personal involvement but instead is manufactured or preselected by others, especially through photographic reproductions. Unlike other Photorealists, however, Estes was less interested in commenting on photography than in using it as a tool. “It’s silly to work from drawings when I can do better with photographs,” he explained with characteristic frankness.[1] “We see things photographically. We accept the photograph as real,” he asserted.[2] His arguments oppose much contemporary theory addressing questions of artificiality in photography.

Among Estes’s most frequent subjects are the streets and shopfronts of Manhattan’s Upper West Side, near his apartment. *Food City,* from the beginning of his career, displays aspects of traditional realist painting in its visible brushwork. It also points to the artist’s later mature style, particularly in the layered reflections and the insistent verticals and horizontals that forcefully divide the painting.

Food City originated in photographs Estes took with a 35mm camera and developed himself to achieve better details. To create his composition he intuitively selected parts of each photograph for his preliminary drawing on the surface of the fiberboard. The result, as the artist has pointed out, is a combination of realism and abstraction, because multiple, disconnected forms are “floating around on a flat surface.”[3] The painting appears to have begun with markings in pencil over which Estes laid a light layer of diluted acrylic paint, like in a wash drawing. Oils were then applied on top of the acrylic, a slower process that likely involved further alterations. Usually Estes then applies a transparent, slightly tinted layer of paint (known as a glaze) to enrich depth and color and to unite the different elements painted on the surface.

While Estes’s images are thoroughly contemporary, his technique harks back to painting in the tradition of Jan Vermeer and other great realists from centuries past. He has given us a visual record of New York in much the same way that Vermeer recorded intimate portraits of Delft. And like Vermeer, Estes draws attention to the difference between the way the eye sees and the way a lens “sees.” Working from multiple photos, Estes can have many areas of the image “in focus,” while the eye can focus on only one place at a time.

Ironically, Estes abandons the humanistic concern at the core of Dutch realism. “I don’t want any kind of emotion to intrude.”[4] The artist’s aloofness is especially evident in the anonymous figures visible through the window. The uniformed, pink image of the cashier is repeated three times, as though a person is as easily reproducible as any of the store’s packaged goods.

Food City is not beautiful; even the arrangement of items and prices in the display window is banal. But the scene is visually enticing and offers a rich array of images to examine: vehicles in the street, consumer staples, price tags, and a sense of both the tedium and energy in city life.

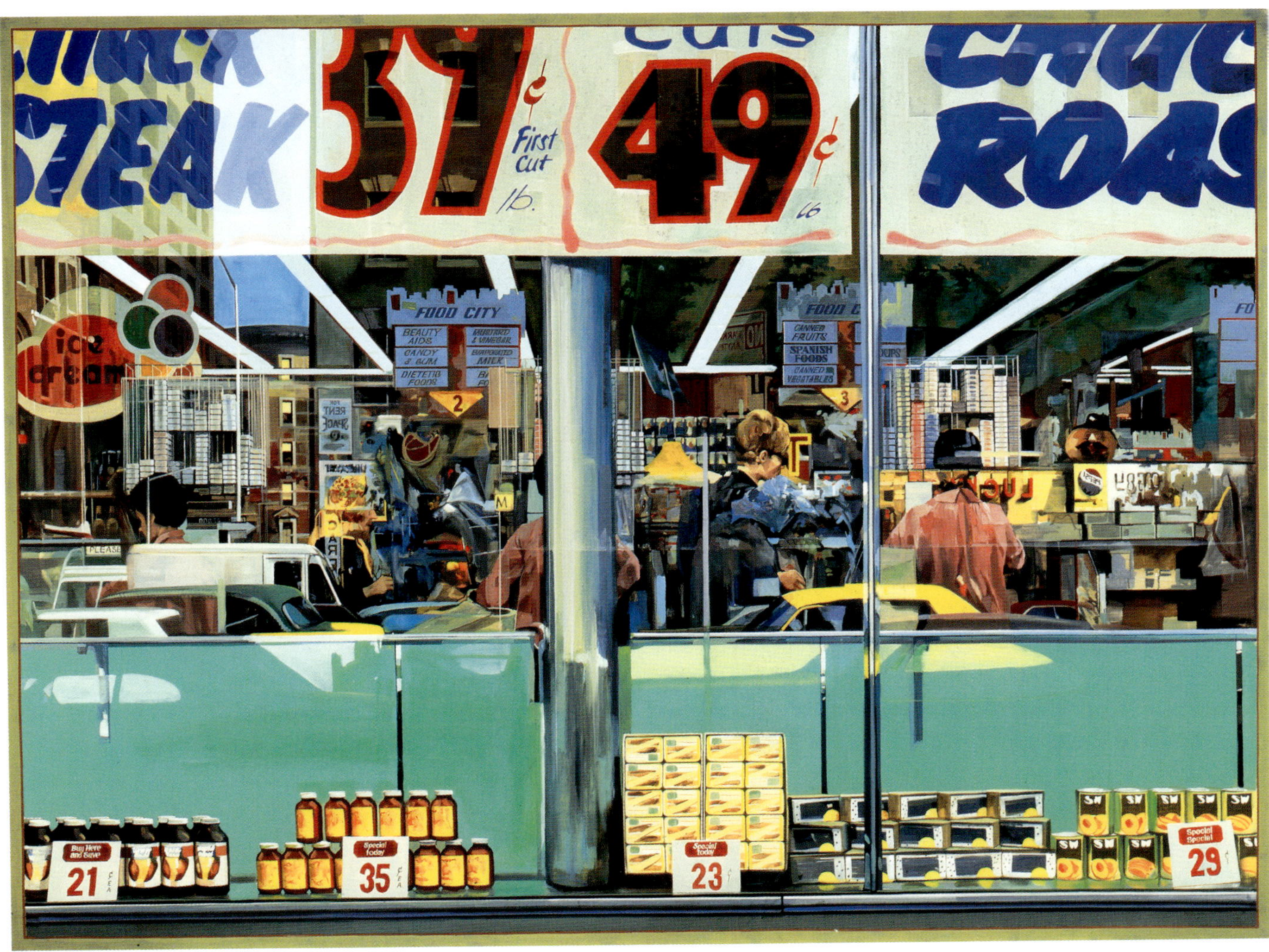

1981.13

Richard Estes
Born 1932, Kewanee, Illinois; lives New York and Maine

Food City, 1967

Oil, acrylic, and graphite on fiberboard; 48 x 68 in.
Purchased with funds raised by the Masked Ball 1955–63, by exchange

Mitchell D. Kahan

John Clem Clarke

John Clem Clarke's canvases evolve from the artist's preoccupations with the nature of painting. During college, he first became interested in how images are transmitted and visual signs are interpreted as stand-ins for real things. His subjects have ranged from shorthand versions of old master paintings to images from television to bucolic scenes of contemporary nudes. From 1967 to 1969 Clarke undertook an extensive series based on European and American old master paintings. *Morse—The Old House of Representatives* is from this body of work.

Clarke had his first gallery show in 1968, and it was an immediate success. A critic described his technique as follows:

> He projects a color slide of a painting, sideways, onto marking paper which is tacked to the wall. He enlarges it to the size he desires. When he has decided what are to be the first areas that "he wants to take off" he draws their outlines in pencil and, using a rotary knife, he cuts them out to form his first stencil. He then takes the paper and lays it on top of a canvas on the floor and sprays or rolls paint onto the exposed areas. Proceeding in this manner, he may put on anywhere from three to seven layers of paint.[1]

Using this basic procedure, Clarke explored the odd way that bits and pieces of abstract pigment are, from a distance, reassembled by the eye into recognizable images.

The painting owned by the Akron Art Museum is based on a well-known work at the Corcoran Gallery of Art in Washington, D.C.: *The House of Representatives,* painted from late 1821 to early 1823 by Samuel F. B. Morse (1791–1872). Morse's picture depicts the moment when the chandelier has been lowered so that the candles can be lit and Congress can begin its session. The white border with curved corners clearly indicates that Clarke's source is a 35mm slide reproduction, the type sold in museum shops around the world. Clarke's composition is close to Morse's original, but he cropped the top of the domed chamber, thereby focusing more attention on the figures and downplaying the neoclassical architecture as well as Morse's references to the Pantheon and the Roman republic.

Morse, a founder of the National Academy of Design, devoted himself increasingly to scientific interests after 1830; he is also known for promoting the daguerreotype and inventing the telegraph. Morse's dual interests in art and technology may have attracted Clarke, who regards painting as the establishment of a visual code to be interpreted by the viewer. Oddly enough Clarke's fabricated images made from spots of stenciled pigment recall Morse's creation of words from dots and dashes.

The notion of what is real and what is a replica is central to Clarke's work. "Our whole world is made up of copies," whether of objects or ideas, the artist explained.[2] Accordingly Clarke paints a work that instantly resonates as a copy of an antique, whether or not viewers recognize its source. Paradoxically the work is not a fake but an original painting—a copycat and a unique work at the same time.

Clarke's decision to use preexisting images was a direct outgrowth of Pop Art, particularly Andy Warhol's silkscreened paintings of familiar commodities and celebrities (see pp. 148–49) and Roy Lichtenstein's comic-book images with their stenciled dots. Clarke, too, challenges conventional notions of originality but at the same time acknowledges the role of tradition, reminding us that painters from the Renaissance to the twentieth century have been trained by copying older art.

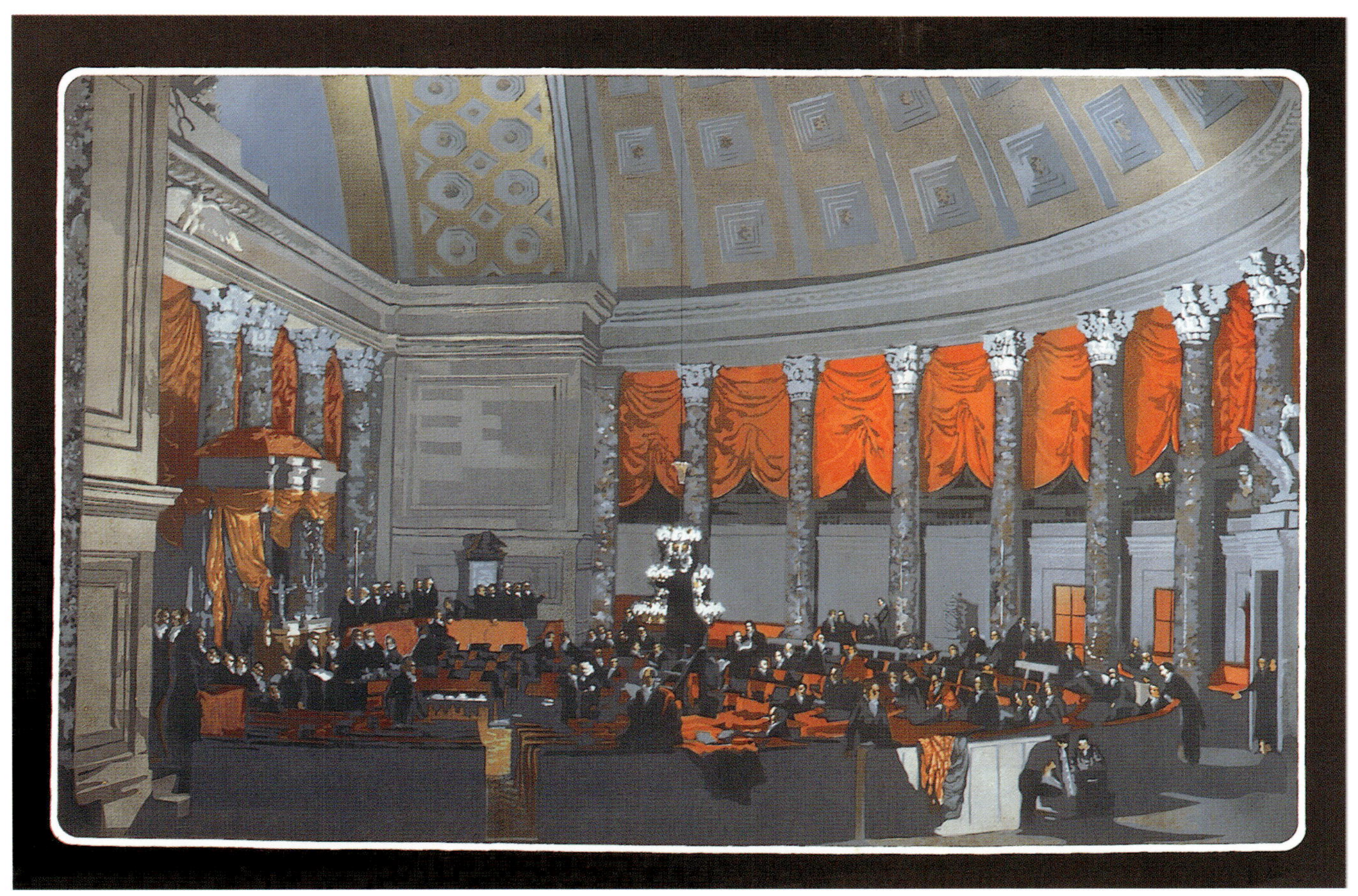

1971.2C

John Clem Clarke
Born 1937, Bend, Oregon; lives New York

Morse—The Old House of Representatives, 1969

Oil on canvas; 90 x 142 in.
Gift of Mary S. and Louis S. Myers

Mitchell D. Kahan

Robert Colescott

As children Robert Colescott and his brother Warrington showed great interest in art and music; both became artists. After army service in France following D-Day, Robert Colescott studied art at the University of California in Berkeley on the G.I. Bill; later, in Paris, he studied with the modernist painter Fernand Léger. Returning to the United States, Colescott received a graduate degree in art in 1951. Over the following decades he taught on the West Coast, in Egypt, and in the Southwest, retiring from the University of Arizona in 1995. In 1997 Colescott represented the United States with a solo show at the Venice Biennale.

Artistic maturity and recognition came slowly to Colescott as he struggled to bring together his personal concerns and his wide knowledge of art and history. In 1971 *Bye Bye Miss American Pie* became a key work in his development, successfully fusing biting humor and a strong commitment to social content.[1] The painting renders images from popular culture and current events in a simplified manner, almost like cartoons. Objects are arranged for symbolic or satirical value rather than fidelity to reality. The composition is dramatic, with bold contrasts of color and huge letters across the top.

While most American Pop Art of the 1960s celebrates consumer culture with a light irony, Colescott's satire engages in a more trenchant criticism, pointing out the inequities between blacks and whites from an African American viewpoint. The painting's title refers to a popular song by Don McLean. Its refrain, "Bye-bye, Miss American Pie," laments the vanished ideals of the Kennedy years and the lost exuberance of early rock music, both replaced by the disillusionment of the Vietnam era.

Here a soldier in a camouflage uniform sprays bullets across what first appears to be white smoke but upon careful observation becomes an outline of Vietnam. Colescott reminds us that those lowest on the social ladder are inevitably the foot soldiers in every war. However, at the same time he exposes the subordinate status of blacks, Colescott demands recognition of their central role in American history.

Even were the United States to win its Asian war, this soldier would not likely get a piece of the tantalizing pie floating like a halo above the nude blonde. Colescott's ribald humor is readily apparent in the gustatory slang of "pie," a reference to the blonde's pudenda. The artist describes the exuberant female as stemming from the myriad advertisements featuring buxom women enticing male consumers to supposed happiness.[2] A new incarnation of the perennial goddess/whore, this triumphant, fleshy fantasy dramatically contrasts with the reality described in McLean's bitter lyrics describing a country where "the music died."

The painting exemplifies Colescott's explosive linkage of social issues with sex. The cliché of fighting for motherhood, apple pie, and the girl next door is turned on its head. "Colescott makes us uncomfortably aware of the implicit arousal in female personification of great American values such as Liberty," wrote Lowery Sims, "and at the same time exposes the raw nerve of interracial sexual politics and of blatant machismo (is it necessary to belabor the metaphor of the gun as phallus?)."[3] Married four times, Colescott pokes fun at women, but he also adores them and acknowledges the humiliating roles they often are forced to play.

Colescott's ironic images of popular song, sex, racial politics, and American history float against a colorful sky that summons visions of Old Glory. His trenchant observations are leavened by an abiding humor and an affection for the realm of folly that is the human condition.

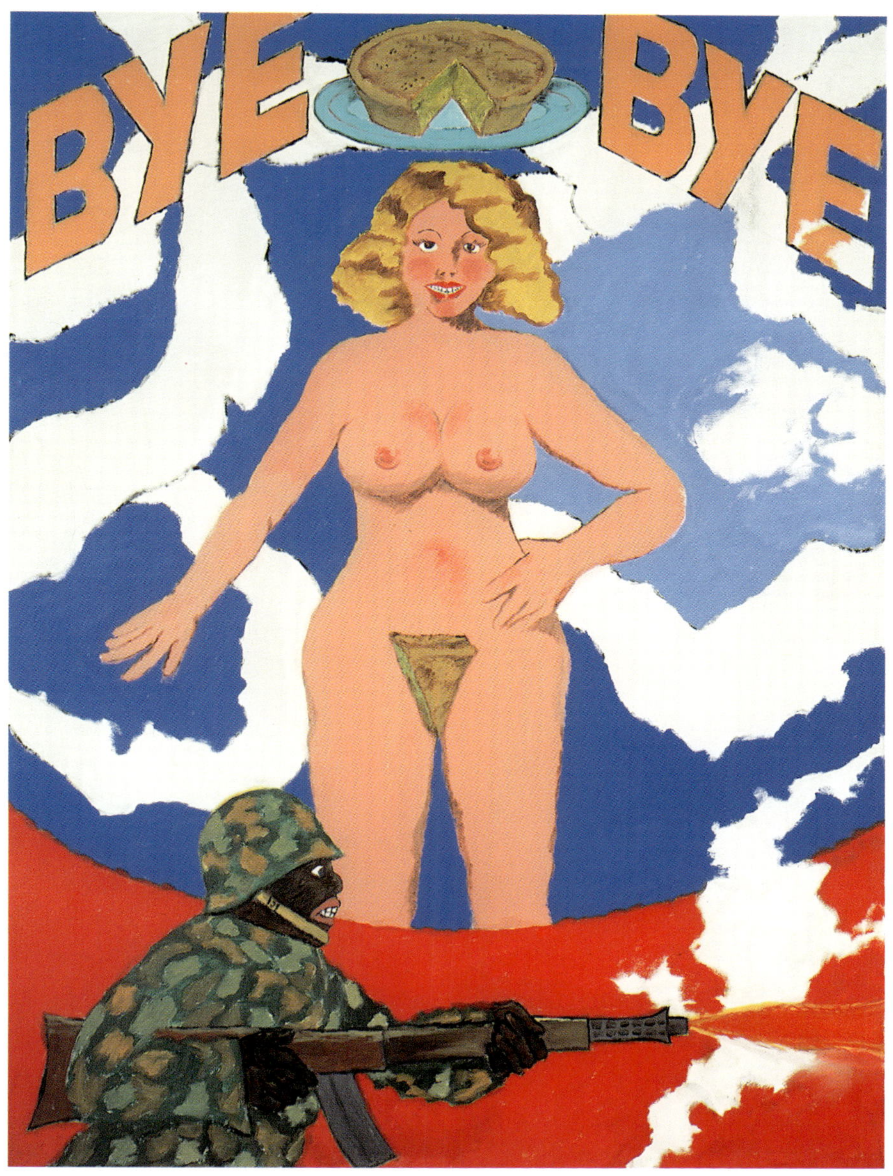

1992.6

Robert Colescott
Born 1925, Oakland, California; lives Tucson, Arizona

Bye Bye Miss American Pie, 1971

Acrylic on canvas; 78 $\frac{7}{8}$ x 59 $\frac{1}{8}$ in.
Museum Acquisition Fund

Mitchell D. Kahan

Duane Michals

Duane Michals has been a leader in creating a new role for the photographer as fantasist, philosopher, and seer. He has been widely imitated for his use of sequential images to unfold a narrative tale and also for the use of handwritten texts to amplify photographic images. Now standard practices in the field, these techniques were anathema to the photographic community in the 1960s, when they first appeared in Michals's work.

Raised in a steelworking suburb of Pittsburgh, Michals took drawing lessons at the Carnegie Institute of Art and later attended college on a scholarship. After military service, he continued studying art in New York and worked as a graphic artist, taking his first photographs in 1958. Three years later he was earning a living as a photographer.

While most artists abandon commercial work after finding artistic success, Michals, who has been greatly influenced by Tibetan philosophy, feels that all experiences are valuable and continues to pursue both gallery exhibitions and advertising gigs. Preferring to use available light, he usually takes just a few shots to capture what he wants with a 35mm Nikon camera. Even on commercial assignments, he does not travel with a battery of lighting equipment.

Acceptance of photography's diverse uses has enriched Michals's work. In fact, his use of photographic sequences to tell a story may be regarded as an evolution of the photojournalistic essays in *Life* and *Look* magazines and of Robert Frank's seminal publication *The Americans.* Referring to newspapers, Michals points out: "Words have always been connected with photographs." Simple bias has evicted words from art photography for most of this century.[1]

The Fallen Angel is one of Michals's classic works. Its eight images are numbered, and the sequence is printed in identical formats. Their characteristic small size provides an appropriate intimacy for the highly personal subject matter and also accentuates a sense of voyeurism by allowing viewers to peer into another world. The first image bears the artist's familiar handwriting, block printing that suggests both childlike awkwardness and elderly vulnerability.

The sequence has elements of an erotic fantasy and is a fable on the loss of virginity and innocence. It might also be a modern lampooning of the Immaculate Conception, for Michals revels in humor and satire, as is evident in the angel's awkward and artificial wings. The blurred details reflect the artist's attitude that "we don't see clearly at all." Michals uses the recording eye of the camera to confirm his abiding belief that visual perception is only a superficial reality. It is art that assists us in seeking the deeper truths that lie beyond mere appearance.

A recurring theme throughout Michals's oeuvre is the attraction, both erotic and paternal, between human beings. In his cast of simultaneously ordinary and beautiful actors we see ourselves and the "other" that we hope to possess. Desire, in all its manifestations, is an essential part of life and art. "Everything is a subject for photography," remarks Michals,[2] an artist who embraces the sacred and the profane, reality and illusion, love and loss.

3

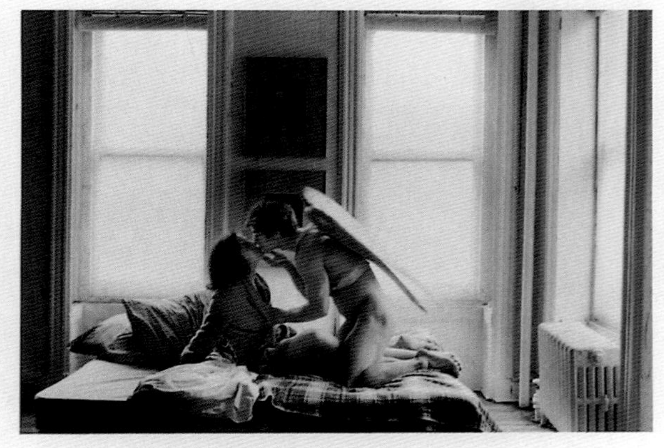

4

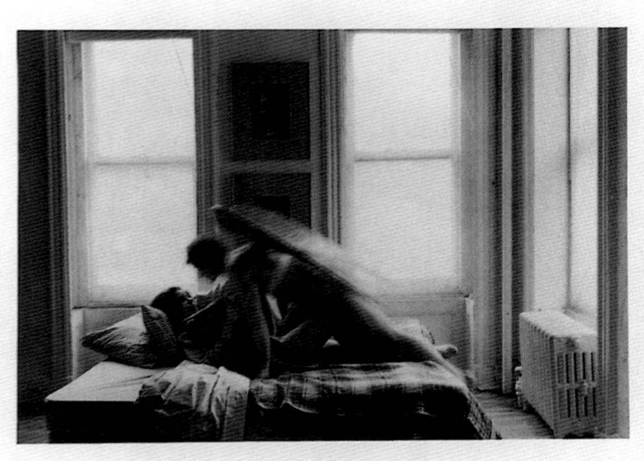

7

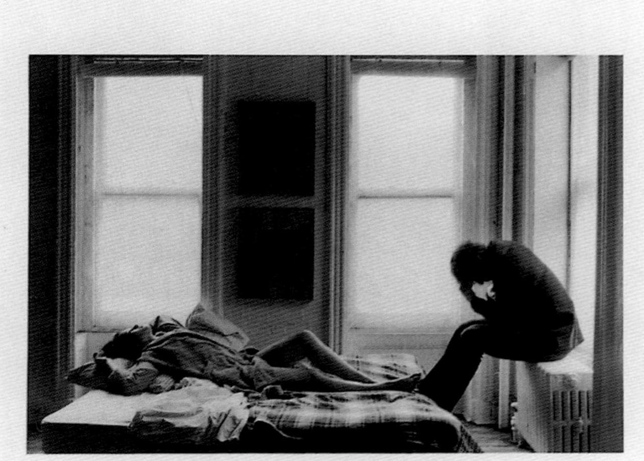

8

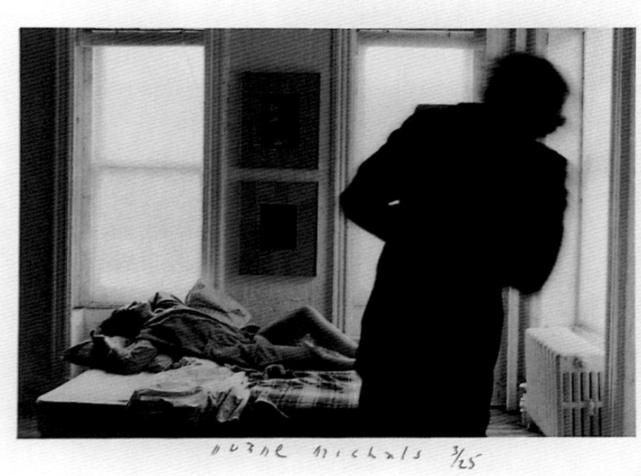

Duane Michals 3/25

1978.42 a-h

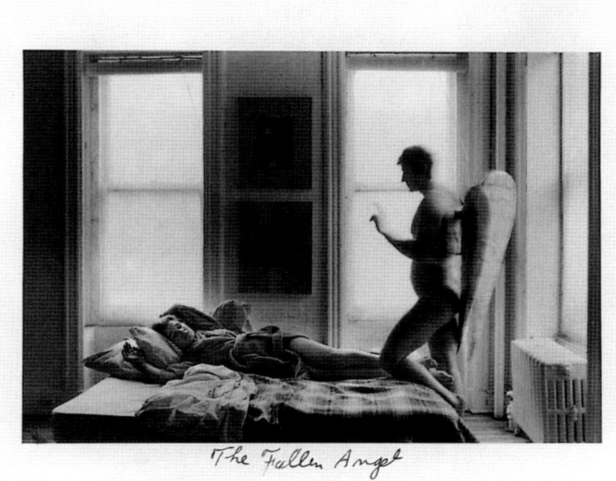

2

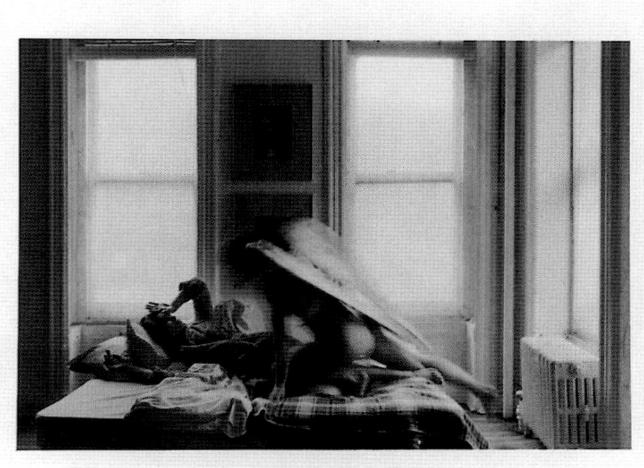

5

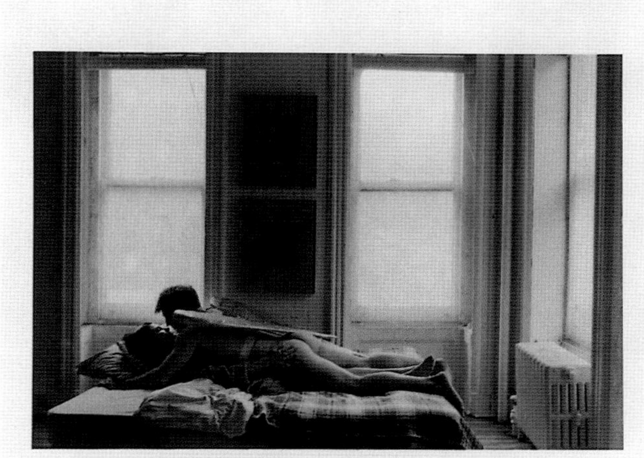

6

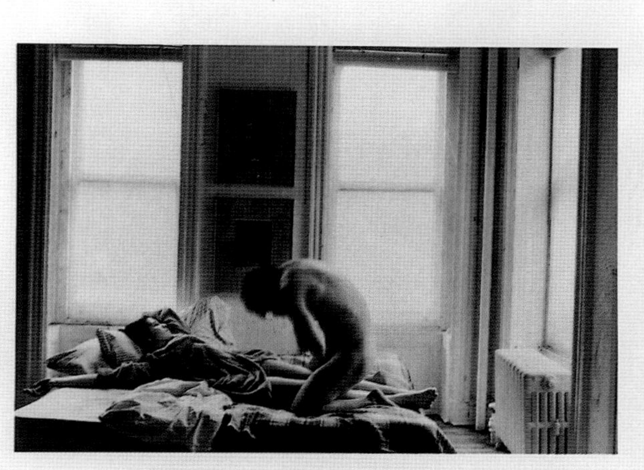

Duane Michals
Born 1932, McKeesport, Pennsylvania; lives New York

The Fallen Angel, 1968

Gelatin silver prints; eight, each $3\frac{3}{8}$ x $5\frac{1}{8}$ in.
Museum Acquisition Fund

Jeffrey Grove

Ernest ("Popeye") Reed

Unlike many visionary or self-trained artists who feel called by God to make art, Popeye Reed was driven to create for reasons more practical than religious. Reed, who was born and lived in the Appalachian hill country of south central Ohio, was a versatile and prolific carver with a flair for self-promotion. After his work was discovered by the art world in the late 1960s, he enjoyed a fairly lucrative career.

Robust female figures were a favorite subject of Reed's, as were American Indians, animals, birds, and mythological figures. (The museum also owns a small sculpture by Reed titled *Harpy*.) The voluptuous subject of *Female Nude* may represent Eve, a hapless player in man's fall from grace. This assumption is supported by the presence of a four-legged reptile ascending the wall next to her. The Bible casts a serpent in the role of Eve's seducer, but the ancient term for serpent suggests a number of creatures, including crocodiles or spiders. Genesis 3:14 indicates that before the Fall, the serpent had legs. Although here Reed appears to have chosen a literal reading of his subject, he is also known to have interpreted his sources freely.

Reed began whittling at an early age but did not start to carve seriously until the early 1960s, when he began to produce wooden pipes and trinkets to sell alongside the road. By the late 1960s he had progressed to using sandstone, flint, and limestone quarried from the land near his home. To shape the stone he used pocketknives, chisels, and mallets, supplemented by more idiosyncratic devices such as stag horn to incise fine lines. As he became increasingly productive in later years he advanced to more modern tools, as incisions from a power drill visible in the hollow between the left breast and arm of the museum's figure clearly indicate.[1] For *Female Nude* Reed chose sandstone, a sturdy yet porous material that is more yielding than most stone and earthier in feeling than the marble traditionally used by generations of academically trained sculptors. Reed added water to the stone as he worked to make it even more pliable.[2]

Solid and stoic, Reed's *Female Nude* reveals neither emotion nor age. Her blunt, nonspecific features range in likeness from vaguely Assyrian to decidedly polyethnic. While the figure's proportions are odd–long arms, chunky toes and fingers–she is stately and primitive. Nonetheless she projects a sense of motion as her body recoils from the serpent. Reed claimed that although he "tease[d] women, he really love[d] them."[3] An erotic sensibility is revealed in his treatment of the figure's sexual characteristics: while some areas are roughly carved, the nipples are delicately shaped and smooth. Likewise the pubic area is almost anatomically correct in detail; with deftly incised hair, it is the work's most richly patterned area.

The purposefully unfinished areas of the *Female Nude,* rather than detracting from the composition, strengthen Reed's self-proclaimed identity as a follower of the "grand tradition" in art. Statuary shaped from a solid mass and left partially unfinished has its antecedent in the work of Michelangelo, an artist whom Reed studied and admired. Like Michelangelo's unfinished works, this is roughly chiseled with varying degrees of finish applied to certain areas. Though some might view such works as simply incomplete, others see them as clear, emotional statements–the equivalent of speaking volumes with few words. Emerging from the stone that serves as both backdrop and support, Reed's unadorned, straightforward figure communicates, in a simple yet powerful way, the biblical account of our origins and our primal connection to the earth.

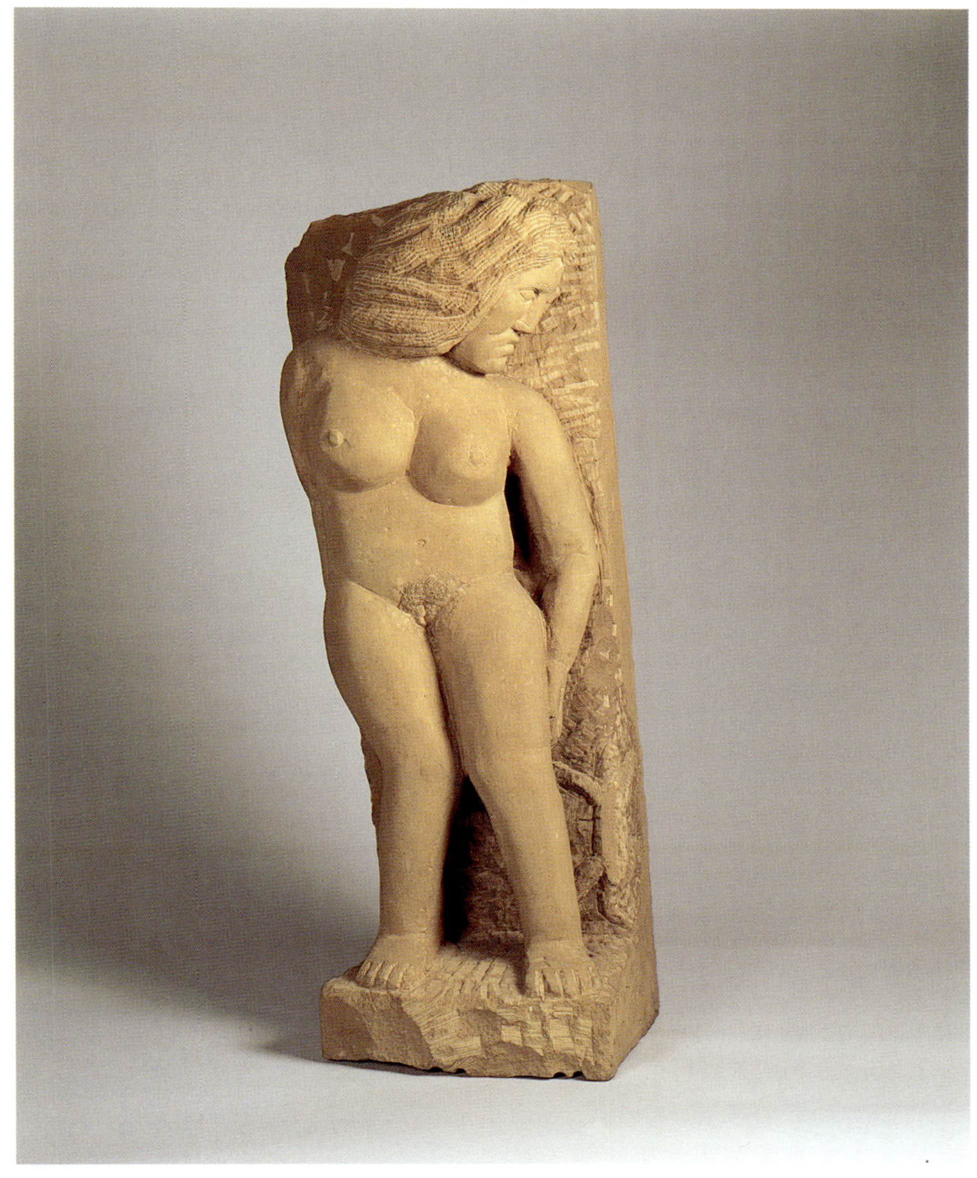

1989.45

Ernest ("Popeye") Reed
Born 1919, Jackson, Ohio; died 1985, Fort Jackson, South Carolina

Female Nude, 1977

Sandstone; 30 x 11 $\frac{3}{8}$ x 9 $\frac{5}{8}$ in.
Gift of Don and Kathy Herron and Museum Acquisition Fund

Barbara Tannenbaum

John William ("Uncle Jack") Dey

Accupuncture Spear Style—Manhunter's [*sic*] is a tongue-in-cheek representation of a skirmish in the infamous, eternal battle between the sexes. Seven women, each bearing a spear and hatchet, chase one man. Just before he runs off the painting's left edge, a redhead gets close enough to plunge her spear into his buttocks, drawing blood. John William Dey (pronounced "dye") reverses the usual relationship between the sexes: the woman sticks a long pointed object into a man as part of a "manhunt." All the participants are naked, which may be appropriate for a sexual conflict, but the nudity is also humorous, given its impracticality for battle—especially in a snow-covered landscape. To confirm the scene's fantastic, ironic nature, Dey wrote its title along the bottom of the image, as he frequently did. He made several "accupuncture" paintings, in each of which the pricking serves to wound rather than heal.

In a short biography Dey wrote in 1975 he claimed that his family had lived in seven different places during his youth, including Akron, Ohio; in actuality he grew up in Phoebus, Virginia. Dropping out of school at age eighteen, he worked at a variety of jobs—among these, trapping and lumberjacking in Maine for two years—before joining the Richmond, Virginia, police force in 1942. Married in 1935, Dey and his wife had no children of their own, but he was a favorite of the neighborhood children, who nicknamed him "Uncle Jack." This was the name Dey used as his signature when he suddenly began painting in 1955. He took up art, with which he had no previous experience, to keep busy following his retirement from the force. Dey, who was only forty-three at the time, had been deemed unfit for service due to psychological problems. His first public exhibition was not until 1973, after which his art began to gain wider attention.

Painting on fiberboard, Dey created smooth surfaces that glisten with the bright, rich colors of enamel, model-airplane paint.[1] Because he used templates to draw animals, his works frequently include the same placid rabbits and circling crows seen here. The template explains their simplified forms, disproportionate scale, and uniformity; though they may be clichés, they are nevertheless reassuringly familiar images from childhood books and school projects. The human figures, seen here only in profile, also have a comforting simplicity, as does the overall design with its repeated forms and rhythms.

Perhaps Dey's major appeal comes from his sense of humor and his skill as a visual storyteller, whether his "stories" are inspired by his own life, popular illustrations, or fantasy. The wintry setting in this work is related to Dey's time in Maine, but the story may come from classical mythology. Are these seemingly single-breasted women the famed Greek Amazons who fought with Hercules? In that context the male figure's long hair and beard may reflect illustrations of ancient times. His skin is considerably darker than that of the women, a convention found on ancient Greek vases. Even the type of image—a battle scene replete with multitudes of naked figures in action—was often used by Renaissance and Baroque painters for mythological subjects and classical history. Of course, in the myths, Hercules won. Although there is no doubt that the women will win this skirmish, Dey leaves it unclear whether this is an act of aggression or vengeance, or simply a case of limited supply and overwhelming demand.

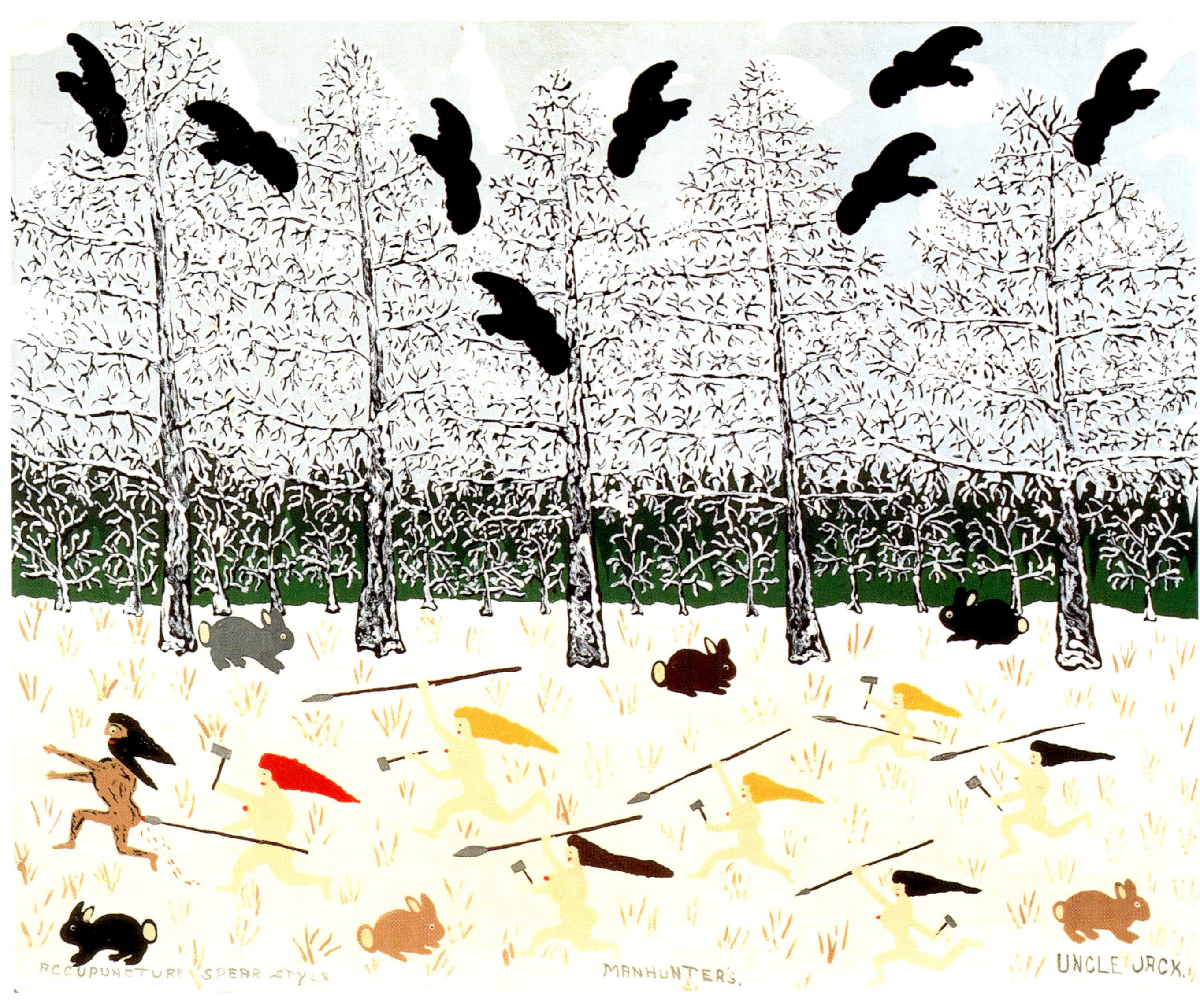

1991.58

John William ("Uncle Jack") Dey
Born 1912, Hampton, Virginia; died 1978, Richmond, Virginia

Accupuncture Spear Style—Manhunter's [*sic*], around 1960–75

Enamel and aluminum paint on fiberboard; 24 $\frac{1}{4}$ × 30 $\frac{1}{8}$ in.
Gift of Herbert Waide Hemphill Jr.

Barbara Tannenbaum

Garry Winogrand

In 1969, Garry Winogrand received a grant from the Guggenheim Foundation to make a photographic study of "the effect of the media on events"; he later titled the resulting series Public Relations.[1] He photographed all sorts of public spectacles, from press conferences and political demonstrations to fancy-dress parties such as the 1969 Centennial Ball at the Metropolitan Museum of Art, where this photograph was taken.

The focal point of the image is an attractive young woman showing off her physical charms in an outrageous costume. A feathery boa, the most prominent feature of her attire, appears to endow her with angel's wings, which likely would be shed by evening's end in the wearer's pursuit of the pleasures of the flesh. Winogrand's camera has captured not only the woman's exuberance but also others' reactions to it; for example, in the awakening of interest (and perhaps desire) on the part of the man at the right side of the image and the surprise (or annoyance) on the face of a woman buffeted by the feathers.

The photographer's own reaction is more ambivalent; his pictures are often "both a slam and an embrace."[2] *Centennial Ball, Metropolitan Museum, New York* certainly has immortalized a woman's youthful beauty. Winogrand included this image in a body of work entitled Women Are Beautiful as well as in his Public Relations series. "Whenever I've seen an attractive woman," he wrote, "I've done my best to photograph her. I don't know if all the women in the photographs are beautiful, but I do know that the women are beautiful in the photographs."[3]

While the image is a paean to the woman's beauty, it also somewhat meanly pokes fun at her exhibitionism and at the evening's excesses. The ball was an important occasion for those with a heightened sense of social performance; people attended it to see and be seen. Winogrand's technique exaggerated the artificiality and sense of facade. Using high-speed film, which allowed him to freeze awkward, but revealing, fleeting expressions, he may have shot five or even twenty exposures of a brief interaction to capture that one decisive moment. Winogrand's use of a flash and a wide-angle lens at a close range flattens the figures so that they appear to be pressed against one another. Physical proximity, however, does not denote intimacy here. These people seem to be strangers, unconnected emotionally to each other and to the photographer.

The practice of photographing strangers on the street or in other public situations without their permission, and often without their knowledge, can be traced back to the late nineteenth century.[4] Initially such shots were considered documentation or photojournalism. By the 1940s fine art photographers purposely began to adopt what had been considered drawbacks to this use of the medium—the awkward or irregular compositions, the grainy image quality—and to turn them into stylistic virtues. In the late 1950s photographers such as Robert Frank (see pp. 134–35) overlaid on this style a distanced, ironic attitude. Similar cynicism and alienation, undoubtedly an aspect of American culture at the time, can be found in the Beat Generation and in "rebels" such as James Dean and the young Marlon Brando.

Winogrand discovered his personal voice when he found street photography. Whatever his degree of physical proximity to his subjects, Winogrand retains a sense of distance in his images. It is not surprising that he should have been interested in the impact of the mass media. In his photographs, the photographer and the viewer are always spectators, never participants.

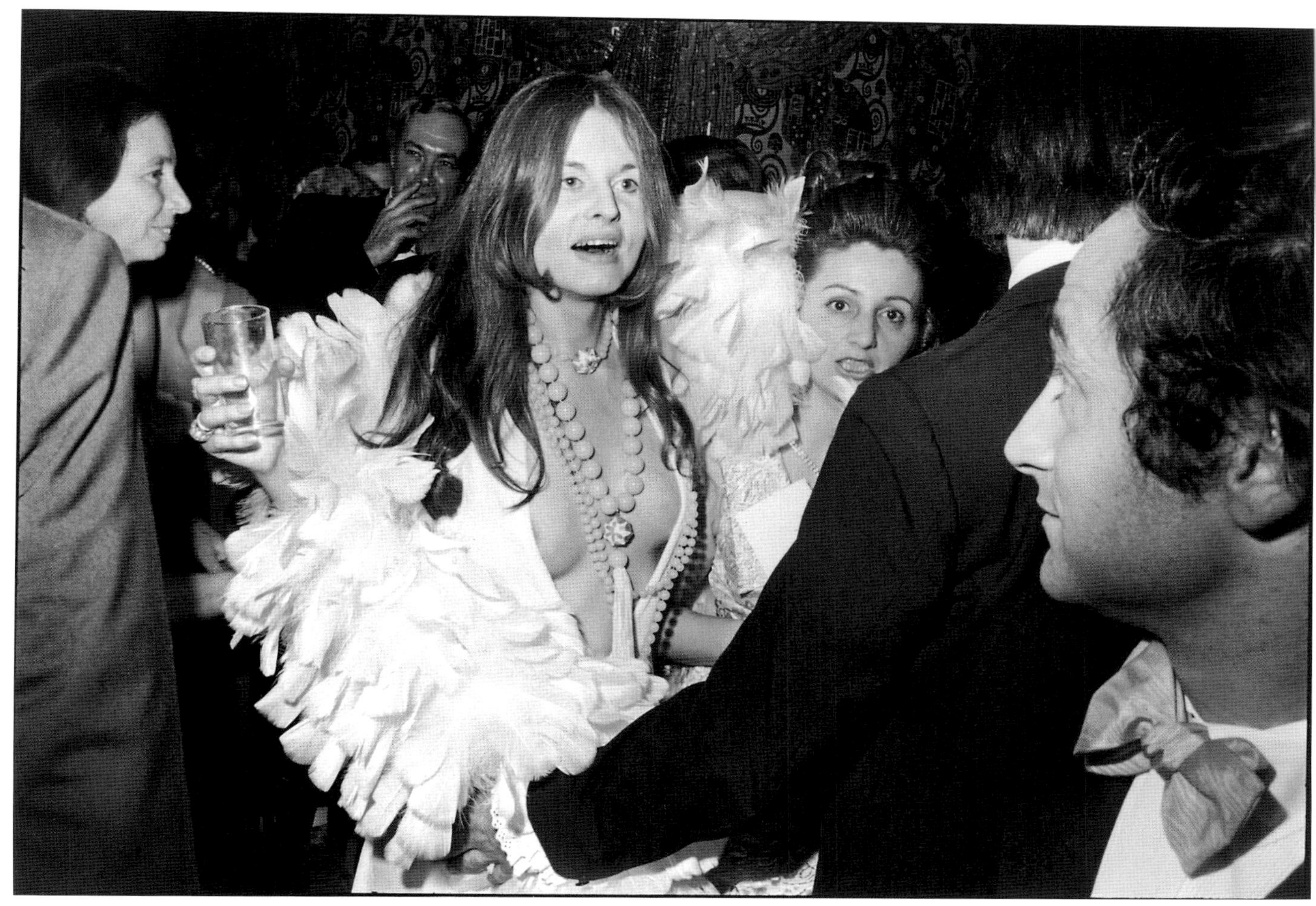

1990.65

Garry Winogrand
Born 1928, New York; died 1984, Tijuana, Mexico

Centennial Ball, Metropolitan Museum, New York, 1969, from the *Women Are Beautiful* portfolio, 1969–80 (printed 1981)[5]

Gelatin silver print; 8 $\frac{7}{8}$ x 13 $\frac{1}{8}$ in.
Gift of Stephen White

Mitchell D. Kahan

George Segal

George Segal depicted the prosaic actions of the human body, seeking to uncover something universal in coarse physical reality and the commonplace. His subjects were most often working-class, perhaps reflecting his immigrant family's humble roots.

Segal attended public schools in the Bronx and Manhattan and later received a B.A. in art education. While pursuing his calling as a painter, he operated a chicken farm in South Brunswick, New Jersey. This farm became legendary when the avant-garde artist Allan Kaprow staged the first "happening" there in 1957, an event that many consider to be the birth of the contemporary discipline known as performance art. The next year, Segal ceased farming and turned to sculpture, modeling his first figures in plaster and eventually converting the chicken coops into a rambling studio.

In the 1960s Segal developed a process of wrapping his models in plaster-soaked bandages. After the wrapping hardened he cut it from the model and reassembled the hollow forms.[1] "Originally, I thought casting would be fast and direct, like photography," the artist explained, "but I found that I had to rework every square inch. I add or subtract detail, create a flow or break up an area by working with creases and angles. I'm shaping forms."[2]

Girl Sitting Against a Wall II is Segal's second version of a female figure seated before a wall and window.[3] It is related to a number of his other nude female figures engaged in private reflection or intimate acts. The apparent intimacy is tempered by aloofness: Akron's figure has a sense of distraction and exhaustion. The emotional quality of such works has often been discussed. Segal's colleague Kaprow described the white figures as "embalmed." "These stark, motionless figures, nearly mummies, frozen in some ordinary hour of their day, remain in an endless trance, blanched of color, communicating with no one."[4]

Unlike idealized marble nudes of the past, *Girl Sitting Against a Wall II* is lumpy and worn. She is not erotic in a predictable way. The girl's exposure is psychological more than sexual; she does not tease or please the spectator. Yet there remains an inescapable sense of voyeurism and eros in presenting any nude subject, which Segal seemed to acknowledge in talking about another nude: "I like her voluptuousness; I like her sturdy construction; I like her massive hips."[5]

Segal typically surrounded his figures with fragments from the real world, creating tableaux of furniture, walls, and signs. Nevertheless, the overall whiteness distances the sculpture from reality. The painted window hints at the world outside while obscuring it from the nude figure, increasing her isolation.

Segal's sculpture possesses many historical resonances, ancient and modern. The process of wrapping bandages around a body recalls ancient burial practices including Egyptian mummification. White plaster, which suggests petrifaction, may remind some of casts made by modern archaeologists from the hollow molds left around the burnt bodies of Vesuvius's ancient victims. And the white nude has, of course, been a mainstay of marble sculpture during several centuries. In this century the painter Edward Hopper pursued a vision similar to Segal's, using architecture and human figures to portray the loneliness and melancholy of American life.

Unlike many contemporary sculptors, Segal did not fabricate by industrial processes. He remained that most traditional type of sculptor, a modeler, employing the pasty white of plaster. Its odd combination of remoteness and tactile physicality points to the timeless dichotomy of all figurative sculpture: it is both realistic and artificial.

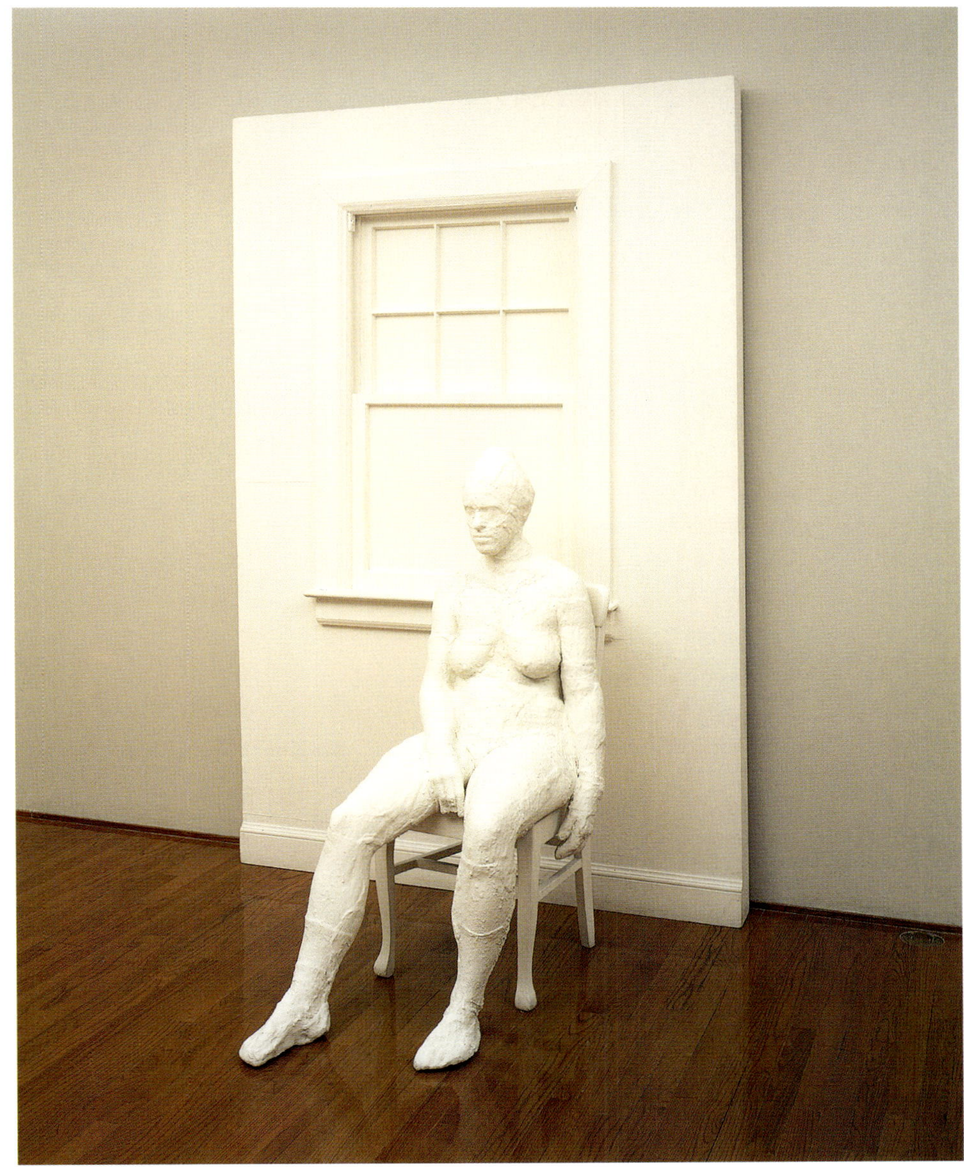

1972.20 a–c

George Segal
Born 1924, New York; died 2000, South Brunswick, New Jersey

Girl Sitting Against a Wall II, 1970

Painted wood, plaster, and glass; 91 x 60 x 40 in.
Purchased with funds from the Fiftieth Anniversary Gala

Mitchell D. Kahan

Chuck Close

Charles Thomas Close has become widely known for portraits that are simultaneously intense and dispassionate. As a child he struggled with dyslexia but received encouragement from his family to pursue his interest in art. While an undergraduate at the University of Washington, Close won a national competition to attend a summer program at Yale University and later enrolled at Yale for graduate study. By 1967 he was settled in New York and experimenting with figure paintings based on his own black-and-white photographs.

Among Close's self-imposed limitations for his paintings of the 1970s are the following: working from photographs, concentrating on the subject's head, centering the image with particular proportions, predetermining canvas size, depicting friends or family members only, using an airbrush, and predetermining the number of colors in his palette. For viewers these decisions deny any excitement over the artist's individual handwork and direct the attention instead to the subject and the process by which the paintings are made.

Close's paintings examine the relationship between photographic reproduction and human sight. Never before has the stationary, monocular quality of photography been so graphically contrasted with the roving nature of human binocular vision.

> I am trying to make it very clear that I am making paintings from photographs and that this is not the way the human eye sees it.... At first I just had everything from the nose back to the cheeks sharp, and that defined the back edge of the focus. Then I decided that I wanted to make it a much shallower depth of field, and have the tip of the nose begin to blur, and I would have a sandwich.[1]

Linda is one of Close's major pieces. Having worked for several years in black and white, he "decided to change the problem," Close explained in the early 1970s. "I decided I would alter one variable and try color. The minimum number of colors to get full color is three.... Every square inch has some of all three."[2] He began by photographing a friend, Linda Rosenkrantz Finch. Color separations in magenta, cyan, and yellow were made from the photograph, as if to reproduce an image for printing in a magazine. From the separations, five dye transfer prints (which are also owned by the Akron Art Museum) were made as a guide. Grids were drawn onto the dye transfers, corresponding to a much larger grid drawn onto the canvas. After covering the canvas with multiple layers of white gesso, Close outlined the head in pencil, then mimicked the three color separations, applying one color at a time—red, blue, and yellow. It took about a year to complete the portrait. The pigment itself is extremely thin, having been dispersed by airbrush on the canvas in tiny droplets. The huge size of the canvas necessitated the use of a motorized lift to reach the top.

In *Linda* Close captures the cold objectivity of photography, revealing pores, creases, and veins to the point of painfulness. But attention to factual description gradually gives way to an appreciation of the work's enormous psychological complexity. Does Close's enlargement heroicize this average, aging face? Or is it a cruel exposure? With her blank stare, is Linda the passive recipient of our gaze or a mammoth and domineering presence surveying our territory? Is the mug-shot format a mere pictorial device, or does it remind us how bureaucracies methodically collect information about individuals? Close's portraits address our fragile sense of identity, first tantalizing our inflated notion of importance, then reminding us that our identities are mere bits of information to be reproduced by color globules and technical procedures.

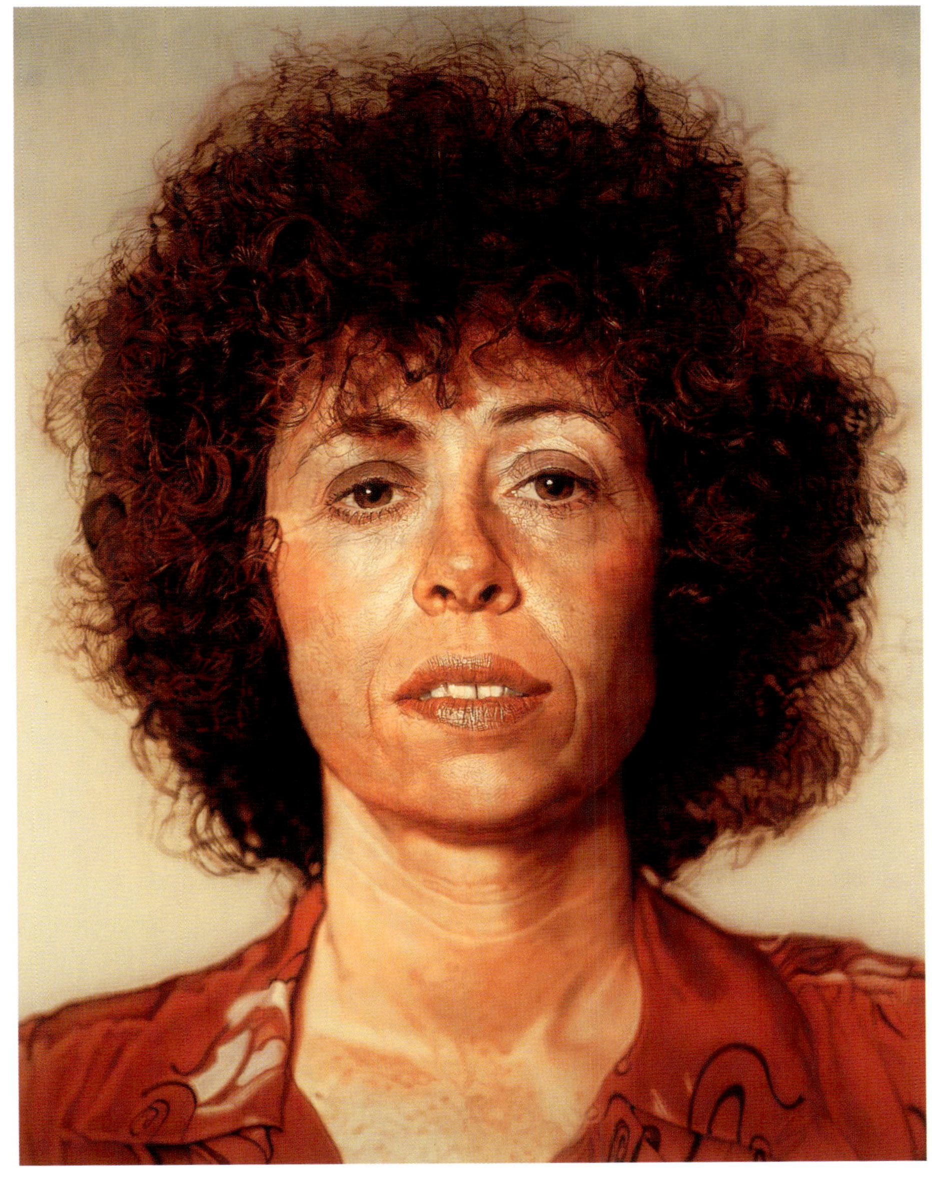

1982.3

Chuck Close
Born 1940, Monroe, Washington; lives New York

Linda, 1975–76

Acrylic and graphite on gessoed linen; 108 x 84 in.
Purchased with funds from an anonymous contribution, an anonymous contribution in honor of Ruth C. Roush, and the Museum Acquisition Fund

Russell Bowman

Philip Pearlstein

In 1941, at the age of seventeen, Philip Pearlstein showed a precocious artistic talent, winning first and third prizes in *Scholastic Magazine's* fourteenth *National High School Art Exhibition* and having his winning entries reproduced in *Life* magazine. He studied both fine art and commercial design at the Carnegie Institute of Art and in 1949 set out in the company of fellow graduate Andy Warhol to seek work as a commercial artist in New York. Soon he was dividing his time between commercial design, painting, and the pursuit of a master's degree in art history from New York University's Institute of Fine Arts.

Pearlstein's first exhibited works in New York were landscape subjects, which were almost lost in a flurry of Abstract Expressionist-inspired painterliness. Following a trip to Italy in 1957 on a Fulbright scholarship the artist tightened his brushwork and joined a group of painters who met regularly to draw from the model. His first figure painting was shown in 1962, the year he published an article in *ARTnews* entitled "Figure Paintings Today Are Not Made in Heaven." The article outlined the modernist proscriptions against illusionism:

> It seems madness on the part of any painter educated in 20th century modes of picture-making to take as his subject the naked human figure, conceived as a self-contained entity possessed of its own dignity, existing in an inhabitable space, viewed from a single vantage point.[1]

Of course, this defines precisely the program he had set for himself.

By 1963 Pearlstein was painting larger scale works in which he recorded the model in his studio in a very direct, almost clinical manner, using restrained color and brushwork. At this time the hallmarks of his style all combined to create a startlingly different "realist" look in which his subjects are shown from a close and "tilted" single viewpoint, and strongly axial compositions paradoxically emphasize both the recession of forms into space and the flat surface of the canvas. Forms are sharply cropped at the canvas's edge, and the three lights of the studio setup cast multiple shadows. Pearlstein's innovations related to those of other American artists known as the New Realists.[2] Their art—especially Pearlstein's—had singular connections to the antiromantic, "mechanical" attitudes and techniques of Pop Art and Minimalism developing simultaneously in New York.

Model with Legs Up is a product of Pearlstein's full maturity and remains one of his most elegant compositions. His works of the 1970s and into the 1980s might almost be described as sensuous, although not in the sense associated with older manifestations of the reclining nude. *Model* employs typical Pearlstein methods—extreme foreshortening, linear composition, surprising cropping, and restrained color. In addition there is the dramatic vertical sweep of the model's legs set against the diagonal of the studio baseboard, the complexity of skin tone and textile pattern, and the almost playful treatment of the shadows falling on the wall. For all its formal rectitude, *Model* has a certain elegance of contour and warmth of tone less evident in other works by the artist.

Pearlstein's works of the last decade could be said to have entered a more convoluted, "Mannerist" phase, with more spatial complexity, rich color patterns, and details of studio props. In fact, Mannerism—in the classic sense of sixteenth-century Italian painting, with its spatial thrusts, sharp contours, and hard, patterned surfaces—has been cited as a possible influence on his work.[3] This connection to earlier painting points to the full relevance of Pearlstein's art in that he has managed to extend both the modernist tradition and the tradition of realist art since the Renaissance.

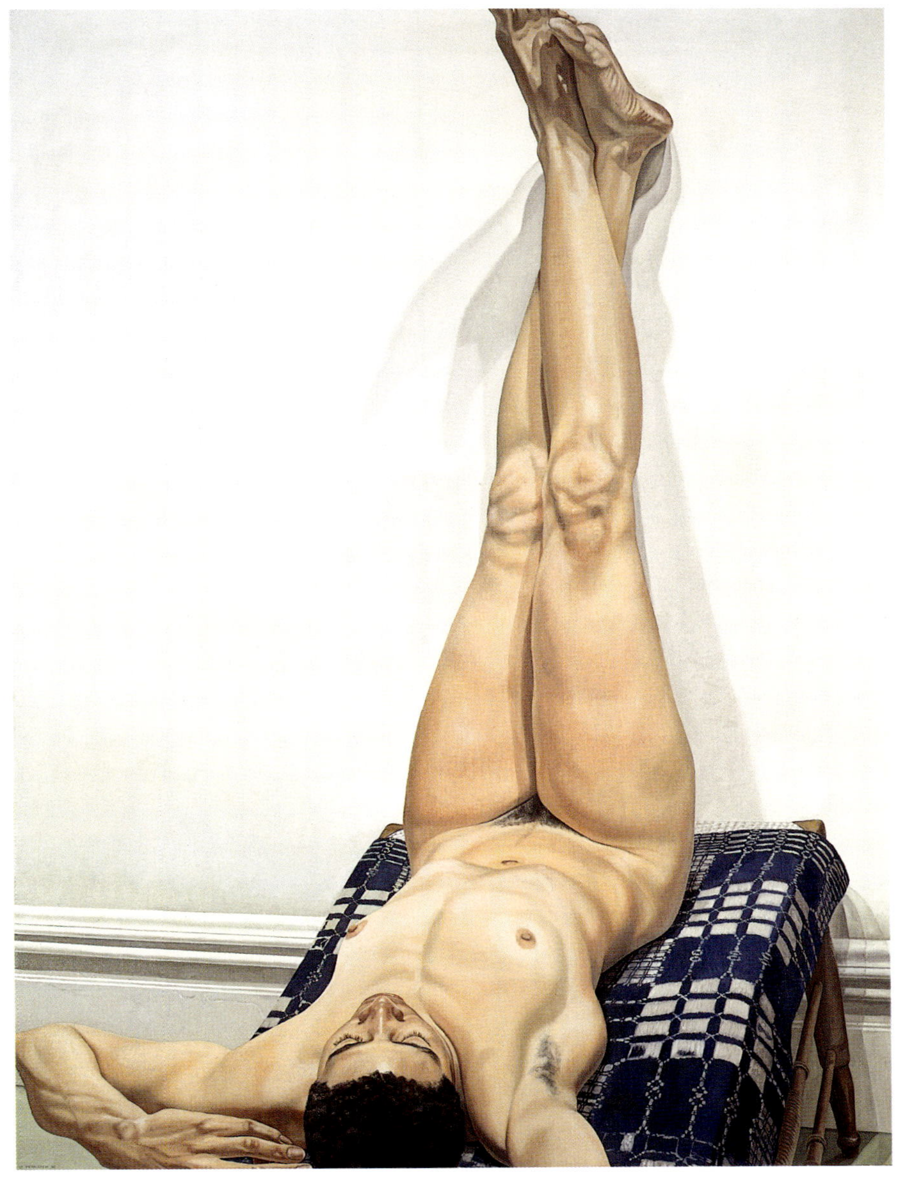

1980.46

Philip Pearlstein
Born 1924, Pittsburgh, Pennsylvania; lives New York

Model with Legs Up, 1975

Oil on linen; 72 x 54 in.
Purchased with funds raised by the Masked Ball 1955–63, by exchange

Mona Hadler

Helen Frankenthaler

Helen Frankenthaler's paintings radiate a powerful atmospheric light. According to the artist, "It's more than light as an element. It's a metaphysical, esthetic light. Every work of art that works, on paper or canvas, happens to have that common denominator. It is a combination of the artist, the medium and the magic—elaborate magic."[1] The "magic" of Frankenthaler's art has continued to be the focus of critical acclaim since her major breakthrough in the early 1950s. Her catalytic work, which grew out of Abstract Expressionism, became seminal for the Color Field artists of the 1960s, such as Washington painter Morris Louis (see pp. 126–27).

Frankenthaler's father was a New York Supreme Court Judge. Growing up in New York, she was nurtured in a learned and cultivated environment. In the early 1950s she formed a friendship with the prominent art critic Clement Greenberg and was catapulted into the city's heady world of Abstract Expressionism.

Frankenthaler's technical breakthrough occurred in 1952 in the painting *Mountains and Sea*. After visiting Jackson Pollock and viewing his technique of pouring and dripping paint on canvas spread on the floor, Frankenthaler laid down a large piece of unprimed cotton duck, thinned her oil paint to the consistency of watercolor, and applied it to the canvas. This "soak-stain" technique was borrowed by a number of her contemporaries, in part because of its unique sense of space. The stained image appears to be neither in front of nor illusionistically behind the picture plane but is literally one with the canvas. Her paintings appear both flat and filled with atmosphere at the same time.

Frankenthaler continued to work with the canvas on the floor. Like her Abstract Expressionist predecessors, she formed the image spontaneously during the process of painting and exerted a high degree of control over the medium, making sophisticated judgments in relation to color, edge, and the cropping of the borders. In *Wisdom* the paint areas appear to flow naturally with curving rhythmic lines, while the central salmon-colored shape descends slowly and asymmetrically into the lower region of the canvas. Organized in three color areas, with subtle variations of primary colors, the painting is clearly controlled. The dominant shape establishes a central focus to the composition. The bold, simplified structural language of the painting relates it to new artistic currents of the times. In the early 1960s Frankenthaler switched from oil-based paints to acrylics, the paint used in *Wisdom*. Acrylics flood rather than stain the canvas, eliminate the turpentine halos sometimes seen with oil paints, and allow sharper lines and crisper contrasts.

Like the Abstract Expressionists, Frankenthaler titles her works after they are finished, using an associative process. That she titles her art suggests that to her content continues to be significant. Often her titles evoke nature, but *Wisdom* suggests a mental rather than a physical landscape. This title harks back to the psychological and mental content of much Abstract Expressionist and Surrealist art before it. The accidental process, practiced to different degrees by both Frankenthaler and Pollock, has its roots in the Surrealist technique of psychic automatism. Accident, and ultimately abstraction, are in part products of the unconscious. Referring to a 1964 painting she said: "It's called *Interior Landscape* because that's what it is—an interior landscape—an abstract picture."[2] The magic of Frankenthaler's radiant canvases is that they attest to the "wisdom" of her art and the enduring meanings to be found in abstraction.

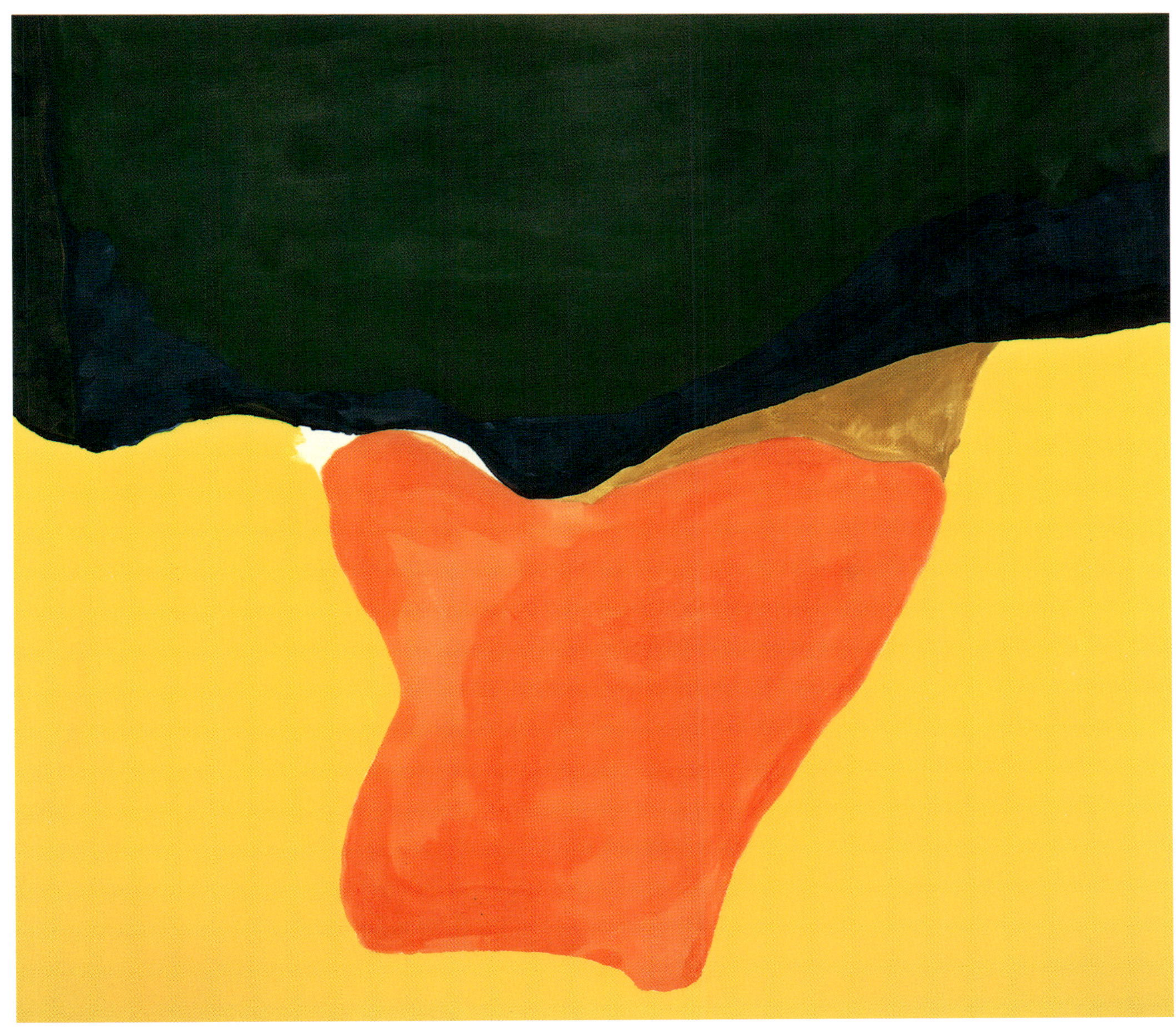

1978.39

Helen Frankenthaler
Born 1928, New York; lives New York

Wisdom, 1969

Acrylic on canvas; 94 x 112 in.
Gift of the Mary S. and Louis S. Myers Family Collection
in honor of Mrs. Galen Roush

Jeffrey Grove

Anthony Caro

Anthony Caro is one of the twentieth century's most influential sculptors. Knighted in 1971, he has been credited with single-handedly reinventing the look of British sculpture in the 1960s. Caro brought abstract sculpture to a new place in the modern age by completely eliminating the traditional base and creating works that occupy the viewer's space in an aggressive manner. Commenting on his approach, he has stated that he likes to work "at the edge of the impossible."

In the winter of 1972–73 Caro was invited to work at the Ripamonte Factory in Veduggio, Italy. Famous for his prodigious output, the artist, with the help of his assistant, turned out twelve sculptures in ten days. At the factory Caro found a quantity of irregularly shaped, soft steel offcuts or scraps. He arranged these components into relatively basic planar configurations and secured them to bases with simple joints. In many of these works, the naturally contoured sheets of steel were presented vertically, their upright nature altering the viewer's relationship from one of observation to one of confrontation.

Stylistically these sculptures are a radical departure from Caro's earlier work, which was characterized by geometric planes jutting into space at all angles. Those animated, architectural works—composed of precisely machined and crisply milled segments welded or riveted together and painted in bright, primary colors—were much more "theatrical" than the quieter shapes Caro initiated in the Veduggio series.

The unusual, melting forms of the Veduggio sculptures border on the organic or biomorphic, and "even carry a suggestion of geological eccentricity...of rocks [or] the exposed strata of cliffs."[2] They also suggest objects such as mirrors, gateways, and paintings. Indeed, comparisons between *Veduggio Wash* and abstract paintings are inevitable. Whereas Frank Stella transformed the properties of painting into sculpted surfaces (see pp. 202–3), Caro may have been attempting to transform traditional sculpture by imbuing it with the concerns of abstract painting. It is no accident that the Veduggio works recall the lyrical abstraction of Helen Frankenthaler's paintings (see pp. 174–75). In fact, Frankenthaler had worked in Caro's studio only a few months before he commenced the Veduggio series. The organic forms created by her soak-and-stain method clearly resonate in the soft and irregular profile of *Veduggio Wash.*

The Veduggio series marks a transition in Caro's development. Finding the unfinished "drawn" edges of the steel sheets uniquely expressive, Caro left their surfaces unpainted, protected only by a thin coat of varnish; thus he amplified the visual and physical properties of the unfinished steel. Caro has maintained that "sculpture and the making of sculpture is 'of the body'; physical; no matter how abstract, it has to have a 'felt' relationship to our bodies."[3] With his emphasis on organic metaphors and more tranquil forms in *Veduggio Wash,* Caro seems to be encouraging a different type of interaction—one that invites an emotional as well as physical engagement between the viewer and the sculpture.

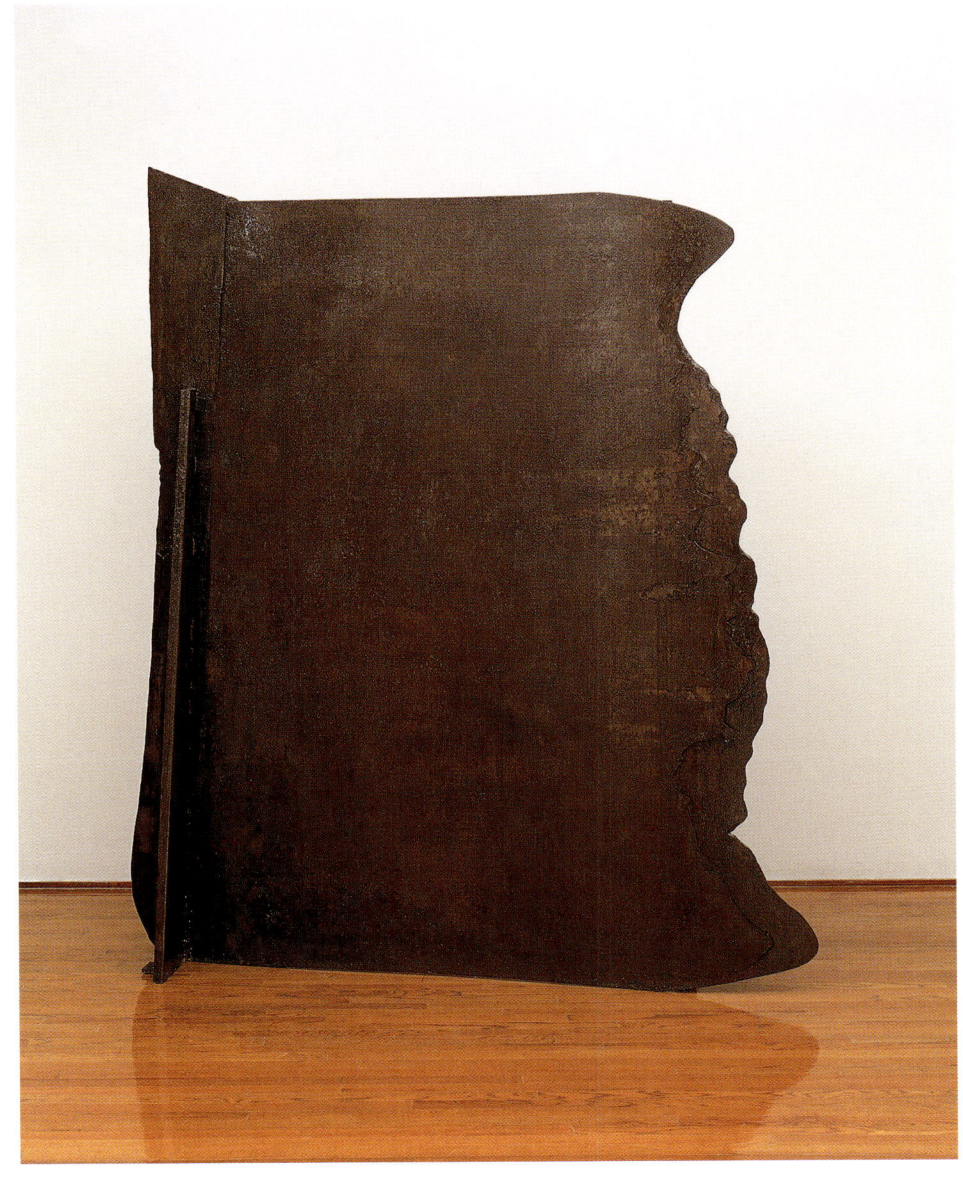

1991.116

Anthony Caro
Born 1924, New Malden, Surrey, England; lives London

Veduggio Wash, 1973

Steel; 82 x 72 x 20 ½ in.
Gift of Mary S. and Louis S. Myers

Sachi Yanari-Rizzo

Alma W. Thomas

A pioneer of her generation, Alma Woodsey Thomas was an African American who allowed neither age, race, nor gender to become barriers in her pursuit of a career as an artist and educator. In 1924 she was the first graduate of Howard University's art department. Thomas became a strong presence in the art scene in Washington, D.C., where she spent most of her life.[1] Among her many accomplishments was the vice-presidency of the Barnett Aden Gallery, the city's first art gallery privately owned by African Americans and notable for its presentation of racially integrated shows.

Thomas earned her living teaching art for thirty-five years in the Washington public schools. "People always want to cite me for my color paintings," she said, "but I would much rather be remembered for helping to lay the foundation of children's lives. I tried to develop them culturally and expand their perspectives."[2] It was only after her retirement in 1960, at age sixty-nine, that she finally was able to give painting her undivided attention. Thomas garnered national recognition in 1972, when she became the first African American woman to have a solo exhibition at the Whitney Museum of American Art.

In the mid-1960s, Thomas began painting impressions of natural phenomena in a highly individualized, abstract idiom. She abandoned oil for the newly developed acrylic paints, which were also the preferred medium of her contemporaries: Washington Color School painters Morris Louis (see pp. 126–27) and Gene Davis. Thomas's dark, heavily painted abstractions of the 1950s were suddenly replaced with explosions of color formed by irregular dabs of paint organized into regularly spaced strips.

In the early 1970s Thomas began to limit the number of colors within a painting in order to further explore color harmonies and contrasts. In *Pond—Spring Awakening* vertical strokes of gray paint tinged with faint casts of green and blue are tightly woven to create a soft gray expanse—an unusual color selection for Thomas. Radiating from behind the gray is a mixture of reds, yellows, and oranges that seem to glow.

For Thomas, color and light were the foremost elements of her paintings. She often quoted Bauhaus teacher Johannes Itten's text on color theory: "Color is life. Light is the mother of color. Light reveals to us the spirit and living soul of the world through colors."[3] Indeed, because of this primacy of color and her preference for geometry and clarity of design, Thomas is often associated with the Washington Color School. However, while the concerns of Louis and Davis were primarily formal, Thomas's work stemmed from another source: nature.

The titles of her paintings frequently refer to flowers in bloom, leaves on the trees, or the seasons, but usually not to specific locations or individual plants. Explaining the critical inspiration leading up to her mature paintings Thomas credited the hollyhock tree outside her kitchen window, which produced colorful patterns and shadows that were transformed endlessly by the sunlight and wind. Washington's renowned gardens and arboretums provided additional stimulation for her.

The desire to present impressions of the beauty and ever-changing moods of nature sustained Thomas's interest for the rest of her life. Former Akron Art Museum director Robert Doty insightfully summarized Thomas's paintings: "The possibilities of interpretation and association are so strong that her paintings maintain a strategic balance between an arrangement of abstract color shapes on a two-dimensional surface and the imagery of a common but exalting experience."[4]

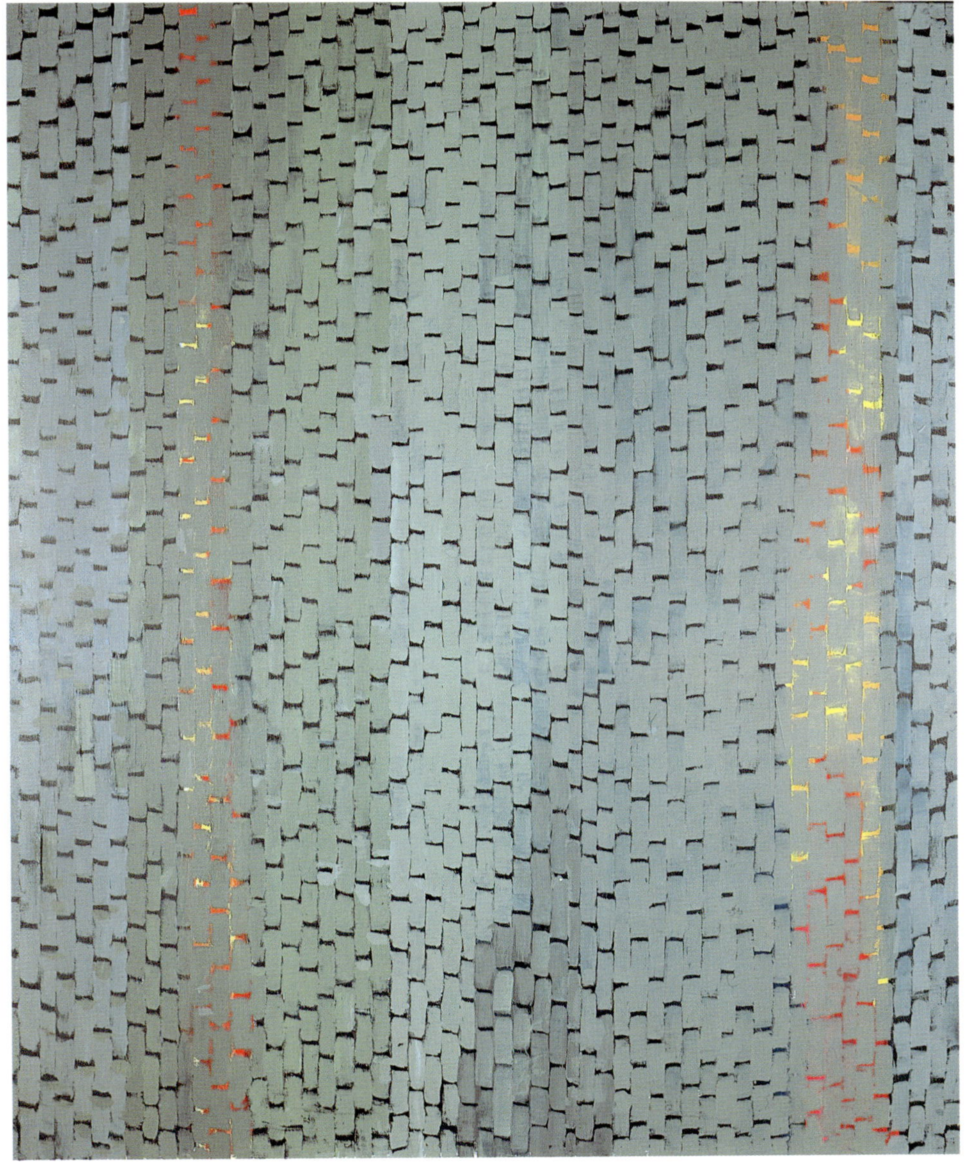

1976.32

Alma W. Thomas
Born 1891, Columbus, Georgia; died 1978, Washington, D.C.

Pond—Spring Awakening, 1972

Acrylic on canvas; 68 × 55 in.
Gift of Mr. and Mrs. David K. Anderson

Mitchell D. Kahan

Sol LeWitt

Best known for his variations of three-dimensional grids and cubes, Sol LeWitt generates rationally plotted structures that range from refined simplicity to hypnotic complexity. He has pursued a wide variety of artistic activities, including book design, printmaking, and photography, consistently approaching each from a conceptual starting point.

LeWitt studied art at Syracuse University, graduating with a B.F.A. in 1949. In New York in the early 1960s, he and other artists developed an approach to art that stressed rigorous design, geometric abstraction, and a rejection of emotional and spiritual content. By 1965 LeWitt had executed his first sculpture based on modular variations of open cubes. In the late 1960s he began working in steel and aluminum as well as wood; most of the sculptures began as drawings in his notebooks. LeWitt also developed a new way of making extremely large drawings. The collector would purchase a set of written instructions and a documentary photograph of a prior installation of the piece, from which LeWitt or others could execute large drawings directly on walls. One such drawing was temporarily installed at the Akron Art Institute in 1980.

Floor Piece #2 is a single cube that has been subdivided into nine smaller cubes along each edge, creating a three-dimensional grid. Eighty-three of the component cubes have been removed from three levels of the central upper section. *Floor Piece #2* is one of eighteen related sculptures—ranging from cubes and pyramids to other forms—all based on the common factor of having their width, depth, and height formed from nine small cubes adding up to 43¼ inches.

LeWitt's cubes belong to two art movements: Minimalism and Conceptualism. "In conceptual art the idea or concept is the most important aspect of the work," LeWitt insisted in 1967; "all of the planning and decisions are made beforehand and the execution is a perfunctory affair. The idea becomes a machine that makes the art."[1] This logically led LeWitt to act as a designer of works made by outside fabricators or assistants.

His structures depend only on basic arithmetic, not number theory or advanced mathematics. Though strongly attracted to rational systems, LeWitt believes that "Ideas are discovered by intuition."[2] He recognizes the inherent contradiction that art based on ideas must still adopt a physical form that viewers regard as an "art object." Accepting this, LeWitt tries to downplay the materials, painting all his three-dimensional works white and giving them flat uninteresting surfaces to reduce any concentration on their visual properties. Risking visual boredom, he creates objects that invite intellectual engagement.

LeWitt's work presents stimulating oppositions. The openness of the grids provides an airiness even when the works are large. Inside and outside are simultaneously exposed. Finite two-dimensional lines create three-dimensional forms and the illusion of infinity. There is both stasis and the sensation of movement. LeWitt is well aware of the contradictions in his work between logic and intuition, between his stated emphasis on concepts and the austere elegance of his objects. His approach is to follow a personal aesthetic, not rigid theory, a course that places him in the realm of art rather than science.

Unlike other abstract artists of his generation, LeWitt feels that his sculptures are not mere visual facts but have a meaning beyond their appearance. "Those who understand art only by what it looks like often do not understand very much at all," he asserts.[3] "Conceptual artists are mystics rather than rationalists. They leap to conclusions that logic cannot reach."[4]

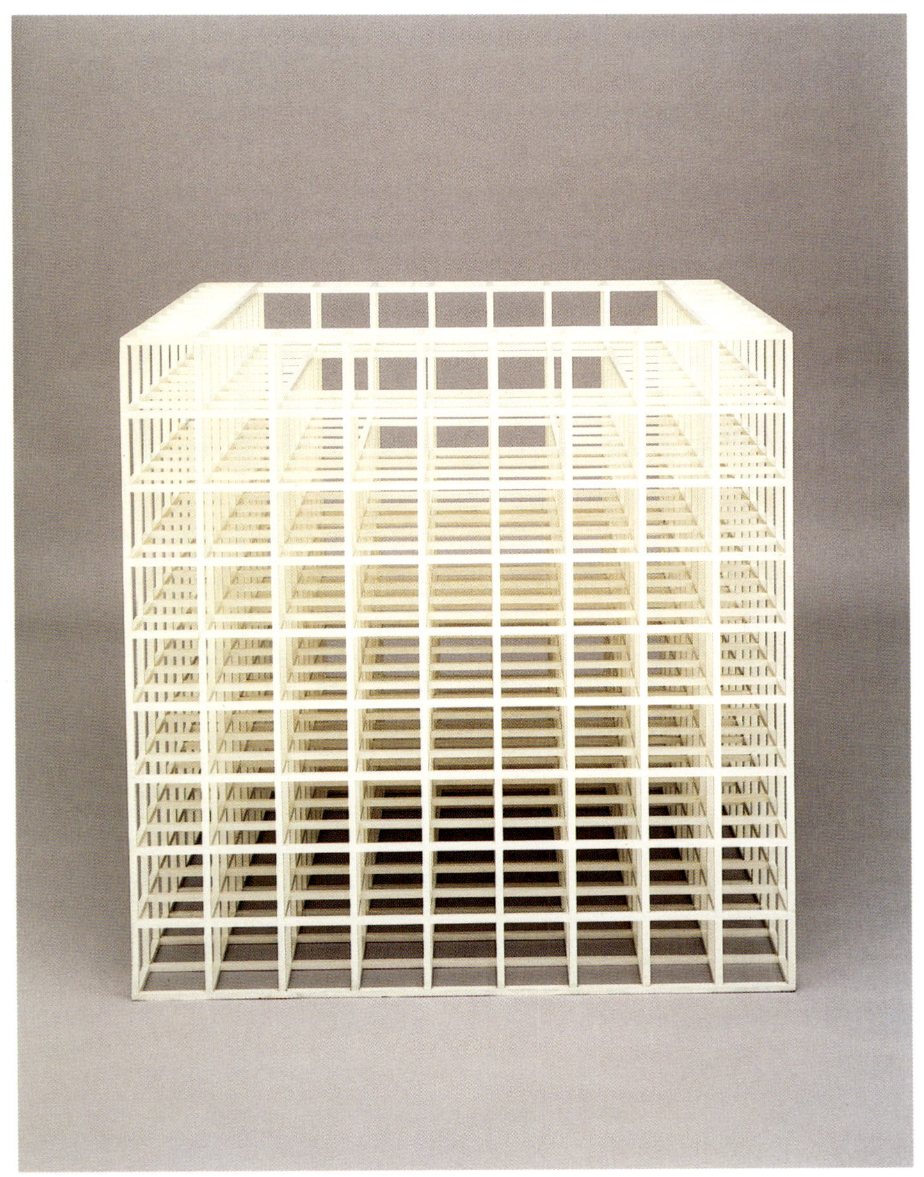

1980.47

Sol LeWitt
Born 1928, Hartford, Connecticut; lives Chester, Connecticut

Floor Piece #2, 1976

Painted wood; 43 1/4 x 43 1/4 x 43 1/4 in.
Purchased with funds from Diana McKean Wallace, by exchange

Mitchell D. Kahan

Jackie Winsor

"Art making is about taking parts and making wholes," Jackie Winsor has explained.[1] Her painstakingly constructed cubes, spheres, and other geometric forms breathe rich life into common construction materials and address compelling human desires for order and unity. She imbues rope and copper, concrete and wood lathe with subtle and sensual effects.

Vera Jacqueline Winsor was born in the provincial capital of the Island of Newfoundland, which later became Canada's easternmost province. In 1952 her father, a self-trained engineer, moved the family to Boston, where Winsor took classes at local art schools. After undergraduate and graduate studies in art, she moved to New York in 1967. She has journeyed to China, India, and Tibet, where she has found both philosophical and spiritual affinities. Her many international exhibitions include two solo shows at the Akron Art Museum.

The process of creating an object is almost as important to Winsor as the finished piece. Unlike many contemporary sculptors, she eschews machine fabrication and working with foundries and factories. Instead, like a traditional craftsperson, she makes objects by hand, investing them with the memory of human touch no matter what material is used. Rarely are her works more than three feet square. Though some may weigh up to two thousand pounds and take several years to complete, they are modest objects, not monuments.

The wrapping of coils to form spheres in *#2 Copper* is typical of Winsor's earliest works, which were formed of rope or carefully bundled balls of twine. *#2 Copper* also forms a cube. Winsor's longtime exploration of cubical structures owes a debt to the Minimalism of Donald Judd (see pp. 150–51) and Sol LeWitt (see pp. 180–81), but her simple forms are metaphorical, not analytical. Winsor's cubes, for example, are about joining six sides into perfect union. She explains that art "is not about the object *per se;* it is a vehicle through which you get to express and experience" other things that are elusive, mysterious, and sustaining.

Winsor rarely produces studies or sketches but visualizes the objects in her mind before commencing. She spends much time searching for appropriate materials. "Just as friends are pulled to you by some magnetic energy that matches up with yours, so materials are drawn to you." Artist and materials "are in partnership with each other, involved in a kind of dance in which no one is leading and no one is following."

In *#2 Copper,* there are two types of materials: one an inorganic, shiny metal, the other an organic, matte wood. Thick #2 gauge copper wire is wound into seventy-two balls on thirty-six wooden staves that are fifty-one inches tall and one inch thick. The heaviness of the copper plays off the lightness of the airy grid. The round shapes contrast with the square ends of the sticks as well as the cubic form of the overall sculpture. This complexity unites into an overall form that is impressive in its calm and silence. The sense of mass and weight, no less than the earth tones of the materials, resonate a sensation of being grounded and complete.

The art world of the 1970s was newly politicized by feminist activity, one aspect of which sought to reestablish an appreciation for the hand labor of women as opposed to industrial fabrication. To rough construction materials typically associated with masculinity Winsor introduced the surprising handwork of winding copper wire into a ball, as if it were a skein of yarn. This union of masculine and feminine sensibilities results in a meditative equilibrium that approaches the spiritual.

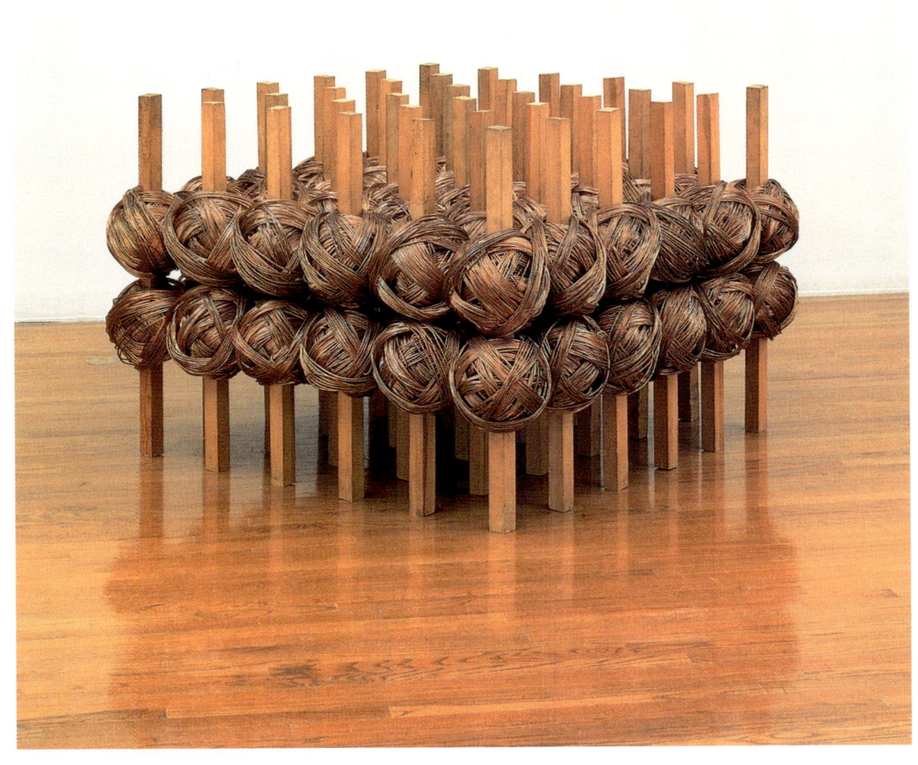

1983.4

Jackie Winsor
Born 1941, St. John's Island, Newfoundland; lives New York

#2 Copper, 1976

Wood and copper; 34 ½ x 51 x 51 in.
Purchased with funds from Mr. and Mrs. Raymond C. Firestone, by exchange

Barbara Tannenbaum

Claes Oldenburg

Akron's former role as a center for rubber manufacturing inspired Claes Oldenburg's *Inverted Q*, but it is to Mary and Louis Myers that the work owes it existence. In 1972 they invited Oldenburg to Akron and asked him to propose a sculpture for a park adjoining the downtown library. A fan of Goodyear's giant balloons in Macy's Thanksgiving Day Parade in New York, Oldenburg was thrilled by the possibility of collaborating with the rubber companies.[1]

The artist was already celebrated for his Pop Art transformations of commonplace objects into a wide variety of media, from drawing and watercolor to plaster, steel, and cloth. Born in Sweden, Oldenburg was raised mostly in Chicago, where his father was a consular official. After attending Yale, he studied painting and drawing at the Art Institute of Chicago. Moving to New York in 1956, Oldenburg became involved with "happenings," a new type of performance art. In 1959 he began to produce sculpture, the medium for which he is now best known.

For the Akron project Oldenburg considered three objects: a cap; an alphabet Good Humor bar; and, his final choice, a "Q." The letter was a perfect fit for a library setting and, with its tirelike shape, was clearly appropriate for Akron and its rubber industry. Oldenburg had first drawn an inverted "Q" in 1968 as part of a tongue-in-cheek proposal to the City of Los Angeles for buildings and monuments in the shape of colossal letters. "An inverted position seemed necessary," he wrote, "because a Q with its tail buried wouldn't be a Q at all."[2]

Multiple meanings and oppositions are characteristic of Oldenburg's images. His *Q* inverts, enlarges, and metamorphoses what is usually a tiny, common, two-dimensional image into a huge three-dimensional object. Oldenburg wanted the sculpture to appear soft, inflated, and light, even though it would be heavy.[3] He felt that *Q* needed to have "its own meaning apart from the context of its Akron surroundings. For example, its reference to the artist's body" (an early sketch is titled *Navel-Akron*).[4] To some viewers, *Q* suggests erotic areas of human anatomy or the body of an imaginary animal.

To arrive at *Q's* final form Oldenburg spent over two years meeting with researchers and technicians at Firestone, Goodyear, and other firms; sketching; making clay and plaster models; and even casting plaster in canvas sacks sewn in the shape of a "Q." In 1975 eighteen-inch models of the final *Q* were cast at Firestone in a synthetic rubber. Much to everyone's disappointment, the costs and technical difficulties of producing a six-foot rubber version were deemed prohibitive.[5]

By this time another sculpture had been found for the library park, but Oldenburg was unwilling to abandon the project. In 1976 he had the large *Q* cast in concrete and covered with a clear, smooth coating. The Myerses bought the first work in the edition to donate to the Akron Art Institute, which organized an exhibition about its genesis.[6]

In 1986, after years of exposure to the elements, *Q* needed refinishing. At the artist's request it was repainted the same shade of purplish pink that graces the other three works in the edition. The color evokes childhood memories of rubber balls and bubble gum and also enhances the references to the human body. Whether clear or pink, *Inverted Q*—the sculpture based on the city's history—has been one of the best-loved works in the museum's collection.

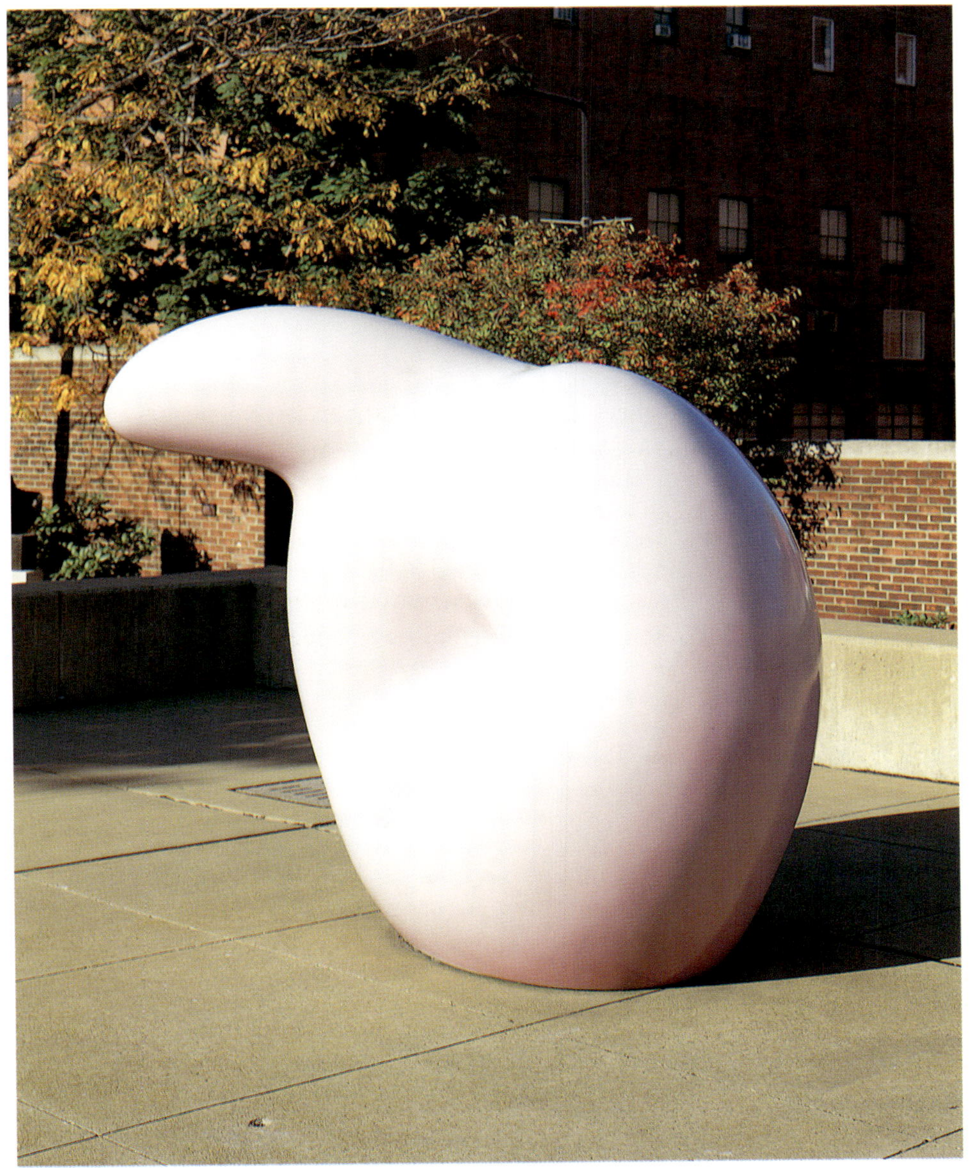

1977.20

Claes Oldenburg
Born 1929, Stockholm, Sweden; lives New York

Inverted Q, 1976

Painted cast concrete; 72 x 70 x 63 in.
Gift of Mary S. and Louis S. Myers

Jeffrey Grove

Mark di Suvero

Since the early 1970s, Mark di Suvero's mammoth constructions of cut and welded steel, recycled timbers, and industrial castoffs have become familiar fixtures on the urban landscape. Unlike much large-scale public sculpture, however, di Suvero's works are not lofty memorials or emblems of civic pride. Instead, using materials and production techniques familiar to tradesmen, mechanics, and factory workers, di Suvero strives to make "the kind of art that joins technology to people's knowledge."[1]

The construction of these immense, kinetic works relies as much on di Suvero's skills as an engineer, metallurgist, and weatherman as on his artistic talents. Most of his sculpture, including *Eagle Wheel*, could not have been realized without the use of cranes, forklift trucks, and welding torches—tools indigenous to the building trades but less common among the fine arts. Likewise, the "studios" where di Suvero and his teams of assistants create these formidable works are actually outdoor sites that more closely resemble industrial scrap heaps than artists' ateliers. He has three such properties: one along the East River in Long Island City, near Manhattan's shipyards; one in Chalon-sur-Saône, France, where he lived from 1971 to 1975 in protest to United States involvement in Vietnam; and one in Petaluma, California, near Berkeley, where he grew up.[2]

Di Suvero is noted for his improvisational approach to sculpture. Using a crane, which he refers to as his "paintbrush,"[3] he frequently revises a composition even after it is initially completed. *Eagle Wheel* is an extreme example of this practice. Originally created in 1976, *Eagle Wheel* was acquired by the Oakland Museum in California in 1977. When that museum opened a new building in 1978, they decided to acquire a larger di Suvero sculpture and *Eagle Wheel* was "traded-in" toward the purchase of another work. It was next exhibited in 1980 (shortly before the Akron Art Museum acquired it), but in the interim di Suvero had altered it significantly, adding four long sections of I-beams, which now connect the two separate bases.[4]

More modestly scaled than much of di Suvero's sculpture, *Eagle Wheel* is nonetheless an archetypal example. It is painted in the artist's signature color, industrial orange. The intense color, commonly associated with caution or safety, unifies the disparate elements and transforms the whole to art. At once oddly balanced and elegantly off-kilter, *Eagle Wheel* joins together a panoply of opposing forms—sharp angles and graceful curves; flat, platelike segments; and protuberant spheres. Most of the parts are vaguely familiar: a bisected flotation buoy (often thought to be a wrecking ball) coupled with a giant chain; an immense, suspended flywheel resurrected from an old sawmill in northern California; and sleek I-beams that might have been used to build a skyscraper.

Di Suvero's resolutely abstract sculptures are carefully designed compositions that balance an unruly jumble of dissonant parts, often incorporating potentially precarious mobile elements. For instance, in *Eagle Wheel* the flywheel swings freely and rotates on a turnbuckle. Although this appeals to di Suvero's egalitarian ambitions—he intends his work to be played upon, crawled over and under, or even swung upon—unfortunately, it is at odds with the museum's mandates to preserve works of art and to safeguard visitors from accidental injury. Di Suvero once claimed that "everything has a center of gravity.... I have to find it, find the balance."[5] Exhibited within the confines of the Myers Sculpture Courtyard, *Eagle Wheel* nonetheless escapes its boundaries to engage in a visual dialogue with Akron's industrial landscape on the horizon.

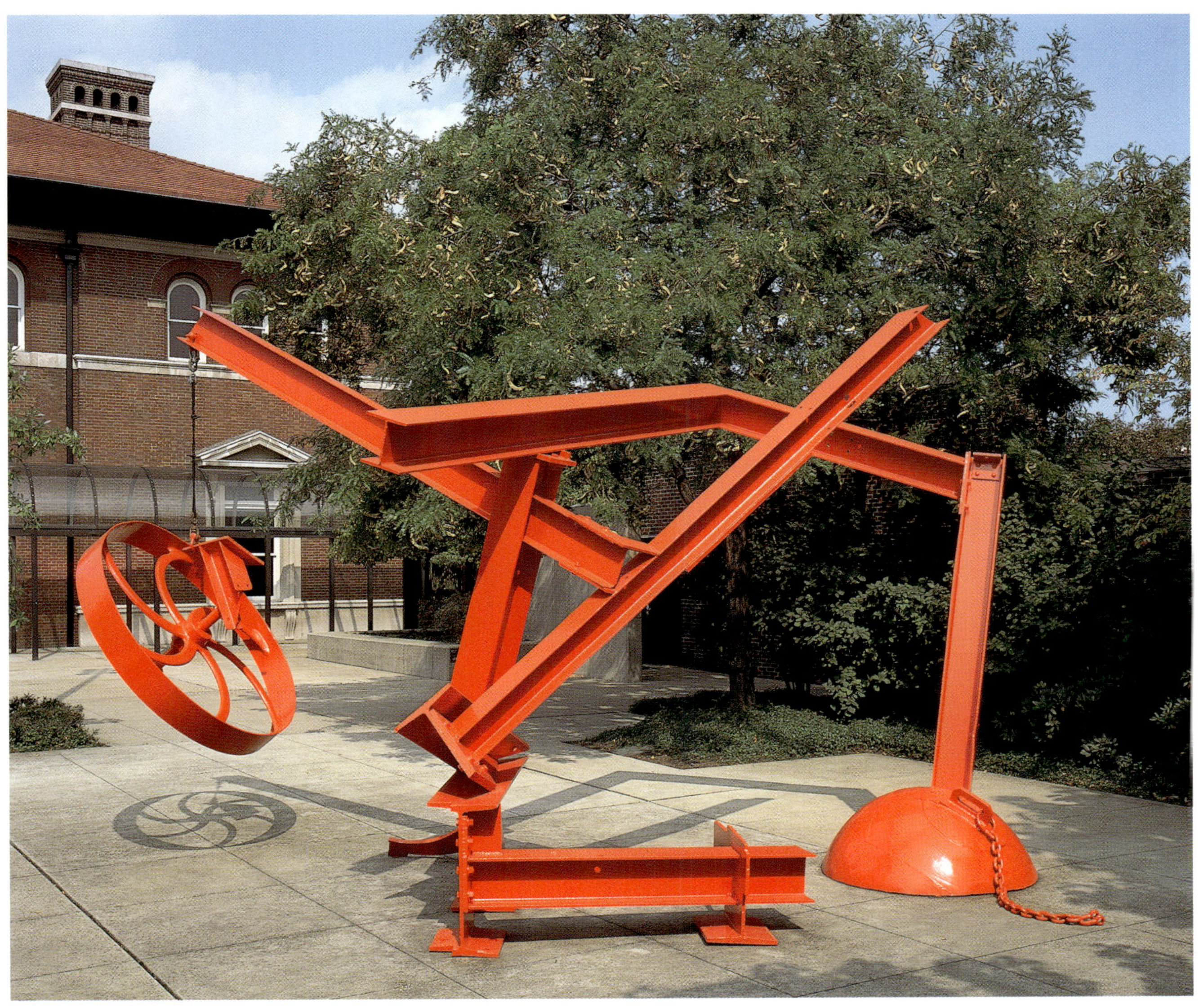

1980.48

Mark di Suvero
Born 1933, Shanghai, China; lives Long Island City, New York

Eagle Wheel, 1976–79

Painted steel; 242 x 96 x 156 in. overall
Purchased with the aid of the National Endowment for the Arts, The Sisler McFawn Foundation, and the Museum Acquisition Fund

Mitchell D. Kahan

Nancy Graves

Pittsfield's Berkshire Museum, where Nancy Stevenson Graves's father worked, presented both art and natural history, a combination that presaged the future artist's interests. Her family encouraged her studies, which led to undergraduate and graduate degrees in art from Yale.

Abroad in Florence, Graves experimented with sculpture while investigating taxidermy and antique anatomical models. Her first sculptures were of camels. She eventually created twenty-five large, realistic camels constructed over wood and steel armatures from burlap, wax, animal skin, and other materials; most of these were eventually destroyed. Relocating to New York in 1966, Graves continued to pursue her interests in anatomy, anthropology, and archaeology. She also worked in film, drawing, painting, and printmaking.

In 1976 a German museum asked Graves to make a permanent version of an earlier sculpture in plaster, which initiated twenty years of experimental processes in casting and coloring bronze. She became a key figure in the revival of bronze as a favored medium for sculpture at a time when most sculptors favored industrial methods and architectural constructions.

Whereas in the earlier life-size replicas Graves examined a camel's external appearance, in *Variability and Repetition of Similar Forms II* she explored the animal's inner structure. The origin of this work can be traced to Morocco and Los Angeles in 1970, when Graves made an eight-minute film showing camels in rhythmic tableaux that seemed "to have been posed and choreographed by sheer will power on the part of the director."[1] Around the same time Graves pursued a longtime interest in fossils by making drawings of an articulated Pleistocene-age camel skeleton at the Museum of Natural History in Los Angeles. These drawings, along with photographs, led her to make thirty-six separate legs formed from wax over steel armatures and colored with marble dust and acrylic paint. Their arrangement into a dancing chorus of legs echoed the ideas of movement and patterning explored in the films.

The Akron Art Museum's piece is not identical to the thirty-six plaster legs of 1970; it is a unique bronze made nine years later. Graves wanted to execute this second version in a material that could be shown outdoors.[2] To transform the piece into bronze she made six wax casts, each subtly different from the others. The resulting bronze legs were bolted onto a Cor-ten steel base and covered with white wax to enhance the bonelike quality.

Though *Variability and Repetition* does not move, the legs, abetted by the elevated arc of the foot and ankle bones, display a delicate sense of balance. Graves explained: "One of the ideas in that piece, as everyone walks around it, is [that] the illusion of motion is introduced so that the legs simply seem to move."[3] The cinematic effect reflects the artist's involvement in film and her interest in the pioneering nineteenth-century photographs of Eadweard Muybridge depicting animal and human movement in stop-action sequences.

To Graves the animal world appeared to represent a superior and more ancient form of life than that of the human body. Her odd subject matter, however, is not the only reason her work is startling. The art historian Linda Nochlin explains that Graves challenges our expectation that zoology and art are separate. "Boundaries between the activities of science—observation-research, systematic investigation, archeological reconstruction—and those of art—invention, creation, construction, imaginative play—are purposely left undefined and open."[4] Graves's scientific curiosity is imbued not only with imagination but with an affecting empathy that eschews morbidity in favor of animation and theatricality.

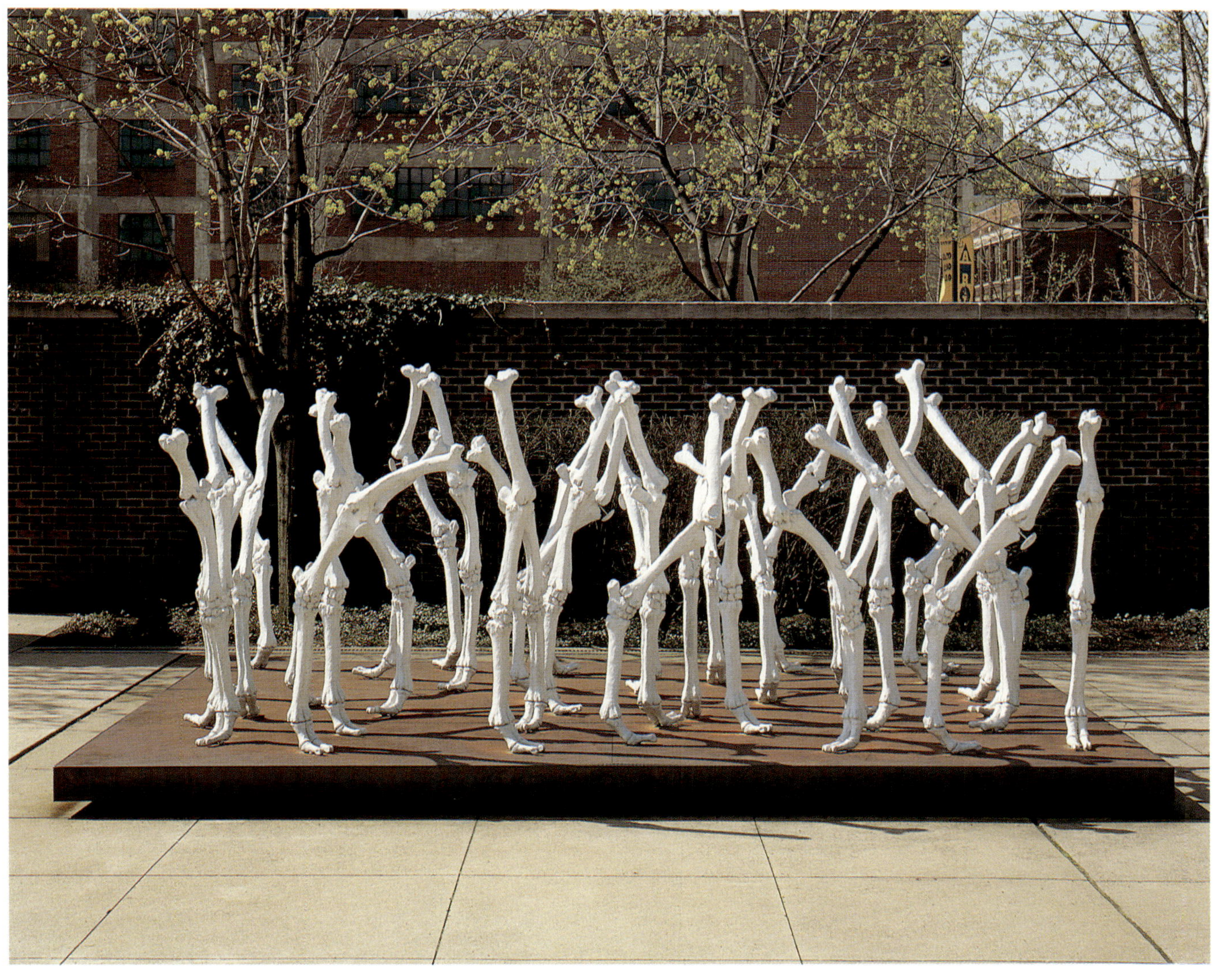

1981.15

Nancy Graves
Born 1940, Pittsfield, Massachusetts; died 1995, New York

Variability and Repetition of Similar Forms II, 1979

Bronze and Cor-ten steel; 72 x 192 x 144 in.
Purchased with funds from the Mary S. and Louis S. Myers Foundation, the Firestone Foundation, the National Endowment for the Arts, and the Museum Acquisition Fund

Mitchell D. Kahan

Philip Guston

Born in Montreal to poor Jewish immigrants from Russia, Philip Guston, whose birth name was Philip Goldstein, moved with his family to Los Angeles in 1919. The artist attended Otis Art Institute and, though he never graduated, later taught at several prestigious universities. After settling in New York in the 1950s, he moved permanently to Woodstock in 1967. Throughout his life he received much recognition, including international exhibitions and awards. In the late 1970s, Guston greatly influenced a return to figurative painting across the United States.

An ideal summation of Guston's work, *Opened Box* is a haunting commentary about the quest for meaning that unites many of his lifelong philosophical concerns. The canvas presents a scene as if it were a stage, but the unfolding drama is not clear. This is a world of allegory, with symbols, not facts.

The whip on the right evokes both art historical and personal references. It directly recalls Guston's love of Piero della Francesca's great Renaissance fresco, *The Flagellation of Christ,* a reproduction of which hung in his home. Did Guston view the whip as punishment reserved for the seer, whether prophet or artist? The whip first appeared in his early drawings of a violent Klansman; later it appeared in an image of a figure flailing himself, a complex vision encompassing a guilt-ridden survivor, innocent humanity, and a suffering artist.

One could hardly construe Guston's ominous wooden box as a toy chest or wedding chest; it seems too much a reliquary or coffin. Its primitive form may evoke the primordial box of Pandora, but instead of devils and pestilence, we see symbols of bedraggled humanity such as tongues and soles of shoes. To the scholar the soles may suggest the upturned horseshoes and shields in Paolo Uccello's Renaissance battle murals, which Guston greatly admired. To the student of recent history the empty clothing may recall the discarded belongings of Jews slaughtered in Nazi gas chambers. Those evil events had a deep impact on Guston. On a more prosaic level, the flat-footed and oversized shoes may suggest the routine tasks of living, the donning of worn clothing to stumble through the coming day.

Draped across the shoes is a knotted rope or chainlike cord. This form appears frequently in Guston's late paintings, usually hanging from the ceiling of an artist's studio with a naked light bulb at its end. The cord can lead to darkness as well as illumination, however; here it may refer to the artist's traumatic childhood discovery of his father, who had hanged himself.

That Guston's paintings contain humor may seem incongruous given his weighty themes. Nevertheless, his bumbling, flattened images with lumpy edges are directly inspired by the artist's youthful interest in George Herriman's Krazy Kat comics. And there are sometimes private jokes in the canvases. In *Opened Box* a tongue emerging from one of the shoes appears to slide toward cigarette butts, a reference to the artist's own nicotine habit. His humor often black, Guston took solace in the intellect but was demoralized by the dark side of human nature, by racial and religious prejudice, by abandonment and suffering.

Guston's rumpled jacket and crumpled shoes in *Opened Box* are pitiful, even grotesque. But the artist was no nihilist. If his paintings reflect a loss of faith after the inhumanity of the Holocaust, his images of beleaguered shoes and suits can also be considered surrogates for human survival. And though he visualized a world where the clarity of reason no longer reigns, Guston refused to abandon hope. Instead, he continued the eternal quest for meaning.

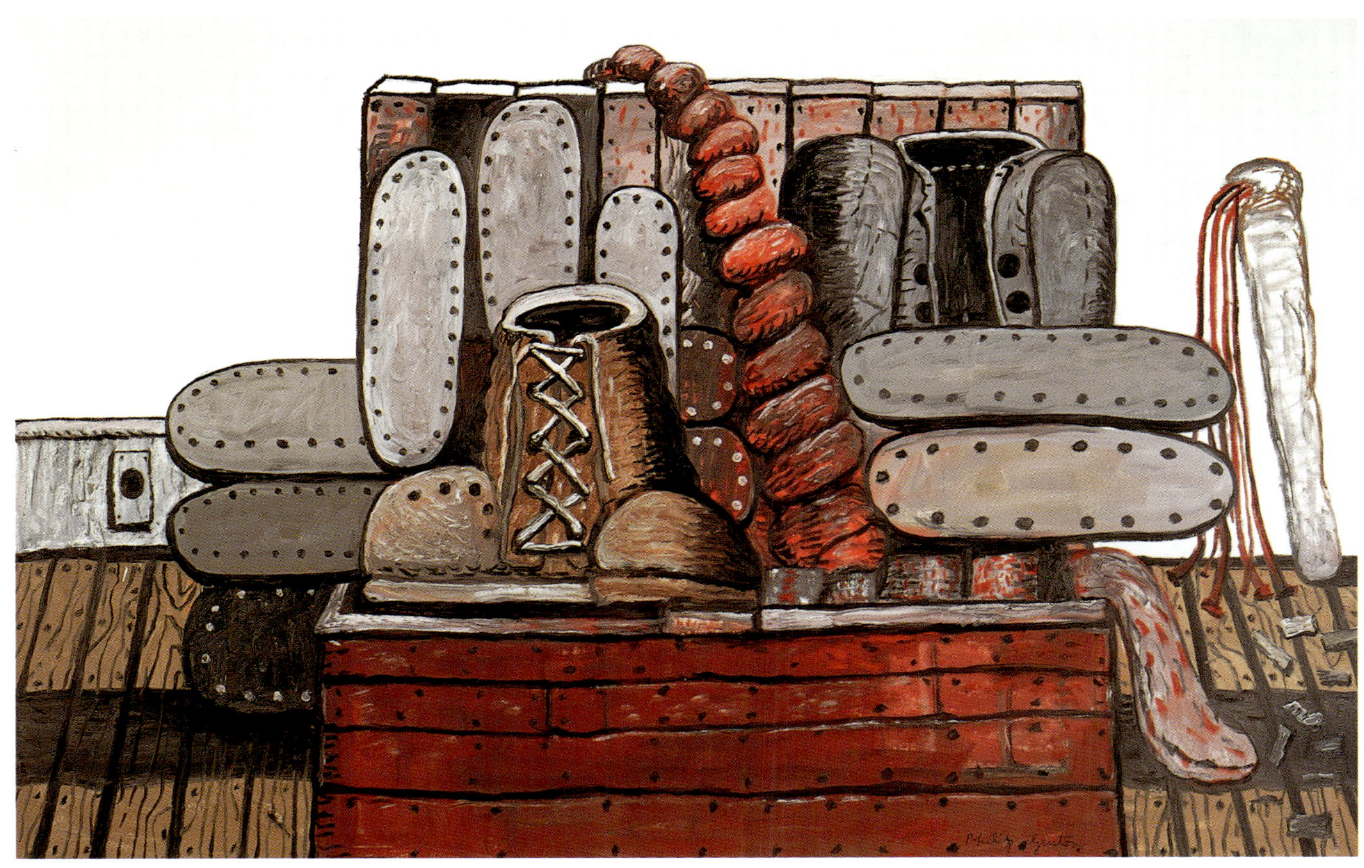

1980.49

Philip Guston
Born 1913, Montreal; died 1980, Woodstock, New York

Opened Box, 1977

Oil on canvas; 67 $\frac{1}{4}$ x 110 $\frac{1}{4}$ in.
Purchased with funds raised by the Masked Ball 1955–63, by exchange

Graham W. J. Beal

William T. Wiley

William Wiley grew up in a nuclear-power boomtown in rural Washington State. He was profoundly influenced by his high school art teacher, Jim McGrath, whose interests included poetry and Native American culture. In 1956 Wiley went to the San Francisco Art Institute, where he encountered the lingering but powerful influence of Abstract Expressionist Clyfford Still. Of the intense atmosphere of the art institute Wiley has said, "If you drew a line it had to be grounded to God's tongue or the core of the earth to justify putting it there."[1] Wiley quickly developed a fluent Abstract Expressionist style distinctive enough to earn him a solo exhibition at the San Francisco Museum of Art in 1960.

As a member of the art faculty at the University of California, Davis, from 1962 to 1973, Wiley encountered an unusually talented group of students, some of whom, he has said, were "better than me: Bruce Nauman...and Steve Kaltenbach...David Gilhooly and Robert Arneson [see pp. 214–15].... It all just bubbled."[2] In the 1960s Wiley's own painting style shifted to a cooler approach indebted to Dada and Surrealism; the sly, interrogative tenor of this new style concealed a growing personal crisis of conscience. By 1968 Wiley found himself artistically immobilized and unable to work for months on end. The crisis ended with his realization—what he has described as "really an amoral thrill"—that "art is something I love doing.... It was surrender, you know? I said to myself 'I can't do it anymore, keep everything separate. I'll just fall over dead.'"[3]

The resulting signature style embraced painting, drawing, sculpture, found objects, words, and symbols, often in the same work. He drew upon incidents of his everyday life as the springboard to explorations of more universal concerns. Using the idea of the artist as nomadic wanderer, he favored objects and imagery—notably maps, hides, and branches—recalling the West and Native American culture. At the same time he drew heavily on Zen philosophy, which he valued, among other things, for its ability to reconcile seeming opposites. The lowly pun became a favorite device, especially in his titles. While some older observers viewed his development with grave misgivings, Wiley's knowing self-rustication influenced younger artists and placed him at the center of the so-called California Funk Art scene.[4]

Dominated by large jagged forms, *Weigh of the Spirit and Flesh* clearly reveals Wiley's grounding in Abstract Expressionism. Closer inspection, however, reveals words and symbols that transform the painting into something like a morality tale. By highlighting the word "flesh," Wiley gives specific meaning to the pink field of color. The void in the center is identified as the "Sea of Solutions...Where Miracles Fester." But what kind of solution? The kind that solves problems or the one that dissolves substances? And how can a miracle fester? Scattered across the terrain are symbols. Some—the spiral, the tic-tac-toe mark, and the figure eight—commonly denote space and infinity. Others—pyramids and precious stones—suggest mystery and wealth. In one corner are two brawling figures whose actions generate similar symbols, here indicating profanity and injury. The words "Raw" and "cuss" (a pun on "raucous") appear above and below the antagonists. Embedded in a painted border around the pink field are impossibly long figures wearing hats: cowboys? gangsters? Do they menace or protect? Everything is ambiguous, yet it seems that when weighed by Wiley the ways of the spirit and flesh are finely balanced indeed.

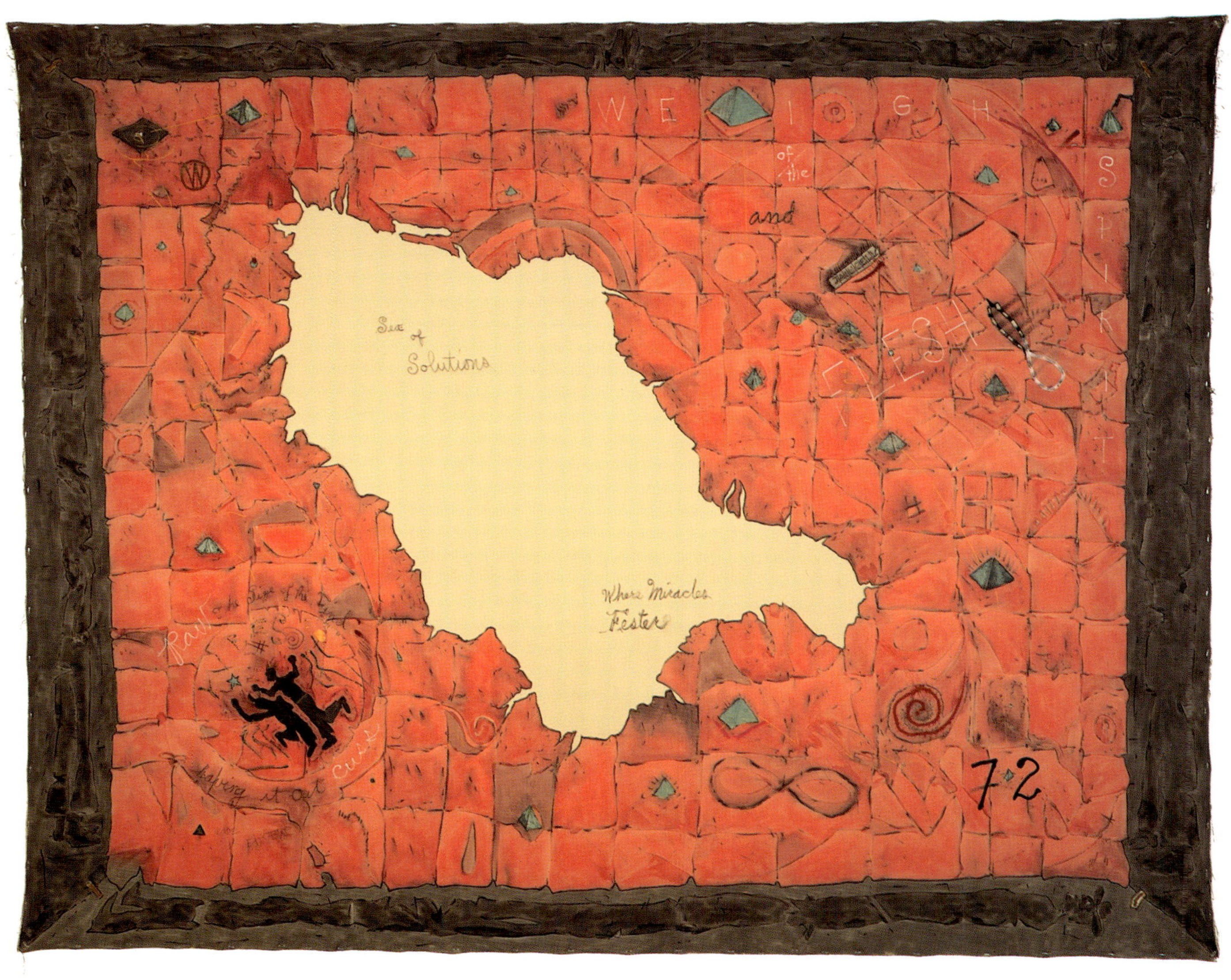

1975.15

William T. Wiley
Born 1937, Richland, Washington; lives Marin County, California

Weigh of the Spirit and Flesh, 1972

Acrylic on canvas; 84 x 111 in.
Purchased with funds from the National Endowment for the Arts and the John A. McAlonan Trust Fund

Barbara Tannenbaum

Christo

Initially, Christo's two-paneled drawing of *Wrapped Walk Ways* provided a glimpse at a sculpture yet to be built. The left panel contains specifications for cloth to cover the park's walkways for two weeks in October 1978. The right panel, a collaged drawing with a sample of the cloth used in the park, shows how the artist envisioned the finished work.

Almost twenty years later this drawing and many others, along with photographs and a film, serve as documentation of a work that no longer exists. Christo (who dropped his surname, Javacheff, decades ago) has adapted planned obsolescence to public art. Best known for his 1995 wrapping of Berlin's Reichstag, he transforms a building or site by temporarily wrapping, veiling, or covering it. At the end of a specified time, all traces of the project are removed. The alterations may be ephemeral, but they leave a lasting impact on the viewer. Christo explains,

> If I live across the street from Loose Park,...and jog on its paths every morning for three years, after a while I cease to pay attention.... Half awake, panting and sweating, I look but I do not see. Suddenly, on the second of October, 1978, teams of young workers...are covering the paths with a loosely draped, luminous saffron cloth. By the fourth all the paths, pavilions and walkways have been transformed into rivers of gold, rippling slightly in the breeze. I notice the curve of a path against the green lawn, the formal rigidity of the garden area with its strict horizontals and verticals. For two weeks I'm awake while running, curious, aware...and then it is gone. The change is almost as radical as the initial transformation. I carry the memory of the *Wrapped Walk Ways* and a deeper appreciation of Loose Park with me every morning as I continue my circuits around the park.[1]

Christo's monumental outdoor projects can be accomplished only through teamwork involving not just the artist's wife and collaborator, Jeanne-Claude, but also industrial fabricators, engineers, politicians, and a large crew of installers—in Kansas City, eighty-four people.

The artist's drawings are more solitary undertakings and demonstrate his exquisite draftsmanship. Christo received a traditional academic education in painting, drawing, and stage design at the Fine Arts Academy in Sofia before leaving Eastern Europe for the West at age twenty-one. Perhaps his theatrical background taught him how to seductively evoke, with simple means, the look and mood of a future creation. In this drawing of *Wrapped Walk Ways*, Christo puts us on one of the park's paths, with the cloth streaming out from beneath our feet. Ahead, in the distance, we glimpse flashes of the brilliant gold cloth winding through grass and trees.

It is crucial that Christo's drawings for projects such as *Wrapped Walk Ways* be inspiring and alluring as well as informative. Not only are they the means to convey a project's overall look and to convince officials to grant permits for it, they are also the major source of revenue for each project. The artist accepts no subsidies, fees, or grants for his projects, instead supporting their entire cost through the sale of drawings such as this. Since 1968 Christo has used the art market to finance his large-scale sculptures. By purchasing this drawing from the artist, Harold and Alice Gilbert helped pay for a work that neither they nor anyone else will ever own, a work that exists in memory and imagination—sparked by photographs or by drawings such as *Wrapped Walk Ways*.

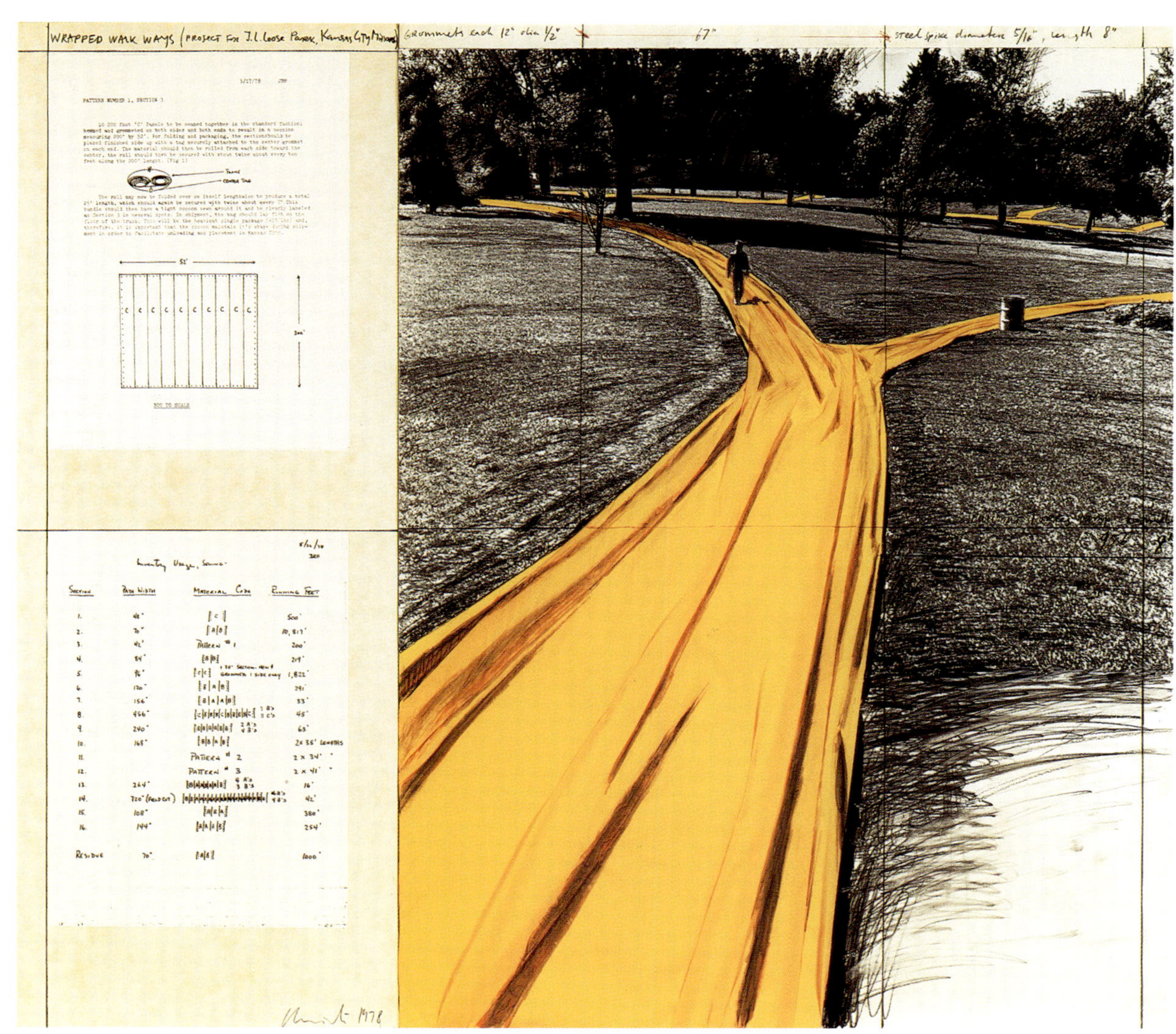

1990.28 a,b

Christo

Born 1935, Gabrovo, Bulgaria; lives New York

Wrapped Walk Ways (Project for J. L. Loose Park, Kansas City, Missouri), 1978

Fabric, photostat, pencil, charcoal, crayon, and technical data; two panels, overall 28 x 33 x 1 $\frac{1}{8}$ in.
Gift of Harold and Alice Gilbert

Barbara Tannenbaum

Lee Friedlander

The "American Ruhr"—the industrial cities from Detroit eastward—was the original subject of Lee Friedlander's 1979 commission from the Akron Art Institute.[1] Already a distinguished photographer, he had won two Guggenheim fellowships, had been given two solo exhibitions at New York's Museum of Modern Art, and had seen six books of his photographs published. Friedlander's career began in the mid-1950s, when he joined other young New York photographers, including Robert Frank (see pp. 134–35) and Garry Winogrand (see pp. 166–67), in the attempt to redefine documentary photography. Following in the footsteps of Walker Evans (see pp. 86–87), these artists considered documentary photography not as a socially oriented genre but as a personal vehicle, one allied more closely with the experimental freedom of fine art than the objectivity of reportage.

Friedlander's approach to the Akron commission, which eventually became known as the Factory Valleys series, included responding to social and personal concerns. Narrowing his focus to Ohio and Pennsylvania, he visited the two states for a total of thirteen weeks throughout 1979 and 1980. He arrived in a region that was suffering a serious economic depression, one symptomatic of a nationwide decline in American industry. Friedlander ignored the region's natural beauty (which was later documented in a second museum commission by Robert Glenn Ketchum [see pp. 206–7]) and chose not to depict the social and cultural benefits resulting from industry-based wealth. Instead, he focused on harsher aspects of the situation: the machinelike repetitiveness of factory workers' daily lives, the environmental cost of strip mining and heavy manufacturing, and the ugliness of the industrial environment.

Pittsburgh, one of eighty-two photographs by Friedlander in the Akron Art Museum's collection, evokes the bleakness of the region. The photographer's concentration on gray middle tones rather than stark contrasts between black and white contributes to a sad, wintry mood. Workers' houses tilt uncertainly on the hillsides. Across the highway is an idle steel mill, the cause of the workers' plight.

The composition is rebellious and disorderly, an affront to traditional notions of what makes a good photograph. The human-made structures are screened by a row of branches and stalks. The dark tree at the center is the first element to draw the eye, but buildings and the highway soon demand equal attention because they, too, are in sharp focus. The visual chaos may echo the emotional and social disruption that Friedlander found in the factory towns. The placement of major elements away from the viewer, in the middle ground, suggests the emotional and intellectual distancing of residents not yet ready to accept the transition from industrial heartland to "rust belt."

Friedlander's interest in visual chaos was not determined purely by expressive needs; it was a device he employed many times in his career. The denial of symmetry and the layering of images may belong, at least in part, to a shared sensibility of the period, for his "closest ally in art is not a photographer; it is the painter Robert Rauschenberg.... Friedlander views his photography as a synthesizing activity: the photograph is an environment constructed like a collage.... [It is] fragmented, discontinuous parts...in a single, coherent moment."[2]

Perhaps because Friedlander was commissioned by an art museum, not a corporation or social service agency, he was free to use his time to explore not only the region and its emotional tenor but also the medium of photography itself. The resulting body of work unites formal experimentation, documentation, and personal expression in a single, though not seamless, whole. Because of that combination, Factory Valleys has come to be recognized as a milestone both in the artist's career and in the history of documentary photography.

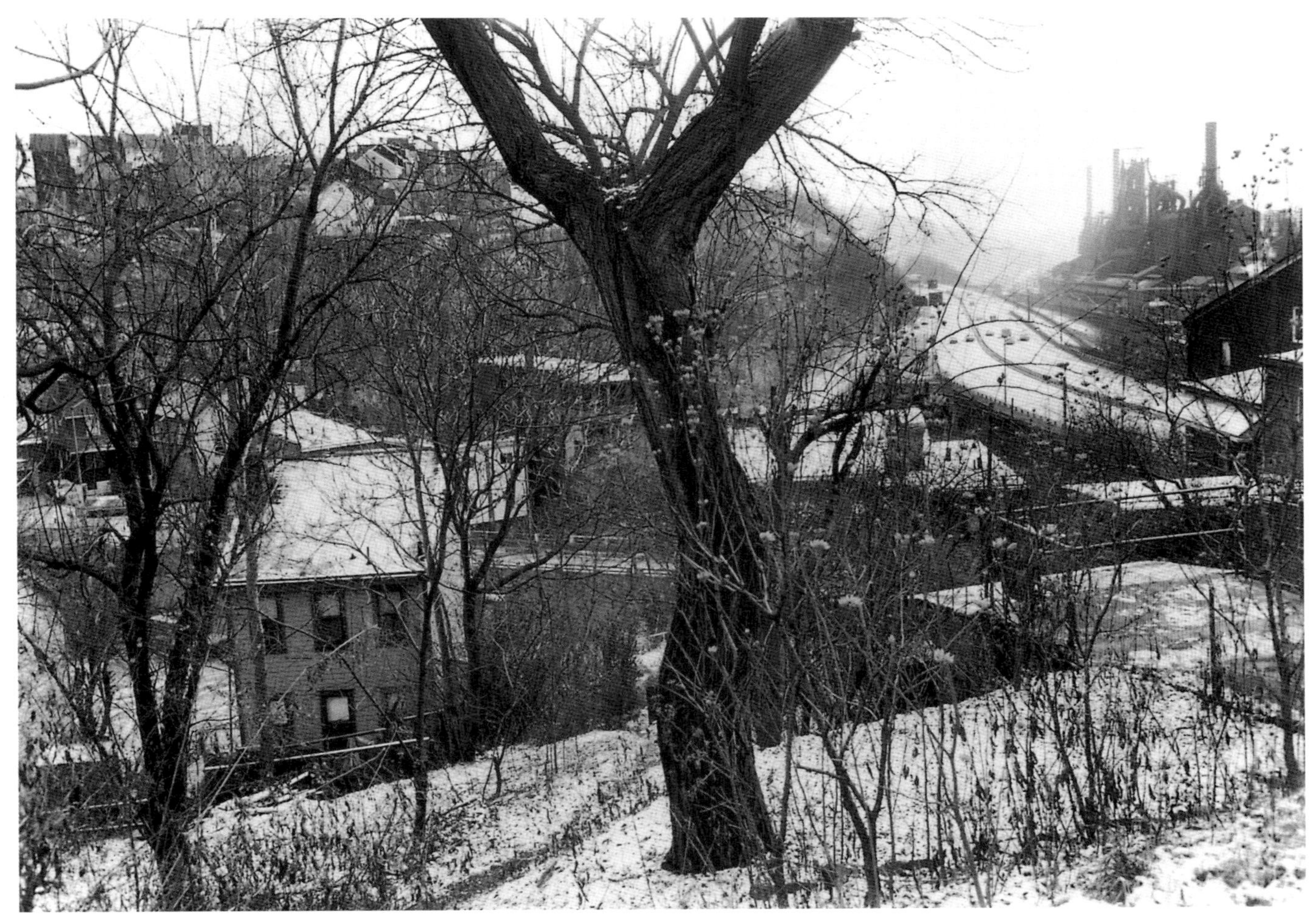

1981.11.38

Lee Friedlander
Born 1934, Aberdeen, Washington; lives New York

Pittsburgh, 1979, from the Factory Valleys series, 1979–80

Gelatin silver print; $7\frac{1}{2}$ x $11\frac{1}{4}$ in.
Purchased with funds from the National Endowment for the Arts and Centran Bank of Akron

Barbara Tannenbaum

Jim Goldberg

"My son, David, always seems to take an amused, philosophical approach to life," wrote Linda Benko on one of three photographs of her family in Jim Goldberg's Rich and Poor series. "He is the kind of son that every mother wishes she had." "But," writes Larry Benko below a picture of himself with David, "he is to [*sic*] fragile for a rough father like me."

Reading the words under the photograph of father and son, it is impossible not to think about what has become of this vulnerable child. One of ten photographs by Jim Goldberg in the museum's collection, the image shows the two males standing in the center of the family's home—a single claustrophobic room in a transient hotel. Larry Benko presses his son against him with one arm; the other is bent behind his back, as if he needs to hide it to restrain his actions. Against the bulk of his father's body, David's long, thin limbs look as easy to snap as twigs.

When Goldberg began photographing residents of San Francisco's transient hotels in 1977, he hoped to "create...a better understanding of a life we either refuse to see or are ignorant of. And I believed that having my subjects write on the photographs would bring...a deeper truth."[1] He returned with the portraits and asked their subjects to comment on them. After editing their words Goldberg went back to ask them to write out his selections in their handwriting. As a final step he made photographic prints that combined the images with the handwriting.

It is the union of image and words that makes us wonder if David's philosophical approach survived life with his father and a childhood spent in rooms with "dark, slanted floors, smelling of piss, alcohol and cheap food, bare light bulbs."[2] Or did he end up like Larry, aware of his flaws but convinced of his inability to change? The Rich and Poor series attempts to explore the effect of environment and circumstance on an individual. Are the poor, or the rich, really different from you and me? Do we get what we "deserve" in life or is it all a game of chance?

After a year of shooting in the hotels Goldberg began to find that "my sense of their powerlessness and of my own helplessness to offer them a way out created a pain that was difficult to accept."[3] As an antidote, he decided to also photograph the wealthy in their homes using the same interactive process. Since he was pursuing an M.F.A. in photography at the San Francisco Art Institute, he chose his rich people largely from the school's board of trustees. Self-doubt, irony, and an awareness of privilege prevail in their comments; in general, the wealthy seem far more self-conscious and reticent to address major issues than do the poor.

By the time Goldberg completed the Rich and Poor series in 1985, it had already begun to renew critical debate about the effectiveness of social documentary photography in our cynical, me-first, image-saturated age. The photograph of David and Larry makes us sad, but does it make us act to help the Benkos and others escape poverty? Will having an understanding of the problems of the rich help solve them? To be fair we must also ask: is there not value in learning about the lives of our fellow humans, rich and poor?

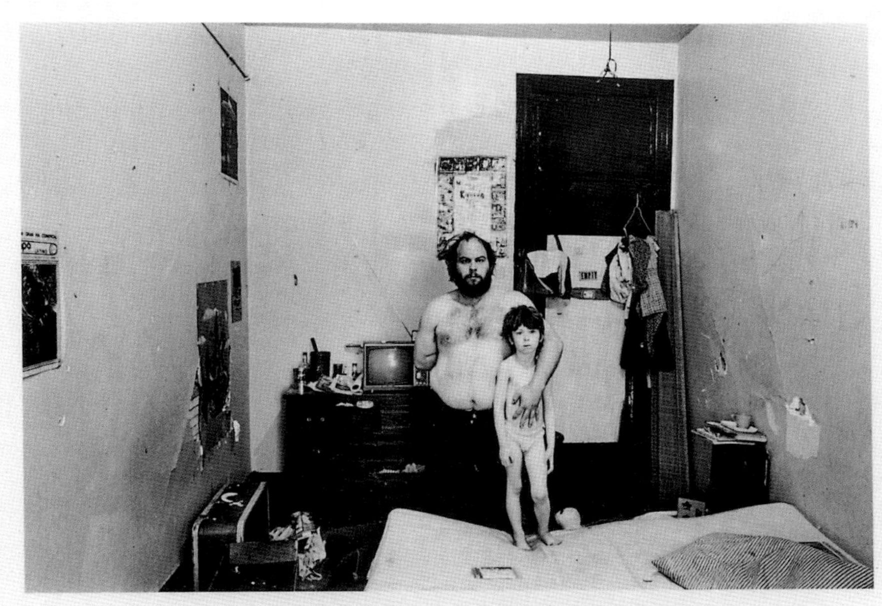

1986.31

Jim Goldberg
Born 1953, New Haven, Connecticut; lives San Francisco

Untitled from the Rich and Poor series, 1979 (printed 1985)

Gelatin silver print; $13\frac{7}{8}$ x $10\frac{3}{4}$ in.
Museum Acquisition Fund

Jean E. Feinberg

Jim Dine

Jim Dine's rise from youthful midwestern art student to internationally celebrated artist was meteoric. Raised and educated in Ohio, Dine remembers with fondness his first visits to the Cincinnati Art Museum as well as the evening art classes he attended as a teenager at the neighboring Art Academy of Cincinnati. He began college at the University of Cincinnati but transferred to Ohio University in Athens, where he was awarded a B.F.A. in 1957.

Moving to New York in 1958, Dine became the youngest among a handful of brash upstarts who would steal the art world's spotlight from the Abstract Expressionists in the early 1960s. What Dine shared with these Pop Art stars—notably Claes Oldenburg (see pp. 184–85), Tom Wesselman, Andy Warhol (see pp. 148–49), and Roy Lichtenstein—was a healthy disregard for the separation between so-called high and low subject matter and a desire to blur the boundaries between art and nonart forms. The Pop mandate was to create art reflective of everyday modern life. Domestic objects, references from popular culture, and modern advertising were embraced and utilized. Over the years Dine has repeatedly used a variety of media to focus on a few familiar motifs, including a heart, a gate, a tree, Venus de Milo, numerous tools, and a man's robe.

Dine created his first robe painting in 1964. Like all of his subjects, the robe was found rather than invented. In an advertisement in the *New York Times,* Dine came across a photograph of a man's bathrobe with the human model airbrushed out. With this as his starting point, he created a number of robe pictures during the mid-1960s. The robe was immediately identified as a stand-in for the artist, a symbol of masculinity as well as a generalized self-portrait.

Multiple robes, as in the Akron painting, provide the artist with additional opportunities to explore the image's communicative power, thereby increasing, in this case fourfold, the intense presence of the male icon. Dine has frequently used the robe and other images in multipaneled works in which an image is repeated or seen as part of a sequence of related images. Through focused repetition comes variation: no two images are alike, despite their thematic consistency. This theme-and-variation approach characterizes Dine's art making.

In the late 1970s a change occurred. Leaving behind Pop's cool reserve and aloofness, Dine turned up the emotional heat in order to exploit the expressive power of his imagery. Simultaneously he fine-tuned his draftsmanship and explored the painterly gesture more enthusiastically, even if always within the context of representation. With these aesthetic shifts in place, the artist returned to making robe pictures after a hiatus of several years.

Painting around Mount Zion, one of a small number of robe pictures created during the late 1970s, was produced during a three-month sojourn in Jerusalem. Dine's studio there was in a neighborhood known as Yemin Moshe; its proximity to Mount Zion gave rise to this painting's title. The artist was enchanted by the Middle Eastern light, even though its intensity was so great that he had to whitewash the windows of his studio in order to work in it.

The Jerusalem robes radiate with the brilliance of the local sunlight. In *Painting around Mount Zion,* four large figures loom out at the viewer, their strident stance seen against a flood of saturated color. These robes serve so potently as receptacles and vehicles for emotional energy, it is easy to see why the late 1970s robe paintings are considered to be among the artist's most expressive and most successful works.

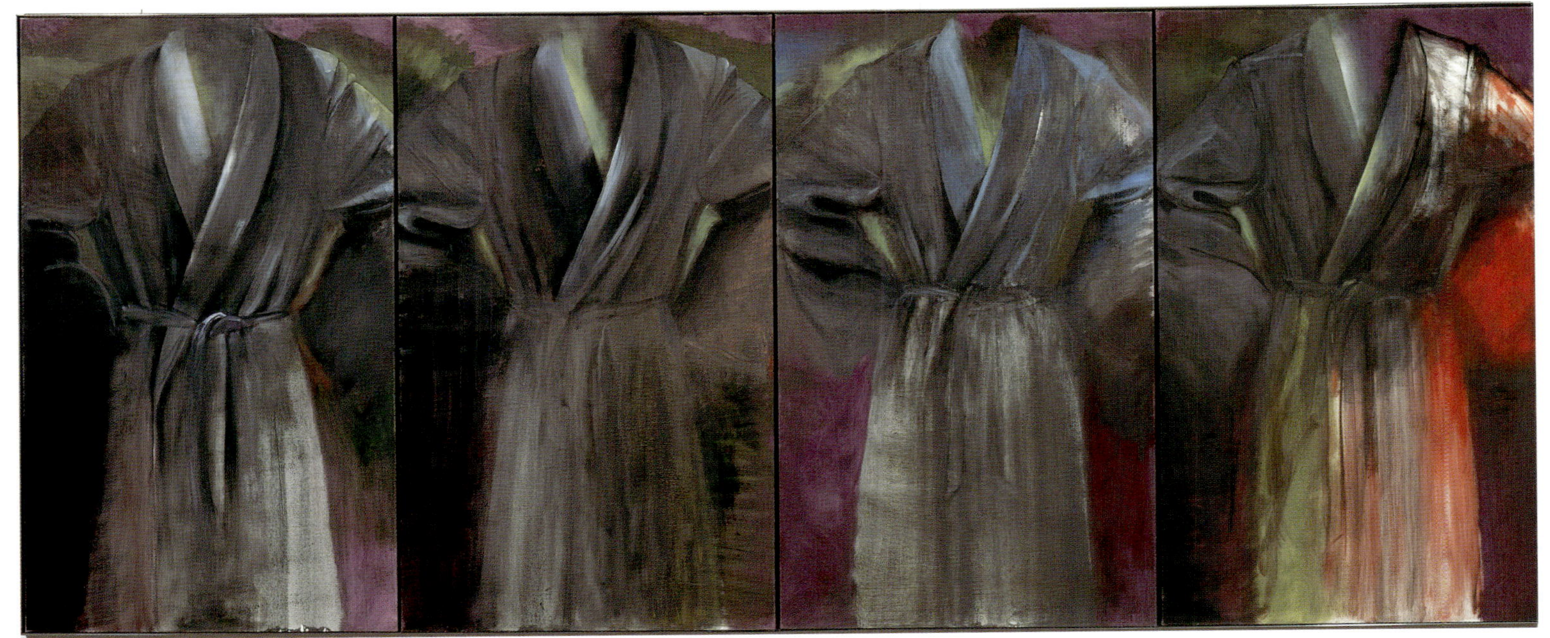

1983.2 a,b

Jim Dine
Born 1935, Cincinnati; lives New York

Painting around Mount Zion, 1979

Oil on canvas; 71 x 173 in.
Purchased with funds from an anonymous contribution and the Museum Acquisition Fund

Mitchell D. Kahan

Frank Stella

Frank Stella, one of the most widely exhibited artists of the late twentieth century, is as perplexing as he is exciting. He refuses to confine paintings to flat surfaces, endowing metal reliefs with an exuberant materialism and overwhelming grandeur.

Stella was raised in suburban Boston and first studied art at Phillips Academy in Andover. At Princeton University he took classes with teachers and students who were to become leaders in the art world of the 1960s. Only one year after his 1958 college graduation, Stella was included in the influential *Sixteen Americans* exhibition at the Museum of Modern Art in New York. Numerous awards and exhibitions have followed. The most prestigious honor was an invitation to deliver The Charles Eliot Norton Lectures at Harvard University in 1983, during which he offered highly creative insights on paintings by old masters as well as contemporary artists.

Diepholz is from a series titled Circuits, a group of ninety-five painted metal reliefs and dozens of prints which the artist completed from 1980 to 1984. What Stella described as "the longest and most concentrated streak of work that I've ever had" may reflect his intense personal interest in auto racing.[1] The individual pieces in the series bear the names of international circuits for auto races. *Diepholz,* named for a course in Germany, is constructed of two layers of honeycomb aluminum to which additional aluminum segments are attached. Begun with drawings and foamcore models, *Diepholz* was ultimately custom-machined by a laser cutter and fabricated in fifteen separate pieces at Swan Engraving Company in Bridgeport, Connecticut. It was then painted in Stella's Greenwich Village studio, where the artist works with several assistants. With its French curves, flexicurves, and other drafting forms, as well as shapes left over from cuts for other works, *Diepholz* conforms to Stella's longtime insistence on using preexisting shapes that avoid personal meanings.

Stella has insisted that "what you see is what you see," that his art is purely visual without reference to anything else. For a time, such a stance was fairly widely accepted by those who rejected both Abstract Expressionism's philosophical ambitions and Pop Art's embrace of everyday life. But it is increasingly difficult to accept Stella's credo that art is only a visual tour de force. Without meaning, there can be no art, only design or decoration.

Although Stella's works are decorative, which accounts for their ubiquitous presence in corporate lobbies, the artist's exploration of a painted surface and how it can dynamically erupt into three dimensions is more than an academic exercise. It is art—and its meaning derives from the works' bureaucratic fabrication utilizing assistants and advanced technology, from their overpowering physical presence, and from the way the works are used by collectors. These attributes proclaim the masculine energy of the artist himself and declare art's ability to confer power, status, and vitality upon those who collect it. If *Diepholz* offers visual thrills more than content, this triumph of style over substance is not unique to Stella. Rather, the artist and his work serve as a brilliant mirror of our times.

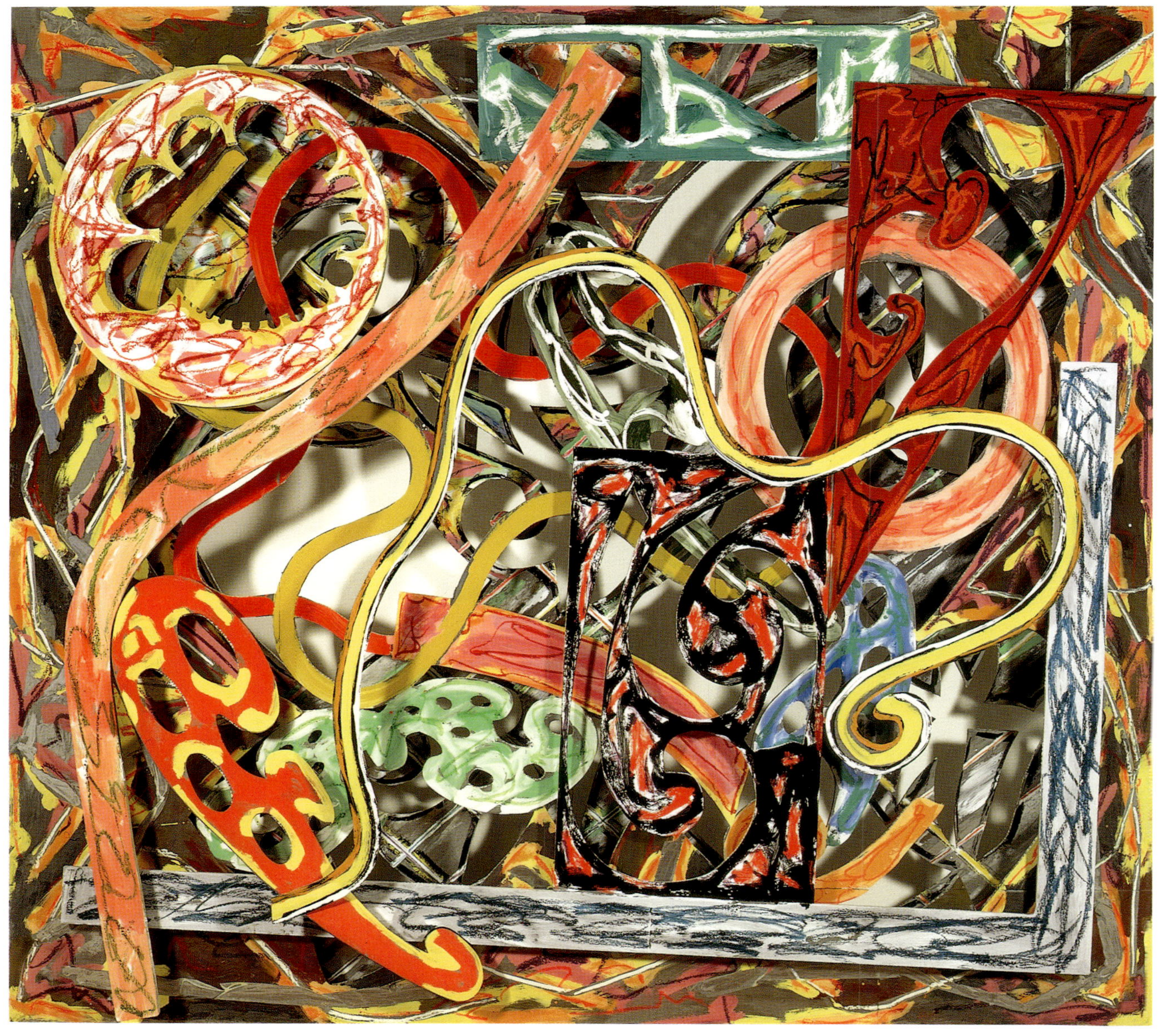

1981.16

Frank Stella
Born 1936, Malden, Massachusetts; lives New York

Diepholz, 1981

Enamel, acrylic, oil, and metal flakes on aluminum; 114 x 128 x 28 in.
Purchased with funds from the John Lyon Collyer Fund and
the Charles E. and Mabel M. Ritchie Memorial Foundation, by exchange

Jeffrey Grove

Louise Nevelson

In the late 1950s, after decades of obscurity, Louise Nevelson burst upon the New York art world with her stunning totemic sculptures painted matte black. Fashioned of wood, they are as unforgettable as their formidable and flamboyant creator. Nevelson's trademark look of tunics, pants, turbans, furs, layers of jewelry, and two pairs of false eyelashes glued together was as exotic and mysterious as her art was dark and theatrical.

Born Louise Berliawsky in Kiev, Russia, Nevelson grew up in Rockland, Maine, a member of one of the few Jewish families in town. Feeling isolated, she married young to escape her surroundings. After several years as a wealthy New York matron and young mother, Nevelson left her shipping magnate husband, defiantly refused alimony, and toiled without recognition as an artist for the next twenty years. During that time she studied at the Art Students League in New York with Hans Hofmann, acquiring the principles of collage and Cubism. Throughout the 1940s and 1950s, Nevelson worked through a succession of styles influenced by Cubism, Surrealism, African, Native American, and Pre-Columbian art before cultivating her mature voice.

In 1958 the artist debuted *Moon Garden Plus One,* a sculptural "environment" that transformed the entire art gallery into a work of art. It brought her instant acclaim. *Moon Garden's* dominant element, *Sky Cathedral,* was a room-size installation composed of stacked boxes filled with fragments of carved wood and found objects such as chair backs, furniture legs, spindles, and sections of architectural ornamentation painted a single color. *The Fugue,* created nearly thirty years after her breakthrough, consists of the same types of forms Nevelson used in the 1950s.

Like her contemporaries, the Abstract Expressionist painters, Nevelson worked without preliminary drawings or models: she allowed the abstract shapes to dictate the form of her box-shaped compositions. Depending on their arrangement, her sculptures might appear brooding and ominous, or quirky and humorous. Whether an individual box was hung upon the wall, like *The Fugue,* or grouped with others in complex architectural assemblages, Nevelson's sculptures had an archaeological quality. The unifying coat of black paint did not erase the history or distinguishing characteristics of the diverse elements, but at the same time, the personality of an individual component never threatened to overwhelm the whole.

In *The Fugue* the primary element is a headboard or frame for a child's bed. Turned vertically, it is bracketed by three sections of zig-zagging plywood and compressed between two rough-cut, two-by-six timbers. Not exactly black, as black is the absence of tone or light, *The Fugue* is painted a warm and reflective shade of very dark gray. What could have been a riotous cacophony of oppositions—antique and new, rough and smooth, baroque and modern—was tamed by the artist into a harmonious composition. In music, a fugue is a composition of two or more parts with independent melodies that harmonize and gradually build into a complex form having distinct voices. *The Fugue* could not be more appropriately titled.

Louise Nevelson was a pioneer. Perhaps unwittingly, she struck an early blow to the authority of New York's male-centered art world. Her sculpture, today so familiar, then stood in radical contrast to the type of abstract, open-form, welded metal sculpture dominating the art scene in 1950s America. A chronic collector, Nevelson recycled society's discards, transforming the overlooked and abused detritus of daily life into art. In doing so she created sculpture that challenged the premises of what constituted fine art in the 1950s and prefigured the dominance of installation and environmental art in the 1960s.

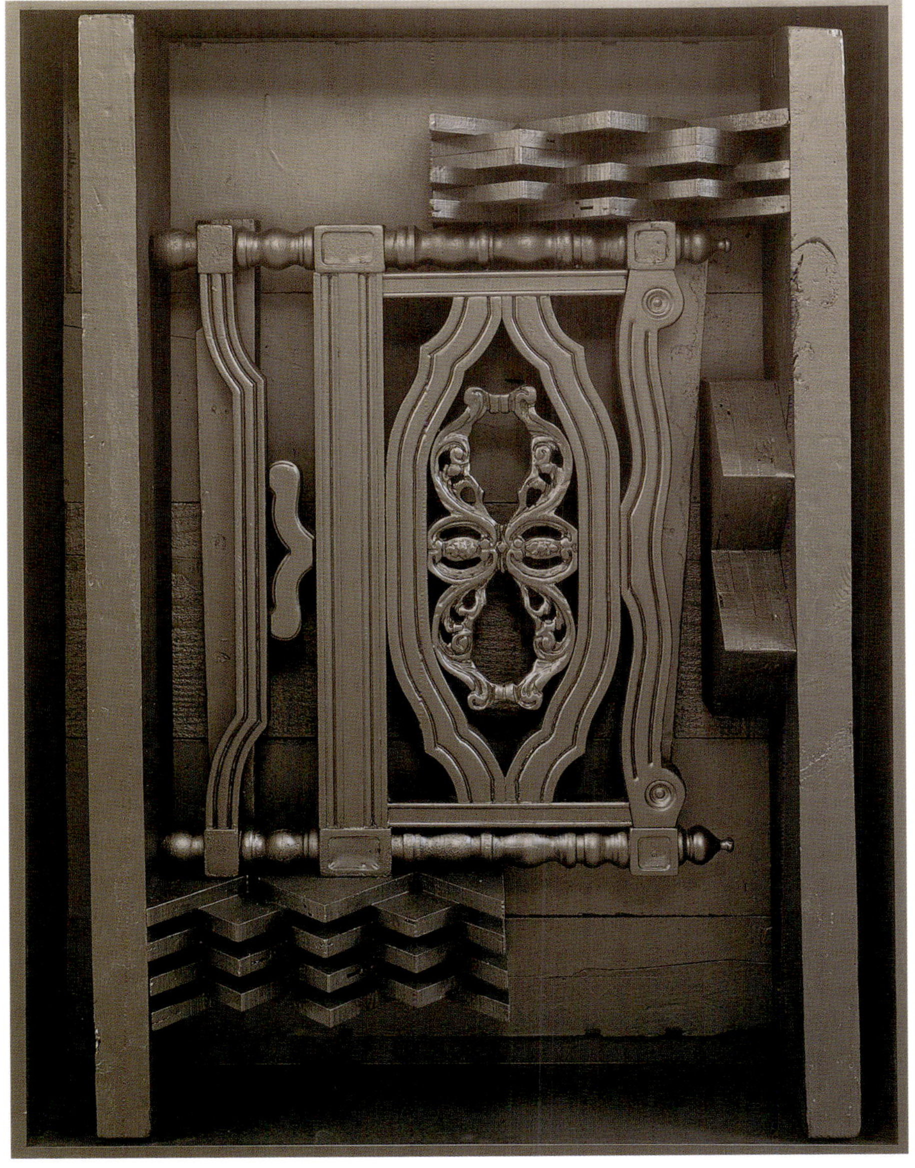

1996.6

Louise Nevelson
Born 1899, Kiev, Russia; died 1988, New York

The Fugue, 1985

Painted wood; 49 ¾ x 38 x 9 in.
Gift of the American Art Foundation in memory of Louis S. Myers

Barbara Tannenbaum

Robert Glenn Ketchum

Rocks and trees jutting precariously from mossy stone ledges; thick, soft mist rising off night-cooled ground—Robert Glenn Ketchum's image perfectly captures the eerie beauty of a summer morning on The Ledges just north of Akron. Commissioned by the Akron Art Museum in 1986 to document the area's natural beauty, Ketchum chose as one of his subjects The Ledges—part of the 33,000-acre Cuyahoga Valley National Recreation Area (CVNRA) extending between Akron and Cleveland.[1] Forty-eight of Ketchum's photographs are in the museum's collection; forty-three of these are from the CVNRA series.

The commission was intended to complement, and perhaps also to counteract, an earlier museum project: Lee Friedlander's Factory Valleys (see pp.196–97). This now-famous series of photographs was a masterful but bleak look at the area as it entered the "rust belt" era. Ketchum's lush color photographs presented a very different view. Concentrating on the region's natural beauty, he not only photographed the park but also examined it as a successful example of federal land use and of the integration of the often opposing forces of man and nature.

Addressing the relationship between humans and the land has been the focus of Ketchum's art since 1969. An important influence was photographer and environmental activist Ansel Adams (see pp. 108–9). Ketchum's work, like Adams's, is straight, or unmanipulated, photography, emphasizing sharp focus and great depth of field. Whereas Adams worked in black and white, Ketchum most often uses color. For the CVNRA project, he worked with a medium format (6 x 7cm) camera and transparency (positive) film from which large-scale Cibachrome prints were made. Cibachrome's high gloss and plastic surface are well suited to record detail and nuances of color, such as the wide range of greens, blacks, and grays seen in *CVNRA #866*.

The photograph's complex composition echoes the site's topography. Like Adams, Ketchum composes in the camera, with no cropping or manipulating later. In this image, he chose a viewpoint that left no empty spaces, no clear sky or distant vista. The ledge blocking the view in the right half of the picture sends the eye left, down the narrow, sloping path. Between the two outcroppings is an obstacle course of rocks and trees. A line of tree trunks, cut off by the picture's top edge and silhouetted by backlighting, flattens out to become repeating verticals, establishing a two-dimensional pattern atop the three-dimensional space. Because of the regular rhythm of the verticals, the viewer becomes intensely aware of how twisted and bent the tree trunks really are. Each curve signals the trees' responses to shifts in the thin layer of soil and the rocky ground of this glacier-sculpted terrain. In order to survive, trees—like people and organizations—must sometimes bend or adapt.

Ketchum wanted to make each of his CVNRA images a metaphor for larger themes behind the park's existence. Hardly wilderness, the CVNRA consists of land that has been occupied for over 12,000 years. Some areas have been reclaimed for nature, but the park has also bent its borders and shaped its administration to include and work in partnership with existing towns, businesses, and cultural organizations. Ketchum hoped his images would raise awareness of this superb natural resource. The seductive beauty of his photographs surely succeeds in that mission, for viewing these works is almost as refreshing and nourishing as a visit to the park itself.

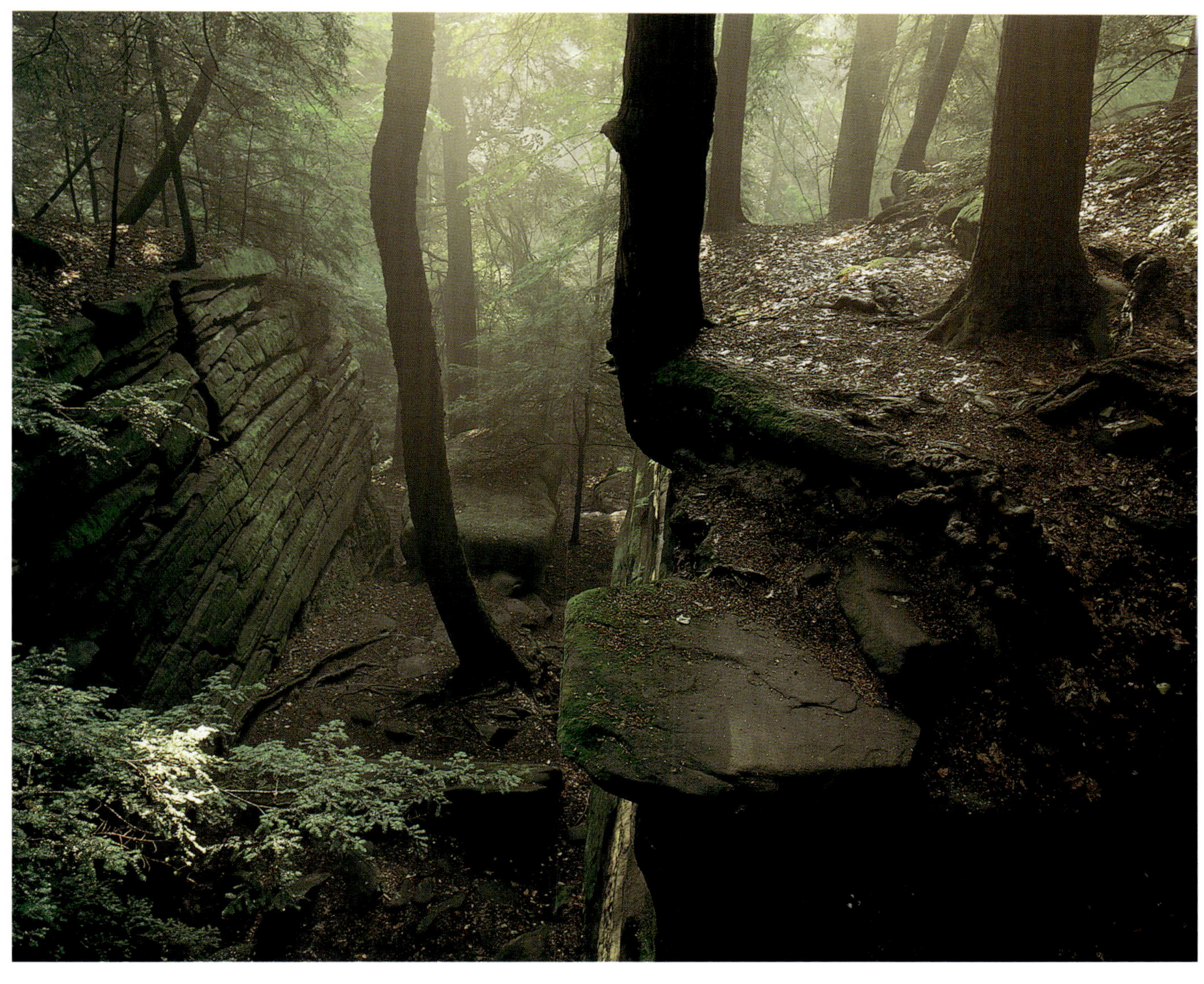

1989.19

Robert Glenn Ketchum
Born 1947, Los Angeles; lives Los Angeles

CVNRA #866 from the Federal Lands series, 1988

Cibachrome print; 24 x 30 in.
Purchased with funds from Kathleen and Gordon Ewers

Barbara Tannenbaum

Hiroshi Sugimoto

Empty or full? The white rectangle of the movie screen in Hiroshi Sugimoto's photograph appears to be blank—ready to reflect the romances, adventures, and tragedies of the Hollywood dream machine of the 1920s and 1930s. The screen sits on the stage of the Akron Civic Theatre, a 1929 movie and vaudeville palace whose interior is designed to evoke nighttime in a centuries-old Moorish garden.[1] The theater's most famous feature—its "atmospheric" domed ceiling of blinking stars and floating clouds—is not visible in Sugimoto's depiction, which centers instead on the white movie screen.

Akron Civic, Ohio is one of a series of images of American movie palaces and drive-in theaters made by Sugimoto beginning in the late 1970s. All the pictures feature a white rectangle, which glows with an otherworldly brightness suggestive of the magical nature of viewing a film. There is indeed magic at work here—the magic of physics and photography. Just as white light seems pure but actually contains all the colors of the spectrum, so each rectangle appears empty but in fact contains an entire film (which one is unimportant).

To make the images in this series, Sugimoto placed his large, 8 x 10-inch view camera at the farthest point from the screen. Sometimes, as in *Akron Civic*, that put him in the balcony. He would then open the camera's shutter and expose his film throughout the entire movie, a duration of one to two hours. Although taken in virtual darkness, Sugimoto's photographs reveal the theaters' interiors because sufficient light is reflected from the screen during the extremely long exposure time.[2] As each frame of the movie danced over the "silver" screen, it also registered on the silver crystals of Sugimoto's film. Viewed all at once, the frames produce a seemingly blank white screen.

Sugimoto's theater photographs contradict the usual notion of photography as a medium that freezes a single moment. Much more time is incorporated into *Akron Civic*: the imagined past of Moorish Spain evinced by the décor, the golden age of Hollywood's dream palaces, and the two hours it takes to view an entire movie. At first glance the theater photographs appear to stop time; paradoxically, however, they capture its flow.

In addition to this theater image, the Akron Art Museum owns eight seascapes by Sugimoto. All of the artist's major series—theaters, seascapes, natural history museum dioramas, and the sculptures of a twelfth-century Buddhist temple in Japan—pose riddles and present opposing dualities that would be at home in the Asian philosophy of Zen. Sugimoto himself has lived in two, often contradictory, cultures. Born and raised in Japan, he received a B.A. from St. Paul's University in Tokyo in 1970, then moved to Los Angeles to acquire a B.F.A. from the Art Center College of Design in 1972. He has resided in New York since 1974 and now divides his time between there and Tokyo.

Sugimoto's theater series documents the American phenomenon of the movie palace, but it also reflects concerns about the nature of photography and the act of looking. While the photographs are impeccably printed, the underlying conceptual process is as important to the artist as the physical object that results from it. Is art illusion or reality? Concept or object? Full or empty?

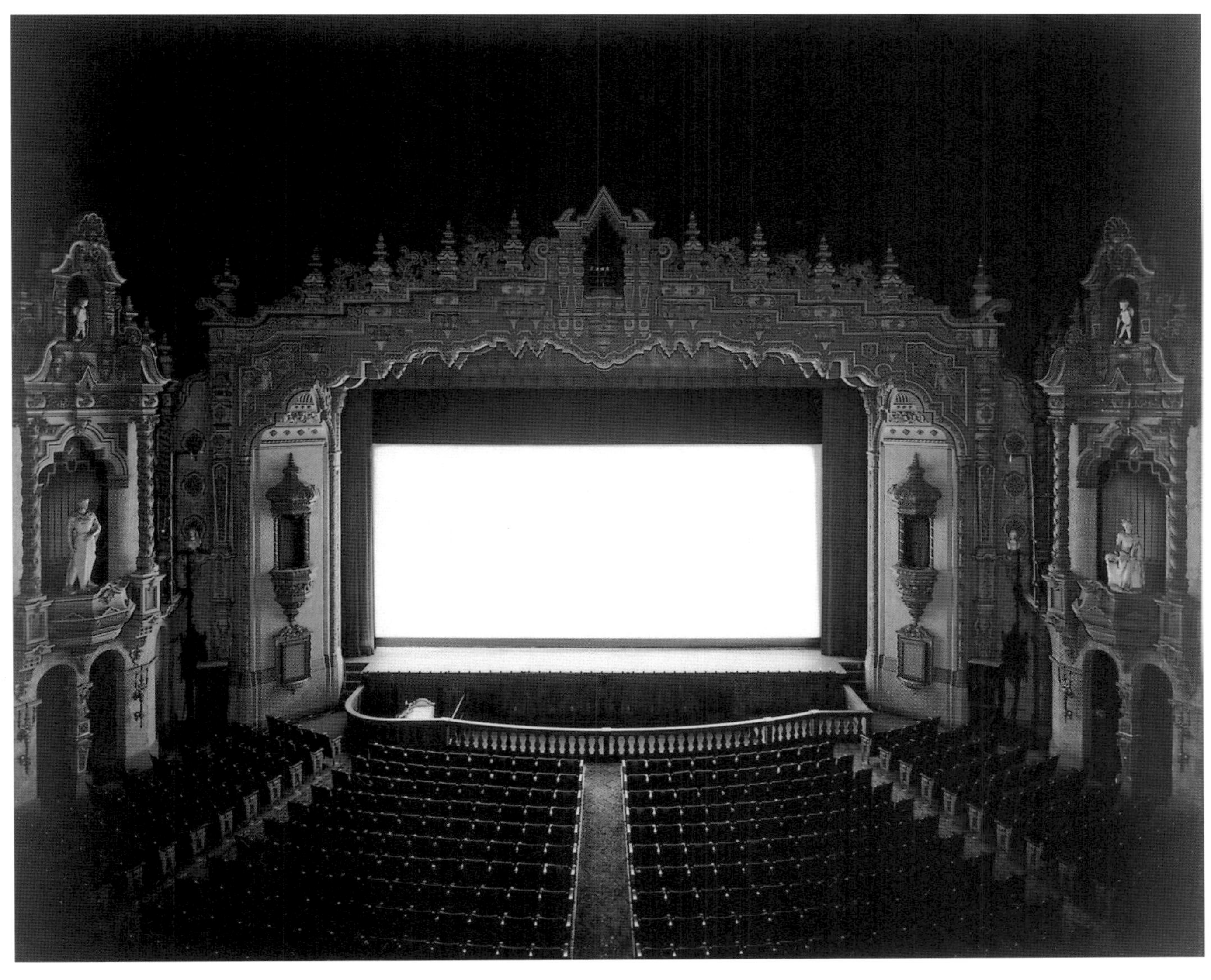

1996.12

Hiroshi Sugimoto
Born 1948, Tokyo; lives New York and Tokyo

Akron Civic, Ohio, 1980

Gelatin silver print; 16 ⅝ x 21 ¼ in.
Museum Acquisition Fund

Barbara Tannenbaum

William L. Hawkins

Even those who have never seen Perkins Mansion would readily agree that William Hawkins's depiction of this Akron landmark is more about the nature of picture making and paint rather than the building's actual appearance. The mansion, completed in 1837 to house the son of one of the city's founders, is now the home of the Summit County Historical Society. Although Hawkins had never visited the site, he had a postcard view of it.[1] Like many artists who work from printed images, he chose to use the photograph as a springboard for his imagination.

When this painting was made, Hawkins at age ninety was just becoming one of the most sought-after, contemporary American, self-trained artists—after over six decades of making a living driving delivery trucks, doing house construction and repair, and holding other such jobs around Columbus.[2] In the 1930s Hawkins had returned to a childhood hobby of making art as a means of supplementing his income, but he did not find his mature style or a national audience until 1981.[3]

Hawkins's economic situation had never allowed him the luxury of indulging in art purely for enjoyment, so he painted subjects he thought would sell, noting, "if you can't sell it, it isn't worth a damn!"[4] Cityscapes, including "portraits" of individual buildings, represent about seventy percent of his output. Hawkins may have been motivated to paint such scenes by his firsthand experience of urban renewal and transformation—a major sociological phenomenon of his lifetime—or simply because he suspected that the pleasure of recognizing a well-known site might inspire a sale. His subject matter often allows viewers to "read" a work in different ways, just as his painting style allows certain latitudes of interpretation.

The printed illustration was for Hawkins a source of inspiration—a familiar tune upon which he could improvise his own riffs and harmonies, like a jazz musician. *Perkins Mansion* is typical in its flattening and abstraction of illusionistic, three-dimensional photographic space. Seen from the side, the house's main entrance, with its two-story arcade of white columns, has been transformed into a set of yellow stripes; the shadowed spaces between them have become black rectangles.

Most strikingly, Hawkins has changed the blue sky of the postcard image into a Jackson Pollock-like swirl of ominous clouds. From about 1981 to 1986, Hawkins painted on fiberboard panel laid flat on a table, a position that allowed such free-flowing swirl patterns. To form a smooth, glossy background, he poured his paint (usually enamel house paint) directly from the can, entirely covering the fiberboard. Next he painted in silhouettes of the images; then he added details. He often painted back into areas of still-wet paint, as he did in the sky shown here.

Hawkins thought of his multicolored skies as realistic, though on a different level than the instant of reality captured by a photograph. Hawkins told an interviewer that "the sky got a million, trillion different colors. Sometimes it's silver, next time it's red, if the sun is way over.... You walk under that sky and it's all kinds of color."[5]

Added to *Perkins Mansion*, as to all of Hawkins's paintings, are reminders that these are created images; here we see a painted border or "frame," a title, and a signature with birthdate and birthplace. To him an image was "real" if it had the ability to attract the viewer's eye and interest. "Real" art, to Hawkins, was taking the commonplace—fiberboard, house paint, and a picture postcard—and making something extraordinary.

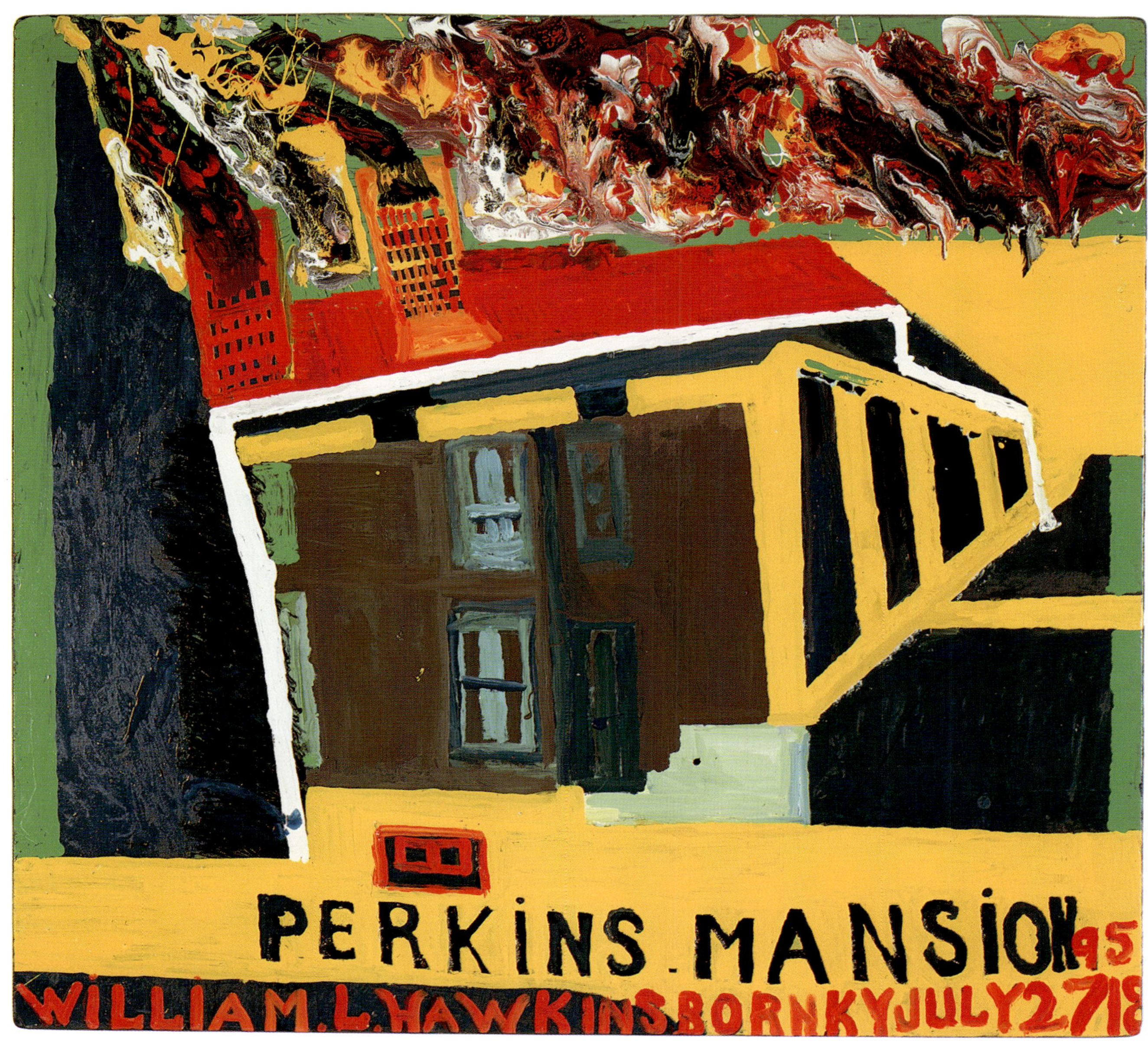

1987.18

William L. Hawkins
Born 1895, Union City, Kentucky; died 1990, Columbus, Ohio

Perkins Mansion, 1985

Enamel on fiberboard; 42 x 46 1/2 in.
Purchased with funds from the Elizabeth Firestone Graham Foundation, Contemporary Art Society of Akron, and Museum Acquisition Fund

Mitchell D. Kahan

Peter Dean

Known for his apocalyptic social satires, Peter Dean described himself as "an interpreter of reality into fantasy and back again."[1] He was brought to the United States by his parents in 1938 to escape the Nazis and raised in New York. As a child he was often taken to art museums. At Cornell and the University of Wisconsin, Dean studied geology, which may account for his lesser known but remarkably intense landscape paintings, such as *Doovekill Poppies* (1984), also in the Akron Art Museum's collection. Dean decided to become a painter in 1959, and for the next ten years divided his time between painting and geological work until he could devote himself full-time to art.

Dean has produced exuberant fantasies and canvases inspired by specific events, both of which can enter the realms of phantasmagoria and violence. He also adored parades and painted that subject as well. *Black Astronaut* is one of two paintings of an astronaut enjoying a ticker-tape parade. Both admiring and sarcastic, it celebrates the triumph of a blond, crew-cut, all-American hero, while combining themes of nationalism and technological prowess with traditional notions of personal heroism and masculinity. The yellow profile in the center is that of the youthful John Glenn, the first American astronaut to orbit the earth and later Ohio's longtime senator. Akron's version is a nighttime scene; "Black" in the title refers not to race but to the artistic practice of designating nighttime scenes or dark paintings as "black" works.

Dean's description of a related painting, *Astronaut in New York,* also applies to Akron's painting:

> I love the total madness and confusion of a ticker-tape parade in New York City. This could be any astronaut but I suppose it's John Glenn (although I don't know if he had a ticker-tape parade). In the painting he has his dog with him. Rockets are going off here and there. The chauffeur is down front with a big-wig from NASA—he sits there wearing a cowboy hat even though he's an Air Force guy.... I wanted a lot of confusing activity in the painting. So I mixed washes with my thick paint and used squiggly lines for the confetti and ticker-tape.[2]

Glenn did indeed have a ticker-tape parade in New York following his flight. He was accompanied by his wife, whose public face, one presumes, was not the white, clownlike mask so prominent in the painting. *Black Astronaut* depicts an historical event, but the details are invented, uniting reality and fantasy.

Dean was interested in both the emotional and technical sides of art. He enjoyed experimenting with different ways to apply paint—spattering, squeezing from tubes, smearing—and would sometimes use his hands in addition to a brush. His thickly applied paint and gestural approach reflect a longtime interest in Abstract Expressionism, in particular the painting technique of Jackson Pollock.

Black Astronaut celebrates, yet also pokes fun at, male fantasies. Phallic rockets frame the scene, raising the obvious association of military prowess with sexual potency. The astronaut was one generation's American hero; the cowboy hat on the NASA official brings to mind an earlier embodiment of American adventure. Another male role model, the cop, takes on a more sinister tone.

Dean's recurring status as an outsider began when he was born a Jew in Nazi Germany. As an artist, he was a figurative painter of social conscience at a time when analytical abstraction and ironic aloofness reigned. And occasionally he was an art professor—with a science degree.[3] Although Dean's art is not yet widely recognized, his impassioned, almost eccentric vision may one day bring him the stature he deserves.

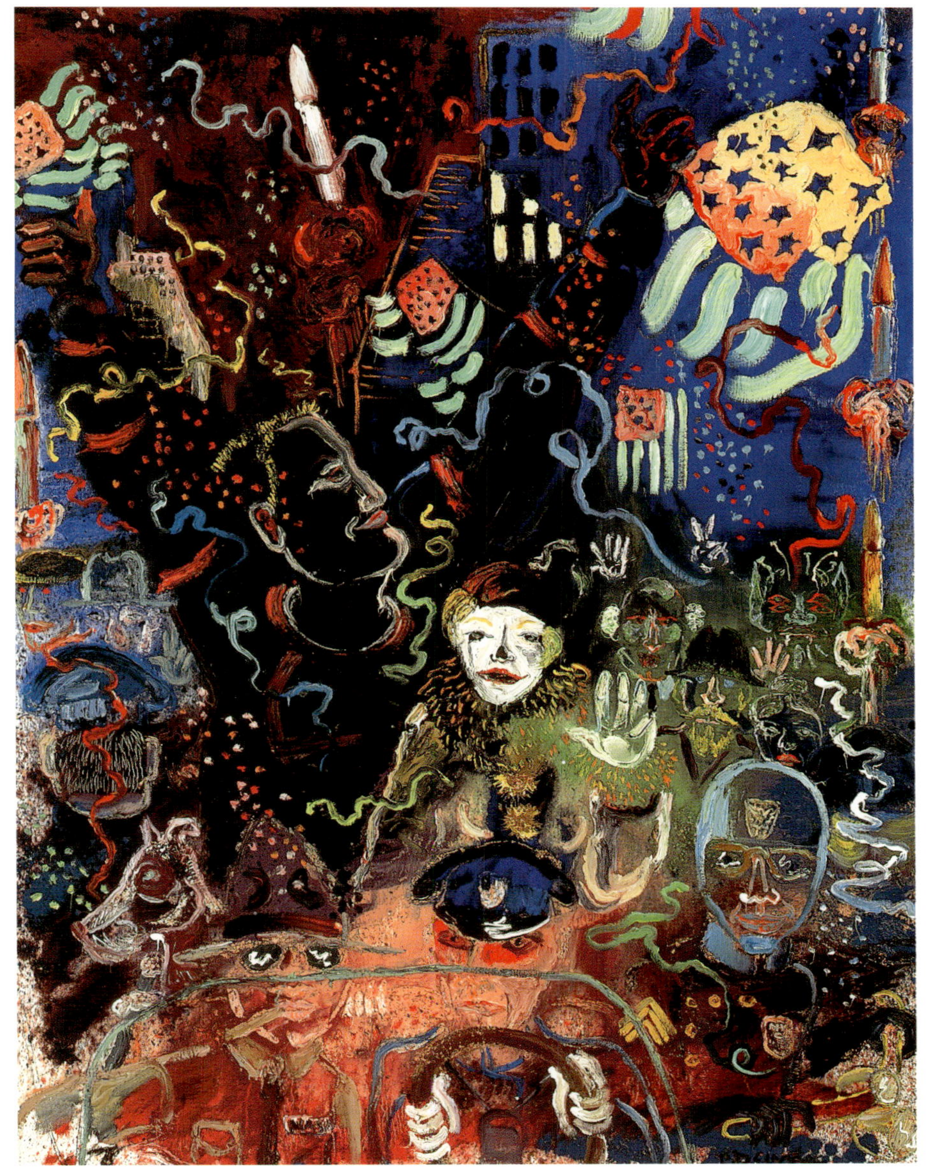

1994.19

Peter Dean
Born 1934, Berlin; died 1993, New York

Black Astronaut, 1985

Oil on canvas; 84 x 64 in.
Gift of Lorraine Dean and Gregory Dean

Mitchell D. Kahan

Robert Arneson

Robert Arneson lived his entire life in northern California. He studied ceramics first at San Jose State University and then at Mills College in Oakland, receiving an M.F.A. in 1958. Most importantly, Arneson taught for almost thirty years at the University of California, Davis, and during that time his role grew from that of regional maverick to influential national leader in ceramic sculpture.

By 1963 Arneson had discovered the distinctive, raucous voice that would characterize his work for the next two decades. Translating the humor of East Coast Pop Art to a California dialect, he injected rough surfaces, gaudy color, and sexual jokes into his ceramic objects, whether toilets, typewriters, or self-portraits. Arneson became the key advocate for the notion that ceramics did not need to be restricted to functional pieces or abstract objects for aesthetic contemplation. Instead, he himself created objects that unmistakably plunged into the Age of Aquarius and the Vietnam War.

Self-portraiture and the history of modern art were two of Arneson's great interests. His innumerable satirical depictions of himself and of famous artists such as Pablo Picasso or Jackson Pollock became well known during the 1970s. In the 1980s, however, a dramatically new dimension appeared in his work. Following continued bouts with cancer and a commission to memorialize the assassinated San Francisco mayor George Moscone, Arneson's preoccupation with violence and militarism led him to create the most powerful works of his career and to explore a new medium: bronze.

Nuke News brings together many of Arneson's concerns. It is thoroughly contemporary in its political impulse but also has strong roots in art history. It is cast in bronze, a traditional medium for major commissions and war monuments, and it is based on Picasso's *Death Head,* a bronze skull that Arneson saw in a 1967 exhibition of Picasso's sculpture at New York's Museum of Modern Art.[1] Cast from a wax model, *Nuke News* is an isolated skull. An alternate version, *Ground Zero,* places the same head on a shallow base that forms a targetlike X. One of Arneson's large drawings related to *Nuke News* is also in the collection of the Akron Art Museum, a gift from the artist.

Although *Nuke News* is serious—even gruesome—it reveals Arneson's noted wit in the poignant black humor of incised phrases memorializing the language of the nuclear age. Reminiscent of surviving graffiti from Pompeii or Rome, the inscriptions range from the names of physicists Oppenheimer, Teller, and Fermi to an enumeration of radioactive elements and the nicknames of the bombs deployed over Hiroshima and Nagasaki. But the colloquial phrases and epithets most clearly reveal Arneson's sardonic vision:

> LETS DROP THE BIG ONE NOW/HELLO RUSSIA/ATOMS FOR PEACE/ARMAGEDDON/GOTCHA/LETS WIN ONE FOR THE GIPPER/M.A.D. MUTUAL ASSURED DESTRUCTION/X-RATED/X-RAYS/NUCLEAR WAR HEAD/MAN UNKIND/ARMS RACE VS. HUMAN RACE/BETTER DEAD THAN RED/ON THE EVE OF DESTRUCTION/FUCK THE WORLD

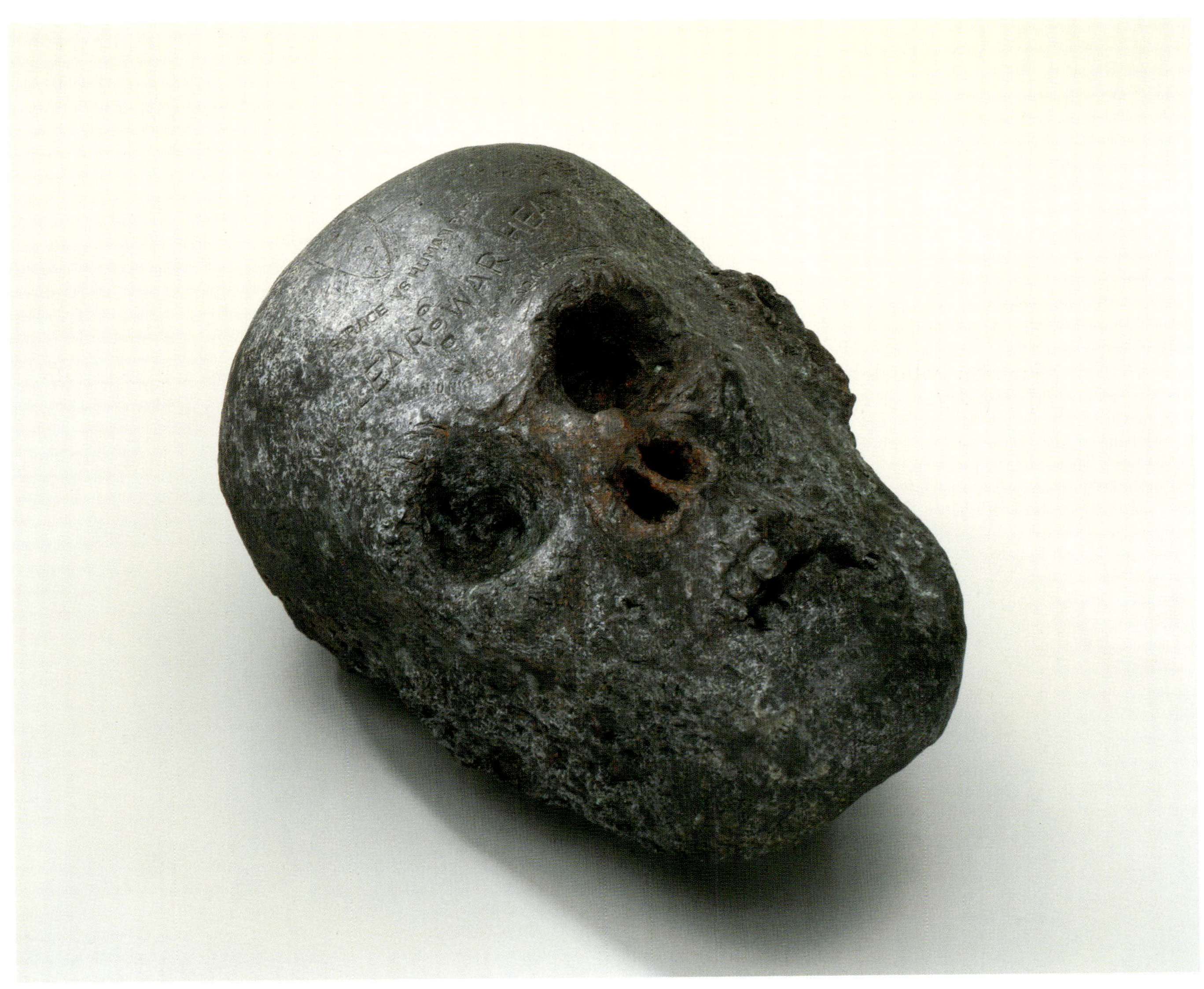

1990.11

Robert Arneson
Born 1930, Benicia, California; died 1992, Benicia, California

Nuke News, 1983

Bronze; 19 x 22 x 28 ⅛ in.
Purchased with funds from the National Endowment for the Arts Purchase Plan Program and the Elizabeth Firestone Graham Foundation

Jeffrey Grove

Cindy Sherman

Cindy Sherman—writer, director, set designer, and actor in a compelling series of single-frame stories—is lauded for her photographs that parody society's expectations of women. Although regarded as one of her country's most famous living photographers, Sherman does not consider herself a photographer; she views herself as someone who uses the camera as a conceptual tool for producing art.

Ironically, Sherman failed her first photography course at Buffalo State College, where she was enrolled in the painting program. She had always enjoyed dressing up as different characters and going to parties in disguise, and at the suggestion of a friend began to document her transformations using photography. This exercise led to the creation of a body of work—images commonly referred to as self-portraits—which first brought Sherman recognition. In reality, these photographs do not actually depict her but show the artist performing in various character roles.

Sherman's first series, Untitled Film Stills, remains one of her best known. To create those images, sixty-nine black-and-white portraits completed between 1977 and 1980, Sherman used wigs, costumes, and interior and exterior settings to effect chameleon-like transformations. The characters she generated were based on archetypes culled from films of the 1950s and early 1960s, including the melodramatic and hysterical women depicted in B-movies and the mysterious ingenues and sex kittens from French New Wave cinema. These photographs, utterly new yet strangely familiar, led one critic to conclude that each represented "a copy without an original."[1]

Sherman's third series, which includes *Untitled #96*, evolved from a never-published commission to create "centerfolds" for *Artforum* magazine. These ten images neatly meshed the artist's interest in the movies with a painterly concern for composition, light, shadow, and hue. In the Centerfolds series Sherman used chiaroscuro lighting, lurid color, and life-size scale to dramatic effect. Exterior props, integral to her earlier works, were pared back; instead, clothing, gesture, and the blank expression in Sherman's eyes offered visual clues. Heightening the psychological effect, the artist employed a horizontal format mimicking the layout of a "girlie" magazine. To achieve a theatrical point of view, she positioned the camera directly above her, visually pinning herself to a floor, couch, or bed, a strategy that has led some critics to associate the Centerfolds with themes of victimization and entrapment.

These claustrophobic, tightly cropped images do suggest emotional narratives, but in *Untitled #96* potential story lines seem dictated by the viewer's own memories and associations rather than Sherman's acting. The character Sherman described as an "adolescent girl"[2] lies sprawled across a 1970s linoleum floor looking pensive and bored. The floorcovering, the subject's hair, poly-blend sweatshirt, and picnic-plaid skirt are all queasy shades of orange. Perhaps an antidote to the girl's dreary existence lies in the torn section of newspaper she clutches—classified ads for dating and psychic services, one of which reads, "Know Yourself, Know Your Future." On the cusp of womanhood, the girl's anxiety is palpable.

Untitled #96 feels almost embarrassingly intimate, yet Sherman cautions against trying to extrapolate stories from her work. She explains that in the Centerfolds, "I want[ed] that choked-up feeling in your throat which may come from despair or teary-eyed sentimentality."[3] In *Untitled #96*, as in all of her work, Sherman shrewdly uses theatrical artifice to explore the artifice of photography. In doing so, she pointedly critiques the truth of the photograph and the honesty of self-portraiture. "It's not like I'm method acting or anything. I don't feel I *am* that person.... There's this distance.... And the one thing I've always known is that the camera lies."[4]

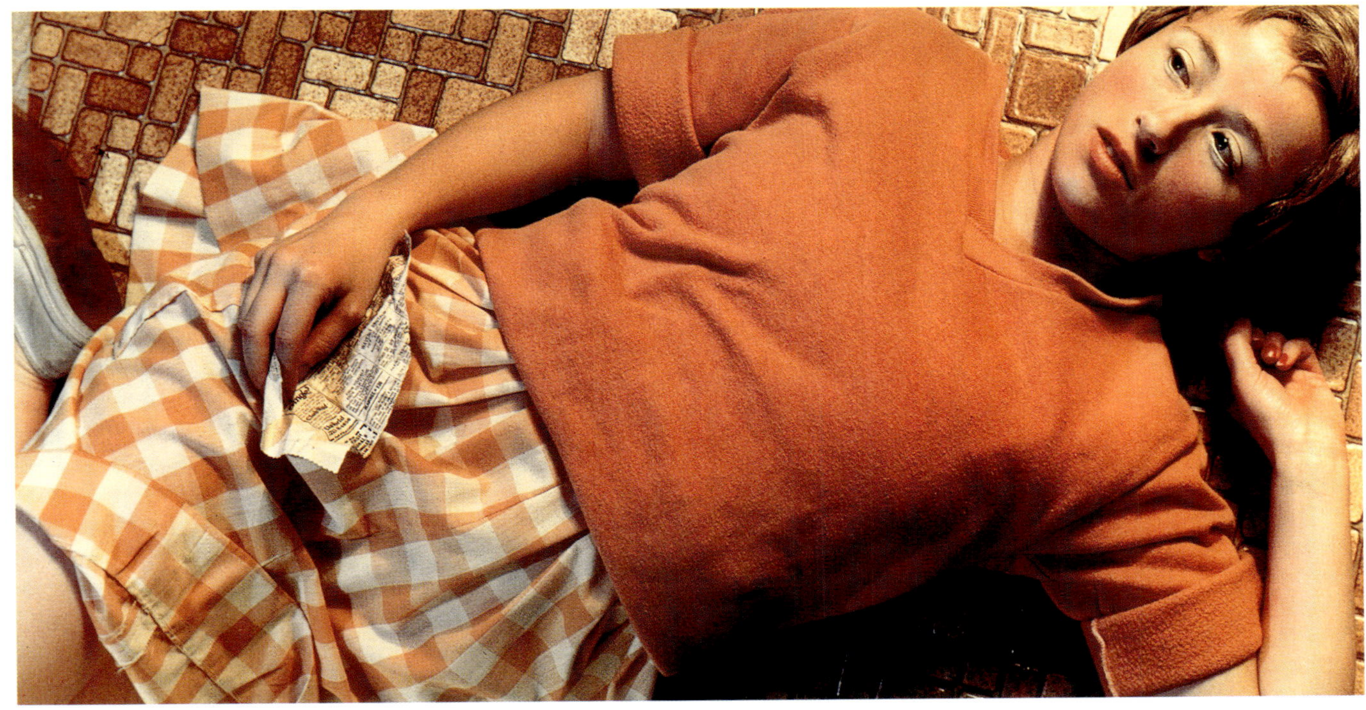

1981.34

Cindy Sherman
Born 1954, Glenn Ridge, New Jersey; lives New York

Untitled #96, 1981

Ektacolor print; 23¾ x 48 in.
Museum Acquisition Fund

Mitchell D. Kahan

Malcah Zeldis

Malcah Zeldis, whose birth name was Mildred Brightman, was raised in Detroit and started painting when she was sixteen. Visits to the Detroit Institute of Arts with her father, an immigrant who was a window washer and Sunday painter, made a profound impression on her. A teenage Zionist, she moved to the new State of Israel in 1949 and changed her name to Malcah, Hebrew for "queen." In Israel she married, had children, and lived on several collective farms. Returning to the United States in 1958 she painted intermittently until the 1970s, when she was finally able to devote her energies to painting and attaining a degree in early childhood education from Brooklyn College. Her paintings have addressed a wide range of subjects from contemporary life to the Old Testament, from the tragedies of the Holocaust and Hiroshima to the joy of her family's Passover seder. She has also written poetry and illustrated children's books.

Malcah Zeldis confounds expectations about self-taught artists or so-called folk painters. Unlike the majority of her peers, she has an advanced education. Moreover, she has shown that an artist may consciously choose to learn about art through books and visits to museums and yet develop a style independent of contemporary art. Zeldis shares a belief widespread among self-trained artists: she believes that she is a conveyor of forces outside herself. "It is as though I am a vessel waiting for the experiences of my life, the lives of others, the meanings of the universe to come suddenly into my being as mysterious visitors telling me about the wonder of their existences."[1]

Zeldis's paintings are distinctive for their vivid, even jarring use of brilliant color, often unmixed and straight from the tube. Simplified outlines, flattened figures, and enormous energy are typical of her works, including *Rita*, which celebrates the moment in the 1946 film *Gilda* when Rita Hayworth sings the sultry "Put the Blame on Mame" while stripping off her gloves. The figure is enlarged far out of proportion to her surroundings, denoting that hers is the key role in the film and suggesting the larger-than-life quality of a star from Hollywood's golden age. The accentuated nose is painted red, which the artist calls the color of "passion and love."[2] In *Rita* Zeldis conveys a perfect combination of energy, fun, and sexiness.

In an odd way, all of Zeldis's paintings are autobiographical, for they come from an intense and personal reaction to an event, whether or not the artist actually took part in it. Hayworth was one of Zeldis's childhood icons, and she remembers being told that she had a "moon face" like Hayworth's.[3] Rita and other characters from Zeldis's paintings such as Miss America and the Statue of Liberty are alter egos for the artist. Like many artists, self-taught or academically trained, Zeldis discovers herself through her work. After completing a painting depicting the biblical Joseph, she commented, "I realized that I was Joseph, the dreamer, and that the coat of many colors is my art."[4]

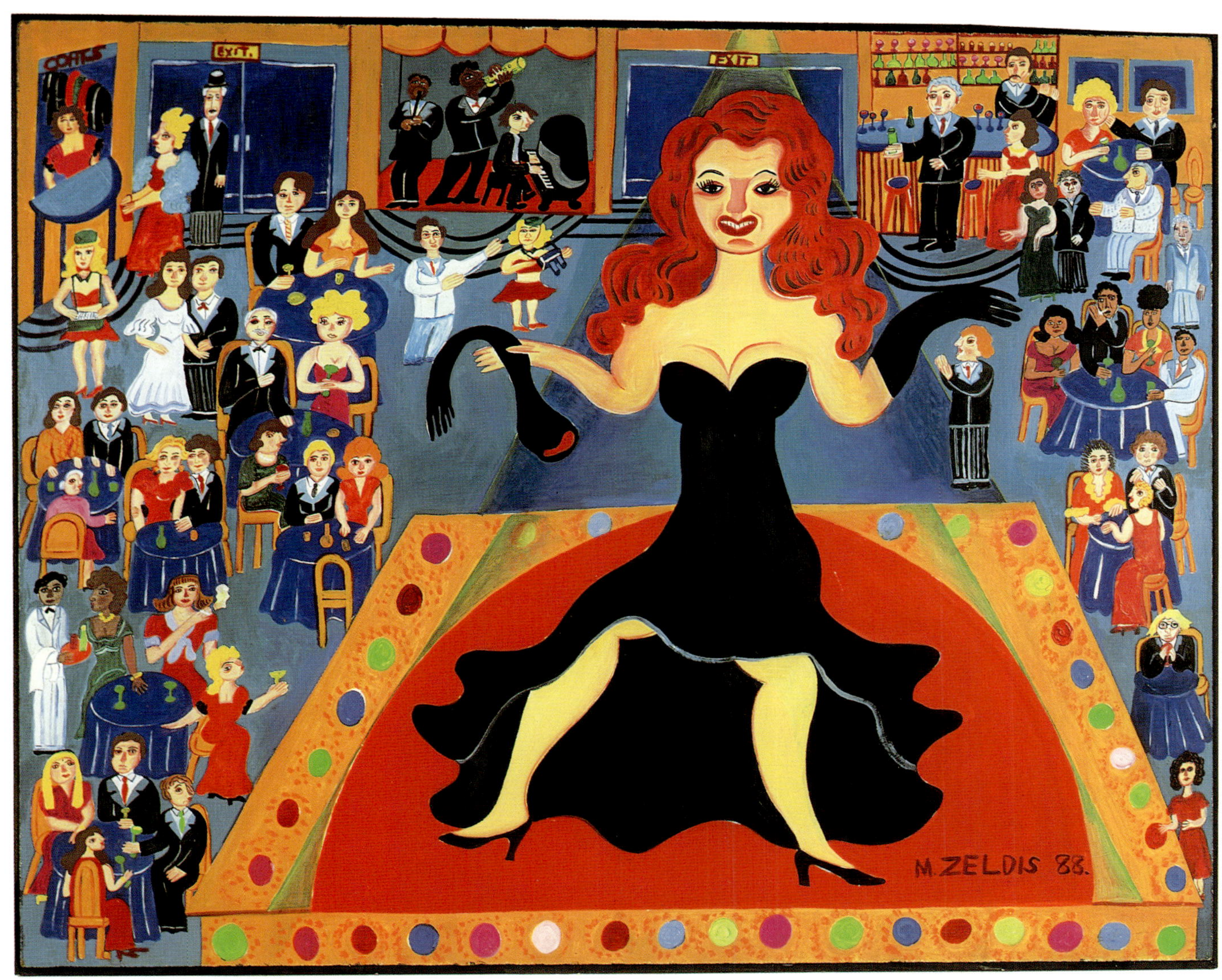

1991.65

Malcah Zeldis
Born 1931, New York; lives New York

Rita, 1988

Oil on fiberboard; 30 x 40 ⅛ in.
Gift of Herbert Waide Hemphill Jr.

Barbara Tannenbaum

Joel-Peter Witkin

It is oddly reassuring to know that art photography still has the power to shock. The photographs of Joel-Peter Witkin have proven that possible, even in an age when scenes of murders, atrocities, and wars enter our living rooms through television's evening news programs. *Courbet in Rejlander's Pool, New Mexico* is one of Witkin's tamest compositions in a body of works that includes images of corpses, the grotesquely obese, and other bizarre subjects. The artist's list of interests ranges from "physical prodigies of all kinds, pinheads, dwarfs, giants, hunchbacks, pre-op transsexuals, bearded women..." to "anyone bearing the wounds of Christ."[1]

Incidents in Witkin's personal history—his upbringing as a Catholic, his encounter at age six with a severed head while witnessing a traffic accident, his one-legged grandmother, and his twin brother's interest in the freaks on Coney Island—help explain his fascination with violence, physical anomalies, and death. However, his work is equally focused on the nature and history of art. Unlike many photographs, the artist's works are not slices of life captured by the camera but instead are elaborate, staged scenes, sketched out in advance—*tableaux vivants* posed for the lens then further worked on in the darkroom. "I make metaphors," says the artist.[2] *Courbet in Rejlander's Pool* is an example of this approach; it is steeped in the history of painting, the history of photography, the relationship between the two, and the artist's own life.

Witkin's photograph looks like a nineteenth-century image because of its warm tone, marks of what appears to be a former arched frame, and scratches and other marks across its surface. The slightly draped, nude female resembles a figurative study made by nineteenth-century photographers for painters. Indeed, the pose, arched frame, and composition are borrowed from an untitled work by Swedish-born English photographer Oscar Gustav Rejlander (1813–75), whose figure study may have been based on Venus's pose in Titian's painting of *Venus and Adonis*.[3] Rejlander believed photography could be an art form. As such, it would be capable of creating fiction that could be used to illustrate a higher truth than mere daily reality. Witkin also ascribes to this belief.

French painter Gustave Courbet (1819–77) vehemently disagreed with Rejlander, his contemporary, about art's purpose, urging instead a realist approach to art. Full-fleshed females such as the one in this photograph are common in his paintings. His *The Source* (which refers to the mouth of a stream that forms a pool) shows a nude female bather from the back in a pose close to both Rejlander's and Witkin's images. It was clearly an inspiration for Witkin, who below his sketch for *Courbet in Rejlander's Pool* pasted a part of a reproduction of the Courbet alongside another image of a nude seen from the back.[4]

The jarring note in Witkin's image, which gives it a different tone than either Courbet's or Rejlander's, is the three dark, angular, slightly smeared lines that mar his model's white back. Suggestive of scarification, they may be ink lines or tattoos. The model for this photograph is Witkin's wife, Cynthia, a professional tattooist. Whereas the photographer gazed through the camera at his mate, the viewer of the image becomes a voyeur, a participant in the scene. Are the woman's "scars" penitent's marks or the suggestion of a lifestyle that deviates from the norm? Beauty—and the appropriate role for art—is in the eye of the beholder.

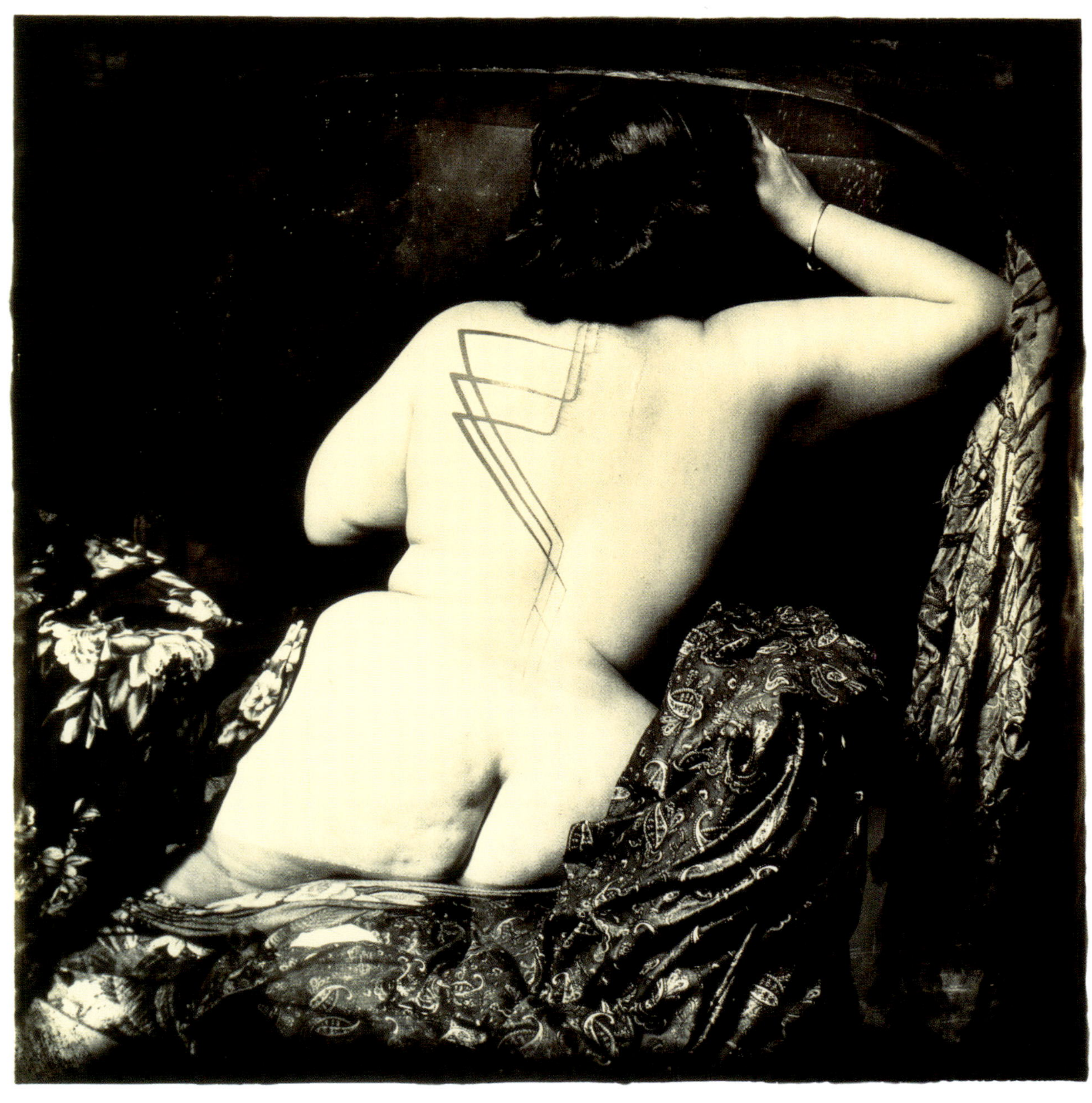

1986.49

Joel-Peter Witkin
Born 1939, Brooklyn; lives Albuquerque

Courbet in Rejlander's Pool, New Mexico, 1985

Gelatin silver print; 15 x 14 7/8 in.
Museum Acquisition Fund

Jeffrey Grove

John Coplans

John Coplans has been staging ruthless photographic examinations of his own imperfect flesh for nearly twenty years. With a single-minded dedication that is either deeply narcissistic or refreshingly selfless, Coplans has created a bracing body of work that challenges traditional standards of grace and beauty. Refusing to glamorize or diminish the idiosyncrasies of his aged skin, Coplans creates photographs that stand in stark contrast to the images of fresh beauties dominating today's culture.

Before devoting himself completely to photography, Coplans enjoyed a long and varied career in the arts, including a stint as director of the Akron Art Institute from February 1978 to December 1979.[1] It was during that time, Coplans recalls, that he "began making photographs in a very intuitive way... I used to photograph myself at night, after work. I'd take my clothes off and photograph my hands, photograph my body, using a camera with a timer. It was a little strange—you know what I mean?"[2]

For an artist who claims that he began making photographs in an "intuitive" way, Coplans has a decidedly programmatic approach to the process that may seem clinical and detached. He assumes the role of a cinematic director, deciding on lighting and equipment and even the poses before actually exposing any film. He employs assistants who use Polaroid positive/negative film (a type that develops both an image and a negative in about thirty seconds) to snap preparatory study photos. Next, checking his image on a monitor connected to a video camera, Coplans refines his pose, compressing and twisting his body into assorted configurations. Sometimes the video camera is positioned to look through the viewfinder of his 4 x 5-inch format camera. When he is pleased with the pose, a final image is taken.

Coplans has used this process consistently to dissect, analyze, and chronicle his body, bit by bit, limb by limb. Some images have focused on his hands, feet, back, and knees, while others depict him reclining, positioned upside-down, or assuming the positions of figures in ancient Greek friezes. Posed against a blank white background, Coplans's hirsute body is always shown headless, a strategy he feels helps make his images more universal.

Coplans often describes his photography in terms of art history, referring to one image as "Melanesian sculpture" and to *Self Portrait (Torso, Front)* as "a seventeenth-century drawing of a face."[3] Approached on a purely abstract level, the wisps and sprays of hair that adorn Coplans's torso might indeed suggest the deft lines of a Renaissance sketch. Those same tufts of hair might be seen to echo, in a humorous manner, the swirling strokes of pigment laid down by the Abstract Expressionist painters of the 1950s. In addition, Coplans's practice of acting out before the camera surely references performance and body art of the 1960s and 1970s, while his straightforward use of the gelatin silver print process to record classic poses recalls the earlier, mostly female, nudes of modernist masters such as Alfred Stieglitz and Edward Weston.

Coplans's characterizations of his photographs as drawings and sculptures and his references to art history clearly reflect a desire to have his work appreciated as fine art rather than documentation. Nonetheless, it is difficult not to see the artist's images as frank and forthright statements of what it means to age in a society that favors youth and beauty above all else.

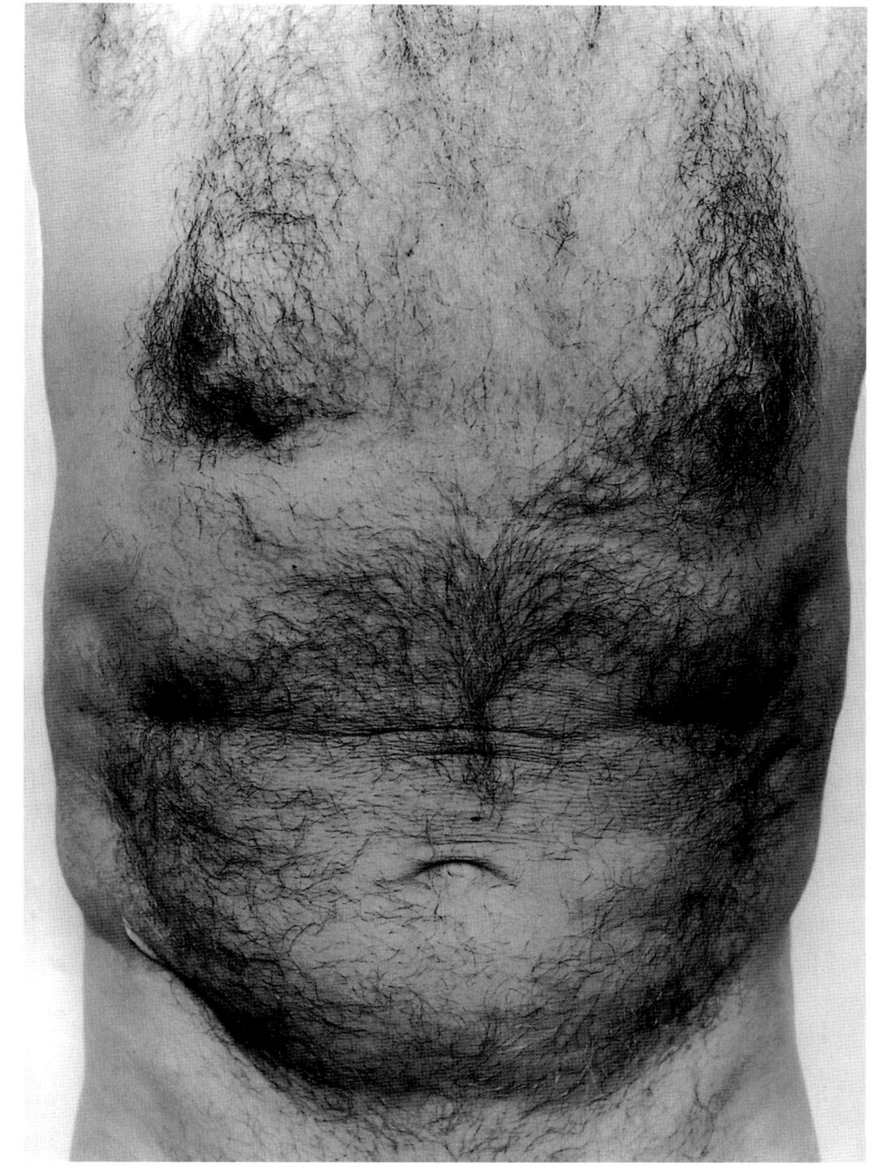

1991.114

John Coplans
Born 1920, London, England; lives New York

Self Portrait (Torso, Front), 1984

Gelatin silver print; 31 $\frac{3}{8}$ x 22 $\frac{1}{8}$ in.
Purchased with funds donated by Walter, Virginia, and Geraldine Wojno

Mitchell D. Kahan

Nam June Paik

The "father of video art," Nam June Paik will quite possibly be regarded in the future with the same reverence that history now accords Michelangelo or Caravaggio, Picasso or Duchamp—as the inventor of a new way of seeing.

Paik was raised in a prominent Korean family during a tumultuous period that included invasion by Japan and war between South Korea and North Korea. Instead of entering his father's business, Paik studied art, music, and philosophy, first in Seoul, then in Hong Kong during the Korean War, and later in Tokyo, Munich, and Cologne. By the end of the 1950s he was deeply involved in the world of avant-garde music as a composer and a performer. In Germany in 1963 Paik purchased thirteen used television sets, altered them, put them alongside pianos and noisemakers, and thus gave birth to a raucous new medium for art. Later that year, he began working with video engineers in Japan and also constructed his first robot, which walked, talked, and defecated plastic capsules.

In 1964 Paik visited New York and decided to stay. The following year, his experiments with altered video images had progressed to the point that he was ready to exhibit his first videotape. Paik never abandoned his interest in experimental music. Throughout his career, he has collaborated with other composers and performers, notably composer John Cage and cellist Charlotte Moorman, capturing them on his videotapes and using their musical compositions as well as his own.

High Tech Child is from a large body of video sculpture collectively titled *Family of Robot*. Paik's irreverent wit pervades the series, lampooning our era of information-overload even as he celebrates it. The family consists of grandparents, parents, aunts, uncles, and eleven similar but not identical children, all constructed primarily of television sets that convey the age of the family member. The grandparents, with old radio cabinets for heads, are composed of 1940s sets. The parents are 1940s and 1950s television sets, while the children are made from recent, miniature metal TVs.

The thirteen small television screens of *High Tech Child* can play either of two energetic, brilliantly colored videotapes produced by the artist: "Heart Channel" or "Robot Channel." The first is characterized by a rotating globe set against synthesized snippets of scenes from around the world. The second tape has a small robotlike figure surrounded by ever-changing colors and shapes; he is a man-child in a technological promised land. Although the tapes are not accompanied by music or narrative, both present the split-second transformation of one image into another for which Paik is known. This rapid shifting and morphing of images has had a pervasive impact on popular culture, particularly music video and advertising. Consumers worldwide have experienced Paik's influence without realizing it.

An enjoyable aspect of *High Tech Child* is its subtle and humorous acknowledgment of art history. The slightly adjustable legs and arms of the TV child assume a frontal pose that recalls the stance of a smiling Greek *kouros* (a statue of an idealized male youth) from the sixth century B.C., a noble ancestry for Paik's new vision of humanity. Most amusing is the fact that this metal-clad kid has as his base a wooden TV from the previous generation. Is this new generation acknowledging dependence on older technology, or is the child stamping out his elders? The glass screen of the wooden set has a reminder of what has been displaced. Paik's hand-brushed painting suggests a landscape or perhaps the defunct Abstract Expressionist movement, but its real message is that painting is obsolete, supplanted by electronic components and a new way of revealing the world.

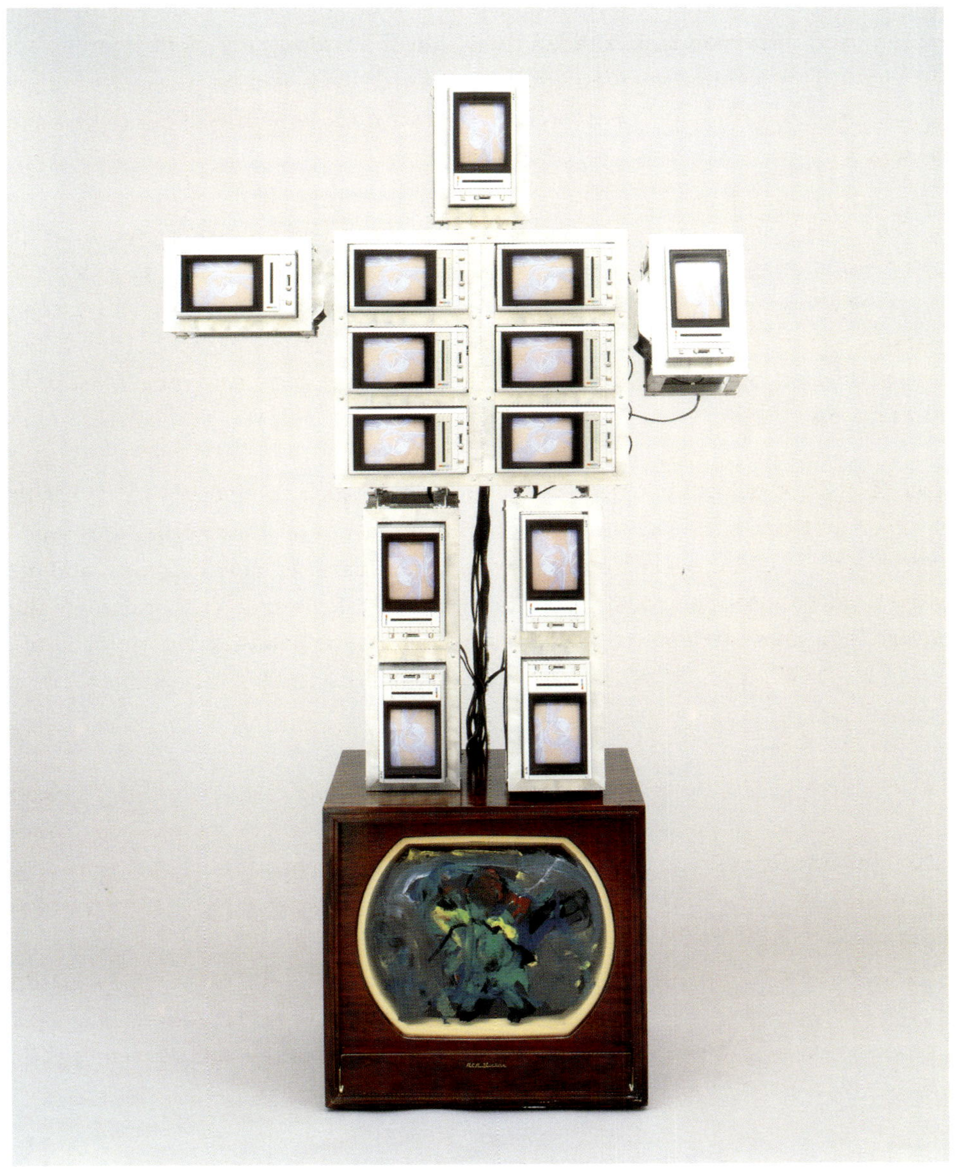

1987.30 a-s

Nam June Paik
Born 1932, Seoul, Korea; lives New York

Family of Robot: High Tech Child, 1987

Thirteen color televisions in aluminum frame on 1950s RCA table model cabinet with paint, video cassette player, and video tapes; 79 $\frac{1}{2}$ x 44 $\frac{1}{2}$ x 26 in.
Purchased with funds from Mr. and Mrs. Irving Sands and the Museum Acquisition Fund

Barbara Tannenbaum

W. D. ("Crazy Mac" or "Mad Mac") McCaffrey

Wayne McCaffrey, who at various times identified himself as "Crazy Mac," "Mad Mac," "Avatar Marsa," "God in Spirit, Plain Mac in the Flesh," and "Gadfly of the City," was a thin man with a huge grin who could talk a mile a minute about himself and his art, cracking jokes, and amusing (and bemusing) all those around him.[1]

McCaffrey earned his living as a house painter, doing remodeling and other jobs, finally working as a truck driver until his retirement in 1981. He had been building things all his life—from a soapbox derby racer to a house in the woods—but it was not until around 1970 that he started making artworks out of wire as a hobby. Though self-trained in art, McCaffrey was not really an "outsider" artist. He became well acquainted with mainstream art through regular visits to the Akron Art Museum, even making pieces in homage to its exhibiting artists. In 1985 he began to receive formal recognition for his work through exhibits in the Akron Art Museum, in regional art galleries, and in New York.

His earliest wire creations were vases and models of antique automobiles and airplanes, but because McCaffrey was a person of strong and highly individual opinions, it seemed inevitable that his subject matter would expand. He had long been sending written missives to area newspaper editors and politicians. Eventually he began to incorporate that commentary in some of his sculptures, using them to express his political views, social critiques, and interpretations of the tenets of Alcoholics Anonymous (AA).

AA, which was founded in Akron, became of central importance in McCaffrey's life in 1971. *Transition*, of which McCaffrey made four versions,[2] is a landscape illustrating his view of some of the organization's principles. According to the artist, the central figure, both flower and butterfly, signifies the blossoming which takes place in the individual as a result of the AA process; a letter "A" tops the tip of each wing. Above and below the butterfly are symbols of the two religions from which AA draws many of its tenets, Judaism and Christianity.

Flanking the flower are two alternative states of existence. The right side presents the virtues of what McCaffrey called "God Power": justice, life everlasting, love, purity, and truth. It is topped by a large star representing Saint Francis (a personal hero of McCaffrey's). The left shows the "Weaknesses of Satan Pride," in McCaffrey's words, including alcohol, drugs, and bigotry, as well as the traditional deadly sins. These are suspended between "Cloud 9" (perhaps a state of intoxication?) and a volcano representing Hell.

Dotting the blue evening sky in the background are stars, each containing a plastic, commercially made eyeball representing the omnipresent eye of God. Although prefabricated eyes had long been a feature of McCaffrey's animals and portraits, the eyes' prevalence here is the influence of a painting by Cleveland artist Scott Miller that McCaffrey saw at the Akron Art Museum and much admired.

According to McCaffrey, *Transition* has a message for all of us, alcoholic or not: the struggle between good and evil is a simple choice, a battle that can be won. After spending most of his life dependent on alcohol, McCaffrey triumphed over his addiction and also over numerous family tragedies and financial problems to make a name for himself in the city, not only as a gadfly but also as one of its valued artists.

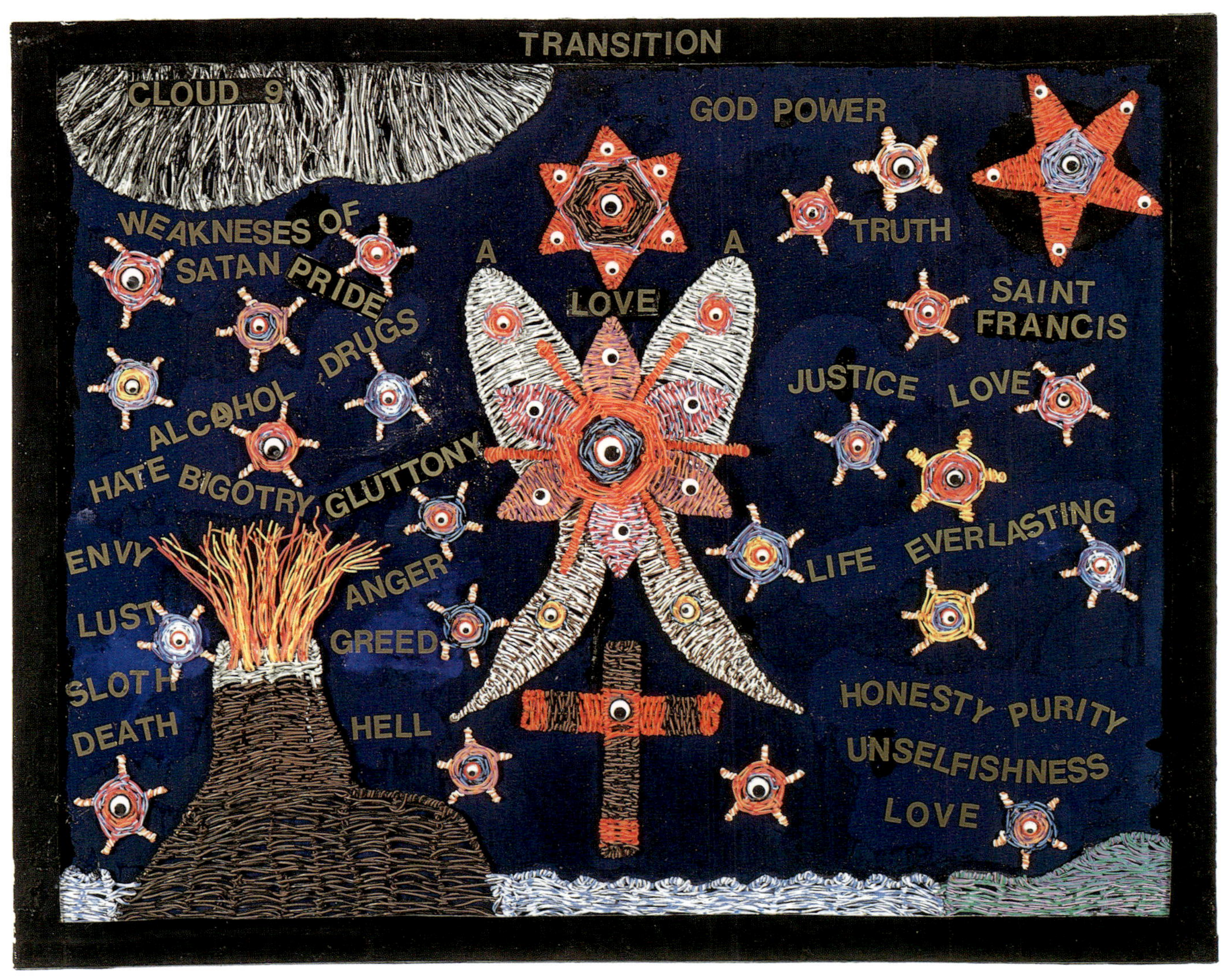

1991.1

W. D. ("Crazy Mac" or "Mad Mac") McCaffrey
Born 1923, Akron, Ohio; died 1993, Akron, Ohio

Transition, 1991

Telephone wire, vinyl letters, paper, plastic eyeballs, fabric glue, and paint on canvas board with painted frame; 22 ⅛ x 28 ¼ x 1 ¾ in.
Museum Acquisition Fund

Barbara Tannenbaum

Anthony Joseph Salvatore

Anthony Joseph Salvatore dedicated himself to fulfilling a divine mission—the illustration of the Holy Scriptures in order to spread God's Word. The subject of *Psalms 25, Verse 4 and 5,* which is a relatively large painting for Salvatore, can also be seen as an allegory of the artist's own life. According to the biblical verses represented, the figures in the blue and white robes say, "Show me thy ways, O Lord, teach me thy paths. Lead me in thy truth, and teach me; for thou art my God and my Saviour; on thee do I wait all the day."[1]

In the course of daily prayer, Salvatore said he received from God not only instruction on which biblical texts to portray but also three-dimensional, full-color, animated visions of the texts—similar to scenes in movies or stage plays.[2] For him, accurate transcription of both text and vision was essential, completely overriding concerns about naturalism, formal structure, or deference to past or present art styles.

Salvatore's lack of shading and use of multiple (often flattened) perspectives are in perfect accord with his work's symbolic function. His forms are sometimes so personalized that they almost seem abstract. The Lord appears here in the Old Testament guise of a pillar of fire—an enormous, dark purple column of smoke broken by bright orange-red flames. In accord with Old Testament proscriptions, the Lord's face is not shown, replaced instead by a light-colored halo with bright yellow "flames." Humans huddle in the pillar's warmth, sheltered from an unwelcoming, symmetrical landscape that yields no hint of the path to be taken. The fact that God answers their plea is symbolized by clouds of breath emerging from his mouth and the top of his head, and by the tiny, dark red, flamelike shapes coming from the humans. The latter device was used by Salvatore to indicate speaking in tongues, which, as a Pentecostal Christian, he understood to be a sign of communication with the divine.

Although first and foremost a visionary artist, Salvatore did receive some training in art, from childhood instruction in school and at The Butler Institute of American Art to a few years of classes at Youngstown State University around 1978. He came to the university with his style already formed. His professors' contributions were to introduce him to some new materials, encourage him to work on a larger scale, and help him develop greater formal sophistication, especially in his handling of color. Salvatore's working process, a combination of painting and drawing on either canvas or paper, began with a pencil or marker sketch, which was often followed by a ground of acrylic paint, then topped with multiple layers of drawing with crayons and oil pastels—media that allowed him to build up a glossy, color-saturated surface.

Salvatore was discovered in 1980 when Rafael Ferrer, a visiting artist at Youngstown State, took his work to a New York art dealer. Since then, Salvatore's work has been widely exhibited and has entered a number of prestigious private and museum collections, usually in the context of work by other self-taught or "folk" artists. Salvatore himself did not care how his art was designated as long as it attracted attention to the Lord's Word, which he felt was a pillar of fire that could provide guidance through the wilderness of modern life.

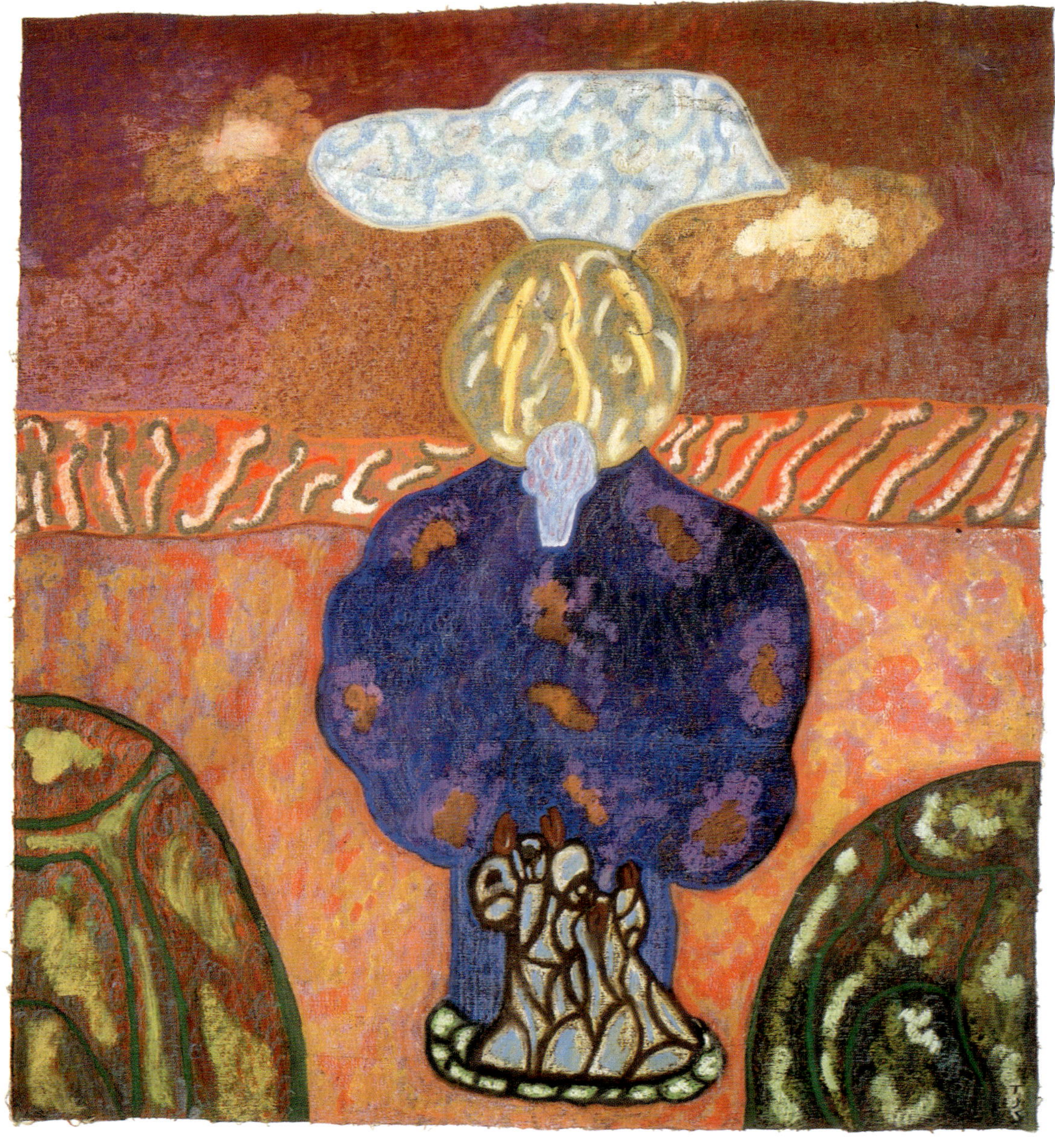

1992.7

Anthony Joseph Salvatore
Born 1938, Youngstown, Ohio; died 1994, Youngstown, Ohio

Psalms 25, Verse 4 and 5, 1991

Pencil, acrylic, oil pastel, and wax crayon on canvas; 64 ½ x 59 in.
Gift of David P. Colts for Anthony J. Salvatore in memory of the artist's father, Tony Salvatore

Barbara Tannenbaum

Nancy Spero

For most of her career, Nancy Spero worked counter to the mainstream movements in art. In Paris from 1959 to 1964, she painted moody, expressionistic canvases while Pop Art's ironic humor and slick style were gaining international recognition. When she returned to the United States in 1964, the art world was hailing Minimalism's purity and detachment. Spero, in contrast, was producing highly emotional drawings protesting the Vietnam (and all) war and violence against women. In the late 1970s and early 1980s, Neo-Expressionist painting, with its macho posturing and predominantly male roster of artists, gained in popularity. Just a few years earlier, in 1974, Spero had decided to focus her art exclusively on women. She had been involved in the feminist art movement since the late 1960s, and wanted "to see what it means to view the world through the depiction of women."[1] Spero's choice of medium also challenged traditional hierarchies. Since 1966 she has worked exclusively on paper, using the technique of collage to merge drawings, written text, painted images, and handprinted images of her own drawings.

Because works on paper are usually smaller and more fragile than paintings on canvas or sculptures, they are often accorded secondary status in the art world. Spero overcame that prejudice in part by making large-scale collages, which, despite their size, do not lose the medium's intimacy and complexity. In *Stalks II (Sky Goddess Totem)*, she joined four sheets of paper to make a tall vertical piece; across them she stamped and pasted images of women. While the overall patterning of the work has a strong impact from a distance, the image's delicacy and the amount of detail in the figures force close and careful scrutiny.

Spero also attacked the lower status of works on paper by using collage as a vehicle for monumental ideas. After years of works about social and political outcasts and the atrocities perpetrated on women, Spero turned in the 1980s to celebrating the vitality of life. *Stalks II* shows women as goddesses of fertility and creation. It includes three images of the Egyptian sky goddess Nut, who is depicted with multiple breasts. She arches over the world, each night swallowing the sun and each morning giving birth to it again.[2] *Stalks II* also contains several figures taken from historic aboriginal art. The mythological women are juxtaposed with idealized heads of contemporary Western females whose sources of power reside in their intellects rather than their bodies.

Several ways of representing the female body are employed in *Stalks II:* all of them depict woman as active and strong. The asymmetrical, overlapping placement of the figures further enhances their dynamism; they dance across this tall "totem" chronicling a sense of transcendent sisterhood that spans generations and cultures. "One of my main strategies," said Spero, "has been to construct a simultaneity of women through time.... I think that many women are now interested in the idea of the Goddess—of a powerful, self-sustaining and autonomous being capable of moving through life as freely as a man."[3]

Stalks II uses images from the past to prophesy a world of women proud of their femaleness and free to celebrate it. In general, true equality is yet to be achieved. In the art world, steps toward equality were taken in the mid-1980s, around the time that Spero's art finally began to receive attention and critical recognition. The multicultural "herstory" (as opposed to *his*tory) that Spero and other feminist artists present is finally moving into the mainstream in the arts and in society.

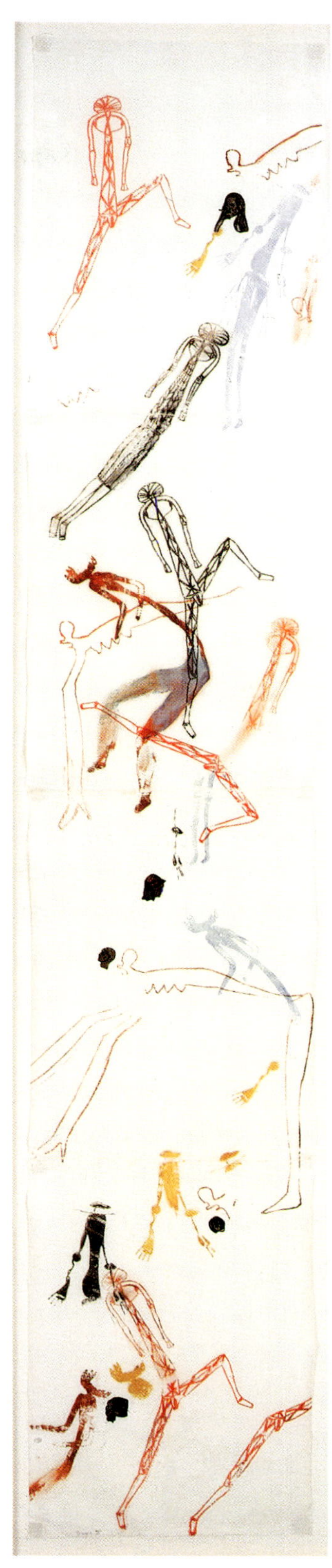

1991.7

Nancy Spero
Born 1926, Cleveland; lives New York

Stalks II (Sky Goddess Totem), 1985

Handprinting and handprinted collage on paper; 111 x 20 ⅜ in. Purchased with funds from the National Endowment for the Arts Purchase Plan Program, the Elizabeth Firestone Graham Foundation, and the Museum Acquisition Fund

Mitchell D. Kahan

Abramović and Ulay

Marina Abramović and Ulay (F. Uwe Laysiepen) worked and lived together for twelve years following their meeting in 1975 on their mutual birthday. They settled in Amsterdam, but the city was less a home than a congenial base for worldwide artistic pursuits. During the 1980s they explored the philosophical issues of ethical living and inner consciousness, rejecting postmodern preoccupations with consumerism and artificiality that characterized so much of the decade.

When they met, both were already engaged in performance art, a hybrid discipline combining a variety of expression—such as poetry, theater, dance, video—into a symbolic artistic experience. In performance art the artist is usually both conceiver and performer. Themes can range from mystical allegory to something verging on cabaret entertainment. Abramović and Ulay eschewed the latter in favor of extreme concentration and meditative, symbolic acts that explore what it means to think, to feel, to love, to trust, and to fear. They poetically summarized their art as "no fixed living place\permanent movement\direct contact\local reaction\self-selection\passing limitations\taking risks\mobile energy."[1]

The title *Modus Vivendi* was first applied by the artists to a 1983 performance in Italy. Moving with extreme slowness, Ulay uttered incantations such as "hearing, hearing; moving, moving; touching, touching," lyrically conveying human conditions like weightiness, loss, separation, or union. The same title was later given to a series of Polaroid photographs, including the major work owned by the Akron Art Museum. Each of the series' four life-size images was carefully staged in Boston in front of a giant experimental camera built by the Polaroid Corporation. Used primarily for research purposes, the camera was made available to artists through a special corporate initiative. Like the familiar hand-held Polaroid cameras, it produces one-of-a-kind photographs employing similar technology.

In *Modus Vivendi* the artists rejected the camera's ability to portray external physical appearances in order to create a gleaming golden atmosphere in which the human body becomes a symbolic icon. The dark silhouettes of the two artists recall certain performances in which, backlit, they appeared as black shapes on a stage. Their slow movements were almost imperceptible; viewers only intermittently realized that the poses had changed, each new gesture summoning rich emotions and some evoking a particular time period or culture. The four separate Polaroid images reflect the restrictions of the camera, but this limitation is used symbolically. The multipart structure suggests how entities—in this case archetypes of male, female, and nature—may appear to exist separately but are in fact part of a whole.[2]

Ulay assumes a dynamic pose, thrusting a pike downward, suggesting both farmer and warrior. The image illustrates humanity's bond to the land and male energy as active penetration. In another print Abramović stands frontally, goddesslike, pointing to both earth and sky. Her dramatic personification of a new kind of Mother Nature is also metaphysical, perhaps suggesting that mankind is the result of joining physical matter with heavenly creation. A third print captures an embrace that brings together male and female forces. And the fourth is of a delicate, haunting tree, which elicits thoughts on fruitfulness and the relation of humanity to fragile nature.

If the golden background implies a timeless, almost fairy-tale allegory of life, the achingly thin tree and the soulful embrace introduce a vein of melancholy. Elsewhere Abramović reminds us that "in the end you are really alone, whatever you do," which, like the work itself, reflects the artist's ancient role as seer, philosopher, and seeker of truth, wherever it may lead.[3]

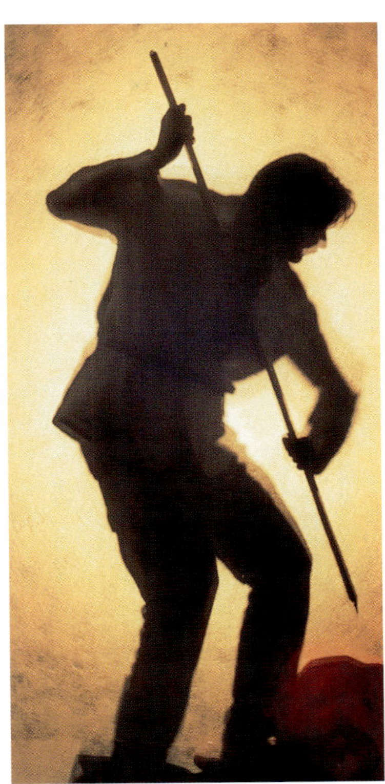
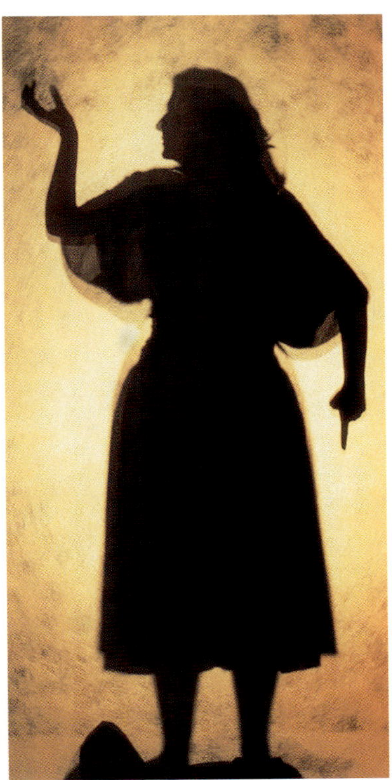

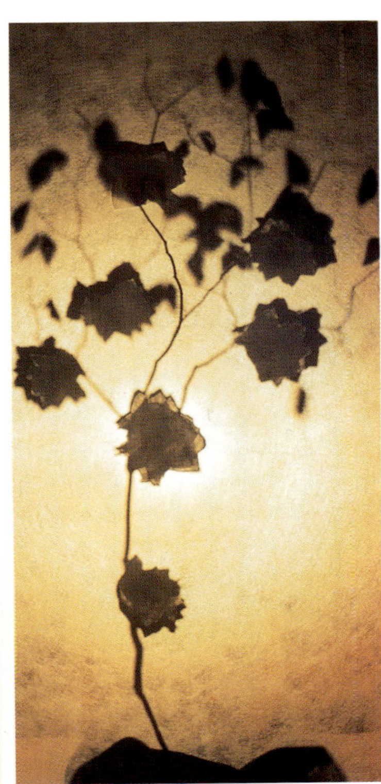

1987.9 a-d

Abramović and Ulay
Marina Abramović
Born 1946, Belgrade, Yugoslavia; lives Amsterdam, The Netherlands
Ulay (F. Uwe Laysiepen)
Born 1943, Solingen, Germany; lives Amsterdam, The Netherlands

Modus Vivendi (Way of Living), 1984

Polaroid prints; four, each 80 7/8 x 41 1/2 in.
Purchased with funds from the estate of Clara L. Knight, by exchange

Mitchell D. Kahan

Richard Deacon

Richard Deacon's labor-intensive methods of fabrication focus attention on the innate physical properties of materials, such as the sensual burnished copper of *Cover.* His sculptures are all unfamiliar abstract forms, without links to any prior experience. Nevertheless, rich psychological associations emanate from the shapes and materials.

Deacon was raised in Sri Lanka and England; his mother was a surgeon and his father a pilot. The artist began art studies in 1968; he received a B.A. from St. Martin's School of Art and an M.A. from the Royal College of Art. He has taught in London and exhibited throughout the United States and Western Europe. In 1987 Deacon received the Turner Prize, awarded to a British artist for exceptional achievement.

"I am a fabricator, not a carver or a modeller," says the artist.[1] Like Donald Judd (see pp. 150–51), Deacon uses industrial and construction materials, not media such as clay and bronze that are traditionally associated with art. But unlike Judd and other American Minimalists, whose techniques embrace industrial technology, Deacon works in his studio using hand tools. He proceeds intuitively, each piece taking shape at full-scale without preplanning or small preparatory models. The result is an energetic fluidity and an awareness of the sculptor's touch.

For Deacon, no choice is made solely for aesthetic reasons, but each bears the added weight of metaphorical possibility. In *Cover* the hammered copper sheets recall armor or sheathing or aged leather. The oxidized surface suggests a natural geological process. Though Deacon rarely works from sketches, the overall contour of *Cover* is based on a drawing he made of Laurasia, one of the hypothetical primordial land masses from which our current five continents divided.[2] That tie to the earth is also seen in the sculpture's gridded divisions, which recall Deacon's interest in mapping, specifically the markings for latitude and longitude.

Implicit inferences about the value of hand labor pervade Deacon's sculpture. The joy of craftsmanship, however, is mitigated by certain factors. *Cover* seems overbuilt, almost armored. The use of multiple staples to attach the copper sheets to the fiberglass understructure finds a parallel in other works by Deacon that have excessive numbers of screws, brackets, and rivets. This extreme craftsmanship borders on a disquieting obsessiveness.

Deacon's titles are carefully chosen. Art may be visual, but language makes us think about art. "Cover" is a noun and a verb at the same time, suggesting a thing and an activity.[3] The word implies that something is hidden. "To cover" is also a term from horsebreeding that means to inseminate. Indeed, viewed from its projecting end, male sexual organs emerge, while from the heavier end a mountainous, crooked spine summons images of a landscape or beast.

Describing several earlier pieces, Deacon made an observation that also applies to *Cover*: "In all the work the organic, the inorganic, and the human, are somehow combined."[4] Appropriately, *Cover* is somewhat larger than a human figure but smaller than a monument; it is neither anthropomorphic nor architectural but an unsettling presence standing on the floor rather than a pedestal. The sculpture inevitably elicits the question, "What is it?" only to summon uncertain and contradictory responses. *Cover* is sensual yet threatening, beautiful and ugly, evoking both attraction and repulsion.

In a catalogue essay on his wife's ceramic work, Deacon wrote that "a confusion between flatness and depth, invitation and rebuttal, characterizes our dealing with the world."[5] His view of life characterizes his own art. Physical attributes are inextricably linked to charged psychological responses.

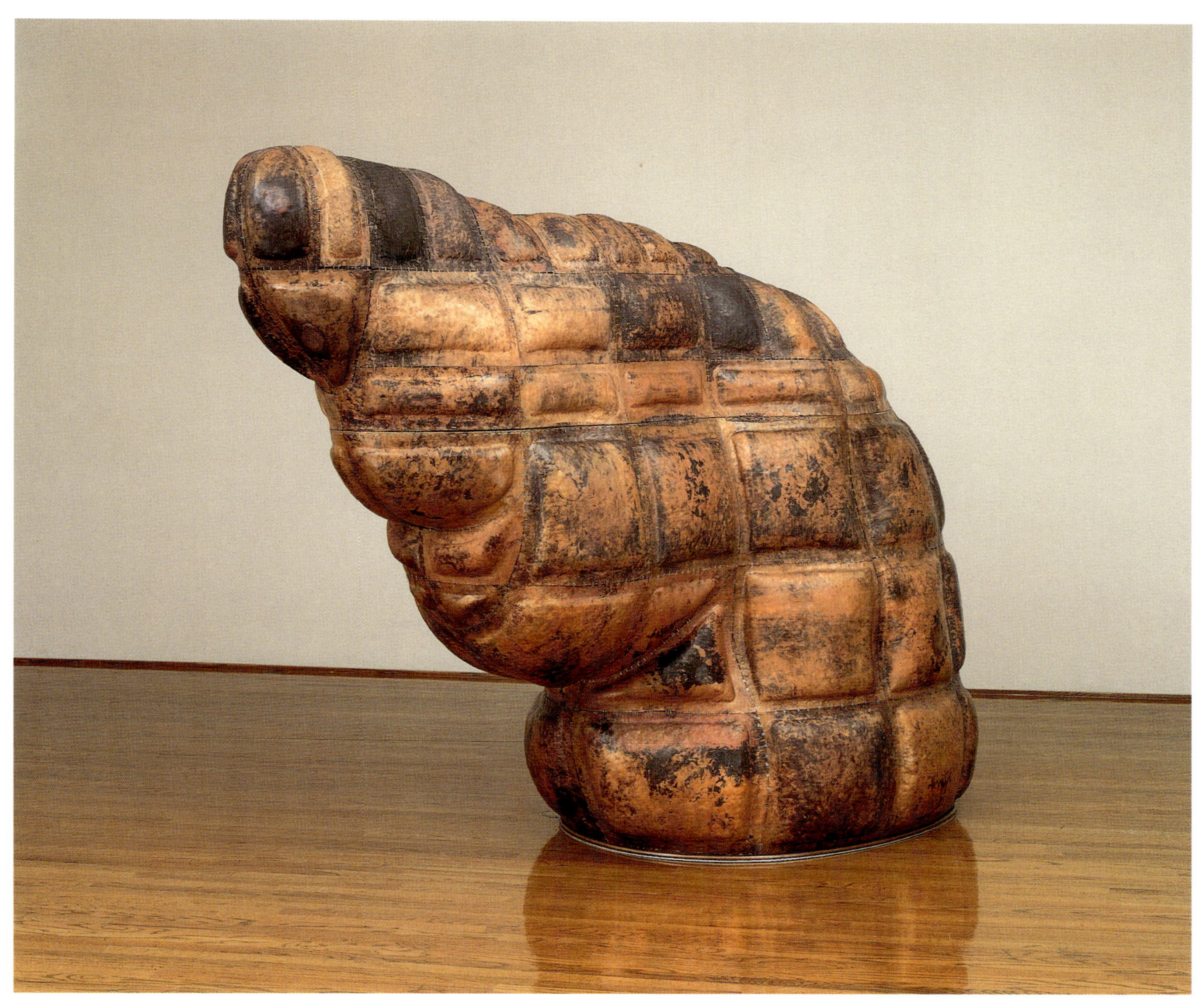

1991.115 a,b

Richard Deacon

Born 1949, Bangor, Wales; lives London

Cover, 1990

Medium density fiberboard, wood, and copper; 72 x 132 x 48 in.
Museum Acquisition Fund and The Mary S. and Louis S. Myers Endowment Fund for Painting and Sculpture

Mitchell D. Kahan

Robert Rauschenberg

One of the most celebrated artists of the late twentieth century, Robert Rauschenberg has been prolific in painting, sculpture, and printmaking as well as performance art, costume, and set design. Insistently combining separate disciplines, he explores what he has memorably called "the gap between art and life."

Born Milton Rauschenberg and raised on the Gulf Coast near Louisiana, Rauschenberg was drafted into the army after being expelled from college. He discovered art and museums while stationed in California, and later studied in Kansas City, Paris, and at the experimental Black Mountain College in North Carolina. By the early 1960s, Rauschenberg had developed numerous innovative techniques: he combined painted surfaces with salvaged objects and transferred images from the print media by various methods including photo-silkscreen. In 1964 he won the prestigious grand prize at the Venice Biennale.

Rauschenberg first conceived the idea of an international tour of his work in 1976. He founded the Rauschenberg Overseas Culture Interchange (ROCI), which organized and funded the artist's travels in the Americas, Europe, and Asia and exhibitions of his work in eleven different lands between 1984 and 1990. Most of the countries had minimal exposure to international contemporary art. For Rauschenberg, "one-to-one contact through art contains potent, peaceful powers...seducing us into creative mutual understandings for the benefit of all." The ROCI project was proof of his belief that "Art is educating, provocative, and enlightening even when first not understood."[1]

In each country, the artist traveled, photographed, and collected indigenous artifacts. Artworks informed by the encounter between the American artist and the host country were then exhibited, some having been made abroad, others in Rauschenberg's studios in New York and Florida. While some critics decried this effort as naive (and even a form of cultural imperialism), Rauschenberg's monumental expenditure of personal funds over a decade and his donation of major works to the host countries should be recognized as a remarkable testament to the power of an individual to act outside of government to promote international communication.

Rauschenberg's trip to the former Soviet Union resulted in two significant bodies of work: fabric wall hangings and seven large photogravures on paper (the Akron Art Museum owns two). The photogravures were made on Long Island at Universal Limited Art Editions following trips to Leningrad, Moscow, Tbilisi, and Samarkand. They bring together photographs taken by Rauschenberg in the Soviet Union and the United States, placing communism and capitalism side by side and forcibly uniting the two former superpowers into one harmonious whole.

Soviet/American Array VII fulfills Rauschenberg's desire to bridge art and life. It refers to the real world but imposes numerous aesthetic choices in the selection of images, their cropping, the distinct blocks of color, and the unusual choice of photogravure for printing. This once-popular commercial process for reproducing photographs allows ink to seep into the paper, yielding a hazy, almost nostalgic quality, as if Cold War rivalry has been relegated to the past.

Some of the artist's favorite themes can be seen in *Soviet/American Array VII,* particularly that of the male figure at work and leisure. The two American construction workers linking hands to attack a bolt perfectly symbolize the artist's own lifelong commitment to collaboration, whether with choreographers, composers, or the masterful technicians who print photogravures. It is no accident that the arrow points up, a sign of optimism to thwart the nearby rubbish. Rauschenberg explained that as a young artist he wanted "to photograph the entire United States." Not hubris at all, Rauschenberg's impossible desire "to look at everything" and to embrace the entire world has impelled him for over forty years.[2] ROCI is the grand, logical outgrowth of such an attitude.

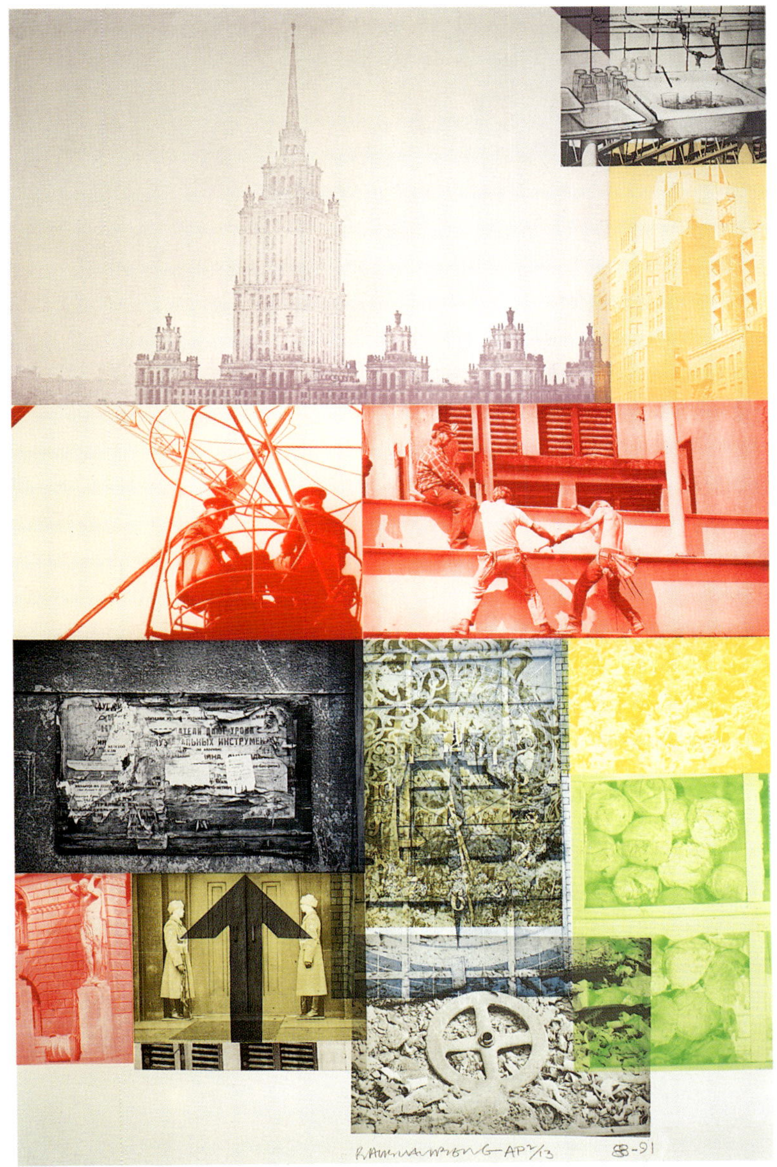

1993.6

Robert Rauschenberg
Born 1925, Port Arthur, Texas; lives Captiva, Florida

Soviet/American Array VII, 1988–91

Photogravure; 78 5/8 x 50 5/8 in.
Knight Purchase Fund for Photographic Media

Jeffrey Grove

Thomas Struth

One of a series of images that Thomas Struth took in museums throughout North America and Europe, *National Gallery I, London* is rich in emotional and psychological content. Struth set up his equipment—a large-format camera mounted on a tripod—in museum galleries, then waited for people to walk in and out of the frame. When the composition suited him, Struth tripped the camera's shutter. He did not pose museum visitors, but given the camera's size and lack of mobility it is hard to believe that most were unaware they were being photographed.

From the start Struth approached his work in a systematic, almost clinical fashion. In the 1970s he studied with leading German artists noted for their intellectual approach to art—among these, photographers Bernd and Hilla Becher and painter and photographer Gerhard Richter. His first body of photographs were black-and-white images that focused on the urban landscape, particularly unpeopled streets and enormous housing complexes. (The Akron Art Museum owns two of those works as well.) His second series, in color, was a group of family portraits that comment on the intimacy and estrangement that often coexist in families. In his third body of work—the museum photographs—Struth focuses on the ways we perceive art and interact both with the artwork and with others similarly engaged.

As lush and luminous as the paintings it portrays, *National Gallery I, London* shows five museum visitors as they scrutinize three Italian Renaissance paintings.[1] Each painting, far removed from its original time, place, and purpose, is presented in a new context. The central painting, for instance, was originally part of an altar in a church, where it served as an object of religious veneration. In the museum, it may again become an object of adoration, now valued more for its aesthetic, cultural, and historical significance than its religious meaning. The works on the left and in the center represent biblical parables; the work on the right portrays a Venetian head of state. This arrangement contrasts secular and spiritual subjects with pointed effect. Discussing the museum photographs, Struth expressed his belief that distinctions separating art, religion, and entertainment have become hopelessly eroded: "Today museums [are comparable] to the sports field or to religion."[2]

Other elements strengthen the idea that art, like religion, has become a form of worship. The young woman in the center appears to genuflect as she views the painting. Further, the photograph itself seems luminescent, as if it were lit mysteriously from within. This curious effect is achieved through Struth's unusual mode of presentation. He attached the front of the photograph to a sheet of Plexiglas using a clear adhesive. Because there is no protective backing, light reflects off the wall and through the image, giving it a seductive, almost ethereal glow. The sensation is similar to viewing a slide projected on a screen—the way many of us first encounter great works of art in an art history course or lecture.

The visitors shown here share the intimacy of a group activity, yet emotionally and physically each remains alienated from the others, silent and alone. Their truest involvement seems to be with the paintings. The pose of some figures and the color of their garments seem to echo those of characters in the paintings. Such details let us know that Struth captured this scene at a strategic moment. Carefully synthesizing his interests in art, architecture, physical space, and the psychology of human behavior, Thomas Struth demonstrates his facility as a thoughtful investigator of the social, emotional, and intellectual forces shaping the role art plays in our lives.

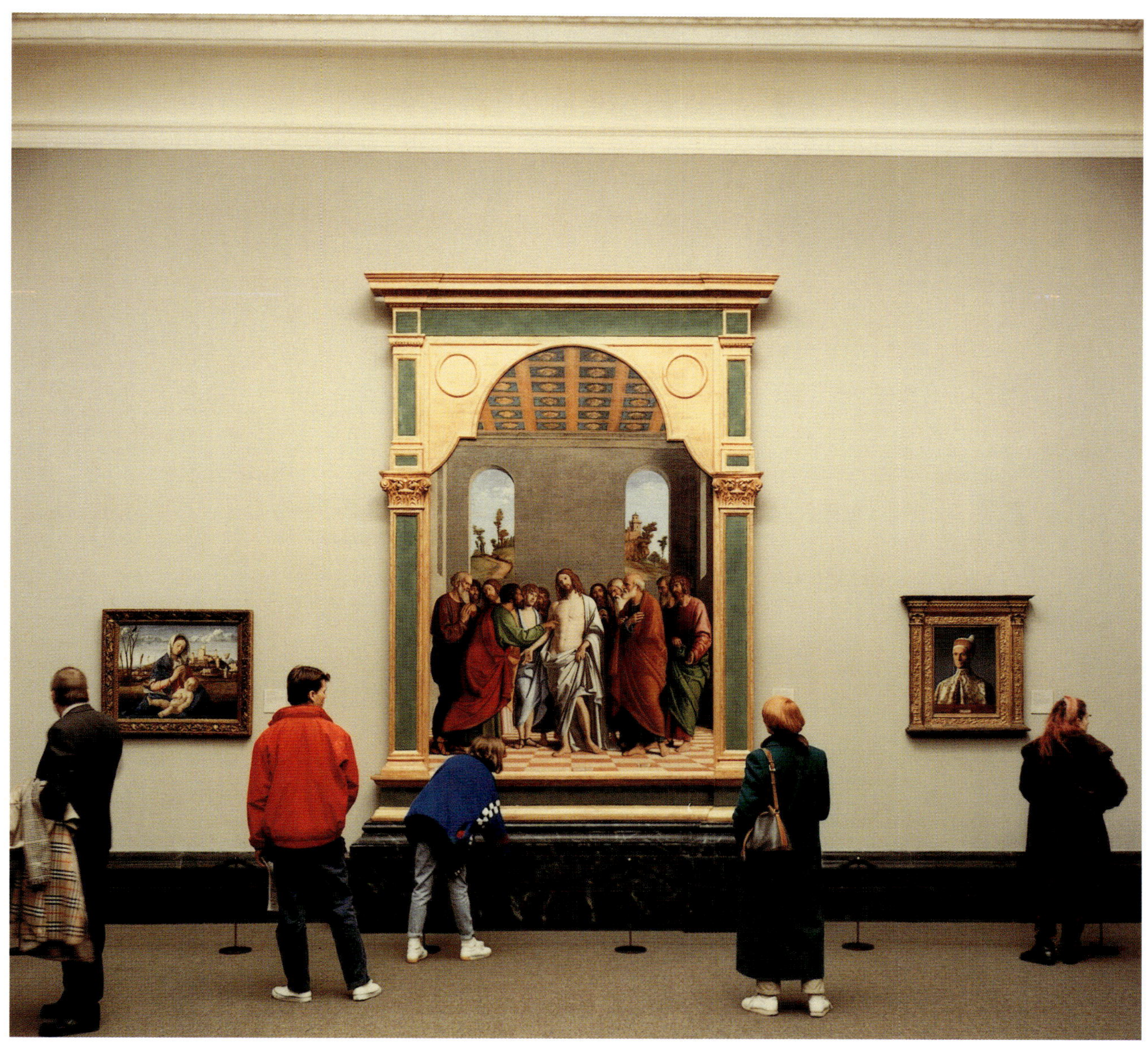

1993.10

Thomas Struth
Born 1954, Geldern, Germany; lives Düsseldorf, Germany

National Gallery I, London, 1989

Type C color print; 71 x 77 ¼ in.
Knight Purchase Fund for Photographic Media

Barbara Tannenbaum

Carrie Mae Weems

Until the Kitchen Table Series, the photography of Carrie Mae Weems focused on her life as an African American. Raised during the Civil Rights era, Weems began photographing in her late twenties. Her early work sought to balance generations of white photographers' depictions of African Americans with documentary images conveying how blacks view and relate to each other. At twenty-seven, Weems entered art school at the California Institute of Arts, receiving a B.F.A. in 1981 and an M.F.A. from the University of California, San Diego, in 1984. During graduate school, she shifted to a conceptually based approach to photography. Instead of recording reality, she began to use staged images combined with text to comment on societal and political aspects of racism.

By 1990 Weems had become interested in addressing the issue of gender.[1] In the Kitchen Table Series, she set out to convey the insider's view of a woman's life through stories of her relationship with her lover and with their child. Like the *Fallen Angel* by Duane Michals (see pp. 160–61), Weems's series combines images with words and has a cinematic feel as it telescopes a complex narrative into twenty photographs and thirteen text panels. And like her contemporary Cindy Sherman (see pp. 216–17), Weems not only writes and directs but also stars in her drama.

The story is that of a man and woman who fall in love and have a child. When they break up, the woman seeks consolation from friends and family. Her relationship with her daughter is also explored. The story ends not with a Hollywood-style reconciliation but with the woman now alone. There are fourteen scenes, some consisting of more than one photograph; all are set at a simple wooden table. Over the table hangs a lamp, which—depending on the mood of the scene—suggests interrogation or enlightenment. The camera viewpoint places the audience in the same room as the protagonist, directly across the table from the central action. Text panels, written in the third person, are rarely synchronized with the pictures. Instead, they complement the photographs by supplying internal dialogues for the characters.

Although designed as part of a larger ensemble, the photographic works in the Kitchen Table Series also can stand alone. The Akron Art Museum acquired one of three triptychs in the series and also owns five other works by Weems from different series. In this triptych the woman is being comforted by her friends, one of whom is black and the other white. In the first panel, they reach out to touch and solace her as she appears to weep silently. In the middle panel, the woman has regained her composure and they all sit solemnly around a table set with full glasses, an ashtray, and (perhaps hinting at discussions of revenge) a knife. In the final panel, the knife remains on the table but humor has lightened the mood, suggesting that eventually there will be an end to the protagonist's grieving. The support of other women has helped her to survive and begin to heal.

The fact that the main characters—the woman, the man, and the child—are black is not incidental to the narrative, but it is not the central focus. "Yes, the individuals are black, but the issues raised are about sexuality in general, the politics of desire—intimacy and domination."[2] "The power of the work comes out of the fact that it's not...about me. It's about us."[3]

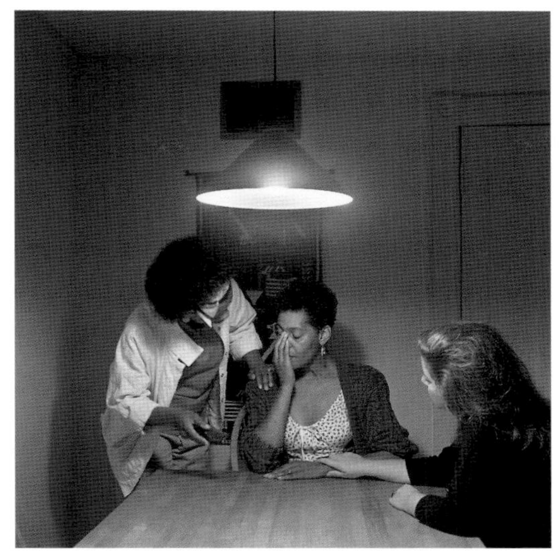

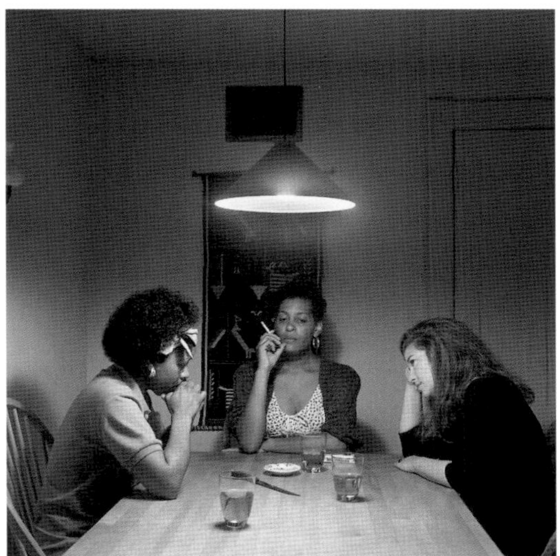

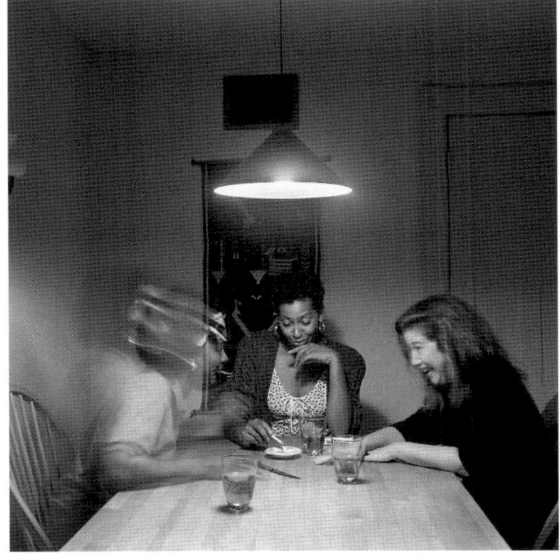

1996.4 a,b,c

Carrie Mae Weems
Born 1953, Portland, Oregon; lives Syracuse, New York

Untitled (Woman with friends) from the Kitchen Table Series, 1990

Gelatin silver prints; three, each 27 ¼ x 27 ¼ in.
Knight Purchase Fund for Photographic Media

Mitchell D. Kahan

Gilbert & George

The British duo known as Gilbert & George have addressed compelling personal and social issues—from private traumas like drunkenness and lust to overarching concerns such as religious fundamentalism, racism, and death. Unifying these diverse issues is the artists' visible and domineering presence in the works: sometimes they appear as victims or witnesses, sometimes as bystanders and perpetrators. Their bold expressions of lamentation, glee, or reckless abandon, which are simultaneously amusing and disturbing, are among the more morally perplexing images of our time.

Gilbert Proesch and George Passmore met while attending St. Martin's School of Art in London. Since 1967 they have lived and worked together in Spitalfields, a working-class London neighborhood. Adopting the name "Gilbert & George," the two men were among the first of a number of artists who began to work as duos or teams in the 1960s. Though best known for their large-scale "photo-pieces," such as *Attacked,* Gilbert & George have also engaged in live performances of a hauntingly robotic nature and produced drawings, films, and works on paper.

By 1980 they had developed a closely guarded technique of dying black-and-white photographs with brilliant hues. George has explained: "We are making a language out of colors. It's not exactly like life. Life's colors are mixed up. Ours are separated."[1] From the start, they regarded the photograph as something purposefully constructed, not an image that captures existing reality. Key figures in the development of postmodern photography, they embraced a carefully manipulated, artificial world characterized by its large scale, strong color, and dramatic images related to advertising and the popular media. The gaudy beauty of their work sometimes camouflages its deeper ambiguities and consciously exploitative depiction of alcoholism, race, and homoerotic lust.

From their earliest efforts, Gilbert & George have combined multiple images or used gridlike structures to divide a single image. This structure is sometimes superimposed over outrageous subjects, joining opposing worlds of order and chaos. Grids, which appear in much twentieth-century abstraction, are more typically used in cool, calculated compositions, as in Sol LeWitt's sculpture (see pp. 180–81). Gilbert & George transform the grid into an emotion-packed structure, like bars on a cell.

Attacked dramatizes multiple threats—psychological assault, urban danger, and viral contagion. It belongs to a group of works first exhibited together as New Democratic Pictures, which depict sardonic fantasies of intimidation, confusion, death, and escape. Gilbert & George told one interviewer that in *Attacked* they were under assault from manhole covers that act like "space invaders" or "stealth fighter-bombers." In their minds, the pair said, "everybody is hiding something" and "some aspect of their life is under attack."[2] The artists stick out their tongues to be rude and defiant, but the gesture also suggests a visit to the doctor's office, childishness, and sexual aggression. The double entendre of the manhole covers and the tapestry of golden droplets inevitably allude to sex and bodily fluids. *Attacked* recalls an earlier series that dealt with the subject of AIDS through riveting images of blood.

"We want our Art to speak across the barriers of knowledge directly to People about their Life and not about their knowledge of art," say the artists.[3] And so they do, employing beauty and artfulness not to comfort but to evoke the spirit of contemporary life. It is not far-fetched to regard Gilbert & George as our century's Dante and Virgil, for these dandies in pink suits chart the depths of heaven and hell. At the same time, they survey the beauty, pathos, and danger of the streets.

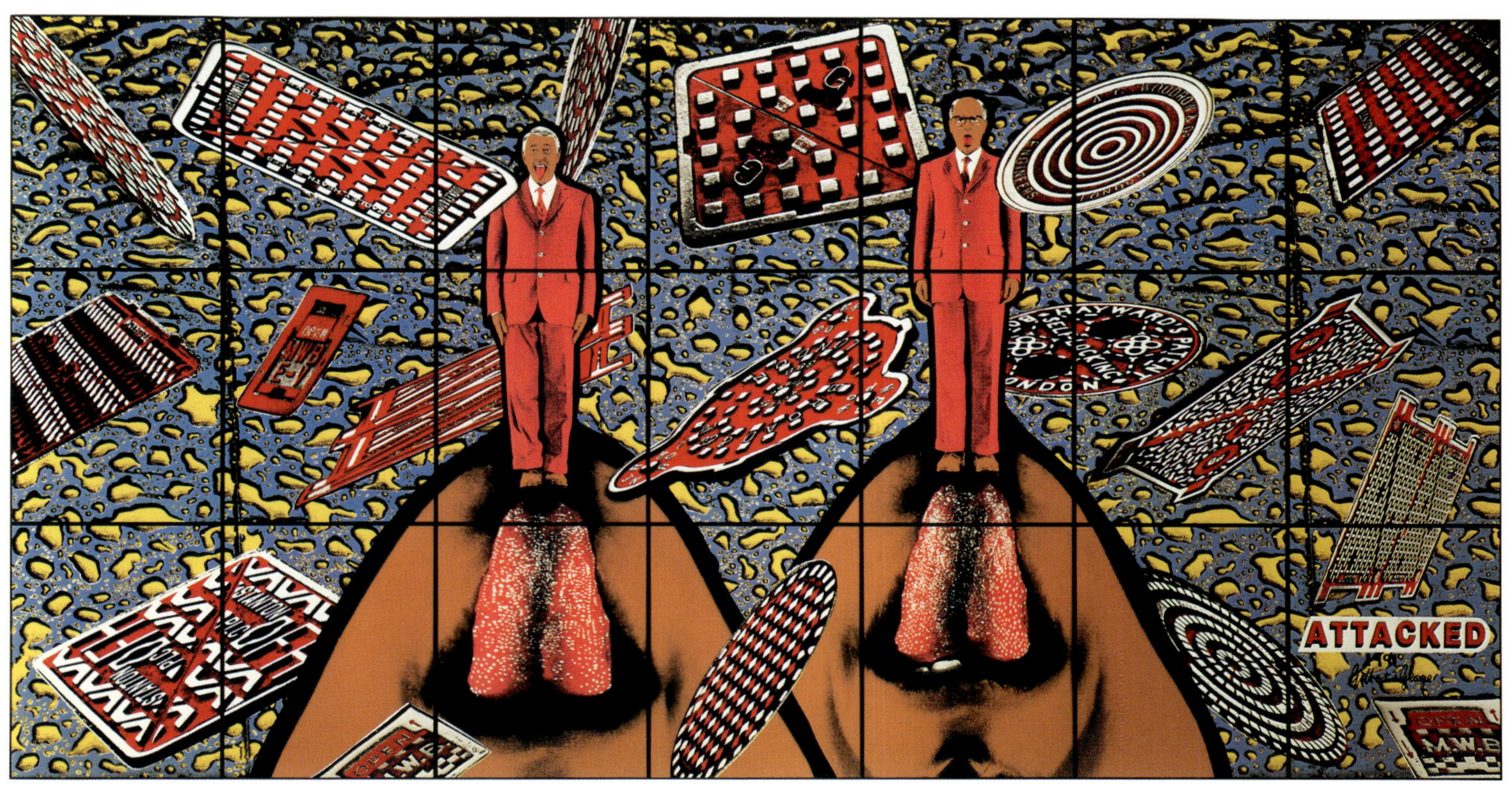

1994 22 a-u

Gilbert & George

Gilbert Proesch
Born 1943, the Dolomites, Italy; lives London

George Passmore
Born 1942, Devon, England; lives London

Attacked, 1991

Hand-dyed photographs in metal frames; 99 3/4 x 195 7/8 in.
Museum Acquisition Fund and Knight Purchase Fund for Photographic Media

Mitchell D. Kahan

Lari Pittman

In contrast to the elliptical tone and ironic stance of much recent art, Lari Pittman's paintings give voice to an independent vision that embraces passion and beauty while reflecting an American culture that is contentious socially and sexually. Deploying a panorama of layered images in his paintings, the artist intends to evoke not chaos but an awareness that many things happen simultaneously in life.[1] Pittman's world does not unfold in linear progression. Even the title combines future and past tenses in a way that defies traditional chronology.

Pittman grew up in two cultures. Born in Southern California, he was raised for the most part in Colombia, where his mother's family lived and his American father worked in the lumber industry. After earning undergraduate and graduate degrees from the California Institute of the Arts in Valencia, Pittman continued to make his own art while working at designer Angelo Donghia's showroom in Los Angeles. Since the early 1990s he has taught at the University of California, Los Angeles. He lives with painter Roy Dowell in a quintessential modernist house designed by Richard Neutra.

The panoramic odyssey Pittman depicts in *Thankfully, I will have had learned to break glass with sound* is part puzzle, part allegory. Images associated with alchemical processes and distilling apparatus are manifestations of the themes of change and transmutation. Pittman suggests that base elements might be converted into gold, and flowers distilled into perfume.

A parade of handsome male faces dominates the painting. Drawn like commercial illustrations, they hover somewhere between the conventions of teen magazines and daytime television. Like all of Pittman's immaculately painted and stenciled forms, they seem manufactured rather than handmade, harking back to the smooth surfaces of 1960s Pop Art. This effect is enhanced by his use of alkyd, an oil paint that adheres smoothly, hiding brushstrokes.

The five younger men in the picture—objects of desire yet barely real—are gazed upon by the older man at the left. Does he shed tears as a sign of mourning, as an allusion to weakness, or as regret over lost youth? Perhaps his weeping relates to the oversize insects, which recall a convention in baroque painting in which flies crawl on flowers and fruit to connote the passage of time and the inevitability of decay.

The array of images and words in *Thankfully* also reminds us of the connection between the personal and the political, the private and the public. The young men sport headgear that elicits thoughts of victory and heroism, martyrdom and loss, masculinity and femininity. Pittman explains that the painting "destabilizes" gender issues and questions why traits positively associated with femininity assume negative connotations when transferred to a male subject.[2] At least one of the veils is inescapably feminine with its flowered embroidery. Another may be a reminder of a secret Masonic society or of hidden sexuality. The still that mutates into a shower head spraying golden rays of "queenliness" emanates from a figure who could represent the "boy next door," someone who might be expected to embark on one of the ships at far right rather than explore his feminine side.

While Pittman's images have multiple, even unfixed meanings, the artist does not share postmodernism's assertion that all meaning is arbitrary. He is instead a bit of a romantic, offering thoughtful meditations with, in his words, a bittersweet point of view.[3] In an age when art's impetus to give pleasure has often been usurped by the responsibility to enlighten and challenge, Pittman's gorgeous surfaces and compelling imagery prove that one can have both pleasure and provocation.

Notes and Further Reading

Abramović and Ulay

1. Quoted in Dorine Mignot, "Marina Abramović/Ulay," *Het Lumineuze Beeld/The Luminous Image* (Amsterdam and Maarssden: Stedelijk Museum and Gary Schwartz, 1984), 93.

2. This key tenet of Tibetan philosophy is discussed in John F. Avedon, "Emptiness, the Two Truths: Excerpts from 'An Interview with the Dalai Lama,'" in *Modus Vivendi*, 75.

3. Quoted in C. Carr, "Where Angels Fear to Tread," *The Village Voice*, February 14, 1989, 32.

Modus Vivendi: Ulay & Marina Abramović 1980–1985. Eindhoven: Stedelijk Van Abbemuseum, 1985.

Ansel Adams

1. Adams, with Alinder, 273.

2. Under the New Deal, instituted during the tenure of Franklin D. Roosevelt, the government sponsored a variety of documentary projects, the best known being that of the Farm Security Administration. The purpose of Adams's project was to provide mural-size enlargements for the offices of the Department of the Interior in Washington. Adams received $22.22 a day for a period of 180 days' work and retained ownership of the negatives with no restrictions on their future use. On the same trip, he did a commercial job in New Mexico for the U.S. Potash Company and made exposures for himself. See ibid., 271.

Adams, Ansel. *Yosemite and the Range of Light*. Boston: New York Graphic Society, 1979.
———, with Mary Street Alinder. *Ansel Adams: An Autobiography*. Boston: A New York Graphic Society Book, Little, Brown, 1985.
Alinder, Mary Street. *Ansel Adams: A Biography*. New York: Henry Holt, 1996.

Laure Albin Guillot

1. Quoted in the "Newsletter," International Museum of Photography at George Eastman House (April 1992), 11.

2. See Bouqueret, 18.

3. Unsigned article, "La Photographie est aujourd'hui la reine de l'illustration," *Photo Illustration* 1 (1934): not paginated.

4. Albin Guillot, using the same subject and process, also produced decorative wall panels for the French luxury liner *Normandie* (later destroyed by fire).

5. Marcel Natkin, "La Nu en photographie," quoted in Bouqueret, 9 (author's translation).

Bouqueret, Christian. *Laure Albin Guillot ou La Volonté d'art*. Paris: Marval, 1996.
Rosenblum, Naomi. *A History of Women Photographers*. New York: Abbeville, 1994.

Lawrence Alma-Tadema

1. Swanson, 211.

2. Lovett and Johnston, 75.

3. Percy Cross Standing, *Sir Lawrence Alma-Tadema, O.M., R.A.* (London: Cassell, 1905), 69.

4. Lovett, in Lovett and Johnston, 76.

5. Ibid.

Lovett, Jennifer Gordon, and William R. Johnston. *Empires Restored, Elysium Revisited: The Art of Sir Lawrence Alma-Tadema*. Williamstown, Mass.: Sterling and Francine Clark Art Institute, 1991.
Swanson, Vern G. *The Biography and Catalogue Raisonné of the Paintings of Sir Lawrence Alma-Tadema*. London: Garton, 1990.

Robert Arneson

1. Benezra, 79.

Benezra, Neal. *Robert Arneson: A Retrospective*. Des Moines: Des Moines Art Center, 1986.
Nash, Steven A. *Arneson and Politics: A Commemorative Exhibition*. San Francisco: Fine Arts Museums of San Francisco, 1993.

George N. Barnard

1. On the margins of this photograph the title is printed as *Destruction of Hood's Ordinance Train*. Since "ordinance" does not reflect correct usage, it has been changed to "ordnance" for the sake of clarity.

Davis, Keith F. *George N. Barnard: Photographer of Sherman's Campaign*. Kansas City: Hallmark Cards, 1990.
Sandweiss, Martha A., ed. *Photography in Nineteenth-Century America*. Fort Worth and New York: Amon Carter Museum and Harry N. Abrams, 1991.

Ruth Bernhard

1. *Ruth Bernhard* (1993), not paginated.

2. Ibid.

3. Ibid. See also Mitchell, 32.

Alinder, James. *Collecting Light: The Photographs of Ruth Bernhard.* Carmel, Calif.: Friends of Photography, 1979.

Mitchell, Margaretta. "Ruth Bernhard." In *Recollections: Ten Women of Photography.* New York: A Studio Book, Viking, 1979.

Ruth Bernhard: Known and Unknown. With essay by Ilee Kaplan and chronology and bibliography by Marina Freeman. Long Beach, Calif.: University Art Museum, California State University, 1996.

Ruth Bernhard: The Collection of Ginny Williams. Denver: The Denver Art Museum, 1993.

Ralph Albert Blakelock

1. Art dealer Robert C. Vose Sr. gave the painting this title in 1922. Letter from Robert C. Vose Sr. to Edwin C. Shaw, January 10, 1922, Edwin C. Shaw Papers, Akron Art Museum archives.

Davidson, Abraham A. *Ralph Albert Blakelock.* University Park, Penn.: Pennsylvania State University, 1996.

Geske, Norman A. *Ralph Albert Blakelock, 1847–1919.* Lincoln, Nebr., and Trenton, N.J.: Sheldon Memorial Art Gallery, University of Nebraska, and New Jersey State Museum, 1975.

Karl Blossfeldt

1. Blossfeldt was included in numerous group exhibitions in the late 1920s, but had few solo exhibitions of his photographs. In fact, until the mid–1980s, scholars believed that while Blossfeldt routinely produced glass slides of his images for use in teaching drawing and sculpture, he created relatively few prints on paper. This notion was disproved in 1984 when a large cache of prints made by the artist was discovered.

2. Blossfeldt's words are from the only statement he published about his art, "Zu meinem Bildern" (About My Pictures), the short introduction to *Wundergarten der Natur.* Quoted in Blossfeldt (1994), not paginated.

3. From "Zu meinem Bildern" (About My Pictures), quoted in George Walsh, Colin Naylor, and Michael Held, eds., *Contemporary Photographers* (New York: St. Martin's, 1982), 81.

4. This information is from the list of plates in *Wundergarten.* A vintage gelatin silver print of this image bears a different description by an unknown hand: *"Frucht einer Losazee, 8 x vergrössert"* (Fruit of a Losazee, 8 x magnified). *Important Avant-Garde Photographs of the 1920s & 1930s: The Helene Anderson Collection* (London: Sotheby's, May 2, 1997), 15.

Blossfeldt, Karl. *Karl Blossfeldt Photographs.* Oxford, England: Museum of Modern Art, 1978.

———. *Art Forms in the Plant World.* Mineola, N.Y.: Dover Publications, 1985.

———. *Karl Blossfeldt Photographs.* With a text by Rolf Sachse. Cologne: Benedikt Taschen, 1994.

Lee Bontecou

1. "Lee Bontecou," *Newsweek* 68 (October 24, 1966): 107.

2. Process art, a movement that arose in the late 1960s, stressed the exploration of the intrinsic expressive and physical properties of nontraditional materials ranging from natural substances such as grass and water vapor to industrial materials such as lead, canvas, and cloth.

3. Lee Bontecou, quoted in Eleanor Munro, *Originals: American Women Artists* (New York: Simon and Schuster, 1976), 384.

4. Lee Bontecou, interview with the author, Pennsylvania, July 19, 1986. All primary information concerning her work comes from this interview and follow-up discussions unless otherwise noted. See also Hadler, 59.

Hadler, Mona. "Lee Bontecou's 'Warnings.'" *Art Journal* 53 (winter 1994): 56–61.

Emile-Antoine Bourdelle

1. It was customary, in nineteenth-century France, for provincial communities to offer monument commissions to local or locally born artists.

2. Albert E. Elsen, *Modern European Sculpture 1918–1945: Unknown Beings and Other Realities* (New York: George Braziller, in association with the Albright-Knox Art Gallery, Buffalo, 1979), 122.

Adams, Philip Rhys. *Antoine Bourdelle.* New York: Charles E. Slatkin Galleries, 1961.

Cannon-Brookes, Peter. *Emile Antoine Bourdelle: An Illustrated Commentary.* London: Trefoil Books and National Museum of Wales, 1983.

Jianou, Ionel, and Michel Dufet. *Bourdelle.* Paris: Arted, Edition d'Art, 1965.

Charles Burchfield

1. Journal entry, July 16, 1934. See Townsend, ed., 52.

2. *Charles Burchfield,* Monograph 13, Foreword by Charles Burchfield (New York: American Artists Group, 1945), not paginated.

3. The quotation and the work's title were handwritten on a piece of paper glued to the back of the original frame. The painting has been published and, until recently, was listed in the museum's records as *Spring Shower.* Research for this book revealed that the notes were probably written by Burchfield himself. Around the time that J. Frederick Seiberling bought this work from the Rehn Galleries, Burchfield mentioned the sale of a work titled *Spring Thunderstorm* in a letter dated January 7, 1957, Frank K. M. Rehn Galleries Records, Archives of American Art, Smithsonian Institution.

Baur, John I. H. *The Inlander: Life and Work of Charles Burchfield, 1893–1967.* Newark: University of Delaware Press, 1982.

Townsend, J. Benjamin, ed. *Charles Burchfield's Journals: The Poetry of Place.* Albany: State University of New York Press, 1993.

Harry Callahan

1. Quoted in Valerie Brooks, "Harry Callahan's True Colors," *ARTnews* 82 (October 1983): 69.

2. Ibid.

Callahan, Harry. *Eleanor.* New York and Carmel, Calif.: Callaway Editions and Friends of Photography, 1984.
Greenough, Sarah. *Harry Callahan.* Washington, D.C.: National Gallery of Art, 1996.

Emil Carlsen

1. Emil Carlsen, "On Still-Life Painting," *Palette and Bench* 1 (1908): 6.

2. Arthur Edwin Bye, *Pots and Pans, Studies in Still-Life Painting* (Princeton: Princeton University Press, 1921), 213, 218. Not only is this book dedicated to Carlsen, but he receives slightly more text than either Courbet or Chardin.

3. Duncan Phillips, "Emil Carlsen," *International Studio* 61 (June 1917): CVI.

The Art of Emil Carlsen, 1853–1932. San Francisco: Wortsman-Rowe Galleries, 1975.

Anthony Caro

1. Anthony Caro, quoted in Yorick Blumfield, "A Conversation with Anthony Caro," *Architectural Digest* 38 (September 1981): 64.

2. Suzi Gablik, "Anthony Caro at Kenwood," *Art in America* 62 (November–December 1974): 126.

3. Anthony Caro, "The Sculptural Moment," *Sculpture* 14 (January–February 1995): 30.

Rubin, William. *Anthony Caro.* New York and Richmond, Va.: Museum of Modern Art and W. M. Brown & Son, 1975.
Waldman, Diane. *Anthony Caro.* New York: Abbeville, 1982.
Wilkin, Karen. *Caro.* Munich: Prestel Verlag, 1991.

William Merritt Chase

1. The painting was dated 1898 by Mrs. William Merritt Chase on the reverse of a photograph, but Edith Dimock Glackens in a January 26, 1923, letter to William Macbeth dates the painting to 1901. From the appearance of the sitter, it is more likely that she was thirteen rather than ten. All correspondence related to this painting can be found in the Edwin C. Shaw Papers, Akron Art Museum archives.

2. This older sister, Edith Louise Dimock, later married painter William Glackens (1870–1938).

3. Letter from Ira Glackens to Carolyn Kinder Carr, January 28, 1982, Akron Art Museum archives; letter from Edith Dimock Glackens to William Macbeth, January 26, 1923, Edwin C. Shaw Papers, Archives of American Art, Smithsonian Institution.

Carr, Carolyn Kinder. *William Merritt Chase: Portraits.* Akron: Akron Art Museum, 1982.
Gallatti, Barbara Dayer. *William Merritt Chase.* New York: Harry N. Abrams, 1995.
Pisano, Ronald. *William Merritt Chase 1849–1916: A Leading Spirit in American Art.* Seattle: Henry Art Gallery, 1983.
Roof, Katherine Metcalf. *The Life and Art of William Merritt Chase.* New York: Scribner, 1917. Reprinted, New York: Hacker Art Books, 1975.

Christo

1. Quoted in Barbara Tannenbaum, "Politics, Economics and Personality as Media: The Art of the Christos," *National Arts Guide* 2 (January–February 1980): 7.

Christo: Wrapped Walk Ways, Loose Park, Kansas City, Missouri, 1977–78. Essay by Ellen R. Goheen, photographs by Wolfgang Volz. New York: Harry N. Abrams, 1978.
Laporte, Dominique G. *Christo.* New York: Pantheon Books, 1986.
Vaizey, Marina. *Christo.* New York: Rizzoli, 1990.

John Clem Clarke

1. Siegel, 44.

2. Quoted in David Shirey, "Copy Cat," *Newsweek* 73 (June 16, 1969): 105.

John Clem Clarke: Comforts, Near Disasters, and Pentimenti. With an essay by April Kingsley. Allentown, Pa.: Allentown Art Museum, 1998.
Reed, Dupuy Warrick. "John Clem Clarke: Another Glimpse of Childhood." *Arts Magazine* 53 (April 1979): 158-62.
Siegel, Jeanne. "An Art of Transmission: John Clem Clarke at Kornblee." *Arts Magazine* 43 (summer 1969): 44-46.

Chuck Close

1. "The Photo-Realists: 12 Interviews," *Art in America* 60 (November–December 1972): 76.

2. Ibid., 77.

Guare, John. *Chuck Close: Life and Work 1988–1995.* New York: Thames and Hudson, 1995.
Lyons, Lisa, and Robert Storr. *Chuck Close.* New York: Rizzoli International, 1987.
Storr, Robert. *Chuck Close.* With essays by Kirk Varnedoe and Deborah Wye. New York: Museum of Modern Art, 1998.

Robert Colescott

1. Humor and fantasy combined with social or personal comment are also key characteristics for a number of Colescott's Bay Area colleagues, such as Robert Arneson (see pp. 214–15), Roy De Forest, and Joan Brown. Works by De Forest and Brown are on public view in Akron's Oliver R. Ocasek Government Office Building.

2. Conversation with the artist, Akron, Ohio, April 11, 1996.

3. Lowery S. Sims, "Bob Colescott Ain't Just Misbehavin'," *Artforum* (March 1984): 57–58.

Roberts, Miriam. *Robert Colescott: Recent Paintings.* Venice: 47th Venice Biennale, 1997.
Sims, Lowery S., and Mitchell D. Kahan. *Robert Colescott: A Retrospective, 1975–1986.* San Jose, Calif.: San Jose Museum of Art, 1987.

John Coplans

1. See introductory essay, 33–37.

2. Christopher Lyon, "Seeing from Inside: John Coplans on *A Body of Work,*" *Members Quarterly,* Museum of Modern Art, New York (spring 1988): 3.

3. Susan Butler, "Rebellions of Age: John Coplans and Anne Noggle," *Ten•8* (April 1987): not paginated.

Coplans, John, with Stuart Morgan, ed. *Provocations: Writing by John Coplans.* London: London Projects, 1996.
———. *A Self Portrait: John Coplans, 1984–1997.* Long Island City, N.Y.: P.S. 1, Contemporary Art Center, 1997.

Edward S. Curtis

1. Edward S. Curtis to Edmond S. Meany, November 11, 1907. Quoted in Davis, 39.

2. Quoted in Graybill and Boesen, not paginated. *The Vanishing Race* is the title Curtis gave to one of the best-known images from *The North American Indian.* It depicts the shadowy forms of a group of mounted Navaho tribesmen seen from behind and illuminated by the last rays of the sun.

3. Published by Curtis himself, the twenty volumes contained 700 large and 1,500 smaller plates printed in gravure on two different papers: a Japanese vellum and a Dutch etching stock. Typesetting and printing were done by University Press, Cambridge, Massachusetts. Morgan first promised $15,000 yearly for five years, which would cover travel, interpreters, and supplies; eventually the Morgan family spent some $400,000 on the publication. Ibid., 45, 75.

4. See Lyman for an exposition of the view that Curtis romanticized his subjects to a dishonest extent.

Davis, Barbara A. *Edward S. Curtis: The Life and Times of a Shadow Catcher.* San Francisco: Chronicle Books, 1985.
Gidley, Mick. *Edward S. Curtis and the North American Indian, Incorporated.* Cambridge: Cambridge University Press, 2000.
Graybill, Florence Curtis, and Victor Boesen. *Edward Sheriff Curtis: Visions of a Vanishing Race.* New York: American Legacy, 1976.
Lyman, Christopher. *The Vanishing Race and Other Illusions.* New York: Pantheon in association with Smithsonian Institution Press, 1982.

Richard Deacon

1. Richard Deacon, in gallery handout for the exhibition *Making Sculpture,* Tate Gallery, London, 1983.

2. Michael Newman, "From World to Earth: Richard Deacon and the End of Nature," in *Interpreting Contemporary Art,* ed. Stephen Bann and William Allen (New York: IconEditions, 1991), 198.

3. Ibid., 199.

4. *Richard Deacon: Talking About "For Those Who Have Ears, No. 2" and Other Works* (London: Patrons of New Art/Friends of the Tate Gallery, 1985), 11.

5. Richard Deacon, *Jacqui Poncelet—New Ceramics* (London: Crafts Council, 1981), quoted in Richard Deacon, ed. Clark, 49.

Richard Deacon, ed. Vicky A. Clark. Pittsburgh: Carnegie Museum of Art, 1988.
Thompson, Jon; Pier Luigi Tazzi; and Peter Schjeldahl. *Richard Deacon.* London: Phaidon, 1995.

Peter Dean

1. Quoted by Lucy Lippard, "Builder on the Edge of a Chaotic World," in Alternative Museum, 12.

2. Quoted in North Dakota Museum of Art, text accompanying plate 29.

3. See Frank Lewis, "Reflections on Peter Dean: A Customer of Culture," in *Peter Dean: Paintings and Stories* (Milwaukee: University of Wisconsin Art Museum, 1992), 10, 12.

Alternative Museum. *Peter Dean: A Retrospective.* New York: Alternative Museum, 1990.
North Dakota Museum of Art. *Peter Dean.* Essay by Carter Ratcliff. Grand Forks: North Dakota Museum of Art, 1989.

Thomas Wilmer Dewing

1. Thomas Dewing to Charles Lang Freer, February 16, 1901, Letter 110, Freer Gallery of Art Archives.

2. Dewing to Edwin C. Shaw, September 9 (ca. 1920), Edwin C. Shaw Papers, Archives of American Art, Smithsonian Institution.

3. Dewing to Freer, January 10, 1894, Letter 40, Freer Gallery of Art Archives; Kathleen Pyne, "Classical Figures: A Folding Screen by Thomas Dewing," *Bulletin of the Detroit Institute of Arts* 59 (spring 1981): 10.

4. Dewing to Freer, September 14, 1899, Letter 100, Freer Gallery of Art Archives.

Hobbs, Susan A. *The Art of Thomas Wilmer Dewing: Beauty Reconfigured.* With an essay by Barbara Dayer Gallati. Washington, D.C.: Smithsonian Institution Press, 1996.
Pyne, Kathleen. *Art and the Higher Life, Painting and Evolutionary Thought in Late-Nineteenth-Century America.* Austin: University of Texas Press, 1996.

John William ("Uncle Jack") Dey

1. Dey started a painting by obtaining a frame, usually purchased at a secondhand store, then making a painting for that frame. Unfortunately, many of these original frames have been removed or lost, which is probably true of *Accupuncture Spear Style—Manhunter's*. The Akron painting is on the back of a reproduction of a painting by the French Cubist Georges Braque.

Rosenak, Chuck, and Jan Rosenak. *Museum of American Folk Art Encyclopedia of Twentieth-Century American Folk Art and Artists*. New York: Abbeville, 1990.

Wright, R. Lewis, Jeffrey T. Camp, and Chris Gregson. "'Uncle Jack': John William Dey." *Clarion* 17 (spring 1992): 34–40.

Jim Dine

Beal, Graham W. J. *Jim Dine: Five Themes*. With contributions by Robert Creeley, Jim Dine, and Martin Freidman. New York and Minneapolis: Abbeville and Walker Art Center, 1984.

Feinberg, Jean E. *Jim Dine*. New York: Abbeville, 1995.

Glenn, Constance W. *Jim Dine Drawings*. New York: Harry N. Abrams, 1985.

Mark di Suvero

1. Howard Junker, "Epics in Beams," *Quest* (April 1981): 79.

2. In a conversation with the author (March 26, 1998), Richard Bellamy, director of Oil and Steel Gallery and di Suvero's dealer from 1960 until 1998, said it was in Petaluma in 1976 that di Suvero constructed the original version of *Eagle Wheel* and two other sculptures, his entire output for that year.

3. Barbara Rose, "A Return to the Heroic Dimension in Sculpture: Mark di Suvero," *Vogue* (September 1980): 162.

4. See William Peterson, "CONSTRUCT at Shidoni's Sixth Annual Outdoor Sculpture Show," *Artspace* (September 1980): 54–58, illus. on cover. Unfortunately, there are no published photographs of the sculpture in its earlier state.

5. Celia McGee, "New Soundings from a Poet of Industrial Debris," *New York Times*, May 14, 1995, 36.

Fournet, Claude. *Mark di Suvero: Retrospective, 1959–1991*. Nice: Musée d'Art Moderne et d'Art Contemporain, 1991.

Monte, James K. *Mark di Suvero*. New York: Whitney Museum of American Art, 1975.

Sandler, Irving, and Maureen Megerian. *Mark di Suvero at Storm King Art Center*. New York: Harry N. Abrams, 1995.

Jean Dubuffet

1. Nathan Rapoport, interview with James E. Young, February 22, l986; cited in James E. Young, *The Texture of Memory: Holocaust Memorials and Meaning* (New Haven, Conn.: Yale University Press, l993), 168.

2. Susan J. Cooke, "Jean Dubuffet's Caricature Portraits," in Dubuffet, 20–33.

3. The outsider artists represented in the collection are American and thus not the artists whose work inspired Dubuffet. Nonetheless, the American outsiders share many values and biographical and stylistic traits with European outsider artists. See entries on John William ("Uncle Jack") Dey (pp. 164–65), Minnie Evans (pp. 138–39), William Hawkins (pp. 210–11), W. D. ("Crazy Mac" or "Mad Mac") McCaffrey (pp. 226–27), the Philadelphia Wireman (pp. 144–45), Elijah Pierce (pp. 136–37), Ernest ("Popeye") Reed (pp. 162–63), Anthony Joseph Salvatore (pp. 228–29), Eugene Von Bruenchenhein (pp. 116–17), and Malcah Zeldis (pp. 218–19).

Dubuffet, Jean. *Jean Dubuffet l943–l963, Paintings, Sculptures, Assemblages: An Exhibition*. Washington, D.C.: Hirshhorn Museum and Sculpture Garden in association with Smithsonian Institution Press, l993.

Wilson, Sarah. "Paris Post War: In Search of the Absolute." In Frances Morris, *Paris Post War: Art and Existentialism 1945–55*. London: Tate Gallery, 1993, 25–53.

Marcel Duchamp

1. James Johnson Sweeney, "A Conversation with Marcel Duchamp,... " taped interview at the Philadelphia Museum of Art. The tape was used as the sound track of a thirty-minute film made in 1955 by NBC, first shown on American television in the program *Elderly Wise Men*, January 1956.

Bonk, Ecke. *Marcel Duchamp: The Box in a Valise de ou par Marcel Duchamp ou Rrose Sélavy*. Trans. David Britt. New York: Rizzoli, 1989.

Hulten, Pontus. *Marcel Duchamp: Work and Life*. Ed. Jennifer Gough-Cooper and Jacques Caumont. Cambridge, Mass.: MIT Press, 1993.

Schwarz, Arturo. *The Complete Works of Marcel Duchamp*. 3d ed., rev. and enl. New York: Delano Greenidge Editions, 1997.

Tomkins, Calvin. *Duchamp: A Biography*. New York: Henry Holt, 1996.

Frank Duveneck

1. Frank E. Washburn Freund, "The Problem of Frank Duveneck," *International Studio* 85 (September 1926): 39.

Duveneck, Josephine. *Frank Duveneck: Painter-Teacher*. San Francisco: John Howell Books, 1970.

Neuhaus, Robert. *Unsuspected Genius: The Art and Life of Frank Duveneck*. San Francisco: Bedford, 1987.

Quick, Michael. *An American Painter Abroad: Frank Duveneck's European Years*. Cincinnati: Cincinnati Art Museum, 1987.

Richard Estes

1. Quoted in Louis K. Meisel, *Photo-Realism* (New York: Harry N. Abrams, 1980), 209.

2. Interview with the artist, in Arthur, 79.

3. Quoted in Meisel, 25.

4. Interview with the artist, in Arthur, 26.

Arthur, John. *Richard Estes: The Urban Landscape.* Boston: Museum of Fine Arts and New York Graphic Society, 1978.
Meisel, Louis K. *Richard Estes: The Complete Paintings 1966–1985.* New York: Harry N. Abrams, 1986.

Minnie Evans

Kahan, Mitchell D. *Heavenly Visions: The Art of Minnie Evans.* Raleigh: North Carolina Museum of Art, 1986.
Lovell, Charles M., and Erwin Hester, eds. *Minnie Evans: Artist.* Greenville, N.C.: Wellington B. Gray Gallery, East Carolina University, 1993.

Walker Evans

1. The FSA, an agency of Franklin Roosevelt's New Deal program, hired photographers to document the impact of the Depression and the government's efforts to help destitute farmers. Evans, despite his employer's instructions, did not restrict his photographs for the FSA to these topics.

2. Hart Crane, *The Bridge* (Paris: Black Sun Press, 1930); Carleton Beals, *The Crime of Cuba* (Philadelphia and London: J. B. Lippincott, 1933).

Hambourg, Maria Morris. *Walker Evans.* New York: Metropolitan Museum of Art, 2000.
Keller, Judith. *Walker Evans, The Getty Museum Collection.* Malibu, Calif.: J. Paul Getty Museum, 1995.
Mora, Gilles, and John T. Hill. *Walker Evans: The Hungry Eye.* New York: Harry N. Abrams, 1993.
Rathbone, Belinda. *Walker Evans, A Biography.* Boston: Houghton Mifflin, 1995.

Robert Frank

1. Greenough, 26.

2. From Robert Frank's Guggenheim application, quoted in Sarah Greenough, "Fragments That Make a Whole: Meaning in Photographic Sequences," in Greenough, 110.

3. *Chicago,* 1956, one of more than 20,000 frames Frank shot on his Guggenheim-funded travels, is not reproduced in *The Americans.*

4. Amy M. Schiffman, "Robert Frank: Politics as Unusual," *American Photographer* 13 (November 1984): 52–57.

5. *Chicago* is one of sixteen Frank photographs about politics in the collection of the Akron Art Museum (others have different subjects). The group consists of ten photographs from 1955–56 and six images of the 1984 Democratic National Convention in San Francisco.

6. Greenough, 121.

Frank, Robert. *The Americans.* Millerton, N.Y.: Aperture, 1978.
Greenough, Sarah, and Philip Brookman. *Robert Frank: Moving Out.* Washington, D.C.: National Gallery of Art and Scalo, 1994.
Tannenbaum, Barbara, and David B. Cooper. *Robert Frank and American Politics.* Akron: Akron Art Museum, 1985.

Helen Frankenthaler

1. Helen Frankenthaler, quoted in Eleanor Munro, *Originals: American Women Artists* (New York: Simon and Schuster, 1976), 220.

2. Helen Frankenthaler, quoted in Carmean, 42.

Carmean, E. A. Jr. *Helen Frankenthaler, A Paintings Retrospective.* New York: Harry N. Abrams, 1989.
Elderfield, John. *Frankenthaler.* New York: Abrams, 1989.
Rose, Barbara. *Frankenthaler.* New York: H. N. Abrams, 1971.

Lee Friedlander

1. The project was conceived by John Coplans, then director of the Akron Art Institute. It was instigated by a request from John McCarter, chairman of Centran Bank (later Key Bank) and a member of the institute's board of trustees. He was searching for art to decorate the Akron branches of the bank and wanted work that was "pertinent to an industrial area—factory workers, American industry, the market in the community that this bank was serving." A grant from the National Endowment for the Arts and support from Centran Bank provided support for the project; in-kind services were donated by the Akron Art Museum. Dorothy Shinn, "A Photographer's Disturbing Vision of Our Backyard," *Akron Beacon Journal,* May 9, 1982, 8–11. For additional information about the circumstances surrounding the commission, see introductory essay, 36.

2. Jonathan Green, *American Photography: A Critical History 1945 to the Present* (New York: Harry N. Abrams, 1984), 107.

Friedlander, Lee. *Factory Valleys: Ohio & Pennsylvania.* New York: Callaway Editions, 1982.
Kao, Deborah Martin. "Lee Friedlander's Factory Valleys: Structure, Artifice, Culture." *Views* (summer/fall 1989): 10–13, 23–24.
Slemmons, Rod. *Like a One-Eyed Cat: Photographs by Lee Friedlander 1956–1987.* New York: Harry N. Abrams, 1989.

Frederick C. Frieseke

Frederick Carl Frieseke: The Evolution of an American Impressionist. With essays by Nicholas Kilmer, Virginia M. Mecklenburg, David Sellin, and H. Barbara Weinberg. Savannah, Ga.: Telfair Museum of Art, 2001.
Gerdts, William H. *Monet's Giverny, an Impressionist Colony.* New York: Abbeville, 1993.
Sellin, David. *Americans in Brittany and Normandy, 1860–1910.* Phoenix: Phoenix Art Museum, 1982.
Weber, Bruce. *The Giverny Luminists: Frieseke, Miller and Their Circle.* New York: Berry-Hill Galleries, 1995.

Gilbert & George

1. Daniel Farson, "Making an Exhibition of Themselves," *Sunday Telegraph* (London), April 29, 1990.

2. Quoted in *"Boot, Blood Heads, Tears, Seen, Eight, Attacked:* From an Interview with Keith Pointing 1995," first published in the poster book *Gilbert & George* (London: Brockhampton, 1996); reprinted in Violette and Obrist, 208.

3. Quoted in *Gilbert & George: The Complete Pictures 1971–1985* (New York: Rizzoli International, 1986), vii.

Aarhus Kunstmuseum. *Gilbert & George—New Democratic Pictures.* Aarhus, Denmark: Aarhus Kunstmuseum, 1992.
Jahn, Wolf. *The Art of Gilbert & George or An Aesthetic of Existence.* New York: Thames & Hudson, 1989.
Richardson, Brenda. *Gilbert & George.* Baltimore: Baltimore Museum of Art, 1984.
Violette, Robert, and Hans-Ulrich Obrist, eds. *The Words of Gilbert & George: With Portraits of the Artists from 1968 to 1997.* London: Violette Editions, 1997.

Raphael Gleitsmann

1. Gleitsmann's family had dropped the second "n" in their surname to "Americanize" it, but he chose to put the letter back.

2. The school is now known as the Cleveland Institute of Art. Travis, knowing that Gleitsmann could not afford tuition there, invited him to sit in on his lectures at no cost.

3. Gleitsmann took two major liberties with the downtown streetscape, probably for formal reasons: he made both the skyscraper and the twelve-story building on the southwest corner of Main and Bowery appear shorter than they really were.

Kendall-Hess, Wendy. *Early Works by Raphael Gleitsmann.* Akron: Akron Art Museum, 1990.
Shinn, Dorothy. "A Wintery View in '32: How a Rising Young Artist Saw Akron." *Beacon Magazine, Akron Beacon Journal,* June 20, 1982, 2–3, 14.

Jim Goldberg

1. "Afterword," Goldberg (1985), not paginated.

2. Ibid.

3. Ibid.

Goldberg, Jim. *Rich and Poor.* New York: Random House, 1985.
———. *Raised by Wolves.* In collaboration with Philip Brookman. New York: Scalo, 1995.

Nancy Graves

1. Lucy R. Lippard, "Distancing: The Films of Nancy Graves," *Art in America* 63 (November 1975): 80.

2. Carolyn Kinder Carr, interview with the artist, 1980; typescript in Akron Art Museum artist files.

3. Ibid.

4. Linda Nochlin, "Nancy Graves: The Subversiveness of Sculpture," in *Nancy Graves: Painting, Sculpture, Drawing, 1980–1985* (Poughkeepsie, N.Y.: Vassar College Art Gallery, 1985), 16.

Cathcart, Linda L. *Nancy Graves: A Survey 1969/1980.* Buffalo: Albright-Knox Art Gallery, 1980.
The Sculpture of Nancy Graves: A Catalogue Raisonné. New York: Hudson Hills in association with Fort Worth Art Museum, 1987.

Harvey R. Griffiths

1. It is possible that the scene is set in Cleveland. On a 1940 label previously attached to the back of *Arrangement with Billboard,* Griffiths's address is given as 3608 Euclid Avenue, Cleveland, Ohio. The Temple Court Building at that address was a residential hotel with some offices. However, the address is crossed out in the same ink with which it was written. It is either a mistake or a temporary address, as newspaper articles from 1930 through 1945 regularly describe Griffiths as an Akron artist who exhibited throughout that period in annual shows of local artists at the Akron Art Institute. Throughout the 1930s he was living at 610 Crosby Street, Akron. His address is given as 73 Rhodes Avenue, Akron, in Reiker, D8.

2. Griffiths may have intended the building to be a Shell service station. The pencil-drawn letters "SHE" can be seen through the dark paint at the edge of the sign on top of the building. At the sidewalk, a hanging sign displays a yellow-orange shell shape. The sign's bracket has a distinctive form that was used by Shell during this period.

"Harvey R. Griffiths, Akron Artist, Taken." *Akron Beacon Journal,* September 9, 1952, 54.

Lengs, Harold J. "Home from 11-Month Trip Abroad, Harvey R. Griffiths Gives Impressions of Famous Art Galleries He Visited." *Akron Beacon Journal,* July 30, 1939, B7.

Reiker, Jane. "Harvey Griffiths Often Neglects Own Creative Work While He Supervises WPA Art Classes in 13 Counties." *Akron Beacon Journal,* September 22, 1940, D8.

Strouse, Don. "Rises from Glass Painting to Fine Art: Harvey Griffiths Finds More and More to Be Learned." *Akron Times-Press,* December 17, 1930, 11.

Philip Guston

Ashton, Dore. *Yes, but... A Critical Study of Philip Guston.* New York: Viking, 1976. Revised ed., Berkeley: University of California Press, 1990.
Mayer, Musa. *Night Studio: A Memoir of Philip Guston.* New York: Alfred A. Knopf, 1988.

Raoul Hague

1. There is no documentary evidence for the source of the wood for this sculpture and thus for the name *Angel Millbrook Walnut.* Given Hague's method of assigning titles, the sculpture may have been named after Angel Mill Brook, a stream about seventy-five miles southeast of Woodstock, in Sullivan County. There is a Millbrook, New York, but it has no feature in or near it with the name "Angel."

2. All quotations in this entry are from "Raoul Hague interviewed by Paula Giannini," *Art International* 24 (August–September 1981): 8–25.

Hess, Thomas B. "Raoul Hague." In *Twelve Americans.* New York: Museum of Modern Art, 1956, 44–50.
Raoul Hague. With an introduction by Dorothy C. Miller and an essay by Gerald Nordland. Washington, D.C.: Washington Gallery of Modern Art, 1964.

Raoul Hague. (Includes a reprint of Paula Giannini and Raoul Hague, "An Interview," *Art International* 24 [August/September 1981]: 8–25.) New York: Raoul Hague Foundation, 1999.

Steinberg, Leo. "Torsos and Raoul Hague." *Arts* (July 1958). Revised and reprinted in *Other Criteria: Confrontations with Twentieth-Century Art.* New York: Oxford University Press, 1972, 272–76.

Childe Hassam

1. Hoopes, 68.

Gerdts, William H. *American Impressionism.* New York: Abbeville, 1984.

Hiesinger, Ulrich W. *Childe Hassam: American Impressionist.* Munich and New York: Prestel, 1995.

Hoopes, Donelson F. *Childe Hassam.* New York: Watson-Guptill, 1979.

William L. Hawkins

1. The card was sent to Hawkins by former Akron Art Museum docent Carol Friedman, who was corresponding with the artist about an exhibition of his work in Akron.

2. Most of the biographical information here is derived from two essays on Hawkins by Gary J. Schwindler, who interviewed the artist extensively and is preparing a monograph on him. See Columbus Museum of Art, 5–10; and Schwindler (1991), 40–45.

3. In 1981 Hawkins befriended a young Columbus artist, Lee Garrett, who suggested that he work larger, use color photographs as well as black and white for inspiration, and paint on fiberboard instead of paper and cardboard scrounged from trash heaps. Garrett also brought Hawkins's work to the attention of the art world, first in Ohio and then in New York.

4. Schwindler, in Columbus Museum of Art, 8.

5. Gary Schwindler, "William L. Hawkins: Myth in the Making?" *Dialogue* 11 (July/August 1988): 13.

Columbus Museum of Art. *Popular Images, Personal Visions: The Art of William Hawkins 1895–1990.* Columbus, Ohio: Columbus Museum of Art, 1990.

Rosenak, Chuck, and Jan Rosenak. *Museum of American Folk Art Encyclopedia of Twentieth-Century American Folk Art and Artists.* New York: Abbeville, 1990.

Schwindler, Gary J. "William Hawkins, Master Storyteller." *Raw Vision* 4 (spring 1991): 40–45.

Charles W. Hawthorne

1. Quoted in Duncan Phillips, "Charles W. Hawthorne," *International Studio* (March 1917): 20, 22.

2. The sitters were identified in a letter from Richard Mühlberger to Barbara Tannenbaum, June 27, 2000. Hawthorne's wife, Ethel Marion Campbell, was a painter. While continuing her own career as an artist, she also helped her husband in his professional endeavors.

3. Letter from Charles Hawthorne to his dealer, William Macbeth, February 20, 1914, quoted in Sadik essay in University of Connecticut Museum of Art, not paginated.

4. Hawthorne in *Hawthorne on Painting,* 17.

Hawthorne on Painting, From Students' Notes Collected by Mrs. Charles W. Hawthorne. With an appreciation by Royal Cortissoz, 1938. Reprinted, with an introduction by Edwin Dickinson and an appreciation by Hans Hofmann. New York: Dover, 1960.

McCausland, Elizabeth. *Charles W. Hawthorne, An American Figure Painter.* New York: American Artists Group, 1947.

Mühlberger, Richard. *Charles Webster Hawthorne.* Chesterfield, Mass.: Chameleon Books, 1999.

University of Connecticut Museum of Art, Storrs. *The Paintings of Charles Hawthorne.* With an introduction by Marvin S. Sadik. Storrs: University of Connecticut Museum of Art, 1968.

Lewis W. Hine

1. The Chrysler Building, completed earlier in 1931, was the tallest, but it was surpassed a few months later by the Empire State Building. See Carol Willis, "Chrysler Building," and "Empire State Building," in Kenneth Jackson, ed., *The Encyclopedia of New York City* (New Haven: Yale University Press, 1995), 221, 375–76.

2. Lewis W. Hine to Frank Manny, "Field Note," around 1906, with added written note, 1938. McCausland Papers, Archives of American Art, Smithsonian Institution.

3. His photographs were used to illustrate the five volumes of *The Pittsburgh Survey* (New York: Survey Associates [Russell Sage Foundation], 1910–13). They also appeared frequently in a number of magazines, primarily *The Survey.*

4. Hine to Florence L. Kellogg, February 17, 1933, Survey Associates Papers, Social Welfare History Archives Center, University of Minnesota, Minneapolis.

5. A plaque in the lobby of the Empire State Building lists the chief craftsmen involved. Hine was recommended for the position by his neighbor, Richard Shreve, a principal in the architectural firm of Shreve, Lamb and Harmon. Kaplan, ed., 34.

6. Hine to Paul Kellogg, November 25, 1930, Survey Associates Papers, Social Welfare History Archives Center, University of Minnesota, Minneapolis; cited in Kaplan, ed., 37.

Kaplan, Daile. *Lewis Hine in Europe.* New York: Abbeville, 1988.

———, ed. *Photo Story: Selected Letters and Photos of Lewis W. Hine.* Washington, D.C., and London: Smithsonian Institution Press, 1992.

Rosenblum, Nina, and Daniel V. Allentuck, producers. Video, *America and Lewis Hine.* New York: Cinema Guild (educational distribution) and New Video (home distribution), 1984.

Rosenblum, Walter; Naomi Rosenblum; and Alan Trachtenberg. *America and Lewis Hine.* Millerton, N.Y.: Aperture, 1977.

Vera Jackson

1. Vera Jackson in a letter to Naomi Rosenblum, March 10, 1993.

2. Ibid.

Moutoussamy-Ashe, Jeanne. *Viewfinders: Black Women Photographers.* New York and London: Writers & Readers Publishing, 1993, 85–89, 180.

Donald Judd

1. "Questions to Stella and Judd," interview by Bruce Glaser, ed. Lucy R. Lippard, *ARTnews* (September 1966); reprinted in *Minimal Art: A Critical Anthology,* ed. Gregory Battcock (New York: E. P. Dutton, 1968), 154.

Donald Judd. Essay by Rainer Crone. Eindhoven, The Netherlands: Stedelijk Van Abbemuseum, 1987.

Elger, Dietmar. *Donald Judd: Colorist.* Ostfildern-Ruit, Germany: Edition Cantz, 2000.

Haskell, Barbara. *Donald Judd.* New York: Whitney Museum of American Art in association with W. W. Norton, 1988.

Robert Glenn Ketchum

1. CVNRA is a national park administered by the National Park Service, Department of the Interior. The commission to photograph the area and the resulting exhibition were made possible by funding from Akron Community Foundation, The GAR Foundation, The George Gund Foundation, The Cleveland Foundation and with the cooperation of the CVNRA. For additional information about the commission, see introductory essay, 36.

Ketchum, Robert Glenn. *Overlooked in America: The Success and Failure of Federal Land Management.* New York: Aperture, 1991.

———. *The Legacy of Wildness: The Photographs of Robert Glenn Ketchum.* With a preface by Robert Redford and an essay by John Perlin. New York: Aperture, 1993.

Yayoi Kusama

1. March 13, 1964, statement by Herbert Read, in Karia, ed., 84.

2. Statement by the artist, in "The Question of Gender in Art," *Tema Celeste: Contemporary Art Review* 39 (winter 1993): 50.

Adams, Brooks. "Proliferating Obsessions." *Art in America* 78 (April 1990): 228–33.

Karia, Bhupendra, ed. *Yayoi Kusama: A Retrospective.* New York: Center for International Contemporary Arts, 1990.

Tatehata, Akira. *Yayoi Kusama.* With an interview of the artist by Tatehata and contributions by Laura Hoptman and Udo Kultermann. London: Phaidon, 2000.

Zelevansky, Lynn; Laura Hoptman; Alexandra Munroe; and Akira Tatehata. *Love Forever: Yayoi Kusama, 1958–1968.* Los Angeles: Los Angeles County Museum of Art, 1998.

Sol LeWitt

1. Sol LeWitt, "Paragraphs on Conceptual Art," *Artforum* 5 (June 1967), 79–83; reprinted in *Sol LeWitt* (1978), 166.

2. Ibid.

3. "Sol LeWitt," in *Flash Art* 41 (June 1973), 2; reprinted in *Sol LeWitt* (1978), 174.

4. "Sentences on Conceptual Art," *Art-Language* 1 (May 1969), 11–13; reprinted in *Sol LeWitt* (1978), 168.

Garrels, Gary. *Sol LeWitt: A Retrospective.* New Haven, Conn.: Yale University Press, 2000.

Sol LeWitt. Ed. Alicia Legg. New York: Museum of Modern Art, 1978.

Sol LeWitt: Structures 1962–1993. Oxford, England: Museum of Modern Art, 1993.

O. Winston Link

1. Much of the information in this entry is drawn from Link (1995) and a biography and bibliographic listing compiled by Thomas H. Garver, last revised in May 1997; typescript, Akron Art Museum files.

2. Thomas H. Garver, "Afterword: O. Winston Link and His Working Method," in Link (1987), 141.

3. In Link (1983), 44, the artist erroneously calls the movie *Sky Taxi.* Garver, however, discovered the film's true title; author's telephone conversation with Garver, November 1997. According to Garver, Link shot about half a dozen sheets of film of different images from the movie before shooting the rest of the picture—i.e., the locomotive and drive-in. A second version of *Hot Shot* may exist, supposedly produced for a Norfolk and Western Railway annual report. In that version, another image may have been substituted for the airplane.

4. Ibid.

5. Ibid.

6. The Akron work is one of the combination prints using a pin registration system.

Link, O. Winston. *Ghost Trains: Railroad Photographs of the 1950s.* With an essay by Carolyn [Kinder] Carr. Norfolk, Va.: Chrysler Museum, 1983.

———. *Steam, Steel & Stars: America's Last Steam Railroad.* With text by Timothy Hensley and afterword by Thomas H. Garver. New York: Harry N. Abrams, 1987.

———. *The Last Steam Railroad in America: From Tidewater to Whitetop.* With text by Thomas H. Garver. New York: Harry N. Abrams, 1995.

Morris Louis

1. The information in this entry is drawn from Upright's catalogue raisonné on the artist.

2. Upright, 37.

3. Russell O. Woody, *Painting with Synthetic Media* (New York: Reinhold, 1965), 29; quoted in Upright, 50.

4. Upright, 55.

5. Ibid.

6. According to Elderfield, 41, some of the black washes in the Veils were applied with a swab.

Elderfield, John. *Morris Louis.* New York: Museum of Modern Art, 1986.
Upright, Diane. *Morris Louis: The Complete Paintings, A Catalogue Raisonné.* New York: Harry N. Abrams, 1985.

René Magritte

1. René Magritte, unpublished paper; quoted in A. M. Hammacher, *René Magritte* (New York: Harry N. Abrams, 1973), 27.

2. René Magritte, quoted in "The Square Surrealist," *Newsweek* (January 3, 1966): 57.

Ottinger, Didier, ed. *Magritte.* Montreal: Montreal Museum of Fine Arts, 1996.
Sylvester, David. *Magritte: The Silence of the World.* New York: Harry N. Abrams, 1992.
Whitfield, Sarah, and Michael Raeburn. *Oil Paintings, Objects and Bronzes.* Vol. 3 of *René Magritte: Catalogue Raisonné.* Ed. David Sylvester. Antwerp: Mercatorfonds, Menil Foundation, and Philip Wilson, 1993. Distributed in the United States by Rizzoli International. *Les Pas perdus* is reproduced as no. 750, p. 174.

Man Ray

1. Schwarz, 205–6.

2. Penrose, 109.

3. Man Ray, *Self-Portrait* (London: Andre Deutsch, 1963), 392.

Baldwin, Neil. *Man Ray: American Artist.* New York: Clarkson N. Potter, 1988.
Foresta, Merry, et al. *Perpetual Motif: The Art of Man Ray.* Washington, D.C.: National Museum of American Art, Smithsonian Institution, 1988.
Penrose, Roland. *Man Ray.* Boston: New York Graphic Society, 1975.
Schwarz, Arturo. *Man Ray: The Rigour of Imagination.* New York: Rizzoli, 1977.

W. D. ("Crazy Mac" or "Mad Mac") McCaffrey

1. Most of the information in this article comes from the author's interviews with the artist. Information was also supplied by Charles Auerbach, an Akron folk art dealer who was one of the artist's early supporters.

2. According to the artist, the museum's collage is the first of four versions. The second is owned by Charles Auerbach; the third is with Father Sam Ciccolini of the Interval Brotherhood Home in Akron and is entitled *Tools of Choice.* The fourth is in an Akron private collection.

Cooper, David B. "Postscript: The Artistic Soul of 'Crazy Mac.'" *Akron Beacon Journal*, Thursday, July 29, 1993, A14.
Haferd, Laura. "The Madness of Mac." *Beacon Magazine, Akron Beacon Journal*, June 2, 1981, 6-8, 10, 14.
Sellen, Betty-Carol. *20th Century American Folk, Self Taught, and Outsider Art.* New York: Neal-Schuman, 1993.

Ralph Eugene Meatyard

Hall, James Baker, ed. "Ralph Eugene Meatyard." *Aperture* 18 (1974). The entire double issue of the journal is devoted to Meatyard and his works.
Meatyard, Christopher, ed. *Ralph Eugene Meatyard: In Perspective.* Tavagnacco, Italy: Art&, Edizioni delle Arti Grafiche Friulane, 1996.
Tannenbaum, Barbara, ed. *Ralph Eugene Meatyard: An American Visionary.* Akron and New York: Akron Art Museum and Rizzoli International, 1991.

Willard L. Metcalf

1. Letter from Willard Metcalf to Thomas Dunbar, March 15, 1917; Edwin C. Shaw Papers, Archives of American Art, Smithsonian Institution.

2. Review in *Evening Mail and Express,* January 6, 1910, not paginated; Metcalf Papers, Archives of American Art, Smithsonian Institution, roll N70–13, frames 516–20.

3. Royal Cortissoz, "Willard Leroy Metcalf," in *Commemorative Tributes of the American Academy of Arts and Letters, 1905–1941* (New York, 1942), 511.

De Veer, Elizabeth, and Richard Boyle. *Sunlight and Shadow: The Life and Art of Willard L. Metcalf.* New York: Abbeville, 1987.
Gerdts, William H. *American Impressionism.* New York: Abbeville, 1984.

Duane Michals

1. Quotes without notes are from a lecture given by Michals at the Akron Art Museum, December 4, 1995.

2. Interview by Paul Lin, "Duane Michals: A Picture and a Thousand Words," *View* (1989): 11.

Kozloff, Max. *Duane Michals: Now Becoming Then.* Altadena, Calif.: Twin Palm, 1990.
Livingstone, Marco. *The Essential Duane Michals.* Boston: Little, Brown, 1997.

Robert Morris

1. The original color specified was Merkin Pilgrim gray, according to *Robert Morris,* 170.

2. Robert Morris, "Notes on Sculpture, Part II," *Artforum* 5 (October 1966): 23.

Berger, Maurice. *Labyrinths: Robert Morris, Minimalism, and the 1960s.* New York: Harper & Row, 1989.
Robert Morris: The Mind/Body Problem. New York: Solomon R. Guggenheim Museum, 1994.

Louise Nevelson

Albee, Edward. *Louise Nevelson: Atmospheres and Environments.* New York: Clarkson N. Potter in association with the Whitney Museum of American Art, 1980.
Lisle, Laurie. *Louise Nevelson: A Passionate Life.* New York: Summit Books, 1990.
Nevelson, Louise. *Dawns + Dusks: Taped Conversations with Diana MacKown.* New York: Charles Scribner's Sons, 1976.

Elmer Novotny

1. Quoted in "Portrait of a Realist," by Robert Downing and William Bierman, in *Beacon Magazine, Akron Beacon Journal,* July 21, 1974, 9.

Robinson, William H., and David Steinberg. *Transformations in Cleveland Art, 1796–1946: Community and Diversity in Early Modern America.* Cleveland: Cleveland Museum of Art, 1996.

Claes Oldenburg

1. Information on the sculpture's genesis and Oldenburg's involvement with the rubber industry comes from three sources: an interview with Mary and Louis Myers by Barbara Tannenbaum, Akron, September 21, 1986 (typescript); correspondence between the artist, the Myerses, and rubber company scientists and fabricators (museum files); and the most comprehensive publication on the work, a catalogue compiled by the Akron Art Institute's director, Robert Doty (see below).
2. Claes Oldenburg, "The Letter Q," in Oldenburg (1975), not paginated.
3. The title of this work at the Akron Art Museum was until recently *Soft Inverted Q.* This choice was based on correspondence and discussions between the staff and the artist during the work's creation. In researching this book, the author discussed the title with Oldenburg. The artist feels that since the *Q* was ultimately produced in a hard material, inclusion of the word "soft" is not really appropriate for the finished work.
4. Claes Oldenburg, "Brief Log of the Soft Inverted Q, 1968–1976," 10–17, in Doty, 11. *Navel—Akron,* 1973, is in the collection of the Akron Art Museum, a gift of the artist.
5. The Akron Art Museum owns a black version of the eighteen-inch model, which was a gift of the artist, as well as six drawings, prints, and multiples by Oldenburg. A rigid foam prototype for the six-foot tall version was produced; it was fabricated by moldmaker Bud Lamont of Plasti-Cast Mold & Products Co., Akron.
6. The six-foot tall version of *Inverted Q* was produced in an edition of four, all of which are now pink. These are owned by the Akron Art Museum; the Städtisches Museum Abteilberg, Mönchengladbach, Germany; the Iris & B. Gerald Cantor Center for Visual Arts at Stanford University, California; and the Samsung Corporation, Seoul, Korea. The latter work is made from cast resin. It was fabricated in 1988 at the same time as a white trial proof (collection of the Wichita Art Museum, Kansas) and an edition of two black *Qs* (private collection and the Yokohama Museum, Japan). *Q's* original six-foot tall rigid foam prototype, which was covered with resin and painted black, is still extant, although its whereabouts are currently unknown.

Doty, Robert, ed. *Oldenburg/The Inverted Q.* Akron: Akron Art Institute, 1977.
Oldenburg, Claes. *The Alphabet in L.A.* Los Angeles: Margo Leavin Gallery, 1975.
———. *Claes Oldenburg: An Anthology.* New York: Guggenheim Museum Publications, 1995.
Rose, Barbara. *Claes Oldenburg.* New York: Museum of Modern Art, 1970.

Nam June Paik

Hanhardt, John G. *Nam June Paik.* With essays by Dieter Ronte, Michael Nyman, and David A. Ross. New York: Whitney Museum of American Art in association with W. W. Norton, 1982.
———. *The Worlds of Nam June Paik.* New York: Guggenheim Museum, 2000.
Stoos, Toni, and Thomas Kellein, eds. *Nam June Paik: Video Time—Video Space.* New York: Harry N. Abrams, 1993.

Philip Pearlstein

1. *ARTnews* (summer 1962): 29.
2. This group should not be confused with the European Nouveaux Realistes, a loosely affiliated group of artists centered in Paris. Rather than depicting objects (or models), they chose to employ the real items in their art.
3. Lawrence Alloway has suggested that Pearlstein's style is related to sixteenth-century Italian sculpture, a proposition that can be extended to include Mannerist painting as well. See Lawrence Alloway, review of *Philip Pearlstein: The Complete Paintings,* by Russell Bowman, *Art in America* (February 1985): 19.

Bowman, Russell. *Philip Pearlstein: The Complete Paintings.* New York: Alpine Fine Arts Collection, 1983.
Georgia Museum of Art, University of Georgia. *Philip Pearlstein.* Essay by Linda Nochlin. Athens, Ga.: Georgia Museum, University of Georgia, 1970.
Perreault, John. *Philip Pearlstein: Watercolors and Drawings.* New York: Harry N. Abrams, 1988.

Philadelphia Wireman

1. The relationship to *minkisi* has been suggested by art dealers John Ollman and Randall Morris and by African art specialist Robert Farris Thompson. For information on *minkisi,* see Thompson, 88–89; Thompson, *Flash of the Spirit: African & Afro-American Art & Philosophy* (New York: Vintage Books, 1983), passim; and the National Museum of African Art, Smithsonian Institution, "The Face of Astonishment and Power: Kongo *Minkisi* and the Art of Renée Stout," exh. brochure (Washington, D.C.: Smithsonian Institution, 1993).
2. This information was provided by Fred Smith, Professor of Art, Kent State University, on March 23, 1993.
3. Quoted in McGonigal, 52.

Jarmusch, Ann. "Mysterious Stranger." *ARTnews* 85 (September 1986): 166.

McGonigal, Mike. "Psychic Magnets: Ruminations on the Philadelphia Wireman and the Nature of the Fetish Object." *Raw Vision* 5 (winter 1991/92): 48–51.

Thompson, Robert Farris. *Face of the Gods: Art and Altars of Africa and the African Americas.* New York and Munich: Museum for African Art and Prestel, 1993, 88–89.

Elijah Pierce

1. Elijah Pierce, quoted in Moore, 30.

2. There is no specific biblical text for the image of the clean and soiled heart, but Romans 1:21 mentions hearts darkened by foolishness and sin.

3. Columbus Museum of Art, 238.

4. In Columbus Museum of Art, 236, the scene in the lower right corner is identified as the raising of Lazarus from the tomb (John 11:1–46), which makes no mention of a bed. The story of the man with palsy seems a more likely source, given that the man in Pierce's carving takes up his bed and walks away.

5. The piece is undated. Boris Gruenwald, who brought Pierce's work to the attention of the art world, assigned it a 1942 date in the exhibition handout "Elijah Pierce: Carvings" (Columbus: not paginated, October 18–19, 1971), where its title is *The Wise and Foolish Virgins and The Man with the Clean and Soiled Heart.* Stylistically, Gruenwald's date seems accurate. Most works in that exhibition were not given dates, suggesting that Gruenwald dated pieces only when he had clear evidence. The work is listed as undated in the most comprehensive study of Pierce's work in print—Columbus Museum of Art, *Elijah Pierce: Woodcarver*—which also disputes the dating of several other works in Gruenwald's catalogue. The work was purchased from the artist's studio by Sarah and John Freeman in 1971 and remained in their hands until the museum purchased it in 1993.

Columbus Museum of Art. *Elijah Pierce: Woodcarver.* Columbus, Ohio: Columbus Museum of Art, 1992.

Hall, Michael. "Elijah Pierce." In Museum of American Folk Art. *Self-Taught Artists of the 20th Century: An American Anthology.* New York: Museum of American Folk Art, 1998, 94–97.

Martin Luther King Jr. Center. *Amazing Grace: The Life and Work of Elijah Pierce.* Columbus, Ohio: Martin Luther King Jr. Center, 1990.

Moore, Gaylen. "The Vision of Elijah." *New York Times Magazine,* August 26, 1979, 28–30, 34.

Lari Pittman

1. Pittman expresses this idea in many of his interviews. See Howard N. Fox, "Joyful Noise: The Art of Lari Pittman," in Fox, 21.

2. Telephone interview with the artist by Jeffrey Grove, December 29, 1999.

3. See Paul Schimmel, "An Interview with Lari Pittman," in Fox, 70–71, 77.

Duncan, Michael. "Flash and Filigree." *Art in America* 84 (December 1996): 64–71, 113.

Fox, Howard N. *Lari Pittman.* With contributions by Dave Hickey and Paul Schimmel. Los Angeles: Los Angeles County Museum of Art, 1996.

Lari Pittman: Paintings 1992–1998. With essays by Alex Farquharson and Christopher Knight. Manchester and Exeter, England: Cornerhouse and Spacex Gallery, 1998.

Robert Rauschenberg

1. *Rauschenberg Overseas Culture Interchange,* 154.

2. "A Conversation about Art and ROCI: Robert Rauschenberg and Donald Saff," November 1990, Captiva, Florida; in ibid., 163.

Kotz, Mary Lynn. *Rauschenberg: Art and Life.* New York: Harry N. Abrams, 1990.

Rauschenberg Overseas Culture Interchange. Washington, D.C., and Munich: National Gallery of Art and Prestel-Verlag, 1991.

Ernest ("Popeye") Reed

1. Information on Reed's technique is largely drawn from Rosenak and Rosenak, 255.

2. This technique was reported by Kerry Schuss, art therapist and folk art dealer, who observed Reed at work. See Meridean Hutton, "Dialogues with Stone: William Edmondson, Ernest 'Popeye' Reed and Ted Ludwiczak," *Folk Art* (spring 1996): 51.

3. Sandy Theis, "Popeye Reed: Having Fun as a Self-taught Sculptor," *Chillicothe (Ohio) Gazette,* June 2, 1981, 7.

Barrett, Didi. *Muffled Voices: Folk Artists in Contemporary America.* New York: Museum of American Folk Art at the Paine Webber Art Gallery, 1986.

Ricco, Roger, and Frank Maresca. *American Primitive: Discoveries in Folk Sculpture.* New York: Alfred A. Knopf, 1988, 263.

Rosenak, Chuck, and Jan Rosenak. *Museum of American Folk Art Encyclopedia of Twentieth-Century American Folk Art and Artists.* New York: Abbeville, 1990.

Milton Resnick

1. Linda Cathcart, *Milton Resnick: Paintings 1945–1985* (Houston: Contemporary Arts Museum, 1985), 4.

2. Quoted in Klaus Kertess, "Postcards from Babel," in *1995 Biennial Exhibition* (New York: Whitney Museum of American Art and Harry N. Abrams, 1995), 25.

3. Jonathan Santlofer, "Lions in Winter: American Artists in their 70's and 80's," *ARTnews* 92 (March 1993): 87.

4. Allen S. Weller, *Art: USA: Now* (New York: Viking, 1962), 83.

Campbell, Lawrence. "Resnick Paints a Picture." *ARTnews* (December 1957): 56, 38–41, 65–66.

Robins, Corinne. *The Pluralist Era: American Art 1968–1981.* New York: Harper & Row, 1984.

Larry Rivers

1. Frank O'Hara, "A Memoir," in *Larry Rivers* (Boston: Brandeis University, 1965), 11.

2. Helen A. Harrison, "Larry Rivers," in Jane Turner, ed., *The Dictionary of Art* (New York: Grove, 1996), 431.

3. Larry Rivers in conversation with the author, July 8, 1997.

4. Fairfield Porter, "Rivers Paints a Picture," *ARTnews* 52 (January 1954): 82.

Harrison, Helen A. *Larry Rivers.* New York: Harper & Row, 1984.

Hunter, Sam. *Larry Rivers.* New York: Rizzoli, 1989.

Rivers, Larry, with Arnold Weinstein. *What Did I Do? The Unauthorized Autobiography.* New York: HarperCollins, 1992.

Severin Roesen

Gerdts, William H. *Painters of the Humble Truth: Masterpieces of American Still Life 1801–1939.* Columbia, Mo., and London: Philbrook Arts Center with University of Missouri Press, 1981.

O'Toole, Judith Hansen. *Severin Roesen.* Lewisburg, Pa.; London; and Toronto: Bucknell University Press and Associated University Presses, 1992.

Anthony Joseph Salvatore

1. Salvatore usually wrote out the citations for biblical text on the back of each work. Beginning in the late 1970s, he relied on the Lamsa Bible, an English translation of the Peshitta (Aramaic or Syriac) Bible, and on scholar George M. Lamsa's Bible commentaries. The Peshitta, probably executed from the original scrolls long before their Hebrew or Arabic translation, is believed by some to be the most accurate version of the Scriptures.

2. Information in this entry is based primarily on the author's interview with the artist in Youngstown on December 5, 1989; quotations are also from that interview. Additional information was provided by David Colts; the artist's gallery, Cavin-Morris, New York; professors James Lapore, Russell Maddick, and John Naberezny of Youngstown State University; and Sister Jean DelBono.

Maresca, Frank, and Roger Ricco. *American Self-Taught: Paintings and Drawings by Outsider Artists.* New York: Alfred A. Knopf, 1993, 206–7.

Rosenak, Chuck, and Jan Rosenak. *Museum of American Folk Art Encyclopedia of Twentieth-Century American Folk Art and Artists.* New York: Abbeville, 1990.

Tannenbaum, Barbara. "Pillar of Fire: The Visionary Art of Anthony Joseph Salvatore." *Dialogue* 12 (March/April 1989): 38–39.

George Segal

1. The year after Akron's piece was made, Segal developed a new technique, casting a material called hydrostone (which is stronger than plaster) from the interior of the shell to give a more refined surface and lifelike rendering. The earlier pieces, like Akron's, reveal the lumpy external shape.

2. "Exhibitions: Presences in Plaster," *Time* (December 13, 1968): 84.

3. The first version of a girl sitting against a wall, from 1968, is in the collection of the Staatsgalerie, Stuttgart. Unlike Akron's all-white piece, Stuttgart's version has a red chair and black window, and the figure's hands are placed differently.

4. Allan Kaprow, "Segal's Vital Mummies," *ARTnews* (February 1964): 33.

5. Phyllis Tuchman, "Interview with George Segal," *Art in America* 60 (May–June 1972): 81.

Hunter, Sam, and Don Hawthorne. *George Segal.* New York: Rizzoli, 1984. Reprinted, Barcelona: Ediciones Polígrafa, 1988.

Livingstone, Marco. *George Segal Retrospective: Sculptures, Paintings, Drawings.* Montreal: Montreal Museum of Fine Arts, 1997.

Van der Mark, Jan. *George Segal.* New York: Harry N. Abrams, 1975.

Cindy Sherman

1. Krauss, 17.

2. "Camera at Work," *Life* 6 (May 1983): 16.

3. Gerald Marzorati, "Imitation of Life," *New York* 16 (September 1983): 81.

4. Rudi Fuchs, ed., *Documenta 7,* vol. 2 (Kassel: D + V Paul Dierichs GmbH, 1982), 411.

Danto, Arthur C. *Untitled Film Stills.* New York: Rizzoli, 1990.

Krauss, Rosalind. *Cindy Sherman 1975–1993.* New York: Rizzoli, 1993.

Schjeldahl, Peter, and I. Michael Danoff. *Cindy Sherman.* New York: Pantheon Books, 1984.

Sherman, Cindy. *Cindy Sherman: Retrospective.* With essays by Amada Cruz, Elizabeth A. T. Smith, and Amelia Jones. New York: Thames & Hudson, 1997.

Aaron Siskind

1. Aaron Siskind, "The Drama of Objects," first published in *Minicam Photography* 8 (June 1945); quoted in Kao and Meyer, 51.

Chiarenza, Carl. *Aaron Siskind, Pleasures and Terrors.* Boston and Tucson: New York Graphic Society/Little, Brown in association with the Center for Creative Photography, University of Arizona, 1982.

Kao, Deborah Martin, and Charles A. Meyer, eds. *Aaron Siskind: Toward a Personal Vision, 1935–1955.* Boston: Boston College Museum of Art, 1994.

Torosian, Michael, ed. *The Siskind Variations: A Quartet of Photographs and Contemplations.* Toronto: Lumiere, 1990.

William Sommer

1. To best comprehend the ideas underlying these styles, Sommer read voraciously and attended exhibitions, most notably the famed Armory Show of 1913, but it is uncertain whether he did so in New York or Chicago.

2. Although Edwin Sommer's signature attests that he worked on this piece, the painting appears no different than those executed wholly by William Sommer. Consequently, it is treated here as a William Sommer work.

3. Convincing evidence for both of these theories, drawn from a number of people who knew both the Bordners and William Sommer, can be found in Wendy Kendall-Hess,"From Mantel to Museum: The History of William and Edwin Sommers' *The Bordner Mural*," in *Cleveland as a Center of Regional American Art* (Cleveland: Cleveland Artists Foundation, 1994), 55–62.

Kendall-Hess, Wendy. *The Art of William Sommer.* Akron: Akron Art Museum, 1993.

McClelland, Elizabeth. *William Sommer: Cleveland's Early Modern Master.* Cleveland: John Carroll University, 1992.

Robinson, William H., and David Steinberg. *Transformations in Cleveland Art, 1796–1946: Community and Diversity in Early Modern America.* Cleveland: Cleveland Museum of Art, 1996.

Nancy Spero

1. Quoted in "Extracts from an interview by Jon Bird, New York, 1986," Spero (1991), 10.

2. Elinor W. Gadon, *The Once and Future Goddess: A Symbol for Our Time* (San Francisco: Harper & Row, 1989), 198.

3. Quoted in Spero (1991), 39.

Spero, Nancy. *Nancy Spero: Works Since 1950.* With an introduction by Dominique Nahas and essays by Jo Anna Isaak, Robert Storr, and Leon Golub. Syracuse, N.Y.: Everson Museum of Art, 1987.

———. *Nancy Spero, Woman Breathing.* With essays by Brigitte Reinhardt, Robert Storr, Noemi Smolik, Achille Bonito Oliva, and Klaus Vierneisel. Ulm, Germany: Edition Cantz, 1991.

———. *Nancy Spero.* With essays by Jon Bird, Jo Anna Isaak, and Sylvere Lotringer. London: Phaidon, 1996.

Frank Stella

1. Quoted in William Rubin, *Frank Stella: 1970–1987* (New York: Museum of Modern Art, 1987), 156. Stella was commissioned by BMW to paint a racing car. He survived a serious crash en route to Le Mans in 1980.

Guberman, Sidney. *Frank Stella: An Illustrated Biography.* New York: Rizzoli International, 1995.

Rubin, William. *Frank Stella: 1970–1987.* New York: Museum of Modern Art, 1987.

Stella, Frank. *Working Space.* The Charles Eliot Norton Lectures; 1983–84. Cambridge, Mass.: Harvard University Press, 1986.

Alfred Stieglitz

1. Quoted in Norman, 76.

2. Alfred Stieglitz, "Four Happenings," *Twice a Year* 8/9 (1942): 128. See also Norman, 75–76.

3. The enlarged version of *The Steerage* appeared in the last issue of Stieglitz's journal *291* (September/October 1915). Five hundred copies were printed, according to Stieglitz, quoted in Norman, 127. Eight thousand copies were printed according to Lowe, 127.

4. Quoted in Norman, 77.

Homer, William Innes. *Alfred Stieglitz and the American Avant-garde.* Boston: New York Graphic Society, 1977.

Lowe, Sue Davidson. *Stieglitz.* New York: Farrar Straus Giroux, 1983.

Newhall, Nancy. "Notes for a Bibliography." In *From Adams to Stieglitz.* New York: Aperture, 1989, 97–133.

Norman, Dorothy. *Alfred Stieglitz: An American Seer.* New York: Random House, An Aperture Book, 1960.

Thomas Struth

1. From the left these are Giovanni Bellini's *The Virgin and Child* or *Madonna of the Meadow,* Ama de Conegliano's (Cima's) *The Incredulity of St. Thomas,* and Giovanni Bellini's *The Doge Leonardo Loredan.*

2. "Interview between Benjamin H. D. Buchloh and Thomas Struth," in *Portraits: Thomas Struth* (New York: Marian Goodman Gallery, 1990), 39.

Belting, Hans. *Thomas Struth: Museum Photographs.* Munich: Schirmer/Mosel, 1993.

Sennett, Richard. *Thomas Struth: Strangers and Friends, Photographs 1986.* Cambridge, Mass.: MIT Press, 1994.

Stack, Trudy Wilner. *Art Museum.* Tucson: Center for Creative Photography, University of Arizona, 1995.

Hiroshi Sugimoto

1. The Akron Civic Theatre, designed by Viennese architect John Eberson, was built as the Akron Loew's Theatre. Information on the history of the building was provided by the Akron Civic Theatre.

2. There is no audience visible in this photograph because, according to the recollections of Patti Eddy, theater manager at the time, the film was run in an empty theater especially for the artist's photograph. Sugimoto rarely had the luxury of such a special showing, so most often would go to an early show and ask audience members to move back to a row where they would not be seen in the photograph.

Contemporary Arts Museum, Houston, and Hara Museum of Contemporary Art. *Sugimoto.* Houston and Tokyo: Contemporary Arts Museum and Hara Museum of Contemporary Art, 1996.

Sugimoto, Hiroshi. *Motion Picture.* Milan, Italy, and Locarno, Switzerland: Skira editore and Galleria SPAS, 1995.

———. *Sugimoto: Photographs by Hiroshi Sugimoto, Dioramas, Theaters, Seascapes.* Japan: Mitsumura, 1988.

Alma W. Thomas

1. Adolphus Ealey, in *A Life in Art: Alma W. Thomas, 1891–1978* (Washington, D.C.: Smithsonian American Art Museum and Smithsonian Institution Press, 1981), 12, recalled Alma Thomas saying, "We artists are put on God's good earth to create. Some of us may be black, but that's not the important thing. The important thing is for us to create, to give form to what we have inside of us. We can't accept any barriers, any limitations of any kind, on what we create or how we do it."

2. Alma Thomas Papers, microfilm, Archives of American Art, Smithsonian Institution. During and after her teaching tenure, Thomas organized extracurricular art clubs for children in which she cultivated an appreciation for art—including African American art—and the rich cultural resources in Washington.

3. Quoted in *Recent Paintings by Alma W. Thomas: Earth and Space Series, 1961–1971* (Nashville, Tenn.: Carl Van Vechten Gallery of Fine Arts, 1971), 4.

4. Robert Doty, introduction to *Alma W. Thomas: Recent Paintings, 1975–1976* (New York: Martha Jackson Gallery, 1976), not paginated [7].

Foresta, Merry A. *A Life in Art: Alma Thomas, 1891–1978.* Washington, D.C.: National Museum of American Art and Smithsonian Institution Press, 1981.

Munro, Eleanor. *Originals: American Women Artists.* New York: Simon and Schuster, 1979.

Thomas, Alma Woodsey. *Alma W. Thomas: A Retrospective of Paintings.* San Francisco: Pomegranate Communications, 1998.

Dwight W. Tryon

1. Letter from Dwight Tryon to Edwin C. Shaw, September 6, 1922, Edwin C. Shaw Papers, Archives of American Art, Smithsonian Institution. Shaw liked to correspond with artists whose work he had purchased in order to obtain information for a series of notebooks on his collection.

2. Letter from Dwight Tryon to Thomas Dunbar, June 16, 1922, Edwin C. Shaw Papers, Archives of American Art. Another related letter in the same archives to Thomas Dunbar, dated July 16, 1922, states that one painting represents spring; it is unclear, however, whether the reference pertains to *The New Moon* or to another work.

3. Letter from Dwight Tryon to Thomas Dunbar, July 6, 1922. Edwin C. Shaw Papers, Archives of American Art.

4. Ibid.

Merrill, Linda. *An Ideal Country: Paintings by Dwight William Tryon in the Freer Gallery of Art.* Washington, D.C.: Smithsonian Institution, 1990.

White, Henry C. *The Life and Art of Dwight William Tryon.* Boston: Houghton Mifflin, 1930.

Elihu Vedder

1. Letter from Vedder to unknown woman, September 7, 1884, Venice; Archives of American Art, Smithsonian Institution, Vedder roll no. 8, frames 936–39. The original letter is in the Century Collection of Manuscripts of the New York Public Library.

2. Letter from Anita Vedder to Edwin C. Shaw, dated June 6, 1922, Edwin C. Shaw Papers, Akron Art Museum archives.

National Collection of Fine Arts, Smithsonian Institution. *Perceptions and Evocation: The Art of Elihu Vedder.* Washington, D.C.: Smithsonian Institution Press, 1978.

Soria, Regina. *Elihu Vedder: American Visionary Artist in Rome (1836–1923).* Cranbury, N. J.: Fairleigh Dickinson University Press, 1970.

Vedder, Elihu. *The Digressions of V.* Boston and New York: Houghton Mifflin, 1920.

Eugene Von Bruenchenhein

1. Most of the information on the artist, his life, and his beliefs comes from Joanne Cubbs, "Eugene Von Bruenchenhein: Obsessive Visionary," in John Michael Kohler Arts Center, 11–23. Cubbs had access to Von Bruenchenhein's art, writings, and tape recordings. She also interviewed the artist's widow, his sister-in-law, and his close friends.

2. Von Bruenchenhein publicly exhibited his art once during his lifetime, in a solo show at an art gallery in Wauwatosa, Wisconsin, in 1965. The show apparently met with neither commercial nor critical success, so he never repeated the experience.

3. John Michael Kohler Arts Center, 13.

4. Information on technique comes from John Michael Kohler Arts Center, 12–13, and James Auer, "Poor, Unknown in Life, Artist Now a Big Find," *The Milwaukee Journal,* March 20, 1983.

5. It is possible that Von Bruenchenhein came by this knowledge firsthand by visiting one or more of the few exhibitions in Milwaukee in the 1940s and 1950s that contained examples of work by Surrealists and Abstract Expressionists. However, since none of the people Cubbs interviewed remembered the artist mentioning visits to museums or galleries, it is more likely that the art world "came to him" in the form of magazine articles.

John Michael Kohler Arts Center. *Eugene Von Bruenchenhein: Obsessive Visionary.* Sheboygan, Wis.: John Michael Kohler Arts Center, 1988.

Stone, Lisa. "Eugene Von Bruenchenhein." *Raw Vision* 10 (winter 1994–95): 32–38.

Andy Warhol

1. Marco Livingstone, "Do It Yourself: Notes on Warhol's Techniques," in McShine, ed., 72–73.

2. "Warhol in His Own Words," selected by Neil Printz, in McShine, ed., 457.

3. Andy Warhol, *The Philosophy of Andy Warhol (From A to B & Back Again)* (New York: Harcourt Brace Jovanovich, 1975), 92.

The Andy Warhol Museum. Pittsburgh: The Andy Warhol Museum, Carnegie Institute, 1994.

McShine, Kynaston, ed. *Andy Warhol: A Retrospective.* With essays by Robert Rosenblum, Benjamin H. D. Buchloh, and Marco Livingstone. New York: Museum of Modern Art, 1989.

Weegee

Barth, Miles. *Weegee's World.* With essays by Miles Barth, Alain Bergala, and Ellen Handy. Boston and New York: Little, Brown in association with the International Center of Photography, 1997.

Kaiser, Reinhard. *Weegee's New York.* Munich: Schirmer/Mosel, 1990.

Stettner, Louis. *Weegee.* New York: Alfred A. Knopf, 1977.

Weegee, with Mel Harris. *Weegee, by Weegee: An American Biography.* New York: Ziff-Davis, 1961. Reprinted, New York: Da Capo, 1980.

Carrie Mae Weems

1. In hooks, 84–85, Weems says that the Kitchen Table Series was in part a reaction to an essay by feminist film theorist Laura Mulvey, which drew the attention of the art world in the late 1970s and 1980s. Mulvey suggested that most previous images of women, even those made by females, were created for "the male gaze" and based on men's expectations and experiences. See Laura Mulvey, "Visual Pleasure and the Narrative Cinema," *Screen* 16 (autumn 1975): 6–18; reprinted in *Art after Modernism: Rethinking Representation,* ed. Brian Wallis (New York: The New Museum of Contemporary Art, 1984), 361–73.

2. Ibid., 78.

3. Quoted in Susan Benner, "A Conversation with Carrie Mae Weems," *Artweek* 23 (May 7, 1992): 5.

Carrie Mae Weems: Recent Work, 1992–1998. With essays by Thomas Piché Jr. and Thelma Golden. New York: George Braziller in association with Everson Museum of Art, 1998.

Contemporary Arts Museum, Houston. *Carrie Mae Weems: The Kitchen Table Series.* Houston: Contemporary Arts Museum, 1996.

hooks, bell. "Talking Art with Carrie Mae Weems." In *Art on My Mind: Visual Politics.* New York: New Press, 1995.

Kirsh, Andrea, and Susan Fisher Sterling. *Carrie Mae Weems.* Washington, D.C.: National Museum of Women in the Arts, 1993.

Julian Alden Weir

1. Letter from Dorothy Weir Young to Edwin C. Shaw, 1922, Edwin C. Shaw Papers, Archives of American Art, Smithsonian Institution.

2. After his heart attack Weir's brushwork also became less controlled; see *Exhibition of Paintings by Julian Alden Weir* (New York: Montross Gallery, 1914), not paginated.

Bolger Burke, Doreen. *J. Alden Weir: An American Impressionist.* Newark: University of Delaware Press, An American Art Journal Book, 1983.

Gerdts, William H. *American Impressionism.* New York: Abbeville, 1984.

William T. Wiley

1. Albright, 119.

2. John Perrault, interview with the artist, August 1979. Cited in Beal and Perrault, 9.

3. John Perrault, "Metaphysical Funk Monk," *ARTnews* (May 1968): 52–53.

4. See Hilton Kramer's review of "Dude Ranch Dada" in the *New York Times,* May 16, 1971.

Albright, Thomas. *Art in the San Francisco Bay Area, 1945–1980, An Illustrated History.* Berkeley and Los Angeles: University of California Press, 1989.

Beal, Graham W. J., and John Perrault. *Wiley Territory.* Minneapolis: Walker Art Center, 1979.

Garry Winogrand

1. From Winogrand's Guggenheim application, quoted in Szarkowski, 32. See also Leo Rubinfien, "The Man in the Crowd," *Artforum* 16 (December 1977): 33–37.

2. Colin Westerbeck and Joel Meyerowitz, *Bystander: A History of Street Photography* (Boston: Little, Brown, 1994), 382.

3. "Winogrand on Women," in Winogrand (1975), not paginated.

4. The development of smaller cameras and faster films and lenses made street photography possible. For a history and analysis of this way of working, see Westerbeck and Meyerowitz.

5. The museum's print is from a portfolio of *Women Are Beautiful* images produced in 1981 by RFG Publishing.

Fraenkel, Jeffrey, and Frish Brandt, eds. *The Man in the Crowd: The Uneasy Streets of Garry Winogrand.* With an introduction by Fran Lebowitz and an essay by Ben Lifson. San Francisco: Frankel Gallery in association with Distributed Art, 1999.

Szarkowski, John. *Winogrand: Figments from the Real World.* New York: Museum of Modern Art, 1988.

Winogrand, Garry. *Women Are Beautiful.* New York: Light Gallery Books, 1975.

———. *Public Relations.* New York: Museum of Modern Art, 1977.

Jackie Winsor

1. All quotes by the artist are from an interview in *Jackie Winsor/Barry Ledoux: Sculpture* (Cambridge, Mass.: Hayden Gallery, Massachusetts Institute of Technology, 1984), not paginated.

Mifflin, Margot. "Jackie Winsor: Pieces of Life." *ARTnews* (summer 1992): 100–105.

Sobel, Dean. *Jackie Winsor.* Milwaukee: Milwaukee Art Museum, 1991.

Joel-Peter Witkin

1. Witkin, quoted in Celant, 175.

2. Witkin, quoted in Susan Zurcher, "Joel-Peter Witkin, A Midwestern Visitation: Interview," *Dialogue* (January/February 1988): 20.

3. The image is reproduced as *Nude Study* and dated around 1857 in Edgar Yoxall Jones, *Father of Art Photography O.G. Rejlander 1813–1875* (Newton Abbott, England: David and Charles, 1973), 60. In Roy Flukinger, *The Formative Decades: Photography in Great Britain, 1839-1920* (Austin, Tex.: University of Texas Press, 1985), 61, it is dated around 1860. Stephanie Spencer, in *O.G. Rejlander: Photography as Art* (Ann Arbor, Mich.: UMI Research Press, 1985), 111, cites it as a study made to prove the lack of realism in the anatomy of Venus in the Titian painting; she leaves the photograph undated.

4. Witkin's sketch is reproduced in Celant, plate 51; the Courbet painting is reproduced in Celant, 38.

Celant, Germano. *Witkin.* Zurich, Berlin, and New York: Scalo, 1995.

San Francisco Museum of Modern Art. *Joel-Peter Witkin: Forty Photographs.* San Francisco: San Francisco Museum of Modern Art, 1985.

Townsend, Chris. *Vile Bodies: Photography and the Crisis of Looking.* Munich and New York: Prestel-Verlag, 1998.

Alexander Wyant

Olpin, Robert S. *Alexander Helwig Wyant, 1836–1892.* Salt Lake City: Utah Museum of Fine Arts, University of Utah, 1968.

———. *Alexander Helwig Wyant (1836–1892), American Landscape Painter: An Investigation of His Life and Fame and a Critical Analysis of His Work with a Catalogue Raisonné of Wyant Paintings.* Ann Arbor, Mich.: University Microfilms, 1978.

Malcah Zeldis

1. Letter from Malcah Zeldis to Julia Weissman, April 16, 1973; in curatorial files, Department of Painting and Sculpture, Smithsonian American Art Museum, Washington, D.C.

2. Telephone conversation with the artist, November 2, 1996.

3. Ibid.

4. Interview with Julia Weissman, April 14, 1975, New York; transcript, 12, in curatorial files, Department of Painting and Sculpture, Smithsonian American Art Museum, Washington, D.C.

Niemann, Henry Paul. *Malcah Zeldis: Her Life and Evolution of Her Work, 1959–1984.* Ann Arbor, Mich.: University Microfilms International, 1991.

Rosenak, Chuck, and Jan Rosenak. *Museum of American Folk Art Encyclopedia of Twentieth-Century American Folk Art and Artists.* New York: Abbeville, 1990, 44.

Notes on the Contributors

Graham W. J. Beal is director of The Detroit Institute of Arts.

Jack Becker is curator of the Florence Griswold Museum.

Russell Bowman is director of the Milwaukee Art Museum.

Carolyn Kinder Carr is deputy director of the National Portrait Gallery, Smithsonian Institution, and was formerly curator of the Akron Art Museum.

Sheryl Conkelton is an independent curator in Seattle.

Keith F. Davis is fine arts program director, Hallmark Cards, Inc.

Jean E. Feinberg is a curator, an arts administrator, and the author of two books on Jim Dine.

Jeffrey Grove, curator for The Malrite Company, Cleveland, was formerly curator of exhibitions of the Akron Art Museum.

Mona Hadler is professor of art history at Brooklyn College and The Graduate Center, City University of New York.

Susan A. Hobbs is compiling the Thomas Wilmer Dewing catalogue raisonné.

Mitchell D. Kahan is director of the Akron Art Museum.

Judith Keller is associate curator of photographs, The J. Paul Getty Museum.

Wendy Kendall-Hess, an independent curator, was formerly assistant curator of the Akron Art Museum.

Nicholas Kilmer, grandson of the painter Frederick C. Frieseke, was dean of the Swain School of Design.

Gerald Nordland is an independent curator in Chicago.

Naomi Rosenblum, a photographic historian, authored *A World History of Photography.*

Luc Sante is an author and photography critic.

Barbara Tannenbaum is chief curator and head of public programs of the Akron Art Museum.

Sachi Yanari-Rizzo is associate curator of collections, Fort Wayne Museum of Art.

Index of Artists

STAFF AS OF JUNE 30, 2000

DIRECTOR'S OFFICE

Mitchell D. Kahan
Director

Lenore DeLong Fiedorek
Executive Secretary

PUBLIC PROGRAMS

Full-time

Barbara L. Tannenbaum
Chief Curator and Head of Public Programs

Arnold Tunstall
Registrar

Thaddeus C. Gregory
Preparator

Kathryn A. Wat
Associate Curator of Exhibitions

Deborah Pinter
Associate Educator

Seth Thompson
Associate Educator

Jason Byers
Assistant Preparator

Gary Setzer
Curatorial Assistant

Part-time

Lyndsey Shaeffer
Librarian

Lauren Space
Program Coordinator

Martha R. Tracy
Education Assistant

ADMINISTRATION

Full-time

Gail E. Wild
Administrator

Patricia Anderson
Bookkeeper/Assistant to Administrator

Susan E. Holliday
Business Office Assistant

James Burza
Security Supervisor

Timothy Kester
Building Supervisor

Part-time

Kara E. Blake
Christopher Coleman
Jenni Jarrell
Carla Lockhart
Stephen Peterson
Aaron Witwer
Maintenance

Robert W. Biesemeier
Denny Carano
Elizabeth Downs
Allen M. Dunlap
Don Jovich
Gallery Attendants

DEVELOPMENT

Full-time

Joan Lauck
Director of Development

John Marzich III
Public Information Officer

Cynthia Kellett
Development Assistant

Part-time

Shirley J. Bolanz
Special Events Coordinator

Michelle Cavanaugh
Reception Desk Coordinator

Nancy Mermelstein
Membership Coordinator

Jane Ann Turzillo
Public Information Assistant

Angela R. Barton
Megan Shaeffer
Front Desk Receptionists

The graphic design of this book employs a conceptual, contextual approach. It reflects the historical range of the works in the Akron Art Museum collection by choosing a sympathetic group of typefaces and typographic conventions for each individual artwork. As you move through the one hundred works from older to newer, front to back, the typefaces and typographic conventions change.

Design: Nicholas Lowie and Sheridan Lowrey